DATE DUE

W9-AVT-087

Folsom Lake College Library

Also by Robert Staib

Environmental Management and Decision Making for Business

Business Management and Environmental Stewardship

Environmental Thinking as a Prelude to Management Action

Edited by
Robert Staib

First published 2009 by
PALGRAVE MACMILLAN

Palgrave Macmillan in the UK is an imprint of Macmillan Publishers Limited,
registered in England, company number 785998, of Houndmills, Basingstoke,
Hampshire RG21 6XS.

Palgrave Macmillan in the US is a division of St Martin's Press LLC,
175 Fifth Avenue, New York, NY 10010.

Palgrave Macmillan is the global academic imprint of the above companies
and has companies and representatives throughout the world.

Palgrave® and Macmillan® are registered trademarks in the United States,
the United Kingdom, Europe and other countries.

ISBN-13: 978–0–230–53561–9
ISBN-10: 0–230–53561–5

This book is printed on paper suitable for recycling and made from fully
managed and sustained forest sources. Logging, pulping and manufacturing
processes are expected to conform to the environmental regulations of the
country of origin.

A catalogue record for this book is available from the British Library.

A catalog record for this book is available from the Library of Congress.

10 9 8 7 6 5 4 3 2 1
18 17 16 15 14 13 12 11 10 09

Printed and bound in Great Britain by
CPI Antony Rowe, Chippenham and Eastbourne

Contents

Part III   Support Operations and Business Case

List of Figures and Tables

Figures

Tables

Acknowledgements

I would like to acknowledge the many organizations and business managers with whom I have worked, who have given me the opportunity to observe, learn and practise business management. To these I add the many environmental managers with whom I have worked, who are helping to change the way business managers think and act about environmental and social issues.

I would like to thank the staff and students from the Macquarie University Graduate School of the Environment in Sydney, Australia with whom I have been associated for over twenty-five years and who have discussed with me many of the ideas that led to the structuring of this book, and in particular Peter Nelson, Ros Taplin, Wendy Goldstein and Ken Cussen. Teaching corporate environmental management at the Graduate School has exposed me to many diverse ideas and has led me to think closely about the relationship between environmental management and business management.

The 14 contributing authors who have given their time freely have brought a wealth of experience to the book across many disciplines and from many countries. This experience is exemplified by the amount of material they have collectively published on the subject of environmental and social management and their contributions to business, environmental and social education around the world. I would like to thank them for their excellent contributions.

I also acknowledge the use of unpublished material from many organizations from which I have drawn to provide background information on current corporate environmental practices. I would also like to acknowledge the following organizations who have given me permission to include their material in the book: Palgrave Macmillan for information from my earlier book (Staib, 2005); Maria Atkinson for use of material from chapter 24 of my earlier book (Staib, 2005); and Routledge and Suzanne Benn for the use of an edited version of Chapter 9 from Dunphy et al., 2007.

I would like to thank Ursula Gavin at Palgrave Macmillan for her invaluable help in managing the development and production of the book particularly the process of external review which helped me to bring a more focused approach to the book. I would also like to thank the four anonymous external reviewers for their time and effort and Vidhya Jayaprakash of Newgen Imaging Systems for her attention to the detail of copyediting.

I would like to thank my wife Roslyn for her patience and her ability to keep me anchored to the earth when the book started to over-occupy me. I dedicate the book to my children and grandchildren. The book is for the coming generations who will not only be business managers but who will also contribute to the stewardship of the earth's environment and its peoples.

Contributors

Suzanne Benn

Dr Suzanne Benn is Professor of Education for Sustainability and Director of Australian Research Institute in Education for Sustainability, in the Graduate School of the Environment at Macquarie University, Sydney. She is a biochemist and social scientist with research interests in organizational change, learning and change for sustainability and sustainability in business education. Her research is published widely in more than 60 book chapters, refereed conference presentations or referred journal articles and two books, one in second edition.

Lorne Cummings

Dr Lorne Cummings is an Associate Professor and Director – Postgraduate Professional Accounting Programs in the Department of Accounting and Finance, Macquarie University, Sydney, Australia. His teaching expertise is in advanced financial accounting theory and practice, which includes the various accounting theories and paradigms of research, professional ethics and International Financial Reporting Standards (IFRS). His area of research expertise and publications include IFRS, stakeholder theory, measurement and disclosure issues associated with environmental accounting and ethical investment. He is also co-editor of the *Journal of the Asia-Pacific Centre for Environmental Accountability*.

Dexter Dunphy

Professor Dexter Dunphy is the Distinguished Professor, Faculty of Business, School of Management at the University of Technology, Sydney. His main research and consulting interests are in the management of organizational change, human resource management and corporate sustainability. His research is published in over 60 articles and 15 books. Dexter has consulted to over 150 private- and public-sector organizations in Australia and abroad and has also 30 years of experience in working with senior executives, managers and other professionals in enhancing their managerial skills through executive workshops, consulting and counselling.

James Hazelton

James Hazelton is a Senior Lecturer, Department of Accounting and Finance, Macquarie University, Sydney, Australia, where he teaches auditing and business and professional ethics. He has presented and published papers on sustainability, triple bottom line reporting and social responsibility. He is currently doing a PhD on *Accounting for Sustainability,* at the Graduate School of the

Environment, Macquarie University where he is being supervised by Dr Ken Cussen, a moral and environmental philosopher with the Graduate School.

Robin Kramar

Professor Robin Kramar is a Professor in Management at the Macquarie Graduate School of Management Macquarie University, Sydney, Australia where she teaches Human Resource Management. She has published research across diversity management, knowledge management, managing change, international strategic human resource management, the employment of managerial and professional staff, strategic human resource management, equal employment opportunity and affirmative action, organizational change and youth unemployment. She has written five books on human resource management, most recently, *Human Resource Management in Australia* (with Helen De Cieri), published by McGraw-Hill. This book won an Australian Book Publishers Award for Excellence in 2003.

Craig Mackenzie

Dr Craig Mackenzie is director of the Carbon Benchmarking Project and a Senior Lecturer in Sustainable Enterprise at the University of Edinburgh. For nearly ten years, he ran socially responsibly investment teams at Insight Investment and Friends Provident. He has been Chair of the Criteria Development Committee at FTSE4Good since inception. He is a member of the Technical Advisory Committee of the Global Reporting Initiative and advises the Carbon Disclosure Project Supply Chain Leadership Collaboration. He has been involved in the development of the Business in the Community (BiTC) Corporate Responsibility Index and influential benchmarks on sustainable housebuilding, responsible supply chain management and biodiversity in the oil, gas and mining sectors.

Alfred A. Marcus

Professor Alf Marcus is Co-Director of the Center for Integrative Leadership at the University of Minnesota, Carlson School of Management, Minneapolis, USA. He holds the Edson Spencer Endowed Chair in Strategy and Technological Leadership. From 1995 to 2001, he was the chair of Strategic Management and Organization Department at the Carlson School. His teaching responsibilities include MBA courses in Business Strategy; Business Ethics; Business, the Global Economy and the Natural Environment; and Macroenvironment of Technology. He has published extensively with over 10 books, 20 book chapters and over 50 journal articles.

Bo Öhlmer

Professor Bo Öhlmer lectures in the Department of Economics at the Swedish University of Agricultural Sciences.

Michael Polonsky

Professor Michael Jay Polonsky is the Chair in Marketing within the School of Management and Marketing at Deakin University, Melbourne, Australia.

He has taught at Universities in the United States, South Africa, New Zealand and Australia. He has published extensively with over 90 refereed publications in international journals and over 100 conference papers. His areas of research interest include Green Marketing, Stakeholder Theory and Marketing, Marketing Education, Cross-Cultural Studies and Marketing Ethics.

Patricia Ryan

Emeritus Professor Patricia Ryan is an honorary professor at the Graduate School of Environment, Macquarie University, Sydney, Australia. She was previously Head of Division and Professor of Business Law in the Macquarie Division of Economic and Financial Studies. She has taught and researched environmental law and management topics for over 33 years. Her current editorship includes Consulting Editor, Local Government Reporter (Planning, Environment, Governance – Law, Regulation & Policy) (LexisNexis Butterworths) and Editorial Board, NSW Local Government, Planning and Environment (Butterworths – LexisNexis).

Arun Sahay

Professor Arun Sahay is a Professor of Strategic Management and Chairman of the Center for Entrepreneurship, Management Development Institute, Gurgaon, India. He has been a businessman in both public and private sectors as well as an academician. He became the Chairman and Managing Director of Scooters India Limited a company he successfully turned around after it was in danger of collapse. He represents the Government of India on task forces in companies like Nuclear Power Corporation of India Ltd, Neyveli Lignite Corporation Limited, Power Grid Corporation of India Ltd, National Thermal Power Corporation Ltd and National Hydro Power Corporation Ltd. He was awarded the MDI Best Researcher of the year 2006. He is on the Governing Council of International Sustainability Research Society headquartered in Hong Kong.

Robert Staib

Dr Robert Staib is an independent environmental management and business management consultant with qualifications in mechanical engineering, business management and environment. Over the last 15 years he has been an Environmental Manager on projects whose combined value exceeds $A1 billion. He has written over 20 papers on environmental management and project management and his book Environmental Management and Decision Making for Business was published by Palgrave Macmillan in 2005, London. He is a Visiting Fellow at the Macquarie University Graduate School of the Environment, Sydney, Australia where he convenes courses in corporate environmental management.

Rory Sullivan

Dr. Rory Sullivan is Head of Responsible Investment with Insight Investment, London, England. He is responsible for leading the team's thematic research and engagement activities on social, ethical and environmental issues with specific responsibility for investment research and engagement relating to climate change and human rights. Rory has written over 200 articles, book chapters and papers on environmental and energy policy, corporate responsibility and related issues. He is the author/editor of six books including Responsible Investment (editor with Craig Mackenzie, 2006) and Between the Market and the State: Corporate Responses to Climate Change (editor, 2008).

Dodo J. Thampapillai

Professor Dodo Thampapillai is an Adjunct Professor in environmental economics at Macquarie University Sydney Australia and at the Swedish University of Agricultural Sciences at Uppsala Sweden and is an economist at the Lee Kuan Yew School of Public Policy National University of Singapore. In 2005, he was included in the list of Eminent Environmental Economists by UNESCAP and was previously a member of the UNEP Expert Group in Environmental Economics. He has over 100 publications including seven books and nine refereed monographs. He has also consulted with World Bank, United Nations Development Programme, Food and Agricultural Organization of the United Nations and International Labour Organization, and the Australian Government. His current research focus is on macroeconomics and the environment.

Wang Yong

Dr Wang Yong is the Managing Director of ERM, China a wholly-owned foreign enterprise since 2002. ERM's China operations provide environmental, social, health and safety services to multinational companies, local industry, government and international development agencies. ERM became the first and only foreign-invested consultancy to be awarded a prestigious *Class A* EIA license by the State Environmental Protection Administration (SEPA) permitting its involvement at the highest level in preparing EIAs that help clients carry out some of China's largest and most complex development projects.

The Need for Change

Robert Staib

1.1 Introduction

Climate change is not the only environmental problem that is facing the world but it is one that is currently focusing the attention of the world's media. Two reports have appeared in recent years, the first by the Intergovernmental Panel on Climate Change (IPCC, 2007) which presents a consensus on the science of climate change and the second by Sir Nicholas Stern on The Economics of Climate for the UK Government (Stern, 2006b) which links the economy to the effects of climate change. From a business perspective they exemplify the significant business risks that are likely to arise if business ignores the environmental and social impacts of their operations. The World Business Council for Sustainable Development acknowledges that for businesses to stay in business they need to address and respond positively to this and other major environmental and social issues facing the world.

Society seems to be accepting and developing a business philosophy of, or concept of, sustainable development with its three divisions of environmental, social and economic. This is starting to pervade the thinking of private business, government business and government bodies. It has the potential to drive societies' organizations in a direction that diverges from a growth at all costs scenario to a direction that, while still encompassing growth, considers both environmental and social issues. It supports a need for a balance between economic, social and environmental factors, especially when one considers the disparities between *developed* and *undeveloped* countries or rich and poor nations.

The sustainability concept is being adopted by business in a pragmatic way. It is one that balances the feel good approach with the prospect or desire of achieving business advantage: lower material and energy inputs into products; establishment of a market advantage with green products or green image;

maintenance of a licence to continue to operate (either formal or earned); maintenance of an acceptable public image; and achievement of greater sales and profits. The environment (or nature) has many values to many people but I believe most importantly that nature should be preserved for its: role in the support of all life, human and non-human; intrinsic and non-anthropocentric values; and role in providing material and energy needs for society. In business, we need to be continually thinking about these values and why it is important to uphold them and how to develop a *stewardship* approach to the natural environment.

Signs of change

There are signs of a moderate change to a more sustainable future in the medium term but it could be slower than the increases in the opposing forces; for example, population growth both in the developed and the undeveloped countries, increasing materialism in the developed countries and a significant increase in materialism in undeveloped countries, an increase in energy use and a further deterioration of the natural environment and depletion of resources. In addition, organizations are becoming more global in their outlook, size and influence and the traditional business drivers are strong, persistent and difficult to change, for example, continuing growth, proactive marketing, maximization of profits, prime responsibility to shareholders' wealth and substantial rewards for top executives. This global power of the multinational organizations is starting to match the power of the individual states. It may be unlikely (e.g. Staib, 1997; Hoffman, 2001) that significant change to a less materialistic society will not occur in the absence of major environmental shocks (either the physical events or a widespread public acceptance of their inevitability). There is a danger (real I think) that we (in the developed nations) are being diverted (by our strong innate hedonistic desires for possessions, wealth, pleasures and varied experiences) away from the real thrust that started the environmental revolution which was to save nature from massive destruction. These hedonistic desires are often equated with happiness and health. We are strongly tempted to embrace the sustainable development philosophy as a panacea that says *we can have our cake and eat it.*

To address the above issues, there is a need in management education to take students behind the theory of sustainability to expose them to its assumptions and to help them develop a strong environmental and social basis for their management actions. This will help them to apply the concepts in the management of organizations with an approach based on defined and understood environmental, ethical and social concepts. They need to understand how nature supports life and why business should have a role of stewardship for nature and for future generations. These ideas focus on big societal issues and one wonders whether people working within business and governmental organizational contexts can really address them. Do they have the time and motivation to do so? I believe that one of the major drivers will be the mounting physical pressure on the public from the results of the deterioration of the natural world (more than the knowledge of such deterioration) or from major environmental shocks. The physical impact will have a greater impact in its ability to change behaviour than the knowledge will have in its ability to firstly change attitudes then subsequently to change behaviour, that is, direct experience is more likely to change behaviour than indirect experience. That is not to say that we should wait for these impacts or shocks before we act. It means that it will be harder to achieve change without the shocks but it does not mean that we should not try.

The implications for business management are that people in business should develop a greater ability to identify these trends and likely scenarios to be able to respond early. They should develop a greater ability to think strategically not only from an economic point of view but also from an environmental and social perspective. This is starting to occur. In the context of a management education there is a need to engage in environmentally and socially focused thinking.

1.2   Theme and objectives

This book is about that *thinking: environmental thinking as a prelude to management action*. Its aim is to direct management students towards this thinking. There is a need to paint a picture that urgent and focused action is required to solve and manage environmental problems and associated social issues. But the impression left with the readers/students should be that they can make a significant difference through understanding the issues, thinking them through and then applying different management approaches to them. There needs to be a certain amount of prescription but the basic message should be that resolving our environmental management problems will take a lot of management foresight and initiative. As solutions are implemented, there should be regular feedback, that is, *environmental thinking as a response to management action*.

This book is aimed at undergraduate, postgraduate and Master of Business Administration (MBA) students undertaking business courses which include material on sustainability, environmental management and sustainable development. It should also be of interest to practising managers and management consultants. It aims to integrate environmental and social issues into business management philosophies and business management implementation. The book intentionally has a stronger focus on *environmental sustainability* than cultural and social because I believe some of the writing and action on sustainability could (or will) result in a diminution of attention to environmental aspects. All aspects are important but I think that while integration is important each area should be treated on its merits. In the end some compromise will be necessary but I believe that it is better to start out with a strong advocacy position for the environment rather that suggesting compromises at the start. Cultural and social aspects of sustainability are specifically addressed in Chapter 4 'Leadership for Sustainability' and Chapter 6 'Human Resources' and by other authors to varying degrees in the other chapters.

I have worked with a number of authors from different countries and backgrounds, all from specialist areas of management education and charged them with the task of discussing how environmental and in some cases social issues can be integrated into or considered alongside the traditional approaches to their management disciplines. It is not possible to cover such broad topics in detail each in one chapter, but some of the important ideas for managers have been developed. The primary objectives of the book for you as management students are to expose you to some of the philosophies and ideas behind the need to achieve corporate environmental objectives and the need to implement environmental management processes; help you to think environmentally as a prelude to management action and to think environmentally as a response to management action; and assist you to acquire the desire, the drive and the skills to consider the natural environment in all business transactions.

Environmental aspects

In this opening chapter I discuss some of the ideas behind the need for business to respond to the major environmental issues facing the world and discuss why business organizations should consider the environment, the impact they make and how much they can influence change to their environmental footprint. I have used the following three aspects to provide the framework:

- Environmental impact *drivers*, for example, growth of population, growth of the use of earth's energy and resources, growth of technology and biotechnology;
- Environmental *impacts*, for example, unsustainable use of the earth's energy, resources and land, loss of biodiversity, climate change, pollution; and
- *Business responses* to environmental issues, for example, growth in the use of environmental management systems, growth of ethical investment, the share market awareness of sustainability.

There are many indicators that could be chosen to illustrate each of the above aspects, and I encourage readers to explore them further especially those that directly affect their own organization. I have chosen representative indicators and included statements from influential organizations. I think it is instructive to consider what people in some of the world's influential institutions are saying about global environmental and social issues and the need for business to respond. The following sections use information and extracts of recent documents produced by private, public and business organizations: the Worldwatch Institute, World Wide Fund for Nature, the United Nations and the World Business Council for Sustainable Development, Intergovernmental Panel on Climate Change and the UK Government (Stern Report).

1.3   Drivers

Two important drivers of increasing environmental impacts in the world are the growth in population (particularly urban population) and the use of energy (particularly fossil fuels). Figure 1.1 illustrates this continuing growth of world population and urbanization, though one observes that the growth rate of world population has slowed since its peak in the mid-1960s.

State of the World

Sometime in 2008, the world will cross an invisible but momentous milestone: the point at which more than half the people on the planet – roughly 3.2 billion human beings – live in cities. The combined impact of a growing population and an unprecedented wave of migration from the countryside means that over 50 million people – equivalent to the population of France – are now added to the world's cities and suburbs each year. More than at any time in history, the future of humanity, our economy, and the planet that supports us will be determined in the world's cities. Urban centers are hubs simultaneously of breathtaking artistic innovation and some of the world's most abject and disgraceful poverty. They are the dynamos of the world economy but also the breeding grounds for alienation, religious extremism, and other sources of local and global insecurity. Cities are now both pioneers of groundbreaking environmental policies and the direct or indirect source of most of the world's resource destruction and pollution. (Flavin, 2007)

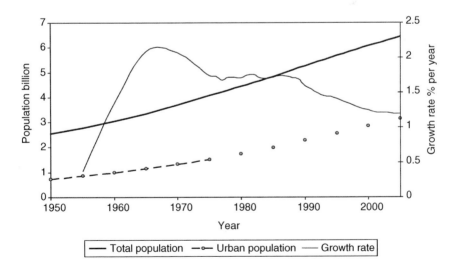

Figure 1.1   World population
Source: The Worldwatch Institute, 2007.

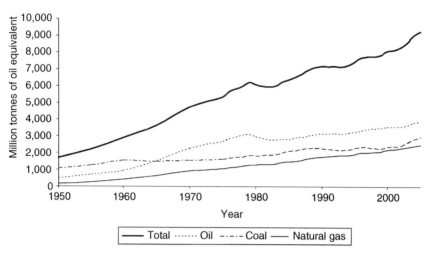

Figure 1.2   World fossil fuel consumption

Source: The Worldwatch Institute, 2007.

Figure 1.2 shows that world fuel consumption of non-renewable fossil fuels continues to grow though other indicators from the Worldwatch Institute show that the production of renewable energy is increasing steadily and in some areas dramatically though it is only a small part of total energy demands.

1.4   Impacts

Impacts on the living planet

The index in Figure 1.3 illustrates that the impact on the earth of human activities is causing a rapid and continuing decline in biodiversity, a 25 per cent reduction in the index since 1970. It shows we are steadily using our natural living resources in a non-sustainable way or in other words we are exceeding the world's production of living resources and we are using our environmental capital. Figure 1.4 illustrates a similar situation where the world's ecological footprint (measured in global hectares) has exceeded the available bio-capacity of the planet (also measured in global hectares).

A Living Planet

WWF began its Living Planet Reports in 1998 to show the state of the natural world and the impact of human activity upon it.... The Living Planet Index, shows a rapid and continuing loss of biodiversity... populations of vertebrate species have declined by about one third since 1970. This confirms previous trends.... The latest data available (for 2003) indicate that humanity's Ecological Footprint, our impact upon the planet, has more than tripled since 1961. Our footprint now exceeds the world's ability to regenerate (i.e., the bio-capacity of the earth) by about 25 per cent.... The message of these two indices is clear and urgent: we have been exceeding the Earth's ability to support our lifestyles for the past 20 years, and we need to stop. We must balance our consumption with the natural world's capacity to regenerate and absorb our wastes. If we do not, we risk irreversible damage.... The Living Planet Report 2006 confirms that we are using the planet's resources faster than they can be renewed. (Extracts from Leape, 2006)

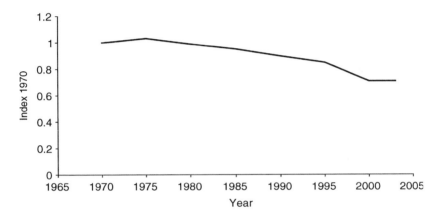

Figure 1.3   Living Planet Index

Source: WWF, 2006.

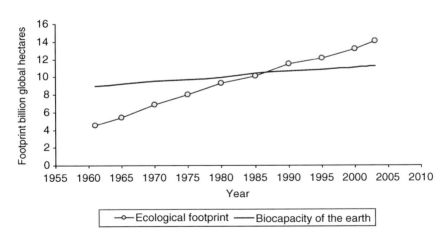

Figure 1.4   Human ecological footprint and earth's biocapacity

Note: Horizontal scales of the figures are different.

Source: WWF, 2006.

Impact on the climate

While climate change is not the only environmental problem the world faces it is one that is currently focusing the attention of the world's media. As mentioned in the first paragraph, two reports have appeared recently, the first confirming a scientific consensus of the science of climate change and the second linking the economy to the effects of climate change. From a business perspective they exemplify the significant business risks that are likely to arise if business ignores the environmental (and social) impacts of their operations and extracts from these two reports are included in the boxes below.

Climate Change – The Science (selected quotes)

Global atmospheric concentrations of carbon dioxide, methane and nitrous oxide have increased markedly as a result of human activities since 1750 and now far exceed pre-industrial values determined from ice cores spanning many thousands of years. The global increases in carbon dioxide concentration are due primarily to fossil fuel use and land-use change, while those of methane and nitrous oxide are primarily due to agriculture.... The understanding of anthropogenic warming and cooling influences on climate has improved since the Third Assessment Report, leading to very high confidence that the globally averaged net effect of human activities since 1750 has been one of warming.... Warming of the climate system is unequivocal, as is now evident from observations of increases in global average air and ocean temperatures, widespread melting of snow and ice, and rising global mean sea level.... At continental, regional, and ocean basin scales, numerous long-term changes in climate have been observed. These include changes in Arctic temperatures and ice, widespread changes in precipitation amounts, ocean salinity, wind patterns and aspects of extreme weather including droughts, heavy precipitation, heat waves and the intensity of tropical cyclones.... (IPCC, 2007)

Climate Change – The Economics

Climate change is global in its causes and consequences, and international collective action will be critical in driving an effective, efficient and equitable response on the scale required. This response will require deeper international co-operation in many areas – most notably in creating price signals and markets for carbon, spurring technology research, development and deployment, and promoting adaptation, particularly for developing countries. Climate change presents a unique challenge for economics. The economic analysis must therefore be global, deal with long time horizons, have the economics of risk and uncertainty at centre stage, and examine the possibility of major, non-marginal change. To meet these requirements, the Review draws on ideas and techniques from most of the important areas of economics, including many recent advances.

The benefits of strong, early action on climate change outweigh the costs. The effects of our actions now on future changes in the climate have long lead times. What we do now can have only a limited effect on the climate over the next 40 or 50 years. On the other hand what we do in the next 10 or 20 years can have a profound effect on the climate in the second half of this century and in the next. No one can predict the consequences of climate change with complete certainty; but we now know enough to understand the risks. Mitigation – taking strong action to reduce emissions – must be viewed as an investment, a cost incurred now and in the coming few decades to avoid the risks of very severe consequences in the future. If these investments are made wisely, the costs will be manageable, and there will be a wide range of opportunities for growth and development along the way. For this to work well, policy must promote sound market signals, overcome market failures and have equity and risk mitigation at its core. (Stern, 2006b)

1.5   Business responses

The business world has been responding to environmental issues for almost 50 years, firstly in response to regional environmental issues and environmental legislation but more recently under its own initiative, though some would argue that this has been patchy and falls short of what will be required. In the boxes below we include quotes from the Secretary-General of the United Nations acknowledging that business leaders are becoming aware of their responsibilities to the environment and from the World Business Council for Sustainable Development (WBCSD) endorsing the need for business to act decisively. In this section I have also included three indicators that illustrate a growing response from business.

Environment and Industry

Rapid environmental change is all around us. The most obvious example is climate change, which will be one of my top priorities as Secretary-General. But that is not the only threat. Many other clouds are on the horizon, including water shortages, degraded land and the loss of biodiversity. This assault on the global environment risks undermining the many advances human society has made in recent decades. It is undercutting our fight against poverty. It could even come to jeopardize international peace and security.... Protecting the global environment is largely beyond the capacity of individual countries. Only concerted and coordinated international action will be sufficient. The world needs a more coherent system of international environmental governance. And we need to focus in particular on the needs of the poor, who already suffer disproportionately from pollution and disasters. Natural resources and ecosystems underpin all our hopes for a better world…. Increasingly, **companies** are embracing the Global Compact not because it makes for good public relations, or because they have paid a price for making mistakes. They are doing so because in our interdependent world, business leadership cannot be sustained without showing leadership on environmental, social and governance issues. (Ban Ki-moon, 2007)

Sustainable Development and Business

Human activity over the past 50 years has changed the world's environment more extensively than ever before, largely to meet growing demands for food, fuel, fresh water, timber, and fiber. The use of natural resources has advanced human development, but at a growing environmental cost. The UN Development Programme has estimated that if the whole world's population were to enjoy a lifestyle similar to that of the industrialized countries today, it would require the resources of 5.5 planet Earths. The 2005 report of the international Millennium Ecosystem Assessment (MEA) group, involving 1,360 experts worldwide, revealed dramatic deterioration in ecosystem services. These include the provision of resources such as fuel and food, processes such as climate regulation, and the aesthetic and recreational values of nature. The MEA found that two-thirds of these services were being degraded or used unsustainably, and described global warming as the change with the greatest potential to alter the natural infrastructure of Earth. Many of the world's natural resources are not owned by anyone or assigned a value. They represent common goods, and failure to halt their depletion is sometimes referred to as 'the tragedy of the global commons'. We believe it is imperative to reverse this trend and operate within the carrying capacity of the earth. Our challenge is to find opportunity in doing so. Encouragingly, this is an area in which **business** is beginning to find ways to turn responsibility into opportunity. We now must do it on a scale that has an impact at the global level.

We believe that the **fundamental purpose of business** is to provide continually improving goods and services for increasing numbers of people at prices that they can afford. We believe that this statement of our purpose unites the interests of business and society at the deepest level. It makes clear that we prosper by helping society to prosper, by innovating to create new goods and services and by reaching out to new customers. We believe that the leading global companies of 2020 will be those that provide goods and services and reach new customers in ways that address the world's major challenges – including poverty, climate change, resource depletion, globalization, and demographic shifts. If action to address such issues is to be substantial and sustainable, it must also be profitable. Our major contribution to society will therefore come through our core business, rather than through our philanthropic programs. We see shareholder value as a measure of how successfully we deliver value to society, rather than as an end in itself. In aligning our interests with the needs of society, we will follow a model based on our own experience and analysis of successful business strategies: we will develop an <u>understanding</u> of how global issues such as poverty, the environment, demographic change, and globalization affect our individual companies and sectors; we will use our understanding of the significance of these signals to search for business <u>opportunities</u> that help to address them; we will develop our core business <u>strategies</u> to align them with the opportunities that we have identified; we will incorporate <u>long-term measures</u> into our definition of success, targeting profitability that is sustainable, supported by a positive record in social, environmental, and employment areas. (WBCSD, 2007)

Environmental management systems

Environmental Management Systems (EMS) are a way of enabling an organization to address and manage the plethora of environmental issues that it is faced with – originating from society or from within the organization. The standard that is being adopted world wide ISO14000 is a series of codes covering environmental management systems, auditing, environmental labels and declarations, environmental performance evaluation, life-cycle assessment and environmental risk management. An organization can use this standard as a basis for its own system or it can adopt all parts of the code and obtain and maintain certification by an external accreditation body (Staib, 2005). By December 2006, approximately 130,000 organizations worldwide had been formally certified to the standard ISO 14001 as shown in Figure 1.5.

Ethical investment

Ethical investment is an indicator of societies' growing interest in how companies conduct their business. This topic is explored further in Chapter 11. Figure 1.6 is an indicator of how the level of investment ethical funds in UK is growing based on data collected and analysed by Ethical Investment Research Services (EIRIS) (2008). It has collected and analysed data since 1989 based on data from investment managers and the Investment Management Association (IMA). The funds included are mainly retail unit trusts available to the general public. Details of EIRIS's selection basis are included on its website. The funds do not include institutional funds (EIRIS, 2008).

Stock market environmental indexes

Chapter 11 discusses investment from the point of view of investors and highlights some of the financial pressures external stakeholders can exert on a company and how this might influence their corporate behaviour. Stock market indicators, especially share price indexes of corporate performance, are an important benchmark against which the investment industry and society judges

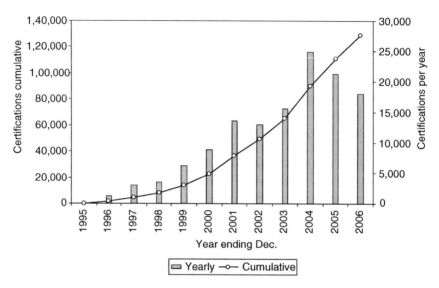

Figure 1.5   Environmental management systems (ISO 14001 certifications)

Source: ISO, 2000, 2006, 2007.

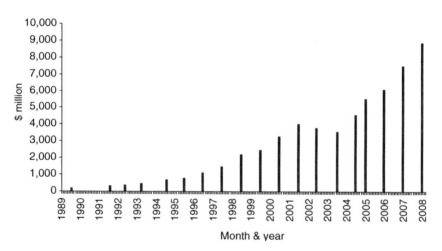

Figure 1.6   Indicator of Ethical Fund Investment in the United Kingdom

Note: Values are now totalled at the end of December but earlier values were totalled at different months of the year.

Source: EIRIS, 2008.

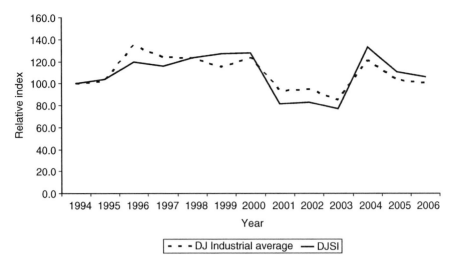

Figure 1.7   Comparisons of Dow Jones Indexes for industrial and sustainability
Source: Dow Jones, 2008.

the financial performance of public companies. In the past 10 years indicators of how companies are performing environmentally have been developed,
for example the DOW Jones Sustainability Index (DJSI) assesses companies
on its Dow Jones Industrial Index (DJII) against a number of environmental,
social and other criteria and only those reaching a certain level are included in
the DJSI. Figure 1.7 shows the performance of these companies on the DJSI
against the basket of all companies on the DJII and indicates that they are performing as well if not better in recent times.

1.6   Sustainable development

The Brundtland Commission of the United Nations (Brundtland, 1987)
described sustainable development as 'development that meets the needs of the
present generation without compromising the ability of future generations to
meet their own needs'. It identified the critical survival issues for humanity
as uneven development, poverty and population growth which were placing
unprecedented pressures on the planet's lands, waters, forests and other natural resources causing a 'downward spiral of poverty and environmental degradation' which was resulting in a waste of opportunities and resources and in
particular a waste of human resources. It said 'What is needed now is a new era
of economic growth – growth that is forceful and at the same time socially and
environmentally sustainable' (Stiener, 2007). Thus the three pillars of sustainable development are economic, social and environmental.

Since that time much effort has been put into defining *sustainable development*
and implementing it at global, national, local and corporate scales, but despite

this 'much of the natural capital upon which so much of human well being and economic activity depends – water, land, the air and atmosphere, biodiversity and marine resources – continue their seemingly inexorable decline' (Mohamed-Katerere, 2007). Since the Brundtland report in 1987 humanity's ecological footprint has exceeded the earth's bio-capacity as shown in Figure 1.4. Sneddon et al. (2006) describe the continuing increases in energy consumption, ecological degradation, growing public mistrust of science, inequalities in economic opportunities within and across societies and fractured institutional arrangements for global environmental governance as seemingly insurmountable obstacles to sustainability. They believe that the world has changed since the Brundtland report in 1987. Despite advancing our knowledge about many aspects of sustainability the challenges of both sustainability and development may be more difficult to master; for example, science has identified that ecological destruction is greater than foreseen (e.g., climate change, losses of biodiversity); equity problems which it was thought would be solved by (economic) growth have in many cases increased with the net growth since Brundtland; and with increased economic activity there has been a simultaneous decrease in the power of national sovereignty and a general turbulence in global order. This is making global solutions increasingly necessary and increasingly difficult to come by.

Despite these critical assessments of the achievements of sustainable development the above-mentioned authors and others still support the concept of sustainable development though they are calling for different approaches to the way it is conceived and implemented (Sneddon et al., 2006; Bass, 2007; Mohamed-Katerere, 2007; Stiener, 2007). Many of the above issues raised in the preceding paragraphs need to be addressed at inter and intra-governmental levels but business organizations still need to address the three aspects of environmental, social and economic. Although the book intentionally has a stronger focus on environmental sustainability, the three aspects of sustainable development (environment, social and economic) are discussed, albeit in different ways, by the individual authors. The social and cultural aspects (from a corporate point of view) are discussed in some detail in Chapter 4 on leadership and Chapter 6 on human resources. The environmental and economic aspects are addressed in Chapters 5 on economics, Chapter 11 on finance and investment and Chapter 12 on accounting. Chapters 2 on philosophy, Chapter 8 on organization, Chapter 11 on investment and Chapter 12 on accounting emphasize the importance of all three aspects of sustainable development.

1.7   Environmental stewardship

The title I have chosen for the book implies that *environmental stewardship* should become a part of business management. The Macquarie dictionary (Macquarie University, 1981) defines a steward as 'one who manages another's property or financial affairs; one who administers anything as the agent of another or others'. The word is very appropriate for business (and for that matter all people) which should be a part of the process of managing the environment for all people, for nature and the maintenance of its biodiversity and for future generations. Stewardship for business can also extend to *product stewardship* where a business can be seen to have a role and responsibility for ensuring that the *use* of its products does not significantly impact the environment or the social and cultural aspects of communities.

Despite much being written about the need for better environmental performance by business organizations, a significant rise in the number of organizations espousing sustainable development as evidenced by their publicly available sustainability reports and the passing of significant environmental legislation over the past 40 years, many indicators of the state of the world environment continue to deteriorate. Section 1.1 raises this issue and some of the authors in this book discuss this important idea.

Other writers say that what we are achieving in the name of sustainable development is mainly an improvement in *eco-efficiency* that is, better use of our natural resources and that this is generally proceeding incrementally but that what we need is more radical changes to address the *total impact* of all our actions and products on the natural world.

To achieve a significant reduction of our impact on the natural environment, it may be necessary for businesses and its customers to better understand their stewardship role. For example, Chapter 5 discusses a way in which the production function of labour and manufactured capital (used in traditional economics) could be extended to include a concept of environmental capital and suggests how *environmental stewardship* could be included as a part of business strategic thinking. Some organizations will incorporate the concept of environmental stewardship into their thinking, but others may have it forced upon them by legislation or by the impact of environmental disasters. The title of the book has been used to suggest that *environmental stewardship* is a concept that we should be able to understand and apply in our business operations whether improvement is incremental or radical.

1.8   Structure of the book

From the starting point of a framework of environmental impact drivers, environmental impacts and business responses, we now consider how the book is structured to support its theme and what management students should aspire to achieve. The book is divided into three Parts:

- Part I: Corporate Strategy and Direction (Chapters 2 to 5);
- Part II: Management of Operations (Chapters 6 to 10); and
- Part III: Support Operations and the Business Case (Chapters 11 to 14).

Authors and their individual chapters are discussed in a following section. At the end of each Part there is a longer case study to illustrate aspects of the text.

Each chapter includes the discussion of ideas illustrated by short case studies and concludes with

- Questions for students to test their understanding of the ideas from the Chapter; and
- Recommended reading for students to broaden their knowledge of how environmental and in some cases social aspects can be integrated into the particular business discipline.

The final chapter, Chapter 14, includes a Capstone Project that encourages students to bring together and integrate the ideas from the book into a Business Case for an organization of their choice. To assist students the chapter also includes an outline of the ideas from each chapter and a list of questions and issues for students to consider while developing their business case.

Learning objectives

I have included below the learning objectives for the book. In attaining them, I assume that students will read each chapter and selections from the references suggested under the 'Further Reading' sections of each chapter; attempt to answer the questions posed by the authors at the end of each chapter in some detail; and finally undertake the Capstone Project in Chapter 14. The learning objectives applying to each of the chapters of the book are for students to

- Develop a broad understanding of how and why businesses can and do impact the natural environment and develop a desire to find out more about your own business organization;
- Develop a broad understanding of how and why environmental issues are likely to directly and indirectly affect your business (now and in the future) through the actions of stakeholders (customers, suppliers, governments, pressure groups, insurers, investors, etc.) and through external changes in the natural environment including climate change;
- Demonstrate an understanding of how environmental issues can change the way the various business management disciplines (as described in the individual chapters of this book) should be managed;
- Develop an ability through discussions and practical examples to apply the diverse ideas of environmental sustainability supported by social sustainability to particular businesses and their management;
- Develop an ability to think deeply and creatively about the broader picture of business interfaces with environmental and social issues and the future of humankind on the earth;
- Develop a skill of thinking about the environmental issues of a business as a prelude to management action and thinking about the environmental issues as a response to management action; and

- Understand how to develop a business plan and business case to support radical greening of a business of your choice, either an existing business or a start-up business.

Summary of authors' ideas

In the following sections, I have summarized each author's approach to his or her particular business discipline.

Part I: Corporate Strategy and Direction

Part I addresses some of the broader environmental and social ideas that a business organization needs to consider, understand and finally apply to its operations.

In Chapter 2 (*Philosophies of Business, Society and Environment*) James Hazelton explores some of the philosophical ideas applied to business and society and other philosophical ideas developed about the environment and about its relationship to business. He does this by considering some of the arguments in respect of moral philosophy, or ethics, that is the ethics of business and of contemporary ethical debates in terms of the social and environmental impacts of business.

In Chapter 3 (*Strategic Direction and Management*) Alfred A. Marcus discusses how establishing a strategic direction and management of a business organization for environmental benefit may help that business to maximize returns to investors and at the same time minimize environmental harm. He also discusses approaches to establishing competitive advantage developed through processes of pollution prevention, product stewardship and sustainable development.

In Chapter 4 (*Leadership for Sustainability*) Suzanne Benn and Dexter Dunphy discuss the leadership of change and the roles that different kinds of change agents can play in constructing the new reality of the sustainable corporation. Transforming the way we do business will require the inspiration, energies and skills of more people than are currently engaged in the task and many more effective leaders.

In Chapter 5 (*Environmental Economics and Environmental Stewardship*) Dodo J. Thampapillai and Bo Öhlmer address environmental stewardship from the perspective of economic theory and suggest that by using modified economic concepts, environmental capital (KN) can be used to help render voluntary environmental stewardship feasible. This chapter may be difficult for readers without some knowledge of economic theory but it is important because it brings environmental stewardship within the ambit of the macroeconomic arena in which businesses operate.

Part II: Management of Operations

Part II addresses some of the disciplines that are integral to putting the management of business organizations onto a sustainable path.

In Chapter 6 (*Human Resources*) Robin Kramar examines some of the issues in human resource management required for progress towards environmental and social sustainability. Human resources management refers to individuals, groups and the relationships between individuals and groups including the systems of practices used to manage and lead within businesses and to build relationships between organizations and external stakeholders.

In Chapter 7 (*Environmental Marketing*) Michael Polonsky discusses the concept of environmental marketing and some of the ideas behind green marketing where firms can seek to minimize negative environmental impacts and in the process create value for themselves and consumers.

In Chapter 8 (*Organization: Structures, Frameworks, Reporting*) Arun Sahay discusses general aspects of organizational management in relationship to environmental and social sustainability with discussions on organizational structures, management system frameworks and organizational sustainability reporting. He includes examples from an Indian company and a multinational company (see also the Indian Case Study at the end of Part II).

In Chapter 9 (*Operations*) Wang Yong and Robert Staib discuss how environmental considerations need to become a part of the operational aspects of companies covering topics such as total quality environmental management, cleaner production and life-cycle assessment. Supply chain management is discussed particularly in relation to China where an increasing amount of the world's manufacturing is taking place.

In Chapter 10 (*Technology Management*) Robert Staib discusses traditional approaches to the management of technology and ways in which environmental issues and environmental management can be integrated into it, including discussions on the management of innovation, research and development, design and production. Also included are discussions on whether incremental technological change can address the major environmental issues facing the world or whether radical technological change will be required. The product stewardship role is discussed in relationship to extended producer responsibility or product take back.

Part III: Support Operations and Business Case

In this final section we outline some of the important disciplines that support a business organization's progress towards more sustainability outcomes. To complete the book we include an outline of the business case for sustainability and a Capstone Project for students to undertake.

In Chapter 11 (*Finance and Investment*) Rory Sullivan and Craig Mackenzie discuss companies from the point of view of investors and highlight some of the financial pressures external stakeholders can exert on a company, and how this might influence a company's corporate behaviour in relationship to environmental and social sustainability.

In Chapter 12 (*Sustainability Accounting and Reporting*) Lorne Cummings discusses the approach the accounting profession is taking to the process of measuring, recording and reporting the environmental and social aspects and performance of business, and the role that accounting systems play in facilitating this process.

In Chapter 13 (*Legal Aspects and Compliance*) Patricia Ryan outlines generally how sustainability issues are addressed by legislation and discusses some of the broad objectives of environmental law and its impacts on business. International environmental agreements are discussed and from a business perspective there is a need to understand how these agreements are translated into the laws and practices of individual nations.

Chapter 14 (*Conclusions and Business Case*) challenges students to make a start by giving you the opportunity to take all you have learnt from the book, the case studies, the readings and the exercises and apply this knowledge to develop a business strategy and a business case that addresses social and environmental issues for an organization either an existing one or a start-up organization.

1.9   Conclusion

Each chapter includes an introduction outlining the subject matter of the chapter and a conclusion summarizing the author's main ideas. In the last chapter (Section 14.5) I have listed the key topics from each of the chapters of the book to assist students to build a framework for the Capstone Project of that chapter.

I have included a diagrammatic model in Figure 1.8 to show a picture for the integration of environmental aspects with business management to help readers keep a focus on how the many aspects of business management and environmental stewardship can and need to come together.

Understanding the complex issues associated with sustainable development (environmental and social) is not easy and implementing sustainable development within a business organization can involve many people in an organization and may be a career-long effort but we need to make a concerted start in all organizations.

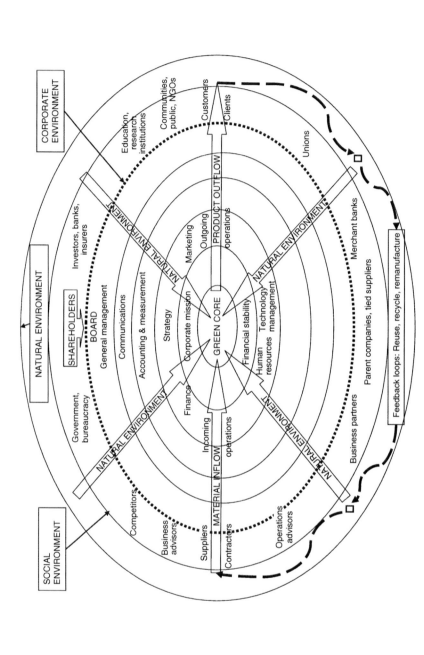

Figure 1.8 Diagrammatic Business Model for the Book

Source: This diagram was developed by the Author R. Staib.

Part I

Corporate Strategy
and Direction

Philosophies of Business, Society and Environment

James Hazelton

2.1 The philosophical approach

In this chapter we explore some of the philosophical ideas applied to business and others that have and are being developed about the environment and about its relationship to business. We do this by considering some of the arguments in respect of moral philosophy, or ethics, that is the ethics of business and of contemporary ethical debates in terms of the social and environmental impacts of business.

What is philosophy and how might it help managers manage? While there are almost as many definitions of philosophy as there are philosophers, a helpful starting point is the Socrates' famous maxim: *the unexamined life is not worth living*. From this perspective, philosophy is above all about critical reflection – the evaluation not only of the objective world but also of subjective beliefs, values and intuitions. Early philosophers such as Plato and Aristotle pursued very broad fields of enquiry well beyond what we consider philosophy today, putting forward theories of astronomy, physics and medicine.

Of primary relevance to the present text is the area of moral philosophy, or ethics. Before considering these questions it will be helpful to clarify the question of whether ethics matters, and whether there can be any agreement on ethical issues. When beginning the formal study of ethics, many people agree that ethics is important, and many have strong views on particular ethical issues such as animal rights and resource conservation. Yet many are hesitant to suggest that their views are 'correct' in an objective sense, especially when confronted by equally passionate and well-informed advocates of an opposing position. In addition, the existence of a wide range of ethical beliefs and customs that operate throughout the world seems to undermine any faith in a universal moral code.

The issues of whether there are absolute, universal moral values are considered in the sub-discipline of 'meta-ethics'. Such issues are important, for if we hold the view that all ethical positions are equally valid, sometimes called *moral relativism*, we seem to lose any ability to move forward in ethical debate. We cannot criticize the practices of other individuals, organizations or countries, as their actions are ethical 'for them'. Slavery, apartheid and terrorist attacks aren't intrinsically evil; it just depends on one's point of view. Indeed, there is no debate at all – I have my beliefs, you have yours, and in the end any arguments have to be settled by force.

Not surprisingly, many philosophers argue strongly against moral relativism. While they accept that there may be a diversity of cultural practices, *universalists* point out that it does not logically follow that all practices are equally moral. Universalists also argue that there are many cultural commonalities – for example, murder and theft are prohibited in virtually every society. Furthermore, the claim by relativists that one should be tolerant of other's ethical beliefs is actually an example of exhorting a universal value (i.e., tolerance). Finally, universalists ask what is the appropriate 'unit' of culture – a country, city, family or individual?

A detailed analysis of this debate is beyond the scope of this book (but for an excellent introduction see Levy, 2002). However, to proceed with a discussion about ethics at least some degree of universalism must be accepted, for if it is not any ethical question reduces to 'might is right'.

Even if universal ethics is accepted, however, determining the morality of a particular action is far from clear. Moral philosophy cannot hope to produce results as clear-cut as those of the empirical sciences. Instead, we have to engage in discussion regarding ethical issues and hope to find the 'better argument'. The conditions for such discussions, and how they might be operationalized, form a major part of the work of contemporary ethicists such as Jurgen Habermas. Shapiro (1998) distils this work into a series of maxims for discussions, including an obligation on those entering into dialogue to justify their ethical positions and be open to the arguments of others. In addition discussions cannot be subverted by including spurious examples or personal attacks, and that those with a stake in the outcome of actions should be entitled to have their views heard. Shapiro cites the US debate on whether stock options should be booked as an expense, and shows that many of these maxims were violated, leading to a sub-optimal outcome. For example, he notes that the legendry investor Warren Buffet's questions ('If options aren't a form of compensation, what are they? If compensation isn't an expense, what is it? And, if expenses shouldn't go into the calculation of earnings, where in the world should they go?') were simply ignored by opponents of expensing options. Such indifference to opposing views is unlikely to be helpful in the long run, especially when considering more complex questions, such as the role of business and the social and environmental obligations of corporations. Entering into a more robust spirit of critical inquiry, the remainder of this chapter considers these questions.

2.2   Philosophy of business and management – early debates

The previous section provided a brief introduction to the philosophical method and critical thinking. We can now apply this approach to one of the most challenging, yet important, questions facing society: what is the role of the modern corporation and its managers? Since the beginning of the twentieth century, the power and influence of corporations have grown to the extent that the sales of many corporations exceed the Gross Domestic Product (GDP) of many countries (Anderson and Cavanagh, 2000). Early corporations had much greater restrictions placed on their activities; citizens granted the corporation limited liability, so expected something of value in return. For example, US corporations were created to fulfil a specific purpose, such as building a rail-road or providing a city with water, and citizens voted annually as to whether the corporation should be allowed to continue to operate in the following year. Ironically, when anti-slavery legislation (the Fourteenth Amendment to the US Constitution) prohibited the restriction of personal liberty, it was successfully argued from the 1880s onwards that corporations were 'people' and therefore entitled to perpetual succession (McIntosh, 2000).

This example illustrates that the debate on the role of the corporation is as old as the creation of the corporate form itself. An early account of corporate social responsibility, but one which remains highly influential in contemporary debates, was provided by the Nobel-prize winning economist, Milton Friedman. Friedman's *Capitalism and Freedom* (Friedman, 1982) discusses the role of the corporation in some detail, but he is best known for an article published in the New York Times in 1970. With characteristic clarity, the title of this work is 'The Social Responsibility of Business is to Increase its Profits' (Friedman, 1970). Friedman follows two broad lines of reasoning to support his position. One is a *normative* line, which presents the reasons why managers are morally obligated to maximize profits. The other is a *positive* line, which presents the reasons why managers are compelled to maximize profits, regardless of their moral predisposition. These arguments are reviewed below, but readers are encouraged to read Friedman's spirited original work.

Friedman's normative arguments for profit maximization

To understand Friedman's arguments it will be helpful to consider the following example. Imagine the CEOs of all the supermarkets in a particular country gather together at a hotel for a weekend convention, where a charismatic animal rights advocate also happens to be staying. Over the course of the weekend, the advocate meets the CEOs and eventually convinces them all that trade in animal products is unethical. On returning to work on Monday morning, the newly enlightened CEOs all issue an edict that all animal products be stripped from the supermarket shelves, leaving only fresh and tinned vegetables behind.

Friedman considers such an act to be wholly unethical for three reasons – agency, competence and democracy. First, he argues that managers are *agents of shareholders* and must therefore follow the preferences of the shareholder. While a manager who supports animal welfare is free to donate her personal funds to this cause, she cannot commit shareholder's funds unless she is certain that this is what shareholders wish her to do. Given dispersed shareholders (Friedman's account is primarily concerned with large public companies) it is unlikely that shareholders would all believe that such action is appropriate. Therefore the obligation is for the manager to maximize profits, and when the profits are distributed back to shareholders via dividends shareholders can allocate their monies according to their particular moral beliefs.

Second, Friedman argues that corporate managers do not have the competency in evaluating the *public good* in the way that government bureaucrats do. Corporate managers are trained in how to maximize profits, and they are promoted on their ability to do so. Therefore to place an obligation on such managers to take the public good into account in their decisions is unwise, as the outcome is likely to be sub-optimal. In the example given above, it is debatable whether public good is enhanced, as any benefits to animals must be weighed against loss of farming jobs and restricted consumer choice.

Third, Friedman argues that while corporate decision-making should abide by the *ethical customs and laws* of a community, it is not a substitute for these customs and laws. Corporate decisions can be made by a few individuals. By contrast, the creation of laws is subject to the debate and scrutiny of the democratic process. In the supermarket example, Friedman would suggest that if the community believed that trading in animal products was unethical, it has the power to elect officials to represent this view who would then implement laws banning such trade. Given that such a law does not exist, the community must consider trading in animal products to be ethical, and a manager does not have the right to subvert this position. The position regarding custom is more ambiguous. Many customs are not embodied in laws, and customs may vary within a community. Nevertheless, Friedman argues that it is not the corporation's responsibility to influence custom.

Friedman's conclusions are clear – a company should act so as to maximize profits. Yet the moral arguments put forward by Friedman have been subject to vigorous debate. For example, the assumption that the law reflects the wishes of society seems simplistic. It ignores the considerable influence that corporations have over the legal decision-making process. AccountAbility (2005, p. 18) estimate that there are over 100,000 lobbyists worldwide, and that in Washington lobbyists outnumber legislators 30 to 1). It also fails to recognize that multinationals may operate in countries which have few laws and limited law enforcement capability. Indeed, the prominent business ethicist Richard DeGeorge (1993) has suggested that one of the moral obligations of corporations operating in the developing world is assist with the development of such a framework, so the suggestion that moral obligations extend only to legal compliance seems questionable. Further, this position ignores the possibility that prevailing laws may be unjust. The decision of General Motors to leave South Africa in protest against oppressive Apartheid laws, or the criticisms of Shell for compliance with the Nigerian military dictatorship (discussed below) are both examples where the community expected corporations to not only comply with, but also evaluate, local laws.

More broadly, Boatright (1994) takes a utilitarian perspective (where the moral action is the one which creates the greatest good for the greatest number, akin to the idea of maximizing the public good). Boatright argues that the interests of wider society are not necessarily best served by corporate profit maximization. For example, a company which pollutes large areas of land and where many employees suffer serious injuries would significantly reduce societal well-being, which is not sufficiently offset by enriching an already wealthy group of shareholders.

Evan and Freeman (1993) critique Friedman using the ethical perspective developed by Immanuel Kant. Kant's ethical theory is both brilliant and complex, and warrants discussion far beyond the space available here, but essentially Kant argues that merely by virtue of being human we possess fundamental rights. Correspondingly, we also have fundamental duties to protect the rights of others, and that societal well-being, or the 'greatest good for the greatest number' is of no moral relevance. Instead, he proposes a 'categorical imperative' (or golden rule) that we should live by, which can be expressed or 'formulated', in a number of ways. The formulation of the categorical imperative central to Evan and Freeman is that people should never be treated merely as means but also as ends in themselves. In other words, we must always recognize that people are intrinsically valuable and not just resources to enable us to meet our personal objectives. Evan and Freeman suggest that a manager focused on maximizing profits treats all other stakeholders as mere means to an end and is therefore unethical. Instead, they suggest 'stakeholder capitalism', whereby the manager does not always act in the interests of shareholders, but rather privileges different stakeholders at different times, as an ideal ethical model. Stakeholder managers play more of a *stewardship role*, ensuring that the interests of any one stakeholder are neither neglected nor made too prominent.

While this stakeholder view may be attractive, it is not without conceptual and practical difficulties. For a start, it must be determined which stakeholders are included. 'Weak' stakeholder theory typically includes only those stakeholders which can affect the corporation while 'strong' stakeholder theory extends the boundary to include those stakeholders who are affected by the activities of the corporation, but who do not have any influence over its operations. A further issue is that the theory seems to offer little practical guidance to managers. When, for example, should the interests of employees become paramount? When negotiating wages? When planning for redundancies? When evaluating workplace safety? Last, but by no means least, is the question of legality. It could be argued that the legal form of a corporation is fundamentally different from the stakeholder collective envisaged by Evan and Freeman, and even they concede that current laws would have to significantly change to realize their vision of a stakeholder-driven firm (Evan and Freeman, 1993, pp. 264–265). This final objection is similar in tone to the second line of Friedman's arguments in favour of corporate profit maximization, which is considered in the following section.

Friedman's positive arguments for profit maximization

Many ethicists engaged with Friedman's account consider only his normative arguments. Yet Friedman also makes the point that even if managers considered it to be their moral obligation to pursue some social or environmental objective, they are compelled to maximize profits by virtue of competitive markets. As he says,

> And, whether he wants to or not, can he [the manager] get away with spending his stockholders', customers' or employees' money? Will not the stockholders fire him? (Either the present ones or those who take over when his actions in the name of social responsibility have reduced the corporation's profits and the price of its stock.) His customers and his employees can desert him for other producers and employers less scrupulous in exercising their social responsibility. (Friedman, 1970, para. 17)

This is a crucial observation, for if true, it renders the moral debate outlined in the previous section largely irrelevant. If corporations are forced to maximize profits by the operation of competitive markets for labour, products, capital and so on, then whether individual managers believe a particular profit-maximizing strategy is social or environmentally ethical is a moot point. The company must execute such a strategy or face oblivion.

A similar point is made by Bakan (2004) on the basis of the legal form of the corporation. While the precise interpretation of what a corporation is varies from country to country, in the United States the precedent is the case of Dodge vs. Ford Motor Co. (1919). In this case it was made clear that directors have a fiduciary duty to act in the interests of one party only: shareholders. Bakan's (highly critical) enquiry into the nature of a corporation therefore likens it to a psychopath, considering only profits and uncaring about the impact of its actions on other stakeholders. Indeed, if a company has no choice in its decision-making, corporations could be conceived as profit-maximizing machines outside the realm of moral consideration at all. Under this (somewhat disturbing) view, what is required is therefore not more ethical corporate decision-making, but rather the provision of goods and services through new organizational forms altogether, such as collectives or NGOs (Hazelton and Cussen, 2005).

One response to this position is to question the assumption that shareholders are only interested in profits. There has been a recent rise in 'ethical' investment, where investors consider factors beyond profitability in making investment decisions (see Figure 1.6). If enough investors allocate capital based on moral considerations, the cost of capital will lower for 'good' companies, making them more successful (and the converse will occur for bad companies). Opinion is divided on the efficacy of ethical investment (for a critical view see Haigh and Hazelton, 2004; Haigh, 2006; see also Chapter 11).

A more fundamental response is to suggest that the interests of corporations and the wider community largely align. This position is sometimes referred to as the 'win-win' view, or 'enlightened self interest', and holds that what is good for the company is good for the world (and vice versa). As the title of one of Shell's earliest sustainability reports put it: Profits and principles: does there have to be a choice? (Shell International, 1998).

Both the competitive markets and legal challenges are neatly resolved under this position. Markets will reward 'good' companies (customers will want to buy from them, employees work for them etc.) and as the interests of shareholders and other stakeholders are aligned, the legal requirement to privilege shareholders is not critical. How plausible is the argument for 'enlightened self interest'? At the outset, it might be noted that for every example of a company where the interests of the company and society seem to be well aligned (renewable energy, medical products etc.) there seem to be others where the alignment is controversial, to say the least (tobacco, armaments, gambling etc.). A recent report by the World Business Council for Sustainable Development suggests that there are a number of challenges for businesses in the years ahead:

> Trust in businesses is at a low ebb, with only four in ten saying they trust global corporations. It could take very little to turn this combination of distrust of business and concern over the world's future into widespread anger. The time is therefore right for progressive businesses to demonstrate not only that we understand and share public concerns, but that we are doing more and more about them. (World Business Council for Sustainable Development, 2006, pp. 6–7)

This statement acknowledges the fact that society may not view the corporate sector as a wholly benign force, and suggests that businesses and their managers face the challenge of operating within the existing frameworks of markets and legislation to deliver outcomes that meet with societal approval. The following sections consider this challenge in more detail with respect to contemporary social and environmental issues.

2.3   Business and society

From the previous discussion, it is evident that critics of corporations point to their adverse impacts on various stakeholders. Charges range from misleading customers, evading taxes and exploiting employees to destroying irreplaceable natural resources. Yet before considering some of these issues, and the implications for corporate managers, it should also be pointed out that the corporate form has been at least partly responsible for the increase in living standards of billions. Many of the items that are so pervasive as to be considered 'essentials' in developed countries (and increasingly in the developing world as well) such as telephones, televisions and even cars, did not exist at all or were restricted to the very rich only 100 years ago.

How can this incredible rise in the material standard of living be explained? One of the seminal texts in this area is Adam Smith's *The Wealth of Nations* (1998). First published in 1776, the full title is *An Inquiry into the Nature and Causes of the Wealth of Nations*, and Smith set himself the task of discovering how it is that nations could become wealthy. He identified two related drivers: specialization and division of labour. In the famous example of the pin factory, Smith suggested that if the various aspects of creating a pin (pulling the wire, cutting the wire, sharpening one end, rolling the ball, attaching the ball to the other end, putting the pins in boxes etc.) were allocated to different people, the productivity of each individual could rise a hundred- or even a thousand-fold. Smith suggested that this division of labour enabled a typical English worker to live at a higher material standard that of an African king (Smith, 1998, p. 20), and even Marx acknowledged its prodigious productive capability (Marx and Engels, 1967, p. 85).

Smith's 200-year-old analysis has proved remarkably prescient. The World Trade Organization (2003) explains the rationale for lower tariffs and integrated global markets in terms remarkably similar to Smith's, and the degree of specialization across the world's labour markets continues to increase. Specialization is not a panacea, however. Even Smith recognized that such division of labour may have adverse consequences on workers whose jobs may become repetitive and routine, rendering them 'as stupid and ignorant as it is possible for a human creature to become' (Smith, 1998, p. 429). Marx expressed a similar idea, suggesting that the worker had been reduced to a mere 'appendage to the machine' (Marx and Engels, 1967, p. 87).

Stakeholder views

In contemporary debates regarding the role of business, one of the most prominent debates has been around 'sweatshops', where manufacturing plants of multinationals have been located in developing countries with pay and conditions far below the norms of the developed world. The issues around sweatshops are complex and fall outside the scope of this text. Suffice it to say that adherents suggest that sweatshops are a stepping-stone for countries to become wealthy, and that working in factories is preferable to the alternative of rural poverty. Critics maintain that sweatshops are inherently unjust, and that given the tiny proportion of labour costs to the retail price of products (shoes selling for US$100 may only have a few cents of labour), corporations could significantly improve working conditions at little economic cost. The issue is further complicated by the fact that many manufacturing facilities are not directly owned by the multinationals who are their main customers, leading to questions about both control and responsibility. In response, companies such as Mattel have been 'in-sourcing' their global supply chain to have greater control over the working conditions they are being held morally (if not legally) accountable for.

A related issue, and one more in line with the themes of the current text, is the exploitation of natural resources. Using the same division of labour argument, countries who are endowed with particular natural resources will use and sell these resources to others who are not so endowed. Oil rich countries, for example, will extract their oil and exchange it for other goods and services in the global marketplace. Such activities, however, are not without controversy. One of the most infamous examples is the activities of Shell in Nigeria. Shell began exploring for oil in the Niger Delta in 1937, by the 1990s it was producing half of Nigeria's output of 2 million barrels per day (Boele et al., 2001a). The billions in oil revenue received by the Nigerian government, however, were largely distributed among the Nigerian military dictatorship rather than the Ogoni people whose land the oil was under and who were most effected by the impact of production (pollution, gas flares and so on) After a series of Ogoni protests, nine of the most prominent Ogoni activists were executed in 1995. Shell was widely condemned both for their conduct in Nigeria and lack of intervention in the harsh response to the Ogoni protests (for a detailed discussion of this case, see Boele et al., 2001a, b; Wheeler et al., 2001).

Such activities therefore raise a number of philosophical and ethical issues for corporate managers particularly in relation to the stakeholders in the countries in which they operate. To what extent are managers responsible for ensuring that the benefits from environmental resource use are appropriately distributed? Should managers only follow the environmental laws of a particular country, or are there minimum environmental standards which universally apply? As Shell commented in their first sustainability report:

> [M]anagers who run a business in this uncertain world have no choice but to make difficult decisions in the face of complex dilemmas. We were all shaken by the tragic execution of Ken Saro-Wiwa and eight Ogonis by the Nigerian authorities... We believe that we acted honourably... But that is not enough. Clearly, the conviction that you are doing things right is not the same as getting them right. (Shell International, 1998, p. 1)

More broadly, to what extent is extraction of non-renewable resources such as oil ethical, and what proportion of such resources should be left for future generations? Given that burning oil contributes to climate change, who should be required to reduce oil consumption and bear the costs of past pollution? How can societal imperatives to reduce consumption be reconciled with corporate objectives for continued growth? To address such issues it will be helpful to consider some of the main conceptions of our moral obligations towards the environment or 'environmental ethics'.

2.4   Business and the environment

Attitudes towards the environment have changed considerably over time. As even Friedman's narrow account of business responsibility suggested that business should operate within the laws and ethical custom of a community, these changing attitudes have already had a profound impact on the way business operates and are set to influence business practices even more in the years ahead. To understand the debates within environmental ethics, it is helpful to consider two broad schools of thought. The first holds the belief that all nature exists for the benefit of humanity and therefore has only *instrumental* value. Within this school are debates as to whether developing or preserving nature will serve humanity's interests the best. In contrast, the second broad school asserts that nature has *intrinsic* value, regardless of the extent to which it serves the interests of humanity. Within this school, there are debates as to whether nature should be conceived at the level of individual animals whose rights should be protected, or at the level of entire ecosystems whose stability should be preserved. This section considers each of these views in further detail and introduces some of the implications for business.

Instrumental views of nature

The *instrumental* (or anthropocentric) position holds that humanity has a special, privileged place in creation. Aristotle held this view in *Politics*, suggesting that nature 'made all animals for the sake of man' (Aristotle, 350 BCE, Book 1, Part VIII). Descartes believed that it was the dualism between matter (nature) and mind (or soul) which enabled human consciousness and free will. By contrast, animals have no soul and are therefore mere machines or 'automata'. Likewise for Kant, animals are outside the realm of moral consideration because they lack rationality (Kant, 1996, pp. 192–193).

An important aspect of this debate is the extent to which nature should be transformed. Some philosophers consider that manipulating the world is not merely useful, it is a necessary condition for the self-actualization of humanity. In other words, tribes that do not intervene significantly in nature are not merely primitive; they are sub-human. For example, Passmore (1974, p. 179) suggests that,

> If we ask, indeed, what human beings add to the world by their presence in it, there is, I should say, only one possible reply: civilization ... man's great memorials – his science, his philosophy, his technology, his architecture, his countryside – are all of them founded upon his attempt to understand and subdue nature.

Many managers might be sympathetic to this position. After all, most corporations aim to transform nature, either explicitly in the case of extractive industries or manufacturing, or implicitly in the case of service organizations. For many, therefore, it almost goes without saying that nature can be improved upon for the betterment of society.

However, while still holding an instrumental view of nature, it has also been argued that human interests are best served when nature is *preserved* rather than transformed. For example, Godfrey-Smith (1979) identified four arguments for the preservation of wilderness:

- The *gymnasium* argument: preservation of wilderness as important for athletic or recreational activities;

- The *laboratory* argument: wilderness areas provide vital knowledge, in particular an understanding of the intricate interdependencies of biological systems. This is important because if we are to understand our own biological dependencies, we require natural systems as a norm to inform us of the biological laws which we transgress at our peril;
- The *silo* argument: the wilderness is a stockpile of genetic diversity, important as a back-up in case something should suddenly go wrong with the simplified biological systems which, in general, constitute agriculture and which also hold the promise of medical advances; and
- The *cathedral* argument: wilderness areas provide a vital opportunity for spiritual renewal, moral regeneration and aesthetic delight.

Manifestations of the instrumental view

While these arguments are certainly important, some commentators suggest that they miss a fundamental point – namely, that preservation of the environment is critical for humanity's very *survival* (or at the very least critical for the survival of civilization as we know it). This survivalist position has deep historical roots. For example, in 1798 Thomas Malthus wrote *An Essay on the Principle of Population*, where he argued that population increases geometrically (i.e., the rate of growth accelerates over time) while food production increases arithmetically (i.e., the rate of growth is constant over time). Therefore he predicted mass starvation (Malthus, 1798). With the benefit of hindsight, it is clear that Malthus significantly underestimated the ability of technology to increase food production, and the extent to which improved technology can mitigate or solve environmental challenges remains hotly contested today.

Another important milestone was the publication of Garrett Hardin's 'The Tragedy of the Commons'. Recall that Adam Smith's basic proposition was that individuals acting out of self-interest will result in collective well-being. Using the example of herders deciding whether to allow their sheep to graze on common land, Hardin suggested the opposite will occur. If, say the carrying capacity of the common is five sheep, it is still in the interests of the sixth herder to graze his sheep as the incremental benefit is realized by the new farmer alone while the incremental cost is shared by all the farmers. Hardin therefore suggests that strong governance is required to ensure the protection of environmental commons as opposed to free markets, and that the absence of such governance is the cause of the widespread environmental degradation observed today.

In 1972, The Club of Rome (an interdisciplinary invitation-only society) released *The Limits to Growth*, a report commissioned from MIT to investigate 'the present and future predicament of man' (Meadows et al., 1972). The report concluded that humanity will run out of resources if economic growth remained unabated. While most of the predictions of the study have not been accurate, the idea that economies operate within biophysical limits remains an important (though contested) idea.

A number of global conferences have attempted to address environmental issues. In 1972, the United Nations held the Human Environment conference in Stockholm, Sweden, which was the first discussion at a global level regarding environmental issues. In 1992, the UN Conference on Environment and Development (UNCED) hosted the first World Summit for Sustainable Development in Rio de Janeiro. The goal was to establish 'concrete strategies that would ensure broad based environmentally sustainable development', articulated in the document 'Agenda 21'. In the same year the World Commission on Environment and Development released *Our Common Future,* commonly referred to as the Brundtland Report, which provided the famous definition of sustainable development as 'development that meets the requirements of the present without compromising the ability of future generations to meet their own needs' (World Commission on Environment and Development, 1992). Ten years later in 2002 the next World Summit for Sustainable Development was held in Johannesburg. The aim of the summit was to examine progress on implementing the goals of the 1992 summit. The then UN Secretary-General Kofi Annan outlined some of the key issues in a speech to the London School of Economics on 25 February 2002:

> Will men and women in the developing world be allowed to compete on fair terms in the global market? How can we mobilise the resources so desperately needed for development? Can the people now living on this planet improve their lives, not at the expense of future generations, but in a way from which their children and grandchildren will benefit? (LeVeness and Primeaux, 2004, p. 190)

The above quote illustrates one of the most interesting aspects of contemporary environmental debates – that they cannot be separated from questions of social justice. This is illustrated by the discussions regarding climate change, unquestionably the single biggest current environmental issue. The environmental dimension of climate change is clear enough – that increasing greenhouse gases in the atmosphere will cause mean temperatures to rise, leading to rising sea levels, changing weather patterns and increasing extreme weather events. Yet there are complex questions of equity in efforts to slow or mitigate climate change. Should nations be held responsible for prior emissions, before it was apparent that emissions had adverse effects? Should newly industrializing countries, such as China, be allowed to increase their emissions to the levels of their more affluent neighbours? To what extent should leaders protect the economic interests of their country versus promoting global environmental interests?

Such debates are complex and ongoing. Before discussing the role of business in such issues, however, it would be remiss not to acknowledge another, competing, perspective on the environment. This position suggests that nature should be preserved not just because of its importance for humanity but also because it holds *intrinsic* value and is discussed briefly below.

The intrinsic value of nature

Some philosophers reject the instrumental view of nature discussed above, arguing instead that nature is *intrinsically* valuable. For example, Desmond Stewart's famous work *The Limits of Trooghaft* (Stewart, 1972) is a fictional account of the Troog, a race of superior intelligence and technology conquering the earth and enslaving humanity. The Troogs use humans as pets, as sport to hunt and for food. They justify such actions to themselves on the basis that they are more intelligent than humans, and that they therefore have the right to use humans in any way they wish. Most readers would be appalled at the actions of the Troog. Yet if we believe the Troog's actions are immoral, how can we defend treating animals instrumentally on the basis of superior human intellect?

Philosophers following this line argue that animals have basic rights, just as humans do. Rather than focusing on the differences between humans and animals (such as the ability to reason or use language), such philosophers suggest that we should consider the commonalities, and in particular the fact that animals can experience pain. Recall that utilitarians believe that the moral act is one which maximizes happiness. Utilitarians such as Peter Singer argue that this happiness should include both human and non-human experience. To do otherwise, suggests Singer, is to be 'speciesist' – analogous to racist – that is, discriminating on the basis of species without justification. According to this view, animal suffering would only be justified where great benefits were going to accrue. Thus while animal experimentation to develop a cure for cancer might be justified, testing to develop new cosmetics might not. Activists typically protest against such activities as factory farming, arguing that human desires for meat and other animal products do not justify the suffering caused to the animals involved. Singer contends that most of humanity is speciesist (Singer, 2001, p. 35).

A different perspective is provided by 'deep ecologists' such as Aldo Leopold. While deep ecologists also consider nature to be intrinsically valuable, they are more concerned with ecosystems and wilderness than individual animals. For example, Leopold (an American forester and later wilderness campaigner) wrote extensively about a 'land ethic' in his famous book *A Sand County Almanac, and Sketches Here and There*. He articulated this ethic as 'a thing is right when it tends to preserve the integrity, stability and beauty of the biotic community. It is wrong when it tends otherwise' (Leopold, 1989, pp. 224–225). According to Leopold, the land ethic 'simply enlarges the boundaries of the community to include soils, waters, plants and animals or, collectively, the land'. For deep ecologists, focusing on individual animals ignores the relationship between all the elements of an ecosystem, or 'web of life' (Capra, 1997). A farm where no animals suffered would still be a gross violation of wilderness, or as Leopold puts it, the biotic community. The culmination of this view is the Gaia Hypothesis, put forward by James Lovelock, who suggests that the entire biosphere could be considered as a single organism (Lovelock, 1991).

Critics of this view present several objections. First, does wilderness actually exist any more? Marx distinguished between 'first nature' which was the untouched canvas upon which humans worked to provide 'second nature'. Even in Marx's time, he considered that first nature no longer existed (Marx and Engels, 1968, I(B)II(2)). More fundamentally, it seems difficult to establish what the interests of a biotic community might be, given that dynamic change is an essential characteristic of natural systems. Further, distinguishing where a biotic community begins and ends is problematic. Nevertheless, deep ecologists do seem to make an important contribution in considering nature collectively, rather than as isolated parts.

Business and the environment

As with the social issues discussed in the previous section, environmental ethics raise some difficult philosophical and ethical questions for managers. From highlighting the positive environmental externalities of activities like video-conferencing, to embarking in explicitly beneficial activities such as renewable energy or land remediation, modern business is increasingly seeking to solve environmental problems within the framework of competitive markets. As noted above, the nature of corporate activity is such that it is generally directed at developing or transforming nature. At the very least, managers must be cognizant of objections grounded in alternative positions, endeavour to make the corporate ecological footprint as small as possible and be transparent in respect of the impact of their operations. A further challenge for corporations is to consider not only their direct impact but also the impact of the entire supply chain. For example, British supermarket chains are experimenting with labelling the 'food miles' that its products have flown, though critics point out that such simple measures may be misleading (Muller, 2007). Fundamentally, however, the message to business is that attitudes to the environment are changing, and that business must respond to such changes. Environmental considerations must be a core part of business objectives, along with social and economic responsibilities. This integrated ethic is represented by the title of the 2006 Sustainability Report of BHP Billiton, one of the world's largest mining companies: *Healthy People + Safe Workplaces + Environmental Commitment + Social Responsibility + Economic Contribution + Sound Governance = Licence to Operate* (BHP Billiton, 2006).

2.5   Conclusion

This chapter has covered much terrain. We began by considering the relevance of philosophy to the modern manager and highlighted the spirit of open but critical inquiry as an appropriate perspective from which to explore ethical debates within business. We then discussed the nature of business itself, and the extent to which business might be considered a moral entity versus a mere profit-maximizing machine. While Friedman's views that the moral obligation of business is mere profit maximization were relatively easy to challenge, his contention that competitive markets force business to profit maximization seems a more robust claim. We then considered some of the main tenants of thought regarding business and society, including historically grounded notions that the interests of managers and employees may not be perfectly aligned, and the contemporary application of this position in the globalization of labour markets. Finally, we touched on some of the major positions regarding environmental ethics, from nature being instrumental to nature being intrinsically valuable. Then we suggested ways in which an argument, philosophical based, could show a strong philosophical link between changing environmental philosophies and business philosophies, for example, how community views on intrinsic and extrinsic values of nature, on the nature of stakeholders rights, on the ideas of sustainable development (both environmental and social as articulated by the United Nations summits) will manifest themselves through *changing the rules of the game.*

The sheer range of issues covered alludes to the complexities that face the modern manager, and more specific aspects of these challenges are considered in the remainder of this book. While acknowledging these complexities, however, it is hoped that this chapter has provided a framework from which managers might engage with these challenges in ways which meet the objectives of business as well as its wider stakeholders, including future generations and the non-human world.

2.6   Questions

- Stating from Friedman's belief that business has a moral obligation to maximize profits, use examples from the World Business Council for Sustainable Development and multinational companies to support or counter this view.
- Using examples from, for example, several companies' sustainability or environmental reports discuss the following: Are the interests of managers and employees inherently antagonistic? To what extent does globalization change the moral obligations of corporations? Does the idea of a difference between intrinsic and instrumental values of nature affect business's approach to sustainability?
- Why does Friedman believe that business will inevitably maximize profits, regardless of any moral arguments? To what extent do you agree with Friedman's position?

2.7   Further reading

Friedman 1970; World Business Council for Sustainable Development, 2006.

Strategic Direction and Management

3

Alfred A. Marcus

3.1 Introduction

This chapter discusses how establishing a strategic direction and management of a business organization for environmental benefit may help that business to maximize returns to investors and at the same time minimize environmental harm.

Among many economists, the idea that expenditures on the environment positively affect firms is controversial (Majumdar and Marcus, 2001). Standard economic assumptions are that spending on environmental protection imposes costs and slows productivity improvements, but Porter has argued that environmental challenges, by inducing firms to economize, can improve their productivity (Porter, 1991). Based on the evidence from several case studies, Porter and van der Linde (1995a) concluded that the environment spending can, in fact, enhance a firms' competitiveness. A considerable body of work now supports this idea that under some circumstances it 'pays to be green' (Gladwin, 1993; Hart, 1995; Shrivastava, 1995; Russo and Fouts, 1997; King and Lenox, 2002; Orsato, 2006). In the years since Porter and van der Linde a number of management scholars have explored these claims and offered their own frameworks for addressing the relationship between environmental protection and competitive advantage (Klassen and Whybark, 1999; Marglolis and Walsh, 2003; Vogel, 2005).

Strategic direction and management

Strategic direction and management of the firm for environmental benefit rests on the assumption that businesses can maximize returns to investors and at the same time minimize environmental harm. Firms can build competitive advantage at the same time that they improve the environment. Examples would be pollution prevention (P2) that lowers a firm's costs and the introduction of environment-friendly products and services that enable firms to obtain premium prices. Pollution is a form of inefficiency – it indicates that scrap, harmful substances and energy are not being used completely or effectively. Introducing new environment-products allows companies to enhance their earnings. They can make big jumps in product development, as innovations are open in such areas as miniaturization, weight reduction, design for reuse and reparability.

Public policies and the values and beliefs of managers exert pressures on firms and contribute in significant ways to the acquisition of capabilities for environmental management like those in P2 and new product development (Marcus and Geffen, 1998). The drivers for acquisition are filtered through psychological and organizational processes, which lead different firms to respond to a set of pressures differently. The overall motivation for the acquisition of competencies in environmental management is pressure and response in which managers perceive, understand and negotiate their solutions (Hoffman, 2000).

3.2   Competencies in competitive environmental management

A large literature deals with business competencies in general and a similar one has emerged with respect to competencies in environmental management. Hart, Shrivastava, Sharma and Vredenburg and Christmann considered environmental management a competency that could provide the firm with business as well as environmental advantages. Hart (1995) took a 'natural-resource-based view of the firm' and argued that firms that developed capabilities in P2, product stewardship and sustainable development could achieve competitive as well as environmental advantage (see Table 3.1). Shrivastava (1995) argued that techniques and methods that minimized environmental impacts, reduced costs and/or enhanced sales were a tool for competitive advantage. Competencies in environmental management are composed of many constituent elements built-up over time. The elements have complex relations among them. To form a coherent whole, the firm's environmental capabilities are brought together and related in intricate ways. The more complex the relations among the elements, the harder to copy or duplicate and the more valuable the competencies may be in providing for competitive advantage. In a study of companies in the Canadian oil and gas industry, Sharma and Vredenburg (1998) found that firms, which took a proactive approach to environmental issues, had unique organizational

Table 3.1   Competitive environmental advantage

Strategic capability	Competitive advantage
Pollution prevention	Lower costs
Product stewardship	Pre-empt competitors
Sustainable development	Future position

Source: Based on Hart 1995.

capabilities, such as stakeholder integration and continuous higher order learning and innovation. Christmann (2000) demonstrated a link between environmental best practices and competitive advantage in the chemical industry based on the existence of complementary capabilities in process innovation and implementation. She found that firms with higher levels of matching assets gained larger cost advantages than firms with lower levels of them.

Competencies in environmental management relate, cohere and are built-up over time to form an overall competence in environmental management. They rest on many constituent capabilities such as P2 and toxic reduction, full cost analysis, auditing, design for the environment, *product stewardship*, industrial ecology, total quality environmental management, collaboration with environmental and other non-governmental organizations, ties to trade associations, relationships with firms in the same and different industries, policy formalization manifested in environmental policy statements and reports, CEO and board involvement and so on. These different elements establish a valuable competitive position that is hard to imitate, reproduce and duplicate. In the retail food industry, for instance, the creation of such competencies might begin with practices like newspaper, plastic recycling, but to these practices others could be added (Marcus and Anderson, 2006). A grocer could engage in advanced recycling (recycling of wooden pallets, cooking oil, meat/fat/bones or plastic bags). It could become involved in consumer education and offer environmental products and services. It might have to provide training to its managers and employees to develop these capabilities. Its employees might be asked to use such techniques as systematically collecting and reporting information on the grocer's wastes and energy usage. Strategic direction and management of the firm for environmental benefit rests on acquiring such capabilities in environmental management.

A firm's capabilities and competencies cannot be taken as given (Ghemawat, 2001). Managers must develop them, but how does this take place? Managers must search for new ideas and methods, compare practices to the best in their industry, evaluate practices in other industries and experiment. Inasmuch as these activities make the acquisition of additional capabilities and competencies possible, they are a dynamic capability (Eisenhardt and Martin, 2000) or an example of 'the capacity of a firm to renew, augment, and adapt its core competencies over time' (Teece, Pisano and Shuen, 1997). A proactive environmental strategy is a dynamic one (Aragón-Correa, 1998; Aragón-Correa and Sharma, 2003).

3.3 Government's role in acquiring competencies in environmental management

Business competencies primarily yield private benefits that firms can fully appropriate. However, with regard to competencies in environmental management, there are likely to be other causes that bring them into existence; this is because the acquisition of these competencies does not produce benefits solely for the firm. When a given level of environmental protection is achieved (Marcus, 1996), there are positive spillovers to the public-at-large. The resulting gain is available to society-as-a-whole, not just those directly connected to the firm. Because environmental protection is a type of public good, whose full value a firm cannot entirely appropriate, factors other than a general dynamic capability that produces business benefit are needed to motivate acquisition. Government's role obviously is quite important.

Government's role

Government's role, however, means more than just regulatory enactments that command firms to act and punish them for refusing to act in accord with government requirements. To capture the richness and complexity of the firm–government interface, the focus should be on a broad array of public policies. Moreover, it must be understood that firms do not merely respond to these policies. They exert considerable influence on the policy process and help create policies to which they must then respond. A key aspect in setting strategic direction and managing the firm for environmental benefit is the role that managers play in creating the public policies to which they must respond.

Whereas environmental regulation generally refers to legally binding mandates imposed by the government on firms and other polluters, environmental policy refers to policies and programmes that include not only regulations but also voluntary government/industry agreements, joint research and development efforts, government information dissemination programmes, grants, subsidies, transfers, taxes and other initiatives. In managing the relationship between competitive advantage and considerations of the natural environment, a conception is needed of the broad policy environment other than just regulation. A firm's acquisition of environmental competencies is impacted not only by environmental regulations but also by the full range of policies and programmes.

In setting strategic direction, managers must try to align their competencies with the full spectrum of public policies. Their aim should be to enhance their competencies so they can obtain sustained competitive advantage from the full range. Within limits, the managers of firms, if they are able to clearly see the linkages between different environmental policy types and their companies' competitive advantage, will try to actively manage the public policy interface to their benefit. Not only will they participate in rule-making procedures with the goal of bringing about regulations that protect and exploit their capabilities and competencies and blocking regulations that threaten their capabilities and competencies, but for the same reasons they also will try to exert influence on voluntary government/industry agreements, joint research and development efforts, government information dissemination programmes, grants, subsidies, transfers, taxes and other initiatives.

Regulation and rules

With regard to regulation, the argument that solutions that are a win for the firm and society-at-large are achievable usually rests on the assumption that a shift in regulations is needed to make the regulations more effective and efficient. A rich literature exists on how to improve regulations. Many authors agree that spending on more rigid requirements is likely to retard productivity, while spending on flexible ones is likely to enhance it (Davis, 1977; Porter and van der Linde, 1995b; Jaffe and Palmer, 1997). A large body of organizational and public policy research supports this view (Marcus, 1988a, b). Several authors have found that flexible rules have a positive effect on performance because they stimulate entrepreneurship, creativity and risk-taking, while an excessively procedures and rule-centred culture stifles innovation (Katz and Kahn, 1978; Lawrence and Dyer, 1983; Burgelman, 1984; Kanter, 1986; Strebel, 1987; Eisenhardt, 1989). Flexible rules allow implementers to move beyond formal compliance to identification and internalization (Kelman, 1961). Linder and Peters (1987), for instance, see value in implementers having the flexibility to adapt and redefine policies as they proceed. They maintain that when those that implement a policy play an active role in their design the results are likely to be better. Several scholars have found that when implementers are given such flexibility, they have greater knowledge of contradictory demands and conflicting imperatives at the point of delivery, and their performance improves (Lipsky, 1978; Elmore, 1979).

Criticisms of the current system of regulation have common elements, which point to the inflexibility of current regulations as being a barrier to the acquisition of environmental competencies by firms (Marcus, Geffen and Sexton, 2002). While the environmental regulatory system in the United States has achieved considerable improvements over the past decades, even those with strong environmental values often view it as being costly and prescriptive, slow in issuing permits, focused on separate media rather than larger problems and in need of updating to meet newly emerging problems. Most US environmental protection laws and regulations, especially those pertaining to emissions to air and discharges to waterways set end-of-pipe technology-based standards based on the level of efficiency of pollution control devices available for a particular production process. Although alternative solutions can be employed, the regulatory outcome is far more certain if a plant manager installs the best available control devices. Thus, innovations in P2, which reduce the use of toxic materials or internally recycle such materials are not sufficiently recognized or encouraged within the current system. Other critiques of the system are insufficient local inputs and a paperwork burden that stifles innovation.

Market mechanisms and environmental impacts

Analysts for a long period of time have been critics of the current US approach and have sketched elements of an alternative that might be more supportive of companies acquiring competencies in environmental management. They base their thinking on the idea that the full harm caused by pollution and extensive use of natural resources are not adequately incorporated into the price system. As a free good with no price, nature tends to be overused. To correct this defect in markets, proposals have been made that move away from rigid command-and-control regulation towards flexible approaches where creativity and innovation can flourish. The model that analysts propose maximizes reliance on market mechanisms when allocation of resources is at stake; imposes pollution taxes (or trading in pollution rights) in proportion to the harms caused by pollution; establishes, to the extent possible, standards based on environmental outcomes and not on current technical solutions; introduces rigorous harm based standards responsive to the latest advances in scientific thinking; provides the public with clear, understandable information about the state of the environment; allows stakeholders a greater role as watchdogs and guardians of the public interest; breaks down the media by media focus of regulatory laws, rules and enforcement so that environmental impact, production and use can be understood holistically; and encourages life cycle analysis, design for the environment, total product responsibility and other system-wide approaches that would enable companies to acquire competence in environmental management. If these reforms were to be implemented, environmental protection would be a more integrated part of the management process. Companies would start with a product's earliest design phase so that the environmental impact and natural resource demands of production, distribution and consumption would be considered at an early stage along with market potential, costs of production and distribution and servicing problems (Geffen and Marcus, 1994).

3.4   Pollution prevention competencies

Would a regulatory system of this nature encourage the further acquisition of innovative environmental management competencies in pollution prevention (P2)? Most US policy, however, has long remained tied to end-of-pipe regulation (Freeman et al., 1992). In theory, the concept of P2, or reducing potential pollution at input stages rather than at the output stage, makes good economic sense. The goal of waste reduction should be a central strategic thrust of the firm. By increasing throughput, lowering rework rates and scrap and using less material and energy per unit of production, a company can save money, enhance efficiency and become more competitive. Right-to-know provisions and the Toxics Release Inventory (TRI) reporting program in the 1987 Superfund Amendments, which were deviations from prior methods, provided an initial impetus to P2.

Chemical manufacturers were encouraged by their manufacturing association to start P2 programs. Many companies did set up these programs. They inventoried wastes and releases, evaluated impacts, established and implemented reduction plans and practiced outreach. Successful P2 demanded attention to product and process design, plant configuration, information and control systems, human resources, and the suppliers' role and organization. A team had to be assembled, a method for measuring P2 determined, process flow diagrams and material-balance diagrams prepared and a tracking system for materials set up. Operational and material changes then had to be considered including process and production changes and material substitutions. A frequent target of P2 programs was reduction of industrial solvents. For such programs to succeed, employee involvement and recognition were important. Companies with notable programs included 3M, Chevron, Dow, General Dynamics, IBM and Monsanto.

Example of Pollution Prevention

A company that started a successful P2 program is Novartis. In 1979 (then called Ciba Geigy), it created 30 units of finished products and 70 units of waste for every 100 units of inputs; by 2000, because of extensive efforts to prevent pollution, it produced 75 units of finished products and 25 units of waste for every 100 units of inputs. To achieve this type of progress, companies rely on material-balance models. They add up their total production inputs and try to minimize them, then they carefully examine production processes to ensure that they are maximally efficient and do not waste inputs. The goal is to increase usable products and decrease waste.

Despite the impressive efforts some firms made, this capability in environmental management was not fully adopted. There are a number of reasons including the following: (1) Despite the financial benefits, managers viewed P2 as an extension of existing regulatory programs that they regarded as costly and burdensome. (2) Many managers believed their environmental accounting systems were not adequate to measuring the true costs and savings. (3) Many managers considered the risks of changing production processes to be too high. (4) Many believed that investments in P2 would yield less return than other investments that they believed to be of greater strategic importance. To fully develop a capacity for P2 and other cost saving environmental management capabilities such as design for the environment, life cycle analysis, environmentally conscious manufacturing, green marketing and industrial ecology these obstacles must be overcome (Geffen and Marcus, 1994).

3.5   Product development competencies

What stalls the acquisition of new product development competencies in many firms? An example would be energy efficiency and renewable energy (EERE) businesses that have developed products and services that would help consumers save or replace traditional forms of energy such as oil, coal, natural gas and nuclear power. The sector includes manufacturers whose products or services: save energy in residential or commercial buildings (e.g., energy efficient windows, lighting components, insulation materials and appliances); save energy in industrial processes or settings (e.g., process controls, thermostats, heat recovery systems, and ventilators); reduce energy use in commercial buildings or industrial settings (e.g., demand side management programmes, energy audits, training and software for energy systems); and/or produce renewable energy or alternate fuel products (e.g., photovoltaic products, wind power systems and whole tree biomass systems). While many EERE businesses are new firms, others are new businesses within larger, more established firms, but even the new businesses within larger firms represent ventures that are entrepreneurial in nature and are subject to the same forces that affect start-up firms.

Many EERE businesses were in a state of 'prolonged gestation' (Marcus and Anderson, 2006) throughout much of the 1980s and 1990s. Unlike other promising sectors (e.g., personal computers), they did not fully take-off. Some of the factors that kept them in a prolonged state of gestation were relatively low energy prices for conventional fuels in this period, a pullback in government subsidies, and partially, as a consequence, a relatively low level of consumer demands. Other factors were performance uncertainties, high costs and insufficient development of infrastructure and supporting industries in the value chain. These supporting industries might have supplied valuable inputs and assisted in manufacturing, distribution, marketing, sales and/or service.

With higher energy prices, will these businesses move through stages of growth and maturity as they are propelled forward by increases in demand and in sales? It is likely that not all businesses will pass smoothly through these stages. To move to take-off, critical mass and momentum are needed and the process can unfold over a very long period of time (van de Ven and Garud, 1989). Some start-up businesses have moved from origin to takeoff in just two years while others take more than 50 years (Aldrich and Fiol, 1994). The range of takeoff time is great, and founders, entrepreneurs and innovators in the area of EERE businesses need considerable commitment if the new products and technologies which they hope to introduce are to succeed.

Since the 1970s many founders of new EERE business gave up, their interest waned, they lost patience and they did not have the determination or the resolution to deal with setbacks that occur. Many were forced to abandon the venture because of circumstances they could not effectively control such as few customers, technological glitches, waning financial support and negative cash flow. This phenomenon is not unique to new product development in the EERE area. In comparison to the number of businesses founded, relatively few survive, and even fewer take-off (Hannan and Freeman, 1989). To increase the chances of success, formidable obstacles must be overcome. The skills of the innovators must be great. Within large industrial concerns those setting strategic direction must cultivate these skills and encourage those who have these capacities.

Examples of Product Developments

Some examples of firms that aimed for new product developments in the environmental area are given below. Consider *Ringer,* a producer of alternative pesticides and lawn and garden products. The company had innovative products but they were high-priced and worked more slowly than conventional ones. Faced with dedicated and resourceful competition from such companies as Scott and True Value, it had problems gaining market acceptance and becoming profitable. After struggling during most of the 1990s, Ringer went bankrupt (Marcus, 1998). *Osmonics,* in contrast, successfully manufactured and sold filtration devices and equipment. These products were used to recycle materials in manufacturing processes and in this way played a role in pollution prevention in industries as diverse as electroplating and dairies. Though Osmonics had its ups and downs, it succeeded as an ongoing business.

Another example is *Deluxe Printing,* which won awards for the development of a new ink system called Printwise. Unlike soy inks, which still rely on petroleum-based products and solvents, Printwise is a pollution-free, vegetable-based ink that uses water. To succeed, Deluxe had to revolutionize the industry as well as transform itself. Never before had it manufactured or sold ink, yet it now had to sell Printwise to its major competitors. Like Ringer, Deluxe relied on a high-price strategy, one that its customers were not willing to accept. Although the company's core check-printing business was in decline, the challenges it faced in the ink business were difficult and it sold Printwise to a French company (Marcus and Geffen, 1998).

Still another environmental innovator is *Alliant Techsystems,* a world leader in the manufacture of conventional munitions. With cuts in Pentagon spending at the beginning of the 1990s, Alliant Tech faced layoffs and downsizing. Therefore, it was searching for new business opportunities. At its Joliet, Illinois, ammo plant, it developed unique methods for recycling out-of-specification explosives. It began to seek customers worldwide for this business, especially in ex-Soviet bloc nations, which had huge stockpiles of antiquated munitions, some dating back to the 1905 Russian–Japanese war. Alliant Tech profited handsomely from recycling and selling the explosives and metals for civilian uses. (Marcus, 1996)

Examples of Product Developments – Auto Industry

Efforts at environmental innovation in the auto industry were less successful. Throughout the 1990s the auto companies struggled to commercialize new, less polluting products. Early research into the feasibility and development of electric cars to reduce petroleum dependence started during the gasoline shortages of the 1970s. By 1990, electric cars were seen as an answer to growing pollution woes, particularly in cities like Los Angeles, which was plagued by smog. Electric vehicles were often hailed as an answer to existing vehicles that release hydrocarbons, carbon monoxide and nitrogen oxide. However, electric cars were not without their problems: They required that coal, oil or natural gas be burned to produce the electricity, and power stations, along with factories, continued to exceed nonelectric motor vehicles with respect to the amount of pollutants they emitted.

Electric vehicles were designed primarily as a response to new clean-air legislation enacted in select states. In September 1990, California enacted new laws tightening emissions standards and mandating that 2 per cent of all new vehicles sold produce no exhaust at all. Zero-emission vehicles (ZEVs) would necessarily be electric – no other alternatives met the California standard. *General Motors* (GM) was a pioneer in developing electric automobiles, investing early research money in a wide variety of environment-friendly, or green, cars, including electric and even solar-powered automobiles. Despite cumulative sales figures in 1998 of only 216 electric EV1s and about 200 electric S-10 pickups, GM indicated that it would continue to work on electric vehicles due to the learning that could be gleaned for next-generation technology in the form of hybrid vehicles (part electric and part conventional) and fuel-cell technology (Marcus, 1996).

In 1998, GM unveiled a prototype hybrid vehicle and started to do serious research on fuel-cell-powered cars. By the year 2000, hybrid vehicles had grown in popularity. Hybrids were being marketed with an emphasis on the environmental benefits of the technology. Honda was the first to actually sell a hybrid, its two-seater Insight, to the public. By 2002, Honda had a hybrid version of the Civic. Toyota's compact Prius hybrid, introduced in the United States in 2000, proved to be more popular than the Insight or the Civic hybrid. Toyota Hybrid sales had taken off (see Figure 3.1 and case study in Chapter 10). The potential for substantial increases in the fuel efficiency of vehicles offered by hybrid electric vehicles were great. They could mitigate persistent and serious environmental problems, improve economic and national security and reduce trade imbalances. (Marcus and Geffen, 2005)

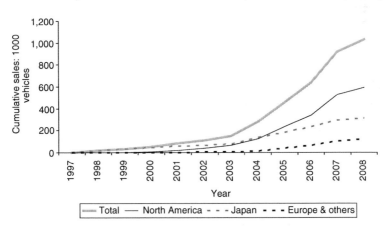

Figure 3.1   World sales of the Toyota Prius

Note: Sales for 2008 are for the first four months, extrapolated to a full year would equal 1240.

Source: Toyota, 2008.

3.6   Values and beliefs

Missing so far in this analysis are values and beliefs that play a critical role in the acquisition of P2 and new product development capabilities in environmental management. Values and beliefs are reflected in how managers define their firms' missions (Sethi and Falbe, 1987). Setting strategic direction a firm's mission is very important. Some firms' missions remain narrow and focused with the main concern being profitability. However, other firms have broad missions that are inclusive of different stakeholders and their needs. Community relations, customer welfare and employee morale are among these firm's top priorities. If a firm's mission is narrow, it is not likely to engage in basic environmental practices, but if it is broad it is likely to go further in the area of acquiring environmental capabilities in such areas as P2 and new product development. The relationship between a firm's mission and its acquisition of environmental management capabilities is critically important.

But what is the origin of the values and beliefs that lead to the managers of some firms broadening their missions beyond mere profitability (Bansal, 2003)? From where do managers get the vision to set such broad goals? It requires that top management take action in educating key business stakeholders in environmental values. Those setting strategic direction in the firm must be proponents of P2 and other management processes internally and of new green products and services externally. They must make the argument that green business practices and products are attractive, that they provide a superior way to do business and that disruptive exogenous change in any case will take place that will compel the firm to engage in the endeavours they have initiated. The more they act to educate key business stakeholders, the more their beliefs and the beliefs of their internal and external stakeholders are likely to grow and the more they are likely to broaden their mission to include concerns outside mere profitability.

By engaging in actions to convince key business stakeholders, managers firm up their convictions and build their own confidence and that of their constituencies in the rightness of their firm's mission and their values and beliefs. In trying to educate key business stakeholders, proponents of green processes and products have to justify their continued commitment to an uncertain opportunity. They must frame an unknown future in ways in which it becomes believable. They compete for the right to be taken for granted by relying on rhetoric – consistent stories, encompassing symbolic language and behaviours to gain legitimacy for their activities (Aldrich and Fiol, 1994). They use their powers of persuasion to overcome resistance and scepticism (Dees and Starr, 1992). They create values, norms, rules, beliefs and new taken-for-granted assumptions.

The role of persuasion is large in the adoption of green practices like P2 and in commercializing green products and services. Optimism is needed to sustain the proponents of green processes and products (Camerer and Lovallo, 1999). This optimism must be based on a conviction that dynamic, disruptive, exogenous factors will alter the existing landscape (Brouwer, 1991). Shocks and upheavals from a variety of sources will fundamentally change the way people live and the system works. The sense, that economic opportunities in the form of new valued products and services from better environmental management and practices, gained momentum in the first decade of the twenty-first century. Many firms have been bolstering their environmental capabilities in response to the challenges of high energy prices and global climate change.

3.7   Negotiating the future

In setting strategic direction, managers have an array of environmental capabilities that they now may acquire and which they can consolidate and build into a competence in environmental management. Public policies and values and beliefs stimulate the acquisition of these competencies. In acquiring these competencies managers confront public policy pressures and must consider their values and beliefs. In light of these pressures, they must negotiate solutions to the problems their firms and society confronts.

The negotiations in which they must be engaged are complex. Environmental negotiations typically are multiparty in nature. Vast differences exist in coming to an agreement in multi-party negotiations as compared to simpler two-party negotiations like employment contracts. With each additional party that joins the negotiation, the complexity of reaching agreement increases as groups and sub-groups form around particular issues and additional bargaining takes place making it more difficult to reach agreement.

Not all the negotiating parties are internally monolithic. In environmental negotiations it is commonly the case that each party might comprise people who are from the same organization but whose interests differ. By design, members of the negotiating team, typically represent different organizational interests. There might be a single person at the head of the team who tries to aggregate these interests but in a complex organization that person will have problems melding together competing factions.

Another factor that adds to the difficulty of reaching agreement is the number of issues on the table. On the face of it, it would seem that the more the issues, the more complex the negotiations and the harder it would be to reach an agreement. If the issues were highly technical, as is often the case in environmental negotiations, it would only add to the difficulty. Different parties with different beliefs regarding the 'facts' – the scientific and technical realities being debated – would have a hard time agreeing. The added complexity can prevent the parties from arriving at a solution. But the upside of ambiguity and of having more than one issue on the table is the potential it provides to satisfy all the parties. It gives the parties more to work within their effort to find joint gains. Joint benefits arise because the different parties attach different values to the different issues. In this way, the pie appears to grow and it may be possible to come to terms when otherwise an agreement was out of reach.

Outside mediators or arbitrators are customarily referred to as 'third-parties', even when there are more than two disputants. If a third party can be brought in – a trained, outside facilitator – then one would think that the prospects for a settlement would go up. Third-party intervention may be able improve the chances for a settlement. However, third parties do not always have this beneficial effect. For example, Leach and Sabatier (2003) examined 50 randomly selected watershed partnerships in California and Washington between 1999 and 2001 and found a statistically significant *negative* relationship between the involvement of a trained outside facilitator and an agreement. They comment that 'despite their best intentions' the paid facilitators evoked 'feelings of resentment'. Their 'professional training in the arts of consensus building' in fact was 'a detriment'. It lead the facilitators 'to devote excessive amounts of time to "getting the process right",' thereby delaying the important substantive negotiations that had to take place (Leach and Sabatier, 2003, p. 167).

Long-standing relationships and history

In most environmental negotiations the parties have a long-standing relationship and a history of negotiating around similar issues. The parties observe each other's behaviour to determine if they can trust each other and work together. Through trial and error they try to discover if mutual rewards are possible. Repeated interactions, therefore, are necessary to forging cooperative solutions. The nature of repeated negotiations amongst the same parties is that each disputant is concerned about its reputation. While this concern with reputation can lead to cooperative behaviour and honesty, it also can lead to friction that builds up over time and spoils the atmosphere for negotiations (Raiffa, 1982). With repetition, each party may want to build a reputation for toughness to obtain long-term rather than short-term rewards.

When parties interact repeatedly, they can develop into long-standing adversaries. The history and content of their prior opposition plays a disproportionate role. The parties seek not just an advance over the status quo but one based on the weight and legitimacy of claims they have historically made. These claims no longer are tied to specific issues but are related to an underlying sense of fairness about their cause (Marcus et al., 2002). If the parties start to think they are dealing with 'strident antagonists' and malevolent, untrustworthy characters whose promises are suspect, then it is unlikely that an agreement can be reached (Raiffa, 1982).

Those setting strategic direction for their firms in environmental management must be particularly skilled negotiators. They must negotiate internally with critics who will resist advances in process innovations like P2 and externally with a full range of societal stakeholders who care passionately about the innovations that firms can unleash in the areas of environmental betterment.

CASE STUDY

Negotiating the Future – Monsanto's Difficult Road to Biotechnology

A good example of the difficulties in reconciling values, public policies and stakeholder perceptions and negotiating towards a more sustainable future where environmental processes and products may be more prevalent is Monsanto. In post-industrial societies, the information component of what is produced increases and the 'stuff', or material component, decreases. The rise of the mind as a source of wealth is among the most important forces with which innovators and entrepreneurs must contend. In a 1996 interview in the Harvard Business Review (Magretta, 1997) Robert Shapiro, former CEO of Monsanto, maintained that the movement from industrial to post-industrial society promised to be one of the most important factors in enabling the world to solve its fundamental problems. This movement could bring into existence a more sustainable society, one where people's basic needs for food and a healthy environment could be better met. Shapiro claimed that instead of being sprayed with pesticides, plants could be genetically coded to repel or destroy harmful insects. He explained that this would be a much smarter way of doing business since up to 90 per cent of what is sprayed on crops is wasted.

Shapiro said that Monsanto was committed to making 'smarter' products that reduced chemical use. It had developed a bioengineered potato that defends itself against the Colorado potato beetle; Btcotton, which kills and repels budworms; and Roundup herbicide, which allows farmers to kill weeds without ploughing, thereby preserving the topsoil (a practice called 'conservation tillage'). Roundup does not harm crops. It sticks to soil particles, but unlike conventional herbicides, it does not migrate into groundwater, it degrades into natural products such as nitrogen, carbon and water, and it is non-toxic to animals.

By the year 2000 in the United States, the production of over half of the soybean crop and more than one-third of the corn involved the use of biotechnology products (Marcus, 2006). Scientists were able to protect crops such as corn, soybeans, cotton, potatoes and tomatoes from pests. They were working on taking genes from fish that swim in icy waterways and injecting them into strawberries to enable the strawberries to resist frost. In addition to its agricultural applications, biotechnology promised advances in other fields as well:

Nutrition. Scientists had extracted genes from one species (e.g., a Brazilian nut) and put them into another species (the soybean) to increase the protein level so that the crops are more nutritional. They also were trying to make crops like soybeans taste better and trying to remove some of the saturated fats so that soybeans offer health benefits.

Pharmaceuticals. Scientists were close to introducing genes into rice that will enable it to produce beta-carotene and thus combat the vitamin A deficiency that is common among people who rely on rice for sustenance. They also were developing vaccines for hepatitis B, diarrhoea and other diseases that could be incorporated into the cells of a banana or a sweet potato and thereby distributed to people in developing nations who might not otherwise be protected against these diseases. Industrial. Ultimately, scientists aimed to make industrial materials like plastics, nylons and other petrochemical by-products from genetically modified plants. These plants would replace world reliance on highly polluting hydrocarbons.

The potential benefits that might ensue from the widespread use of biotechnology were very large. Indeed, scientists and entrepreneurs were not shy about hyping the chances of success. However, they also had trouble focusing on which products to make first. With regard to the use of biotechnology for pharmaceuticals, five federal agencies in the United States had some jurisdiction and guidelines were unclear. While waiting for regulatory approval of a product, companies had to maintain manufacturing facilities that they cannot run at full capacity and sales forces that could not yet market the product. Many therefore moved to other applications and allied themselves with large drug and chemical companies that are experienced in dealing with the regulators. The large manufacturers helped biotech companies shoulder the risks, and the biotech companies benefited from the manufacturers' marketing capabilities.

Monsanto made a huge early investment in biotechnology, but it was disappointed when the governor of Wisconsin banned a bovine growth hormone (BGH) that Monsanto had developed to boost cows' milk production. The ban came after opposition from dairy farmers, who were supposed to be the product's main customers. BGH is a protein similar to one cows make naturally. It is injected into the cows twice a month and increases yields by 10 to 20 per cent. Farmers, however, feared that a milk glut would lower prices. Consumers' anxieties about artificial foods and retailers' fears that people would not buy milk from cows injected with BGH prevented the product from being widely used.

Environmentalists widely criticized genetically engineered food as being 'Frankenstein' in quality, and they warned against eating these foods. European governments imposed regulations. They called for the separation of approved and unapproved strains, required labelling and prevented the sale of some products. European companies like Novartis and Aventis, which were once very active in biotech R&D, left the industry because of the controversy. Still, the competition in the biotech industry was intense. Du Pont saw genetic engineering as a means of using its R&D capabilities to deal with global challenges like hunger and ageing. It financed research in the life sciences with the profits from its mature businesses such as nylon and polyester. It reset its corporate portfolio to carry out this strategy, selling a large petrochemical company, Conoco, and buying a controlling interest in a seed company, Pioneer Hi-Bred.

Meanwhile, as the prospects of biotechnology went up and down, Monsanto was bought by Pharmacia and then spun off again as an independent company (2002). Along with Du Pont, Monsanto remained one of the two major players in the industry. It had partnerships with companies like Cargill to develop animal feed and Mendel Biotech to develop technologies for controlling genes. Start-ups in the industry included Sangamo Biosciences, which was working on gene switches, and DNP Holding Company, which was working on banana rot and cancer-protecting substances in tomatoes. Monsanto and Du Pont continued to compete over what should be the best product to commercialize first – corn for chicken feed, soy oil for healthy hearts or feed stocks for bioengineered chemicals. Whether the industry would fulfil its promise depended on whether its top executives could negotiate solutions that would win public acceptance and overcome regulatory hurdles, especially in Europe.

The European Union (EU) in 1998 imposed a moratorium on approving new types of genetically modified crops for import because of a concern about mad cow disease. It ended the ban in 2004, partly because of US protests that the prohibition was a trade barrier. Nonetheless, EU law that mandated that any food that contained more than 0.9 per cent of genetically modified (GM) ingredients had to be labelled kept a lid on the market. Big supermarket chains refused to sell products about which their consumers were anxious. Critics worried about the impact on people, though almost all GM grains were being fed to cattle, and they worried about contamination of adjacent fields. Greenpeace 'detectives' marked fields of farmers who used GMO seeds. The fields then became the target of eco-activists who vandalized them.

But in France there were signs of change as more farmers were planting the single genetically modified seed the EU permitted, transgenic corn. They planted it because it lowered their costs and increased pest protection. The French farmers were planting the genetically altered seeds despite opposition from the environmental activists and the politicians. In 2006, they grew 12,350 acres of genetically modified corn, more than 10 times as much as they did in the previous year. Other countries such as the Czech Republic, Portugal and Germany were following in France's footsteps. Spain already had 148,200 acres of genetically modified plants under cultivation, the largest amount in Europe.

The seed companies might have another path to expansion. A new biotech revolution appeared to be in the making. Turbo charged selective breeding (TCSB) meant finding plants with desirable traits and mating them. Rather than gene splicing, it did not require taking genes from one set of organisms and inserting them into another. Rows of robotic devices examined DNA in slices from thousands of plants. Scientists examined the slices to find subtle genetic differences that might explain why some plants were better than others at dealing with the cold, suppressing insects, surviving droughts or reproducing seed, for instance. With this knowledge, they tried to breed better plants. The new methods halved the time it took breeders to create marketable seeds. Claims were being made that TCSB could greatly speed the rate at which major crops increased their productivity. The new technology rested on computer power and the seed companies were starting to hire PhDs in mathematics. Once a gene that imparted a desired trait was identified, a probe or marker was attached to it to monitor breeding and determine if it was inherited. The new technology so far had not generated resistance from environmental activists in Europe or elsewhere. (See also Table III.3) (Kilman, 2006; Miller, 2006)

3.8   Conclusion

To what extent can environmental problems be opportunities for business? To what extent do they impose constraints? At one time, corporate leaders regarded environmental issues primarily as a threat to their profitability. However, if extracting more economic value from fewer natural resources and raw materials can improve existing products and services and lead to the development of new ones, environmental challenges can be catalysts for innovation and entrepreneurship. Win-win solutions would mean that both the environment and society would be better off. While the conventional view was that spending on the environment imposed costs, slowed productivity growth and hindered global competitiveness, the revisionist view sees it as a driving force for corporate efficiencies and for entrepreneurship and innovation. Some firms, indeed, have started to change from resisting environmental pressures to incorporating, and even profiting, from them. Environmental considerations have played a role and the optimization of production processes to minimize pollution, especially in pollution sensitive industries like petrochemicals and electric power and in basic manufacturing industries such as auto, steel, paper and cement and in capital investments, new product development. These developments are important ones from which to learn in setting the strategic direction of the firm. For some companies, excellence in protecting the environment has created opportunities for achieving competitive advantage. These companies are able to achieve cost leadership by pursuing environmental efficiency or by pursuing a differentiation or focus strategy based on developing 'green products' for niche markets.

Walley and Whitehead criticized the idea of win-win environmental solutions being a way to spur entrepreneurship and innovation. They claimed that the concept was unrealistic, as at many companies environmental costs were rising and there was no chance of economic payback. However, in a Harvard Business Review symposium (Walley and Whitehead, 1994), participants pointed out that complying with the law was not expected to yield a positive economic return but that, nonetheless, basic changes in products, services and business strategies carried out for environmental reasons often offered financial as well as ecological benefits. Most companies would welcome opportunities to increase shareholder value through environmental spending, but ensuring compliance often dwarfed the possibility of win-win solutions. Sometimes shareholders gained from higher environmental standards, as in the case of companies serving the 'green consumer'. However, most consumers thought 'green' only in buying a small range of products, and the products often did not work as well as others and cost more.

Being early to a market does not guarantee success if the products are too far ahead of customer tastes. Achieving entrepreneurial breakthroughs and innovation by means of a firm's responses to environmental challenges is not easy. Nonetheless, establishing a distinctive competence for managing the physical environment is important, as it can mean less waste, fewer emissions, less accidents, lower costs and better integrated systems. To the extent that this competence is tacit, casually ambiguous, rare, firm specific and adds value to customers through product differentiation or lower costs, it provides competitive advantage. Indeed, many companies have made substantial advances in reconciling their business and environmental goals. They have created 'win-win' solutions where being 'green' rather than a cost of doing business has become an impetus for reduced costs and the development of new market opportunities and innovation.

3.9   Questions

- Source current information on Monsanto's biotechnology approach (see case study box) and critically analyse its journey from pollution prevention to product stewardship to sustainable development.
- Develop a business case and strategy (for a company of your choice) that would lead the company along the pathway from pollution prevention to *product stewardship* to sustainable development.
- Outline a framework and strategy to develop competency in competitive environmental management to support the business case.

3.10   Further reading

Hawken, 1993; Stead and Stead, 2004; Laszlo, 2005; Howard-Grenville, 2007.

Leadership for Sustainability

*Suzanne Benn and Dexter Dunphy**

4.1 Introduction

In this chapter we discuss the leadership of change and the roles that different kinds of change agents can play in constructing the new reality of the sustainable corporation – human sustainability and ecological sustainability. Transforming the way we do business will require the inspiration, energies and skills of more people than are currently engaged in the task. To create a sustainable world, we need many more effective leaders.

In raising the issue of change leadership, we cannot ignore how easier it is to accept the status quo, to respond to our fear of change and our desire for certainty, to opt out rather than to engage actively in attempting to change the organizational world. Change of the order we are advocating here threatens us with uncertainty and chaos. It is much easier to hold on to traditional ways of doing things and to accept the leadership of others who don't question the status quo. The past, because of its familiarity, seems to offer us security but many past practices are unsustainable. If we want the world we know and love to survive, and if we are to survive and thrive ourselves, we must change.

Choosing to lead change involves courage, risk-taking and the development of high levels of skill. This chapter is designed to help you answer some basic questions about your own potential role as a leader of sustainable change: How do I equip myself to be an effective leader? Where shall I start? Who can I work with to have the most impact?

* Edited version of Chapter 9 from Dunphy, Griffiths, S. Benn, 2007.

4.2   Key factors in change agent competency

Effective change leaders need clarity of vision, knowledge of what they wish to change and the skills to implement the changes. None of these can be fully effective without maturity and wisdom. In the end it is who we are, not what we know or can do that makes the crucial difference in effecting organizational change. In the following sections we list and then discuss characteristics of ideal change agents.

Goal clarity

I know what outcomes I want to produce. Yes, we do need to know what we want to achieve, but our understanding of the goal doesn't have to be precise when we begin. What we need is a 'strategic intent', a direction, an intuitive response to the organizational situation in which we find ourselves, an aspiration to nudge our organizational world a little closer to the ideal of sustainability. This aspiration entails a clear understanding of core values and core purpose (Palmer et al., 2006).

Core Values

At Insurance Australia Group (IAG), Australia's largest insurance group, the CEO, Mike Hawker, has defined corporate social responsibility as a core value and sustainability as a shared purpose across the organization to ensure that the organization is around in the future for its customers, employees, community and shareholders. This involves

- economic sustainability – building value for shareholders;
- human sustainability – safety, work–life balance, diversity;
- environmental sustainability – advocating climate change, reducing impact on environment;
- social sustainability – reducing risk in the community such as crime, fires, car accidents etc. (Benn and Wilson, 2006)

Role clarity

I know what to do to produce change. But when we start, we often do not know what to do to make change happen. To overcome this paradox we need to find a viable and effective role to play in midwifing the future when things conspire to block us.

Corporate Responsibility

Nike initially floundered in finding its response to the boycotts and activism associated with poor working conditions in subcontractor factories in developing countries such as Vietnam. In 1998, Nike established a global corporate responsibility function and created the specific role of Vice-President of Corporate Responsibility, covering labour compliance, global community affairs, stakeholder engagement and corporate responsibility, strategic planning and business integration. Tangible sustainability outcomes for Nike include an environmental sustainability policy and initiatives, targeted to give 3 percent of the company's pre tax income to communities around the globe ($37.3 million in cash and product in 2004). They also developed an internal and external contract factory monitoring program and integrated corporate responsibility into the business. (Nike, 2004b)

Relevant knowledge

I have or can access the knowledge required to produce the outcomes I want. Corporate change processes demand depth of knowledge, and in the area of sustainability that knowledge is often not gained easily. Sustainability cuts across traditional disciplinary boundaries. We may need knowledge about the political processes of the organization, energy conservation, water purification, chemical pollutants and the attitudes of key external stakeholders. He/she would be an unusual person who had this knowledge at the beginning of a change programme. But we don't need all the knowledge before we start; we can acquire it as we go along, in partnership with others more knowledgeable than ourselves in some of these areas.

Strategy

Nike's Mark Parker and Charlie Denson, co-presidents of Nike's brand, state that its decade-long journey in understanding its impact has enabled the firm to clearly enunciate its three-pronged strategic goals to

- Use sport as a tool for positive social change and campaign to turn sport and physical activity into a fundamental right for every young person;
- Effect positive, systemic change in working conditions within the footwear, apparel and equipment industries;
- Create innovative and sustainable products. (Nike, 2004a)

Relevant competencies and resources

I have or can assemble the skills and resources to make it happen. We may not have the skills we need when we first take up a role as an organizational change agent. Acquiring skills is a lifetime endeavour. So, we need to be realistic about the skills we have and start the change process that builds on our current skill level through experimentation and practice. We may take faltering steps at first but, with practice, our steps will become firm and purposeful. Mentors and models can help with the necessary skills. To begin with, we need only a subset of the skills demanded by the full change programme.

Self-esteem

I believe I can do it. Sometimes this one is the toughest call of all, but a passionate belief in the profound importance of the change is a great help. Being a change agent is not for the faint hearted. Emotional resilience is a fundamental requirement. We are often called on to persist in the face of adversity, derision, contempt and anger. Changing entrenched power structures can be a career-threatening experience. But abandoning the cause of sustainability is a planet-threatening experience. If we choose to undergo some adversity, at least in the end we have the satisfaction of knowing that we stand for life, hope and a viable future for us all.

4.3   Achieving mastery

The characteristics of the preceding sections are ideals to be worked towards setting a direction for our learning. They define mastery in this field – it is a long path where we learn primarily by doing. We also learn from others more experienced and skilled than ourselves and by finding models and mentors. We need to learn to live with ambiguity and a degree of chaos. Managing corporate change is rather like white-water rafting, that is, not to try to control the environment but to move with it. Success in change leadership comes from being willing to change our internal psychological world. Table 4.1 outlines the stages in achieving mastery as a change agent.

Chatterjee writes of the need for change agents to develop personal mastery – a journey towards a destination we may call an *integral being*. Integral beings experience a life of oneness with themselves and their universe. They act from the wholeness of this experience. There is harmony and a unique synchronicity between their beliefs and their actions. Their bodies, minds and senses orchestrate themselves to the effortless rhythms of the universe (Chatterjee, 1999).

Similarly Handy (2001) talks of change agents as 'alchemists' who don't react to events but shape them. He characterizes them as passionate about what they are doing because they have a conviction of its importance and are able to leap beyond the rational and logical and stick to their dream, if necessary against the 'evidence'. They are changing the world as they go, building excitement and momentum. Like water finding its way down a hillside, they simply go around obstacles and dissolve resistance.

Table 4.1   Stages in achieving change agent mastery

1 Novice: learning 'the rules'	We seek clear guidelines for how to act in different situations; for example, many novices are drawn to The Natural Step (2008) programs which offer simple rules for instituting sustainable practices. We seek the codified knowledge of others who have done it.
2 Advanced beginner: beyond rules to strategies	We realize that in many situations, the rules don't work. Making change is more complex than we thought. Rules become more blurred and evolve into thoughtful strategies.
3 Competence: disciplined effectiveness	We develop a 'feel' for the complexity of change, select cues and respond to them on the basis of our accumulating experience. Our knowledge now is more tacit; our strategies are now evolving to include deeper levels of awareness.
4 Proficiency: fluid, effortless performance	We have internalized the strategies and they are backed up with high levels of skill. Intuition now dominates and reason is secondary.
5 Mastery: acting from our deepest intuition with confidence and flow	We become one with the changes we are making and are changing ourselves and our organizational world at the same time. Our inner and outer worlds are one. What we do often seems effortless and spontaneous.

Starting with self-leadership

Being a change agent means living in and between two worlds: the world of inner experience, of personal meaning, of selfhood and the outer world of action. The inner world is the real challenge for change agents. Mahatma Gandhi had a very clear idea about where his leadership began. He said: 'I must first be the change I want to bring about in my world' (Chatterjee, 1999). Our ability to model in our own lives – in our attitudes, words and actions – the changes we wish to bring about is the most powerful intervention we ever make. If we cannot bring about the changes within ourselves, do we have the right to ask others to make these changes, and what chance do we have of success in changing others?

Quinn (1996) says 'To make deep personal change is to develop a new paradigm, a new self, one that is more effectively aligned with today's realities.' He sees a vital link in our ability to make deep change within ourselves and the effective leadership of organizational change. Leaders who are prepared to make this change make transformative organizational change possible.

Research on leadership effectiveness reinforces the notion that change leadership requires particular kinds of psychological strengths. Several authors (Luthans, 2002; Luthans et al., 2002) draw on developments in positive psychology – a field which emphasizes building on people's personal strengths rather than focusing on their weaknesses. They find that these characteristics include 'realistic hope, optimism, subjective wellbeing/happiness and emotional intelligence'. These are the characteristics of mature, emotionally healthy human beings as well as effective change agents.

Through reviewing the change agent literature and discussions with change practitioners, Dunphy (2001) identified the following as important personal characteristics for change agents: personal resilience and persistence; realistic self-esteem, self-direction and initiative; tolerance of ambiguity; flexibility and adaptability; clear focus; enthusiasm and motivation; ability to inspire others; political awareness and sensitivity; empathy; sense of humour; a helicopter view; and commitment to continuous learning. We may fall short of this ideal, but attempting change leadership is one way to acquire these characteristics.

Seeking cosmocentric consciousness

In bringing about deep change leading to sustainability, the old Newtonian worldview of a mechanistic universe doesn't help; nor does the 'objectivist' stance inculcated by a traditional, scientific worldview, based on the myth that knowledge is created by scientists who stand outside the universe they are studying.

Chatterjee (1999) draws on Indian spiritual tradition in describing the importance of meditation in helping us relinquish both our belief that the world is made up of discrete objects and the egocentricity associated with this belief. In his view, we can progress from being egocentric personalities attached to material objects to cosmocentric individuals in a harmonious relationship with nature. The egocentric person feels empowered by the objects he or she can possess. By contrast, cosmocentric consciousness frees us from the clutter of objects and possessions so that the universal consciousness that flows through the entire universe also flows through us.

Organizations have their collective consciousness. Quinn (1996) writes of the change agent listening to the inner voice of the organization which calls for the realignment of internal values and external realities. He regards the inner voice of the organization as 'the most potent source of power in the organization'. Preparation, reflection and courage are needed to hear the inner voice. The inner voice will provide direction if people have the courage to listen and the commitment to change.

In our view, responding to the inner voice includes voicing the unspeakable – speaking for the interpersonal underworld that exists in most organizations but fails to gain official recognition. This is the world of collective fear and despair, of latent rebellion, of long-remembered anger, of irreverent humour and cynicism. This is also the world of high dreams and ideals: people's hopes and yearnings for more fulfilling and meaningful work. These aspirations have often been submerged by disappointment and discouraging experiences but can rise to the surface again with compelling power. To develop cosmocentric consciousness is to care, and caring is an important part of effective leadership. Effective change leaders are passionate about the changes they support. They care about the environment, the community and the individuals with whom they work.

Empathy, caring and love are not popular terms in the current managerial vocabulary but without empathy, caring, compassion, respect, tolerance and love, organizations cease to be communities and relationships become calculative. The nature of modern organizations means that they don't operate effectively without trust. But trust does not grow automatically. In organizational life, it is built purposefully over time by those who care.

4.4   The skills needed for diagnosis and action

Self-leadership is necessary, but is not enough. As well as self-knowledge and an empathy for others, effective change leaders need skills. To attempt to change an organization we must understand where the organization is on the path to sustainability and where it needs to go. Making the right diagnosis is as important in achieving organizational well-being as it is in achieving individual physical health. One of the major challenges for organizational change agents is that they usually have to make the analysis themselves and they have to do it on the run and *in situ*. It would be nice if our organizational change efforts began with a neatly packaged Harvard Business School case analysis, but unfortunately they don't.

If we work in the organization, then we are part of what we are analysing. Our viewpoint will be biased by the position we occupy – the view from below is always different, for example, from the view from above; the industrial engineer's view is different from that of the salesperson in the field. If we are external to the organization, for example, a consultant – we may have a more open mind; but we don't have the advantage of inside information. Whatever our role, as we start actively to find out more about the organization, looking at records and interviewing personnel, we are already intervening in the ongoing system.

We are studying a dynamic system of which we are part or become a part as we study it. As we immerse ourselves in it, we understand that our own view will be biased and try to offset that by an empathetic identification with others who occupy very different positions. Moving around the organization helps, as does cultivating an open mind, observing and listening. In some cases we may wish to add more formal means of analysis such as surveys and financial analysis.

Diagnostic skills

The diagnostic skills we need are the ability to

- *develop a systematic theoretical position*, a framework or model of how organizations operate to help us select the data that are useful for understanding and for future action. This model is always partial and limited and open to revision on the basis of experience;

- *develop a model of the ideal sustainable organization* combined with openness to others' ideal models. The future is mostly a collective creation, emerging from the active dialogue and interaction of interested parties. We need to be clear so that we can engage fully with others, but we need to be open to any emerging shared vision. There may be competing visions and resistance to visions in general: conflict is simply an element of the unfolding drama through which the future is defined; conflict is a signal that something important is at stake; it is a measure of progress on the path;
- *question and listen to others* for factual, value-based and emotive information; all three kinds of information are useful. Moving to sustainability necessarily involves values and emotions as well as facts;
- *use varied data sources and methods of analysis*, to apply critical insight and make balanced judgements. If we want to make a map, it is useful to view the landscape from different viewpoints;
- *convey a concise diagnosis* to others in their terms. The field of sustainability studies is already developing its own language – some useful as shorthand and for technical precision. But to influence others, we need to be able to translate what is important into the everyday language of the workplace;
- *monitor and evaluate the change process.* Diagnosis becomes crucial in checking whether we are achieving what we set out to achieve and whether we need to change the path we travel along as we reach a fuller understanding.

Management skills

Diagnostic skills help define the path to sustainability. Moving down that path requires change agents to develop other management skills:

- *effective communication*: the willingness to listen and ask skilful questions and adopt multiple viewpoints; the commitment to keep people informed; the ability to communicate clearly and simply with all stakeholders in speech and writing; the ability to use images and emotions as well as facts in communicating with others;
- *management of stakeholder relationships*: direction setting (visioning); defining the scope of responsibilities for parts of the vision; influencing and networking; delegating; developing, mentoring and coaching; performance management and monitoring; team building;
- *project management*: making and taking opportunities; updating technical and organizational knowledge; problem-solving; resourcing.

These skills will be in great demand as more organizations embrace what Hirsh and Sheldrake (2001) refer to as an 'inclusive leadership', which derives from adopting the stakeholder perspective on organizations. It involves managers developing and maintaining an interactive exchange with all those who have a stake in the organization: investors, employees, suppliers, customers, the community and representatives of the environment and future generations.

Organizations need to perform instrumental tasks and to reach financial objectives. But this is most effectively achieved by creating a wider set of outcomes that meet the needs of key stakeholders.

Communicating

In a recent interview, IAG's CEO, Mike Hawker, demonstrates his skilled role in communicating sustainability both in terms of a core organizational value for all stakeholders and in terms of a value proposition to customers: The bigger the organization the more important it is to have a set of control structures to ensure that you are consistent in what you do and the two control structures that work are firstly values (a set of corporate values that don't change, they stand the test of time and the values describe the nature of people in the organization and describe how people will act; and the second one is a clear understanding throughout the organization of what it is you offer as a value proposition (purpose) to your customer. We think that the only way you get the consistent delivery is through a control mechanism which is value based and purpose based. (Benn and Bone, 2005)

4.5   Making it happen

Creating dialogue and shared scenarios

One of the central tasks of change agents is the creation of visioning capabilities in the organization. 'The capacity to create and develop a vision of the future that is compelling and engaging [is] at the very centre of creating a human approach to organizations' Gratton (2000). Vision emerges from dialogue – inner dialogue within ourselves and dialogue within the organization and its external stakeholders. The task of the change agent is to work with others to create new meaning and new realities. Weick (1995) calls this 'sensemaking'. Dialogue begins with cultivating awareness and with listening; it continues with responsiveness and an exchange that is a catalyst for creative change (Schein, 1999).

Dialogue can change people's perceptions of themselves and their organization. From these new perceptions a sense of collective identity and purpose emerges that can renew or transform the existing culture of the organization. If this happens, the leadership of change passes from the handful of change agents to a much larger network within the organization. Leaders create leaders.

Community Network

One of us is a member of Australia's Westpac Bank's Community Consultative Council. The CEO of Westpac, David Morgan, meets annually with 20 community leaders from not-for-profit organizations. For two and a half hours he, and some of his staff, listen as each leader in turn discusses what issues concern them when they think about the next five to ten years. The key issues raised at this meeting become an input to Westpac's Corporate Planning Process – measurable goals are set and reported on the next year. This is a simple and cheap environmental scanning process, and creates an ongoing dialogue with some key stakeholders who are often then drawn in to contribute to the resulting actions plans. (Westpac sustainability performance is recognized internationally – being included in the Dow Jones Sustainability Index and in the international ethical index FTSE4Good. (Westpac, 2008))

Leadership is about 'bringing everyone along' in a balanced way, not just in their minds so they understand it, but emotionally as well, in their hearts, so they are really energized and identify with it, and they themselves take part in the leadership (Blount, 1999).

Our own experience in working with effective change leaders at all levels of organizations is that they have a profound belief in the capability of others, manifests through challenging others to contribute even beyond what they thought was their best and supporting them in doing this. This is a part of the process of creating organizations where everyone has the opportunity to lead in developing a sustainable workplace that offers exciting and meaningful work. Some conflicts of interests in organizations are intractable. Leadership becomes the art of achieving what you believe is the best possible outcome in the circumstances, even if that does not match your ideal. Negotiations and compromise may be necessary to produce small wins that can be built on later.

Resistance to change

All change agents encounter resistance to change. There is an extensive literature on how to deal with it. Much of it is written for senior executives with the assumption that positive change is mainly initiated by senior executives, who encounter resistance to change from middle management or the workforce. Our own experience is that senior executives are as resistant to change as anyone else and the initiative for change often comes from elsewhere in the organization. The reality is that most people resist change when others are attempting to change them; few do when they feel that they are in charge of change.

People are particularly likely to resist change when they see it as threatening their interests and when they believe that their knowledge and skills may be made irrelevant as changes take place. As we move towards sustainability, there will be those whose interests are threatened and whose current knowledge and skills become obsolete. Not all resistance to change is irrational. As change agents we need to understand that change is a political process in which people's power and status are implicated. There will always be those whose identification with the old order is so strong that they will actively oppose or passively resist change. There can also be legitimate disagreements – value conflicts – about the best way to proceed in progressing sustainability: disagreements about priorities, about facts such as the potential danger of certain substances and about strategies and tactics. As change agents, we need to work to create an evolving consensus among interested parties. Active engagement of those who will be affected by the changes is often the most effective way forward. However, it does not always work. There can be delays, obfuscations, sidetracks and subversions. As in many fields of endeavour, persistence is a large part of success and persistence comes from a deep commitment to a meaningful view of the future.

Learning as we go

Quinn (1996) recalls a time when he and a student were writing a case study of a company and interviewed the CEO. The CEO recounted the story of the company's first five years as if it had been the unfolding of a clear strategic plan. This didn't match Quinn's understanding of how the changes took place and he challenged the CEO by giving his own version: Quinn saw it as a rather chaotic learning process. The CEO was somewhat taken aback by this, but then smiled and said 'It's true, we built the bridge as we walked on it. Initiating and managing a change process, particularly in the area of sustainability where there are no standard models, will always be an evolving process and, despite our best efforts will sometimes be disorganized and discontinuous. Learning as we go is the way we become skilled change agents.'

Making it Happen

The implementation of change for sustainability requires relentless attention to the detail of corporate responsibility. At Nike for instance, a team of approximately 150 people are charged with corporate responsibility either solely or as a significant part of their workload. A key task is to identifying risks and opportunities concerning corporate responsibility. Each leader in the team has a reporting line to a business unit and to the responsibility team. As well, sourcing managers bring corporate responsibility data into their decisions about what factories merit increases or decreases in production orders. (Natress et al., 2006)

Contributing to living networks

An important part of making change happen is networking with like-minded people. Change agents spend real time in building networks to provide information about the systems they are working in, to act as channels of influence and support. But where do we find like-minded people?

Values researcher Ray Korten (1999) has identified three major groups in the United States: the *modernists* embrace mainstream materialist values, try to acquire property and money, are value winners and are cynical about idealism and caring for others; the *heartlanders* hold conservative values, reject modernism, favour traditional gender roles and fundamentalist religion and are volunteers who care for others; the cultural *creatives* reject modernism and support the values of an integral culture that seeks to integrate life on the basis of diversity. They have a well-developed social consciousness, and they are optimistic and committed to family, community, internationalism, feminism and the environment. They are concerned about health, personal growth and spirituality. Cultural *creatives* share with *modernists* openness to change and, like *heartlanders*, care about community and personal relationships. Ray's surveys estimate that 47 per cent of the US population are *modernists*, 29 per cent *heartlanders* and 24 per cent cultural *creatives*. Ray argues that the 50 million cultural creatives in the United States are the leading edge of cultural change in the country. There is at least that number in Europe (Futures Foundation, 2001; Novo Group, 2001).

In another study of changing values (Korten, 1999), Ronald Inglehart analysed data from the 1990–1991 World Values Survey and showed a shift towards the values of an integral culture in a number of societies. He concluded that there was a global trend towards values that includes less interest in economic gain, less confidence in hierarchical institutions and a greater commitment to sustainability. The value shift also involves a search for more personal meaning and a deeper sense of purpose in life. Part of our networking can be a process of finding those who share these values so we can build the momentum for change most readily through networks of those who are committed to the values that support sustainability.

Networking

In response to government inaction associated with climate change, six Australian CEOs (from major companies IAG, Westpac Banking Corp, Visy Industries, BP Australasia, Origin Energy and Swiss Re) met to form the Business Roundtable on Climate Change. In contrast to the Business Council of Australia, which has not been able to develop a position on climate change, the Roundtable Group argues that climate change is a major business risk and that action is a business imperative. They have produced research showing that it is possible for Australia to cut its greenhouse gas emissions by 60 per cent from 2000 year levels before 2050 and still have strong economic growth. Their Roundtable Report argues 250,000 jobs could be at stake if greenhouse action is delayed. Delay will also mean the need for much more drastic and costly action later on, they argue. The momentum for change is likely to come from their call for a national, market-based carbon pricing mechanism, which it wants the Government to sketch out a framework for next year. (Snow, 2006)

4.6   Leaders and change agents

What roles do leaders and change agents occupy and how do these roles affect the contributions they can make to the sustainability movement? Change agent roles include:

- *Internal line* roles: the board of management, the CEO, the senior executive team, other managers and supervisors, general employees;
- *Internal staff support* roles: human resources (HR), organizational development (OD), industrial engineering and environmental specialists, life scientists and information technology (IT) specialists; and
- *External*: politicians, bureaucrats and regulators, investors, professional business consultants, customers, community activists, concerned citizens and intellectuals, environmentalist activists and those who speak for future generations.

Boards of management

Boards of management can play a crucial role in setting the operating rules for an organization. Directors have heavy legal responsibilities and may be liable to major penalties if the organization is not compliant. They also have ultimate responsibility for appointing the CEO and signing off on the organization's business strategies. The relationship between the Board and the CEO appears to be critical if an organization is to act more responsibly towards its stakeholders. Research by KPMG's Corporate Citizenship and Business Ethics Unit (Lagan, 2006) indicates that directors of public companies see the CEO as playing the key role in setting the ethical and accountability agenda of the organization and that interaction between the Board and the CEO is crucial to communicating and embedding this agenda across their organization. This interaction could include determining CEO selection criteria, corporate values and ethical performance criteria.

Boards of management often lack sufficient diversity to deal effectively with the shift from sole focus on shareholder value to meeting the expectations of a wider set of stakeholders. The changes we are advocating mean that the membership of boards needs to change so that they sample the diversity of stakeholders whose interests the board must now represent.

Line managers

Line managers include the CEO, senior executives, managers and supervisors or team leaders. Gratton (2000) views the line manager's role in the change process as being courageous enough to create broad involvement, to support the process of change and to ensure that HR is centrally important to the business (see also Chapter 6). The CEO and senior executive team's central task is to ensure that sustainability strategies are an integral part of business strategy and that they contribute to profitability, to customer satisfaction as well as to the welfare of other stakeholders. Their role involves communicating that corporate objectives include sustainability and outlining what this means for the integrity of organizational structures, processes, products and services. Their actions must also match policy statements rather than contradict them: it is important that they model what they are espousing, allocate resources to support the change process and ensure that measures of business unit performance include progress on sustainability goals. As strategies are implemented successfully, line managers also have the responsibility for seeing that the resulting learning is communicated across the organization so that successful sustainability innovations are adopted and adapted.

The CEO

The role of the CEO is vital in terms of both symbolic and practical leadership.

CEO Role

Elkington (2001) describes the dilemma faced by Ford Motor Company Chairman William Clay Ford. Ford made a series of major sustainability initiatives, including a model citizenship report called *Connecting with Society* in which he gave his view that the popular sports utility vehicles were unsustainable given the petrol they consumed. He said that Ford aimed to be a model company for the twenty-first century, particularly in the area of sustainability. However, the report had only just been released when there was a recall of 6 million defective Firestone tyres that were shown to have triggered many accidents, including deaths. Ford vehicles, particularly sports utility vehicles, were the major users of the tyres. Firestone had attempted to cover up the growing history of accidents and is now mired in lawsuits as a result. Firestone was the supplier but Ford's reputation was also affected. The Ford Explorer was equipped with the Firestone tyres and had been a major profit generator, so profits slumped. Addressing the 2000 Greenpeace Business Conference, William Ford said: 'This terrible situation – which goes against everything I stand for – has made us more determined than ever to operate in an open, transparent and accountable manner at all times.'

The CEO of a public company faces the dilemma that many market analysts and investment funds seek short-term returns. The CEO who is attempting to build a sustainable and sustaining corporate culture faces a daily performance evaluation by a share market which traditionally places little value on this. Ethical investment funds have demonstrated consistently superior returns and the size of these funds is growing (see also Figure 1.6 and Chapter 11). Nevertheless the CEO must deliver in the short term and find resources to invest in the future. This is no easy task. Many CEOs do manage to generate short-term gains by 'picking low-hanging fruit' while quietly investing in building the capabilities of the corporation to generate medium- to long-term performance, including performance due to sustainability initiatives.

Hart and Quinn (1993) saw CEOs playing four kinds of leadership roles in the change process: motivator, vision setter, analyser and taskmaster, directed respectively to people, the future, the operating system and the market. They linked these roles to three measures of firm performance: short-term financial performance, growth and future positioning of the organization and organizational effectiveness (non-financial measures of performance such as employee satisfaction, product quality and social responsibility). CEOs used the *taskmaster* role the most but the role did not influence any of the three performance measures. The *analyser* role, directed at creating improved efficiency, and the *vision setter* role were significant predictors of business performance and organizational effectiveness, but not of short-term business performance. The motivator role was, however, a particularly strong predictor of organizational performance on all three dimensions. The research results (which hold true regardless of firm size) also demonstrate that those CEOs who used all four roles achieved higher levels of performance than CEOs who did not. Being an effective CEO demands a varied role repertoire and the flexibility to move in and out of different roles as the needs of the situation change. These leadership qualities of the CEO are the qualities of any organizational leader who need to be able to understand the issues (analyser), inspire others (vision setter) and help them focus their energy (motivator).

CEO and Change

If transformational change associated with redesigning the organization around sustainability principles is chosen as appropriate then the CEO and other corporate figures must be able to face the realities of what the organization is and what it needs to change. Ray Anderson, Chairman of the carpet manufacturer Interface Inc., is such a leader. Through his leadership and with the advice of designers who can envision business models based on the creativity of Nature, Interface has saved US$255 million in the last decade by implementing innovative manufacturing processes aimed at eliminating hazardous wastes. (Debold, 2005)

Managers, supervisors and team leaders contribute to the strategic process and actively translate the strategies into practical action plans. To be effective, these plans will include achievable but challenging sustainability goals and involve the introduction of processes and systems that embody ecological and human sustainability principles. Supervisors and team leaders, in particular, are the critical front line of both incremental and transformational change. Their support and feedback is vital to a successful change programme.

At any level of the organization, leaders who recognize the importance of sustaining the diversity and interconnectedness of life forms and who value their employees and the wider community must address organizational issues of gender, diversity and power. Benn, Dunphy and Ross-Smith (2006) argue for a new mode of thinking about leadership that recognizes the importance of leadership for diversity in achieving change for sustainability. In evidence, they quote a series of empirical studies of organizations where women have achieved a critical mass at senior and leadership levels. These studies show that the presence of women in senior management roles not only adds to diversity but also facilitates more effective accessing of the creative potential of that diversity (Chesterman et al., 2003, 2004).

General employees

General employees often see themselves as having more limited power than executives and managers. They certainly have more limited authority; but general employees make or break organizational strategies. A strategy that is not translated into the moment-to-moment, day-to-day operational work of the organization may never get off the ground.

Employee commitment

No 1 in the list of 100 Best Corporate Citizens selected by Business Ethics Magazine in 2006, Green Mountain Coffee Roaster, provides a good example of the power of employee commitment to make a difference in the sustainability strategy of the firm. According to Winston Rost, Green Mountain Coffee Roaster's director of coffee appreciation, taking a number of its 600 employees on an annual trip, to coffee-growing cooperatives in Vera Cruz and Oaxaca, Mexico has given them an appreciation for how hard the coffee growers work and has dramatically raised staff awareness of the value of the firm's long held commitment to social and environmental issues. According to Rost, many employees now say they will never spill another bean again. As well as being a good corporate citizen, the firm is also showing economic sustainability. Its 2005 revenue of $161.5 million with net income of $9 million was a 15 percent increase over the year prior. (Raths, 2006)

Staff support roles

Staff support roles are usually occupied by specialists who do not have the authority held by line managers. Their impact is achieved through expertise and influence rather than authority.

HR specialists are an integral part of the change planning process, including working with the senior executive team to create and maintain the guiding coalition that leads the change process. They need to provide technical expertise on HR issues such as performance reward systems and training and skills development needed to build the competencies required to progress through the sustainability phases (See also Chapter 6).

OD specialists are particularly important in the organizational reshaping process. They are change agents with highly specialized skills around the process of corporate change. They are professionals with training and experience in techniques such as team building, conflict resolution, counselling and intergroup relations. They are accustomed to working with the human process of change as it occurs; taking emotional reactions as a normal part of any significant change process; working in ambiguous situations where they have little authority; and collaborating with others to design the ongoing process of change.

Industrial designers and engineers

In manufacturing and other industry sectors, specialists with an engineering or industrial design background play key roles in process design, planning and operations. Where they have a grounding in business process re-engineering, this can prove invaluable in redesigning product flows to make them more efficient and sustainable. Their technical knowledge needed in moving to sustainability can combine with the skills of HR and OD specialists to be a winning combination. Where such specialists have a working knowledge of the principles developed by the 'cradle to cradle' design experts (e.g., McDonough and Braunghart, 2002) they can be instrumental in redesigning the firms business model around the 'eco-effective' concept of zero waste. Cars, for instance, would be returned to the manufacturer. Materials would either be composted or recycled into new models. The concept is dependent upon design for ready disassembly and the minimal use of toxic materials (Doppelt, 2003). Designers working according to the 'biomimicry' principles developed by such experts as Benyus (2003) can also radically reconceptualize the firm's business model to integrate sustainability (see also Chapter 10).

IT specialists

IT is an enabler of corporate success. No large, complex modern organization can afford to lag behind the leading edge of change in IT, particularly with the rapid development of e-commerce and virtual organizations. IT specialists are vital to the construction of the computer-based systems needed for coordination and control of a wide variety of processes, including complex supply chains. They need to understand the imperative for building sustainable systems which are efficient and user friendly.

External change agent roles

In the sustainability movement, external change agents have played major roles in bringing pressure to bear on organizations to adopt more sustainable strategies. This has been at times adversarial in both the human and ecological areas.

While there will be a place for adversarial activists in the foreseeable future, a shift in emphasis has taken place as more organizations move beyond compliance to launch sustainability initiatives on a voluntary basis. New collaborative alliances are taking place across the boundaries of organizations and external change agents have important roles to play in these alliances. Major and minor consulting companies have also moved to set up specialized practices to provide advice on a variety of sustainability issues.

Politicians, bureaucrats and regulators

The role of politicians, bureaucrats and regulators is to create 'third wave' economies that support 'third wave' organizations. This means having the courage to challenge the narrow assumptions of 'second wave' economists who dominate departments of finance in most Western economies. It means being open to the new fields of ecological economics, industrial ecology and intellectual capital. The countries making most progress in this regard are the Netherlands, Germany, Finland and Denmark. Japan, too, has highy developed national strategies in place concerning *product stewardship*. These countries are already creating national policies that shift first- and second-wave corporations forward into the growth industries of the third wave and are developing new export industries in, for example, alternative energy generation. In Denmark, for example, the wind power industry alone generates over US$6 billion a year and employs 15,000 people. Developments like the diversification of energy sources represent significant strategic opportunities for both countries and companies.

China has enormous challenges in addressing the problems of regulating such a huge number of firms, many of which are Small and Medium Enterprises (SMEs) in far-flung areas of a huge country. Yet some of its laws are highly advanced. Labour laws, laws controlling emissions in new cars, laws controlling traffic movement in and out of central Shanghai – all are in advance of most countries in the West. Implementing these laws is another question and one the central government is acutely aware of.

Investors (see also Chapter 11)

Investors control the flow of capital to corporations directly and through brokers and funds. There is no more powerful pressure for change than the withdrawal of investment from public companies or the flow of capital to them. It is vital therefore that investors support companies that are working to implement sustainability policies and withdraw investment from those that are not. Companies with sustainable policies can give better returns overall than those without such policies so, on financial grounds alone, this is a viable investment policy. Customers can exert similar pressures through shifting their buying to favour sustainable products and services. As these products and services are healthier, this is also a sensible pattern of consumer spending. Consumers are increasingly demanding transparency in terms of ingredients and components in products (e.g., information on genetic modification of foods). Supporting increasing transparency makes an important contribution to advancing the sustainability movement because transparency makes informed consumer choice possible.

Community activists

Community activists, concerned citizens, intellectuals and scientists also have important roles in demanding transparency in company operations, assembling the best available knowledge about the impact of particular kinds of products and services, and bringing external pressure to bear on companies that avoid their responsibilities to their workforces, communities or the environment. In addition, as more companies move to an 'inclusive leadership' approach that welcomes the participation of a range of stakeholders in achieving corporate sustainability, there are emerging opportunities to collaborate on new initiatives. Community activists also have a vital role in speaking for the natural environment.

Community

Green Mountain Coffee Roster, for example, the firm rated No 1 Corporate Citizen in 2006 by *Business Ethics Magazine*, began to improve its environmental performance in 1989 when it formed an environmental committee and created a rainforest nut coffee to support the Rainforest Alliance, a non-profit dedicated to protecting ecosystems. The company has grown increasingly active in the countries where coffee is grown and has been a pioneer in the fair trade movement, which pays coffee growers stable, fair prices. (Raths, 2006)

Future generations

We have included future generations as change agents. The unborn generations are not, of course, yet present and so are unable to act for change that will serve their interests. They need spokespersons to stand for intergenerational equity. In our view, those best equipped to play this role are parents, educators, youth leaders and others who strongly identify with the children of the future and can speak for them.

Building alliances of change agents

Many change agents feel isolated and unsupported in working towards the creation of a sustainable future. Their activities often have little impact and are lost in the ongoing operations of large-scale, complex organizations. As the sustainability movement advances, there are increasing opportunities to lead by forming alliances between change agents working within an organization and others outside it. It is vital to keep in mind that this is a social movement that extends beyond the corporation and, like all social movements, its success demands a disciplined cooperation despite inevitable differences of values and skill bases.

4.7   Conclusion

This chapter has taken us through a discussion of leadership for sustainable change and to a more sustainable organization both human sustainability and ecological sustainability. We have identified some of the key factors necessary for leadership of this change, some of the stages in the change process and the skills needed for diagnosis, action and management of the change. We have emphasized the importance of continuing dialogue with all stakeholders to make sustainability happen. Finally the leadership roles required in all levels of an organization were discussed.

Underpinning all organizational change for sustainability is the need to embrace the concept of self-leadership. Change leadership involves owning our own power and using it responsively and responsibly.

4.8   Questions

- As a new CEO, how would you go about establishing a network for communication and dialogue with your stakeholders? Who would you personally talk with?
- Will your own personality allow you to make the deep personal change to sustainability as a precursor to leading others down the path to a sustainable organization?
- Using an organization of your choice, identify a major sustainability change that has occurred in it and analyse how the change has been brought about and what role leadership at different organizational levels has contributed.

4.9   Further reading

Benn and Dunphy (2007); Dunphy, Griffiths and Benn (2007).

Environmental Economics and Stewardship

5

Dodo J. Thampapillai and Bo Öhlmer*

5.1 Introduction**

In this chapter we address environmental stewardship from an economic theory perspective. Environmental stewardship by firms is either induced through pecuniary incentives including ownership rights or enforced by regulation. Voluntary stewardship is virtually non-existent. We attribute the absence of voluntary stewardship to flaws in the theory of the firm as conveyed in economics programs including business schools. The flaw is the omission of *environmental capital* (KN) as an essential factor in the firm's production function. The appreciation of modified conceptual premises that recognize KN would render voluntary stewardship feasible.

Addressing the issue of environmental stewardship from an economics perspective is inevitably difficult. This is because traditional economic theory rests squarely on the principles of self-interest (Frank and Bernanke, 2002). That is, a firm's decisions are guided by rational expectations which in turn are defined in terms of profit maximization and cost minimization. Hence the display of environmental stewardship tends to follow one or more of the following measures:

1. A system of incentives (or disincentives) including rights to ownership that would prompt the adoption of custodial tasks that maintain environmental

*With the usual disclaimers we remain grateful for funding support offered by the Swedish University of Agricultural Sciences and the National University of Singapore.

**For those not familiar with the economic principles used in this chapter, the following text provides a basic introduction: Frank and Bernanke (2006) and for more information on the ideas expressed in this chapter see Thampapillai (2002).

resources; (see the literature on environmental taxation and property rights – for example, Ashiabor et al. (2005), Quiggin (1988)); and/or

2. The recognition of market opportunities that generate added pecuniary gains; (see the literature on business and the environment – for example, Hart (1997) and Lovins et al. (1999)); and/or

3. Enforcement of stewardship by recourse to regulation; that is, each firm that exploits environmental resources can be required, by law, to undertake certain custodial tasks; (see the literature on environmental regulation – for example, Porter and van der Linde (1995a)).

Taxes, subsidies and regulation have been long-standing instruments of environmental protection and conservation as identified in a multitude of environmental economics texts (Hartwick and Olewiler, 1986; Hanley et al., 1997; Titenberg, 2004). Proponents of regulation (Porter and van der Linde, 1995a) argue that stringent regulation can lead to innovation. The literature on business and the environment highlights 'win-win' situations where environmental challenges can be transformed into business opportunities. Such opportunities include the much-touted carbon trading markets that have recently become very news worthy. The prevalence of various schemes of incentives, regulations and the promotions of pecuniary opportunities suggests that voluntary stewardship by firms is virtually non-existent. Hence a germane question is *Why is it that firms do not readily and voluntarily advocate environmental stewardship?*

In this chapter we argue that the absence of voluntary environmental stewardship is partly due to the fact that the economics concepts conveyed in various tertiary institutions (including business schools) are flawed. The flaw is that standard concepts in production economics pertaining to the behaviour of the firm exclude KN as an explicit factor that is utilized in output decisions. The production function in microeconomics explains a firm's *output* (Y) in terms of *manufactured capital* (KM) and *labour* (L); that is $\{Y = f(KM, L)\}$. This mathematical expression is equivalent to saying that level of output is some function of the level of inputs from manufactured capital and labour. Such a function is significantly different from one that recognizes KN; that is $\{Y = g(KM, L, KN)\}$. This is because the laws of nature especially the laws of thermodynamics will play a role in explaining the relationship contained in $\{Y = g(KM, L, KN)\}$.

A change in the conceptualization of the production function to include KN will also lead to changes in the conceptualization of two related tools, namely isoquants (see Section 5.3) and cost functions (Section 5.4). As we indicate in the three sections that follow, the changes are distinct and significant. Therefore, firms may be prompted to voluntarily adopt different types of production decisions. We conclude with the argument that an appreciation of the varied concepts when KN is explicitly included will invariably prompt voluntary environmental stewardship, especially from those firms who are seeking to achieve better environmental outcomes or to achieve environmental sustainability. Internalizing KN into the firm's production decisions is normally voluntary but governments can force it to be internalized by introducing environmental taxes, legislation, penalties and by schemes of trading rights, for example, emissions trading.

5.2   The production function

As indicated, the standard theory of production in economics relates production (Y) to the utilization of only L and KM. This theory, which is based on the law of diminishing marginal returns, identifies three zones of production as illustrated in Figure 5.1. The first zone commences from the nil utilization of factors, and in this zone an increase in the utilization of factors is rewarded by increases in output at an increasing rate. In the second zone, the increase in factor usage returns increases in output, but at a decreasing rate. Finally, the third zone is one where increases in factor utilization results in a decrease in output. Economic theory describes the second zone of production as the rational zone, since it is in this zone that producers could choose profit maximizing allocation of factors. However, this theoretical framework gets altered when we incorporate KN as a factor of production as exposited in Thampapillai (2002).

Without any doubt, KN is a factor of production in every production context. Whether it is a factory or an office building, indoor air quality and drinking water are clear factors of production. Similarly soil, water and air are important ingredients of agricultural and related industries. Prior to conceptualizing the characteristics of a production function (Y), we need to explain how one would define and measure KN.

As an example, consider the Industrial Park at Kalunborg in Denmark. This park is located on the shores of Lake Tissø, which serves as a source of water for the park as well as a receptacle for effluent discharges from the park. Activities in the park include coal-fired power generation, refining of crude oil, manufacture of plasterboards and biochemicals. Lake Tissø is one of the items of KN that contribute to the generation of output from the industrial part. There are of course several other items of KN that are interconnected with the lake; for example, tree density on the lake shores and adjoining areas, micro- and macro- organisms in

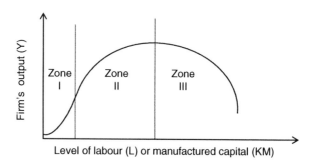

Figure 5.1   The standard production function and zones of production

Note: The diagrams in this chapter are based on the work of the authors
e.g. see Thampapillai and Öhlmer (2000).

the lake and so on. For illustrative purposes, we shall confine our consideration to Lake Tissø as the only item of KN. We could state that the maximum amount of KN is available, if at least the following criteria are satisfied:

- The lake is free of any contaminants;
- It has a stable ecosystem and biological population as one would expect for its given location and topography; and
- It is at its maximum capacity based on ground water hydrological characteristics.

Conversely, when untreated effluents degrade the quality of water and species are lost, and the extraction of water exceeds the rate of ground water recharge and rainfall, we would conclude that the quantity of KN is declining. Therefore, the size measurement of KN has to be a composite measure that accounts for the multiple attributes of the lake including the quality and quantity of water. This measure usually takes the form of an index. In a production function, we hope to explain the relationship between the size index of KN and the output generated from the Industrial Park. Note that an increase in the size of the index means that overall quality and quantity of the lake water is increasing. A decrease in the size of the index implies the reverse; that is, that the lake is degrading. When an increase in KN occurs, we would expect the magnitude of output from the Industrial Park to increase. The historical evidence from the Industrial Park at Kalunborg confirms this to be the case. The Industrial Park has developed a symbiotic relationship between several large industries on the site and has been able to significantly reduce the use of water from Lake Tissø by internally recycling and reusing water in industrial processes thus effectively increasing the value of KN (Symbiosis, 2008; UNEP, 2008). The definition and measurement of KN usually follows the development of an index that attempts to account for as many environmental attributes as possible.

Attributes of *environmental capital* (KN)

Consider now the production function: $\{Y = g\ (KM, L, KN)\}$. When one attempts to conceptualize the relationship between Y and KN (whilst holding KM and L constant), it is possible to argue that the production function will assume a specific shape, which is distinct from the standard production function shown in Figure 5.1. This distinctiveness has much to do with the multiple attributes of KN. This special function is illustrated in Figure 5.2, and it displays the following features.

First, the function has a fixed domain. It is for this reason that the curve describing the changes in output has a bold circle (the large dot) at the end of it. The fixed domain exists because there is a fixed upper limit for KN as dictated by the laws of nature. For example in the case of air quality, the law of nature dictates that we cannot have more than 20 per cent oxygen in the air. Similarly, it is not possible to exceed a certain level of dissolved oxygen in water.

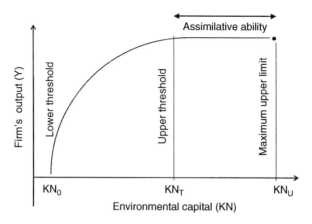

Figure 5.2   The production function relating to KN

An increase in KN contributes to the growth of Y. But, beyond a certain threshold level of KN, denoted by KN_T in Figure 5.2, increases in KN, have no effect on the size of Y. We can explain this in the reverse order as well. That is if we let KN to deteriorate from its maximum upper limit, KN_U, output remains unaffected until KN reduces to KN_T. When KN reduces below KN_T, then output begins to fall. This can be explained by the fact that KN possesses the characteristic of assimilative ability. So, the range between KN_T and KN_U can be described as the region of assimilative ability. At the same time, we can also observe another threshold value for KN, namely KN_0. As the size of KN reduces to KN_0, output approaches zero. In the case of air quality, KN_0 could represent a level of oxygen concentration that is far too low for people to survive. For convenience, we will refer to KN_T as the upper threshold, and KN_0 as the lower threshold.

In Figure 5.3, we show two curves for the production function (Y), that is, $\{Y = f(\overline{KN}, \overline{KM}, \overline{L})\}$, where $\overline{KM}$ and $\overline{L}$ are held constant but at different levels. Here $(\overline{KM}_1, \overline{L}_1) < (\overline{KM}_2, \overline{L}_2)$. As the level of $(\overline{KM}, \overline{L})$ gets higher, the size of Y becomes bigger (though only in Zones I and II of Figure 5.1), but the range of assimilative ability becomes smaller, that is, KN_T to KN_U becomes smaller. That is, at higher intensities of $(\overline{KM}, \overline{L})$, we expect KN to become increasingly fragile. This is consistent with the second law of thermodynamics explained, for example, by Daly (1992), and we can easily relate this feature of increasing fragility of KN to a variety of business contexts regardless of whether it is a farm-firm or a factory floor with a production line. In the example of Lake Tissø, the value of KN_U is fixed and the production Y has increased.

Another feature in Figure 5.3 is that the gradient of the production function (Y) at a given value of environmental capital (KN) is shown to be steeper at higher levels of $(\overline{KM}, \overline{L})$ than at lower levels. This implies that when KN deteriorates to a level below its threshold level, then the fall in output is much faster at higher $(\overline{KM}, \overline{L})$ levels than at lower levels. Also note that both the upper and

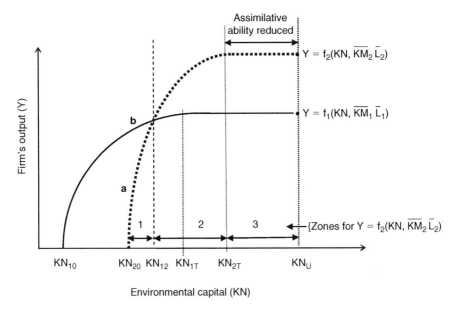

Figure 5.3   Family of production functions and increasing fragility of KN

lower threshold values for KN move progressively to the right as we move to higher levels of $(\overline{KM}, \overline{L})$.

The different rates of change in the gradient result in the curves intersecting each other. In Figure 5.3, this intersection is denoted by the dotted line at KN_{12}. The important feature here is that, to the left of KN_{12}, it is possible to increase Y by cutting back on KM-L; for example, the move from point **a** to point **b**. Hence KN_{12} becomes another important threshold quantity. The converse is true to the right of KN_{12}. We can envisage the existence of a series of such thresholds (for example, KN_{23}, KN_{34}, KN_{45}, ...), which progressively shift to the right at higher levels of $(\overline{KM}, \overline{L})$.

For reasons of illustrative convenience, we have shown only two curves in Figure 5.3. In the context of a continuous function, it is possible to envisage the existence of an infinite number of curves continuously placed on each other and intersecting with each other. However, for clarity and simplicity, we return to the discrete case of two curves. It is possible to make a generalization for a single curve in terms of the next curve that has a lower level of KM-L. For example, consider the curve that has $(\overline{KM}, \overline{L})$ fixed at $(\overline{KM_2}, \overline{L_2})$. It is possible to identify three zones for this curve on the following basis:

- Zone 1 is defined by $KN_{20} < KN < KN_{12}$. In this zone, Y increases rapidly in response to an increase in KN. It is also possible to increase Y by reducing $(\overline{KM}, \overline{L})$ that is, by going from point **a** to point **b**.

- Zone 2 is defined by $KN_{12} < KN < KN_{2T}$. In this zone, Y increases at a diminishing rate in response to an increase in KN. It is not possible to increase Y by reducing $(\overline{KM}, \overline{L})$.
- Zone 3 is defined by $KN_{2T} < KN < KN_{U}$. This is the zone of assimilative ability.

The above-mentioned conceptualization is based on two sets of premises. The first is the premise that entropy increases as the usage of the stock of $(\overline{KM}, \overline{L})$ increases and this in turn causes KN to be more fragile. The second is the numerous cases of anecdotal evidence where the reduction of $(\overline{KM}, \overline{L})$ has rendered KN to be more productive. This is common sense as well. A room full of workers leaves them with little space to move and breathe and hence they produce little output. (An increase in entropy of a system is an increase in disorder of that system or a decrease in the availability of energy from that system.)

Productivity increase of KN

A factor becomes more productive when the same quantity of the factor is capable of yielding higher quantities of output. A car that uses a litre of petrol to traverse 60 kilometres is indeed more productive than another that can go only as far as 40 kilometres. The question is how do we explain this concept with reference to KN? A car that is more productive than the other is so because of the design and organization of the various components of its engine and other parts. Similarly the productivity of KN is a manifestation of its organization/configuration in terms of the specific ecosystem and entropy. Lower the entropy, higher the productivity. Suppose that in its present configuration, Lake Tissø has a set of wetlands which were established when the Industrial Park was reorganized in terms of the symbiotic existence. However, should these wetlands be repositioned and the assimilative ability and capacity of the lake increases, then its productivity has increased. That is, the same lake with the same number of wetlands – but configured differently is able to absorb greater nutrient loads.

To explain the productivity increases of KN, consider Figure 5.4. Here we illustrate that for a given level of $(\overline{KM}, \overline{L})$ intensity, productivity increases can be achieved by extending the function outwards as depicted by the dotted curve. Thus there are two ways in which the productivity of KN increases. First is by extending the region of assimilative ability or capacity; that is, the upper threshold is shifted to the left from KN_{2T} to KN_{2T*}. Second, the region of response is shifted outwards resulting in the lower threshold being moved from KN_{20} to KN_{20*}.

Hence should a firm be positioned at point **a** in Figure 5.4, a productivity increase could move it to point **b**. Should this firm now add to its stock of KN by investing in an amount of ΔKN, then due to the productivity increase it could be positioned at point **c**. We can define degradation as the loss of KN;

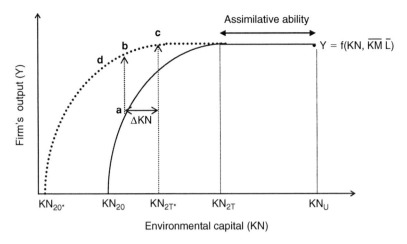

Figure 5.4   Increasing the productivity of KN

that is, a leftward movement along the horizontal axis of the production function. So, once a firm has positioned itself at, say point **a**, then a movement to point such as **d** would entail environmental degradation despite the increase in output.

Degradation of *environmental capital*

We can further explain investment and degradation with reference to Figure 5.5. If a firm is positioned at say point **a** on the curve where $(\overline{KM}, \overline{L})$ is fixed at $(\overline{KM}_1, \overline{L}_1)$, then a move to a point such as **e** on the curve with the higher $(\overline{KM}, \overline{L})$ intensity achieves an increase in Y, but at the same time environmental degradation due to the loss of KN. This type of environmental degradation could be explained as externality arising from output increases that are centred on KM-L alone. On the other hand, a move from **a** to a point such as **g** achieves an increase in Y from increasing all three factors and hence includes an investment KN as well. Note that the increased productivity of KN reflected in the move from **a** to **b** in Figure 5.4 is in the context of a fixed stock of $(\overline{KM}, \overline{L})$ and is due to innovation and technology with reference to KN.

The move from **a** to **g** in Figure 5.5 also represents an increase in the productivity of KN. But, this move is due to a higher accumulation of KM-L and is at the expense of rendering KN to be more fragile, that is, the length of KN_T to KN_U becomes smaller. For example, suppose that the Industrial Park at Kalundborg erects another factory that would employ more labour. So the stock of KM-L has now increased. At the same time, the Industrial Park authorities also establish two more wetlands and thereby increase the biodiversity of the lake. But increasing the intensities of KM-L to achieve higher levels of output may not always prove to be prudent, because with the increasing fragility

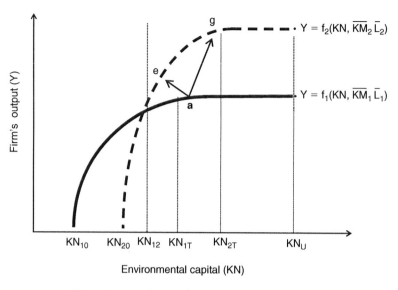

Figure 5.5   Explaining degradation and investment

of KN, the manager can easily lose his/her production capability. These pressures become more explicit when we consider substitution behaviour within the framework of isoquants.

Investing in Environment Capital (KN)

Raft Creek Bottoms of White County in Northeast Arkansas was once a hardwood forest. In the 1960s, this forest was almost all cleared by farmers for crop cultivation. Over the years, the intensity of cropping had denigrated the land to a marginal one with little output capacity. In 1997, some 70 per cent of this marginal land was reforested with bare root seedlings of species such as Willow Oak and Green Ash. The remaining 30 per cent of the land was converted into a shallow herbaceous wetland. A one-day survey in July 1999 revealed that the wetland was a host to, amongst others, some 3000 shore birds (sandpipers and stilts), 30 white pelicans and 22 wood ducks. Restoring forests and wetlands has benefits like improving water quality, recovery of threatened species, sequestering carbon, decreasing erosion and reducing air pollution which can bring economic benefits to industry as well as to a community. In this example the investment in KN not only enriched the quality of adjoining croplands and improved their productivity, but also yielded another good, namely increased biodiversity, which is important for recreationists as well as scientists.

Source: United States Department of Agriculture (*circa* 1999, 2001)

5.3   Isoquants substitution and input mixes

An isoquant is a contour taken out of a multidimensional production surface. For purposes of illustrative convenience, we shall confine ourselves to a two-dimensional surface. In Figure 5.6, we present the isoquants that correspond to the standard production function in economics, namely $\{Y = f(KM, L)\}$, where $Y_2 > Y_1$. Each isoquant describes a locus of points along which output (Y) remains constant for various mixes of the inputs. The region of an isoquant that is convex to the origin represents zone II in Figure 5.1. In this region there is positive substitutability between inputs of KM and L. As explained in most economics texts, it is the region of positive substitutability that is relevant. The ridgelines are usually constructed to separate the region of positive substitutability from the remaining regions.

As one would expect, the business manager would confine his/her decision-making to the region of the isoquant that is convex to the origin, that is, that part between the ridgelines. A manager who is restricted to a fixed budget of B, and facing input prices P_{KM} (unit cost for manufactured capital) and P_L (unit cost for labour), would optimize the selection of inputs at the point where the budget line (defined by $B = [P_{KM} * KM] + [P_L * L]$) is tangent to the highest attainable isoquant. This is illustrated in Figure 5.6. A familiar result in micro-economics is that at the point of tangency, the marginal rate of substitution (MRS), which is the ratio of the marginal products, equals the ratio of input prices. That is, $\{MRS_{L, KM} = (MP_L/MP_{KM}) = (P_L/P_{KM})\}$. As the business manager's budget improves, he/she can move to a higher isoquant and thereby trace an expansion path.

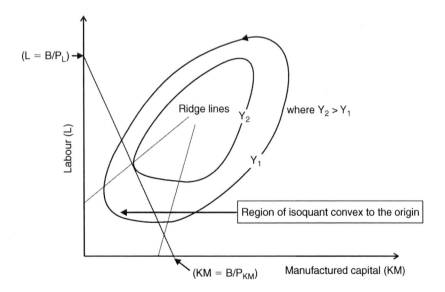

Figure 5.6   Isoquants in Standard Theory

We need to now consider how the explanation given above would change when the business manager begins to recognize KN as also a factor of production. Because we want to keep our illustration to a two-dimensional level, we shall regard manufactured capital and labour as a composite factor input of *manufactured capital* and *labour* (KM-L). So, the production function will be modified to read as $\{Y = g_1[(KM\text{-}L), KN]\}$. The isoquants that describe this production function are shown in Figure 5.7. Note that there is a correspondence between these isoquants and the production function shown in Figure 5.3. Because zone 1 is of little relevance, we have limited the display of isoquants to represent only zones 2 and 3 of the production function. To explain these isoquants consider the isoquant labelled I_2I_2. Substitutability between KN and (KM-L) begins, when the size of KN falls below its threshold level KN_{2T}. That is, there is no substitutability between factors in the region of assimilative ability, which is defined by $\{KN_{2T}<KN<KN_U\}$, that is zone 3 in Figure 5.3. The region of substitutability in the isoquant I_2I_2 is confined to region $\{KN_{12}<KN<KN_{2T}\}$. This is zone 2 in the production function described in Figure 5.3. Further, as we move to a higher isoquant, say I_QI_Q, we note that the region of substitutability becomes smaller and threshold quantities KN_{QT} and $KN_{Q(Q+1)}$ begin to appear sooner.

On the subject of the ridgelines, one ridgeline can be clearly constructed along the boundary between zones 1 and 2; that is, KN_{12}, KN_{23}, ..., $KN_{Q(Q+1)}$. If we place the other ridgeline to connect the upper threshold quantities $(KN_{1T}, KN_{2T}, ..., KN_{QT})$, we imply that it is rational for the business manager to allow KN to degrade and allow input choices to be confined to the region of

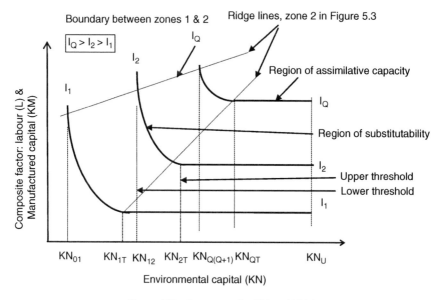

Figure 5.7   Isoquants for KN and KM-L

substitution only. Alternatively, it is possible to describe the next ridgeline as a vertical line representing the fixed domain for KN. This would ensure that conserving KN or rather exploiting the assimilative ability of KN is also an input option choice for the business manager.

However, we are unable to resolve one major issue of strategy that gets resolved with other factors of production. This is the determination of the input mix as illustrated in Figure 5.6. This difficulty is of course primarily due to the absence of a price for KN. But, the manager may nominate the upper threshold levels (that is, KN_{1T}, KN_{2T}, ..., KN_{QT}) as the basis for an expansion path, but, needs to be cautious of the fact that the gap between the upper and lower thresholds becomes progressively narrower. However, being on the upper threshold is not too far from selecting a strategy for KN that places it within the region of assimilative ability. Further, if the price of KN is deemed to be zero, the budget line is always horizontal, and the input strategy for KN would always be within the region of assimilative ability.

One major implication of the framework we have considered here concerns the relationship between the government and business. If governments wished to force business managers to operate within the region of assimilative ability and higher stability, then they would have to place taxes on KM-L so that the budget line shifts to a stable level of output. This type of government intervention can have a positive spin-off. It forces industries to innovate and extend the productivity of KN by way of technology instead of by accumulating more KM-L (see Lake Tissø example). Recall that within the conceptual framework we have presented here, increasing the accumulation of KM-L renders KN more fragile. The limit on substitutability when KN has been rendered fragile at high intensities of KM-L has implications for the theory of costs, and we consider this next.

EXAMPLE

How does one define substituting between KN and KM-L?

Suppose that the premises of an industrial plant contain six buildings dispersed across a land area of several hectares. Further, suppose that two of these buildings need to be renovated and refurbished. The CEO can explore the following option. Demolish the two buildings completely and extend the remaining buildings to accommodate the activities that are being conducted in the two buildings to be demolished. Use the land area rendered vacant by the demolition to establish a wooded area of recreational value to the workers as well as visitors to the plant. One might say that the CEO would have to spend much more than in renovating the two buildings. Therefore this would be tantamount to investment in KN. However, another way of seeing this is that once before the entire industrial estate would have been a wooded area and the erection of the buildings and construction of the industrial infrastructure had reduced the magnitude of KN. Hence the establishment of a wooded area can be seen as substitution between KM and KN.

Sometimes, the distinction between 'increasing KM' and 'increasing KN' can be elusive. Return to earlier example of the Industrial Park on the shores of Lake Tissø in Denmark. Here again if the CEO has to choose between allowing the installation of a mechanical plant to increase daily production as against planting trees, then he/she has an issue of substitution. But this clarity diminishes with some activities that are designed to maintain the quality of KN. For example, suppose that the problem facing the CEO was to choose between setting up a plant that would increase the daily output of electricity and plasterboards as against upgrading the plant that treats effluent and used water. Doing the latter would prevent the degradation of the lake. Hence if the CEO chose to upgrade the effluent-treatment plant then it could be seen as substituting KN for KM.

Note that not all cases of KN are found outdoors. Indoor air quality is equally important in a production context. Many firms have invested in air-cleaning devices to ensure that indoor air quality is maintained at an acceptable level. Hence another example of substitution is one where a manager has to choose, say between hiring a worker and upgrading the air-cleaning device.

5.4   Analysis of costs

As indicated, the theory of costs has its foundations laid on the underlying production function. The total cost (TC) function (which comprises of fixed costs and variable costs) is usually described as one which displays an S-shape reflecting varying returns to scale at different levels of production. In decision-making, apart from TCs, managers are also interested in the shape and properties of average costs (AC) and marginal costs (MC). Whilst TC is the sum of all relevant costs during a production period, AC is the average cost per unit of output produced; that is (TC/Q), where Q is the quantity of output. MC is the TC of producing one extra unit of the good and is usually denoted by (dTC/dQ) that is, it is the slope or gradient of the total cost function graph.

For decision-making, managers would usually compare the TC with total revenue (TR) and select a production quantity that maximizes the departure between TC and TR functions. The relationship between AC and MC also plays an important part in decision-making. As Q increases, both AC and MC initially decrease and then increase beyond a certain value of Q, which represents the shift from the first to the second zone of the production function. However, there is one important property of cost functions that should be noted. That is, *when costs are falling, AC is greater than MC, and when costs are increasing MC is greater than AC.* This is illustrated in Figure 5.8. It would be irrational for a decision-maker to produce in the region where AC is greater than MC, because in this region TR falls short of TC. Therefore, decision-makers would choose their production strategies in the ascending region of the cost functions. It is for this reason that the *supply curve in microeconomics is often described as the ascending segment of the MC curve.*

Consider now the implications of the conceptualization we have introduced above with KN as an additional factor of production. If the business manager were to increase output by increasing the quantities of L and KM, he/she would be shifting upwards from one production schedule to another, as in Figure 5.3; whereby the fragility of KN progressively increases. At some level of KM-L, output capability completely disappears due to the complete breakdown of KN. Hence we can describe the cost curves very much the same way as they are done in standard texts, but with one exception. This being that the manager's costs will tend towards infinity, at the point where KN breaks down completely. Hence the supply curve of a business will be upward sloping as expected in theory, but, turning vertical at some limiting point (see Figure 5.9). In other words, recognizing KN as a factor of production makes the supply curve of

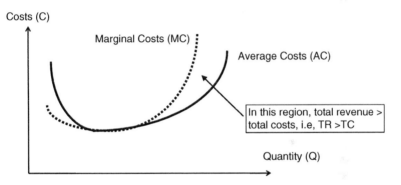

Figure 5.8   Average and marginal cost in Standard theory

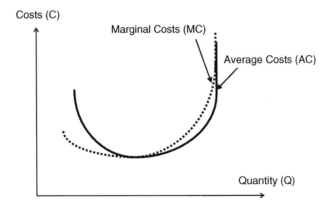

Figure 5.9   Average and marginal cost that tends to infinity

most goods resemble that of exhaustive non-renewable resource in natural resource economics.

5.5   Conclusion

As exposited in microeconomics, the theory of costs and that of isoquants emerge from the theory afforded to production. We have shown above that a reformulation of the theory of production to explicitly recognize *natural capital* results in a distinct as well as significant change in the definition of isoquants and cost function. Because retaining the assimilative capacity of KN and improving the productivity of KN become clear policy options, voluntary stewardship becomes feasible.

One should also recognize that the origins of neoclassical economics had KN firmly rooted as a factor in the production function; for example, see Marshall (1891) and Fisher (1904). The removal of KN for reasons of analytic convenience in the neoclassical models of growth (Solow (1956); Swan (1956)) had extended to the theory of the firm as well. Since then a progression of economics texts such as those by Samuelson and Nordhaus (1994) have confined the theory of the firm to L and KM. Our conceptualization above represents merely one of many methods to explicitly account for the role of KN in the behaviour of the firm.

In any event, the actions of individuals are ultimately governed by their psyche which is strongly influenced by the system of beliefs. These in turn are largely governed by what one learns. A recent anecdote from Singapore appears pertinent. A busy suburban mother was wheeling her shopping trolley in a supermarket with her primary school daughter tagging along. The child was vocal and visibly unhappy with her mother's shopping behaviour. The mother was hurriedly throwing items into the trolley. The child wanted the mother to read the labels and ascertain whether the items were nature-friendly. Either Singapore's Ministry of Education or a well-meaning school teacher had taken on the task of instilling environmental values amongst school children. Professional economists are no exceptions to such responsibility.

5.6   Questions

- Consider two of following sectors of the economy: tourism, manufacturing, fisheries and mining and illustrate how the chosen sectors can conceptualize the existence of a production function: Y = g(KM, L, KN).
- In the examples chosen above, illustrate the substitutability between KM-L and KN and describe how firms could utilize the KN more efficiently.

5.7   Further reading

Thampapillai (2002); Frank and Bernanke (2006).

End of Part Case Study: Internet Sources

Robert Staib

There are a number of organizations, accessible through the internet, that provide online case study material that is worth reviewing and considering for the development of curricula for environmental management or sustainable development management courses. Much of the case study material is in the form of achievements (i.e., good news stories) with less emphasis on the issues and processes of corporate management. But with critical assessment and a selection of different types of material (from different sources, companies, countries and industries) the material can be used to develop course readings. A selection of sources is listed below. In addition, each of the authors of the chapters of this book summarize case study material and the reader is encouraged to explore some of these references in more detail.

Internet sources

The *Centre for Business Education* at the Aspen Institute has material that includes audio material, references to books and book chapters, concept papers, magazine and newspaper articles and some more detailed case studies. Some of the case studies are available on line but many appear to be available for purchase from the suppliers of the case studies (Aspen Institute, 2008; http://www.aspencbe.org/).

The *World Business Council for Sustainable Development* has information that can be used to develop case studies. Their material includes reports on sustainability (environmental and social) from different organizations from around the world and includes a selection of case studies. The cases studies are generally good news stories, not detailed or critical studies, but they can provide examples of achievements that could be used to stimulate critical assessment by students (World Business Council for Sustainable Development, 2008; http://www.wbcsd.org).

The *Corporate Register* is an online directory that facilitates access to corporate social responsibility (CSR), sustainability and environmental reports from around the world. It also includes some comments and assessment of the reports but not as far as I can see a critical assessment of reporting.

It is a good link to corporate reporting that would allow students to assess companies' reporting performance and benchmark it against other companies, industry standards and global reporting frameworks including the Global Reporting Initiative (GRI), the AccountAbility AA1000 Assurance Standard and the Global Compact (Corporate Register, 2008; http://www.corporateregister.com/).

The *Coalition for Environmentally Responsible Economics* (CERES) is a 'nonprofit coalition of investors, public pension funds, foundations, labor unions, and environmental, religious and public interest groups, working in partnership with companies toward the common goal of corporate environmental responsibility worldwide'. It is the convener and secretariat of the Global Reporting Initiative (GRI) an approach to standardizing of sustainability reporting (social, environmental, and economic). Its internet site includes reports on various aspects of sustainability, sustainability reporting and industry performance, for example, the report on the USA automobile industry contains data that would allow benchmarking within the automobile industry of individual companies or other countries (Ceres, 2008; http://www.ceres.org).

The *Business for Social Responsibility* (BSR) is a 'US-based global resource for companies seeking to sustain their commercial success in ways that demonstrate respect for ethical values, and for people, communities and the environment'. Its internet site contains reports on various aspects of sustainability management and reporting (Business for Social Responsibility, 2008; http://www.bsr.org).

Organizations and the Natural Environment (ONE) is a division of the Academy of Management that 'is dedicated to the advancement of research, teaching, and service in the area of relationships between organizations and the natural environment'. Its web site provides links to teaching resources including case studies (ONE, 2008; http://www.one.aomonline.org/).

Case study exercise

Select a company that you are familiar with (from a *specific industry*). If you using a small to medium sized company, it may be harder to find good information but the exercise will present an interesting challenge. Review the web sites listed above (or similar ones) and:

- Identify case studies or reports for the *specific industry* and from these information sources develop quantitative benchmarks for good sustainability performance both environmentally (e.g., energy use per unit of product, greenhouse gas emissions per unit of product) and socially (e.g., level of participation of women in management, level of employment of indigenous people) for an industry participant;

- Develop an outline management strategy to help the chosen company achieve the benchmark level (if it is below the bench mark) or improve its own performance (if it is above the benchmark);
- Develop a philosophical argument and a corporate justification (quantitative if possible) to support your strategy; and
- Identify the organizational changes that might be necessary to implement the strategy.

Part

II

Management of Operations

Human Resources

6

Robin Kramar

6.1 Introduction

This chapter examines some of the issues in human resources required for progress towards environmental and social sustainability. Human resources are an essential component of promoting sustainability in general and environmental sustainability in particular. Human resources are more than people. In this chapter it refers to individuals, groups and the relationships between individuals and groups. It includes the systems of practices used to manage and lead within businesses and to build relationships between organizations and external stakeholders.

Environmental sustainability is defined as the protection and renewal of the biosphere for present and future generations. It can be furthered through the policy decisions of international organizations and governments which provide incentives or sanctions for particular business activities and processes. However, while these policies are important as a means of driving change, they will not result in the embedding of attitudes, values and behaviours which are essential for a business in which environmental sustainability is an integral part of the way business is conducted.

Changes require challenging many of the ideas and practices widely used in organizations, particularly with regard to the way people are managed. Social and human sustainability are an integral part of an organization becoming environmentally sustainable. Social and human sustainability comprise the development and fulfilment of people's needs (and wants?) and the maintenance of social relationships. The systems and processes used to manage employees and other people who do the work of organizations, such as performance management, health, safety, fair treatment and equity are critical to the sustainable organizational outcomes. The first part of the chapter examines these *systems and processes*.

Similarly, progress towards environmental sustainability challenges traditional forms of leadership and interactions in organizations. Such progress requires *individuals*, including leaders to demonstrate skills such as critical and reflective thinking; personal attributes such as self-knowledge and empathy; and an ability to analyse underlying structures in which organizations operate such as power and gender relations. There are therefore implications for the way people behave in organizations, their personal attributes and abilities and the way they integrate work into their non-work life. These issues are examined in the second part of the chapter.

The promotion of environmental sustainability by an organization requires that management involve a variety of *stakeholders*, including those that are essential to the business (such as customers) and also those who influence the organization (government bodies) or who are impacted by the organizations actions (the families of employees). It also involves an ethical, more transparent way of conducting business. The implications for stakeholders are discussed in the third part of the chapter.

6.2   Corporate

Human resource management practices have for many years been identified as critical for the success, particularly the financial success of businesses. Research (Delery and Doty, 1996; Becker et al., 1997; Becker and Huselid, 1999; Ezzedeen et al., 2006) has demonstrated this impact and explained the causes of this impact in a number of ways. Regardless of these explanations, the term strategic human resource management (SHRM) has been used to refer to an approach to the management of people which seeks to further the achievement of business strategy and objectives by explicitly identifying the human resource elements of important business problems and developing practices to solve these problems. SHRM has the potential to be a source of sustained competitive advantage if particular conditions are met (Sparrow et al., 1994; Pfeffer, 1998). This part of the chapter describes briefly SHRM, its potential as a means of furthering environmental, human and social sustainability and the implications for the development and implementation of particular human resource practices.

Strategic human resource management

Central to the concept of SHRM is the view that business performance can be improved by using particular human resource practices. Typically business performance has been interpreted in a narrow way. It has focused on performance in terms of financial and product/service market outcomes and the interests of particular stakeholders such as shareholders (Dowling and Schuler, 1990; Boxall, 1998). SHRM has been shaped by an economic rationale (Walsh et al.,

2003, p. 866). SHRM has also focused on the enterprise as the primary unit for the development of human resource policies and the way these policies contribute to business outcomes rather than societal, human or environmental outcomes.

The concepts of *fit* and *alignment* which are central to SHRM provide the opportunity to be interpreted in a way that contributes to environmental sustainability. *Fit* operates at three levels: external, internal and human resource management. External fit refers to the organization's capabilities and the opportunities and constraints in the external environment. Internal fit refers to the consistencies between the features of the organization, such as its mission, strategy, structure, technology, values, products, services, culture and workforce characteristics. Human resource management 'fit' refers to the various aspects of human resource activities such as recruitment criteria, performance feedback, and rewards consistently influencing behaviour to enable strategy to be implemented and achieved (Collins, 1994). *Alignment* refers to matching the organization's strengths with the opportunities available in the external market.

Outcomes

The concepts central to SHRM could be interpreted and applied in a broader way so that human resources could be applied to environmental, social and human performance and to outcomes. For instance, when environmental factors, such as scarcity of energy, water and disposal of waste are explicitly recognized as factors that impact the business and which could be influenced by the expectations organizations have of their employees and suppliers, the concept of 'fit' takes on a broader dimension. When alignment includes developing employee behaviours which support not only the achievement of financial performance objectives but also environmental and human performance objectives, the opportunity exists to further sustainable performance and outcomes.

In this chapter the term performance refers to the achievement of outputs which can be measured, for instance, an indicator of social performance in an organization could be the average number of days of training each employee receives per year. Outcomes 'represent the joint product of organizational performance and environmental response' (Griffin, 2000, p. 481) and reflect satisfaction or perceptions of effectiveness by stakeholders (Lenz, 1981). The specific indicator of training identified above does not provide information about the quality of the training, its effectiveness in the workplace or whether it is the training that needs to be done.

Competitive advantage

The impact of SHRM on competitive advantage and business performance has been explained in a number of ways. The behavioural-based view of SHRM claims that particular corporate strategies require particular types of *employee behaviours* to achieve these outcomes and that human resources practices can be developed and implemented to achieve these outcomes (Dowling and Schuler, 1990). The configurational view argues that organizations gain their competitive advantage from *cultures* which are unique and difficult to imitate. Therefore, it is the people and the culture created by 'bundles' of human resource practices which are critical for the achievement of financial outcomes (Barney 1991; O'Reilly and Pfeffer, 2000). Another view proposes that *human resource systems* of specific human resource practices produce financial outcomes, that is, they are 'systems producing profits through people' (Pfeffer, 1998, p. 73). This view is known either as the 'universalistic' view (Glinow et al., 2002) or 'high performance work systems (HPWS)'. The practices that typically make up these HPWS are employment security, rigorous selection of new personnel, self-managed teams and decentralization of decision-making, comparatively high compensation contingent on organizational performance, investment in training and management development, sharing of information about financial and organizational performance throughout the business and 'symbolic egalitarianism', that is, reduced status distinctions, such as dress, titles and office layout (Pfeffer, 1996). These views are not mutually exclusive.

Corporate social responsibility

SHRM provides a basic framework for human resources. When the framework is modified to explicitly include the following it could enhance environmental and social sustainability. First, a number of dimensions of performance, rather than just financial performance need to be specified in the model. There are systems which measure organizational performance along a range of dimensions, including financial, social and environmental performance (Dahlsrud, 2008). These systems are typically used to measure an organization's Corporate Social Responsibility (CSR). An extreme view of CSR conceptualizes CSR from a purely economic perspective in which the interests of the owners should be of paramount importance and the business should focus on wealth creation (Friedman, 1970; Windsor, 2006, p. 94).

It has been argued that because there is no one commonly agreed definition for CSR, the concept is of little use, providing limited basis for action (Henderson, 2001, pp. 21–22). Alternatively organizations could describe their own definition of CSR. The definition could then suit the organization's particular circumstances, values and level of awareness (van Marrewijk, 2003). All the definitions, however, would reflect the principle that organizations need to balance the requirements of and are accountable to a number of stakeholders (Freeman, 1984) and reflect a view that businesses are responsible to the society in which they take part (van Marrewijk, 2001).

There is evidence that CSR has a positive impact on a business's financial performance by providing internal benefits such as developing capabilities, efficiencies and culture and that it also has external benefits such as influencing corporate reputation (Orlitzky et al., 2003; Branco and Rodrigues, 2006). It has been shown that these internal benefits can result from an enhancement of employee morale, an ability to attract and retain employees and subsequently a reduction in costs associated with turnover such as training, recruitment and lost productivity (Albinger and Freeman, 2000; Greening and Turban, 2000; Bachaus et al., 2002; Peterson, 2004). Therefore, performing well on social, human and environmental indicators represents a form of strategic investment and has an impact on financial outcomes. This is supported by research that demonstrates companies involved in ethical investments had better financial performance than other companies (Collison et al., 2007) and it also reveals that the market rewards companies that are environmentally responsive (Schnietz and Epstein, 2005; Wahba, 2007).

This suggests that when companies display good CSR practices they satisfy a range of stakeholders' needs and shareholders benefit from good CSR performance. Therefore the shareholder view promoted by Friedman (Friedman, 1970; Bakan, 2004) and the stakeholder view of CSR might not be mutually exclusive or incompatible which suggests that the SHRM model could be extended to include measures of performance other than just financial measures.

Social performance

Approaches to CSR go through stages of evolution, with early stages focusing on the link between CSR and financial performance, while later stages address a link with social outcomes. Walsh et al, demonstrated this in their overview of the research conducted on what they call corporate social performance (CSP). They found that the predominant orientation had sought to understand the relationship between CSR and CFP, rather than social performance. Of the 121 papers which empirically examined the relationship between CSR and CFP, 100 of these 'attach CSR to an economic rationale' (Walsh et al., 2003, p. 868). A more advanced approach to understanding the relationship would be to examine how practices contribute to broader social outcomes, stable institutions and how they balance competing social interests. For instance, the development of individuals could contribute to the public interest. Similarly, HRM practices that equip individuals to exercise active, democratic citizenship (Sennett, 2000) or enable them to function in an increasingly complex world could also contribute to the public interest.

Environmental, social and human sustainability have been shown to be interrelated in another way. It has been shown that there is a relationship between the implementation and maintenance of the environmental management system of an organization, its human resource policies and the development of capabilities necessary for an organization's sustainability (Dunphy et al., 2000; Daily and Huang, 2001; Wilkinson et al., 2001; Benn and Dunphy, 2004b). The development and implementation of advanced environmental policies and capabilities are dependent on the implementation of human resource policies that create trust between employees, management and the communities in which the organization operates.

Culture change

Benn and Dunphy (2004b) found in their study that progress towards environmental sustainability can be considered in stages. They found that movement through the early stages of environmental sustainability could be promoted by human resource processes which

- build competence through awareness raising and information about human and environmental compliance requirements;
- provide clear definition of the roles and responsibilities of every employee, including line and senior management;
- include sustainability targets in performance evaluations, staff training on the compliance requirements; and
- develop formal and informal champions who foster employee commitment to sustainability.

Later stages of development require human resource processes which foster the growth of a culture which encourages innovation, sharing of learning and knowledge, proactive collaborative leadership involving both internal and external stakeholders and visionary leadership.

This type of culture can be built using programmes which encourage employees to suggest new ways of working or becoming more efficient; sharing of learning and knowledge through team-based learning and problem-solving; designing roles which are multi-skilled and team-based; developing community partnerships and involving employees in volunteering programmes with the community and building attitude change through change agents who are specifically concerned with promoting change for sustainability.

Another way in which the SHRM model could be developed is to start from the perspective that organizational performance will depend on the extent to which the human resource system effectively manages multiple stakeholder relationships (Way and Johnson, 2005). Rather than viewing SHRM as a process which seeks to tightly align HRM, internal and external factors and a corporate strategy which focuses on financial outcomes, this broader perspective enables the identification of a range of performance outcomes. Benn and Dunphy (2004b) develop this idea in the later stages of their model of the relationship between environmental and human sustainability. They demonstrate using case examples that in the early phases which they label rejection and non-responsiveness, financial factors dominate corporate decision-making. They claim in the non-responsive organization, the focus is on 'ensuring that the workforce is easily moulded to the corporate will in order to derive maximum financial return' (Benn and Dunphy, 2004b, p. 99). To move into the level 3 stage, compliance and through into the later three stages of efficiency, strategic proactivity and the sustainable organization, there needs to be organizational culture change in which attitudes and values change and a range of stakeholders are identified for the organization. Human resource activities and support, as well as involvement of community stakeholders with employees are essential for this development.

Sustainability and culture

Performance on social outcomes has also been shown to impact on financial performance. An SHRM model could be broadened to identify a number of measures of performance, the interrelationships between these measures and the outcomes for a range of stakeholders of this performance. It would also need to identify the way these stakeholders were involved in decision-making and in contributing to organizational performance and outcomes. Culture change is at the heart of this SHRM model. This culture change can be facilitated by the processes and programmes which engage people who do the work of the organization, define the activities that are performed, influence the way people interact and are involved in the workplace, reward and recompense them, shape working conditions and expected behaviour, provide feedback on performance, foster learning between people and new ideas, remove competency gaps and develop people. These processes and programmes are interrelated as briefly revealed below.

Some specific examples of these processes and programmes include practices that do more than ensure the workplace at least complies with legislation such as occupational health and safety, discrimination, equal employment opportunity, industrial relations and environmental legislation. These processes and programmes could be used in a proactive way to integrate a range of stakeholders in the determination of safety management and well-being programmes, diversity management programs, workplace management programs and environmental awareness programs, all of which go beyond legal compliance and use them as a way of achieving organizational performance and outcomes with benefits for a variety of stakeholders. Studies (see boxes below) indicate that these initiatives can contribute to financial, human and environmental sustainability. At Lend Lease, the planning, design and construction of The Bond Building in Sydney involved a number of features that represent the later stages of Dunphy's and Benn's development model, including engagement of employees and members of the community (Orsato et al., 2006). At Fuji Xerox environmental sustainability was promoted through organizational learning.

EXAMPLE

Stakeholder Engagement

Lend Lease Australia is an Australian company that has been operating for more than 50 years. It operates in the public and private sectors and is involved in the development, construction and management of real estate assets. Lend Lease has had a long-standing commitment to environmental and social sustainability and the expression of this commitment has evolved. In the 1980s Civil & Civic (its predecessor) sought to change safety and health standards in the construction industry by leading change. More recently, the Lend Lease organization has expressed its dedication to making environmental and social sustainability an integral part of the way the construction industry operates. This determination was one way of competing in the product and the labour market.

Stakeholder engagement was a central part of the process of the development of The Bond Building. More than 100 employees were engaged in Blue Sky workshops and eight task forces of 20–25 people were established to address issues such as technology, the environment and leadership. Lend Lease negotiated with the community about what the company could or could not do and prepared legal agreements. The building was also designed to reduce occupant health problems, increase social interaction and reduce silos between staff. One of the major design principles integrated into the building was energy efficiency and indoor work environment quality enabling it to achieve a 5 Star rating by the Green Building Council of Australia. (Orsato et al., 2006)

EXAMPLE

Organizational Learning

Another example illustrates the importance of organizational and individual learning as part of building a culture that fosters sustainability. The Fuji Xerox Eco Manufacturing Centre at Zetland in Sydney provided a range of development opportunities to a range of stakeholders. A systematic approach to building capabilities of staff was an integral part of the use of eco-manufacturing business strategy at Fuji Xerox. Most staff undertook training in 'people management', support for professional and technical courses was provided and almost 350 courses were available through the intranet. In addition collaborative relationships with customers were developed by training talented employees of their customers so they were able to identify problems, install remanufactured and return damaged components for remanufacturing. (Benn and Dunphy, 2004a, p. 9)

Systems of HR practices and values

A number of factors can be taken into account when making choices about HR policy. For instance, choices are made about the indicators used to assess individual and team performance or what types of performance are rewarded. Factors such as the desired culture, the mission and vision, the strategy and goals of the organization, workforce characteristics and the stated values of the organization are some of the main influences on the choices that are made. Values facilitate choosing between the policy options and they provide a reference point for making decisions (Schuler, 1992).

Values can also be captured in codes of conduct or policy statements which set out how members of the organization are expected to behave and do business. These represent ethical statements which are used as a way of influencing the behaviour of employees and other stakeholders. They could and should also influence the way employees behave with their external stakeholders. Westpac provides an excellent model of the way to integrate values, human resource management and sustainability outcomes. At the heart of Westpac's approach is 'Our Principles for doing business'.

EXAMPLE

Principles for Doing Business

At Westpac (an Australian bank) sustainability is regarded as an overarching management approach which requires understanding the true value drivers of the business, the need to operate according to ethical standards and to take a broad view of risk and opportunity. The financial institution's dedication to sustainability is reflected in their detailed 'Our Principles' which specifies how members of Westpac behave with regard to governance and ethics, employee practices, customer practices, care for the environment, community involvement and supply chain management. It states that 'Woven throughout everything we do are our values of teamwork, integrity and achievement.' Westpac states that profitability and improved performance outcomes will be achieved through the quality people, supported by performance management processes, employee commitment and behaviours that reflect the Westpac values. Trust between a variety of stakeholders is at the heart of Westpac success. The Code of Conduct outlines seven principles which build the trust. These principles are:

- Acting with honesty and integrity;
- Respecting the law and acting accordingly;
- Respecting confidentiality and not misusing information;
- Valuing and maintaining professionalism;
- Working as a team;
- Managing conflicts of interest responsibly; and
- Being a good corporate citizen. (Westpac, 2007a)

Business Ethics

Ethics is a difficult concept. It is not clear cut, unlike the concept of compliance. Compliance refers to behaviour that conforms to laws and regulations.

Ethics can be considered at the individual level and it refers to an individual's personal measure of what is right and wrong. At the collective organization level it expresses a consensus about behaviour that is right and behaviour that is wrong (Kramar and Martin, 2007). Ethics captures a set of principles which describe obligations to others within and beyond the organization. When the natural environment is considered as part of an organizations moral responsibility it has the potential to change the choices managers and employees make.

An ethical business environment can be created by developing managers and employees as moral, ethical individuals and by developing a culture of shared values, strategy and standards of conduct. Leaders that role model behaviour are very important for building this culture (Thomas et al., 2004) as are the development, implementation and observance of ethical policies (Andrews, 1989). Individuals need to internalize ethical policies in order to observe them. Actions that encourage internalization include formal assessment of the corporate culture, identification of the desired culture (which expresses the ethics code) and actions taken to reduce the gap. These actions can include developing human resource criteria and policies which reflect these values and behaviours. Senior management have an essential role to play. They should publicly commit to an ethical organization, talk with employees often and provide resources to train employees on their ethical responsibilities (Gagne et al., 2005). There also needs to be monitoring of the implementation of the policies and evaluation to see that they are achieving the desired behaviours. An essential, integral part of management is therefore ethical leadership, decision making and corporate governance (Swanston, 2004).

EXAMPLE

Governance and Ethical Practice

Westpac specifies that the principles described in the previous example should be reflected in practices with regard to governance and ethical practice, employees, customers, the environment and the community. It identifies a number of aspects in each of these areas in which Westpac policies seek particular outcomes. For instance, in relation to 'Employees' area, Westpac specifies the way in which people in Westpac should work together, the way they should be managed, the promotion of equal opportunity, diversity, training, learning and development, work–life balance, occupational health and safety, job restructuring, protecting employee entitlements, fair remuneration, respectful and dignified working conditions and freedom of association (Our Principles for doing business, 2007b, pp. 12–13).

Westpac then measures the extent to which results are achieved in these areas in terms of outcomes such as employee satisfaction, the representation of women in management, employee turnover and the percentage of employees with accumulated annual leave, employees accessing paid parental leave, external tertiary training and Westpac childcare centres and the lost time injury rate. The results of Westpac's performance are reported in the Stakeholder Impact Report (Westpac, 2007b). The results are provided over time so it is possible to see trends (Westpac, 2007b, pp. 61–63). Westpac has achieved recognition as one of the Global 100's most sustainable corporations at the World Economic Forum (2008).

Assessment: approach to ethics

An organization's approach to ethics can be considered in terms of seven stages of development (Kramar and Martin, 2007). These seven stages show how organizations differ in their views of the world and how this is manifested in their attitude towards laws and social responsibility. At one end, organizations are concerned about their survival. At the other end the organizations believe they exist to serve the world and improve it. During the later stages of development organizations behave in a collaborative way with a variety of stakeholders.

This collaborative behaviour displays similar characteristics to the behaviour of organizations at later stages of sustainable development described by Benn and Dunphy (2004b) Organizations at the strategic proactive and the sustainable organization stages seek to develop a values based stakeholder strategy and also develop a social contract through its interactions with its stakeholders. This is evident in written policies about human resource development, community relations and the ecological movement (Benn and Dunphy, 2004b, p. 67). However, although some stakeholders might be treated in a way that reflects later stages of development in the seven-stage model, this might not be the case with all stakeholders. Table 6.1 provides a framework which can be used to assess an organizations orientation to various stakeholders. Some examples of particular orientations to environmental responsibility are provided in this framework.

Environmental ethics raises a number of questions and issues that particularly concern the responsibility of organizations for the environment. Environmental ethics has traditionally been concerned with the relationship between human beings and the natural environment. There are well-established links between issues associated with environmental ethics (biodiversity, ecosystem health and environmental sustainability) and economics (Brennan, 1995; Brennan and Lo, 2002). More recently the impact of the built environment, on areas such as workplaces and cities and poverty have been included as part of environmental ethics (Brennan and Lo, 2002).

Table 6.1 Assessing the organization's orientation to various stakeholders

Organizations					Stakeholders
Stages of development	Employees	Customers, suppliers	Social responsibility		Environmental responsibility
1 Survivalist	–	–	–		Prime focus of the business is financial with no regard for the impact of the business on the environment, e.g., contamination of industrial land in Sydney
2 Paternal/Machiavellian	–	–	–		'Us and them' culture – in this situation Greenpeace and WWF would constitute 'them' and the business 'Us'
3 Orderly/bureaucratic	–	–	–		Laws are complied with in a minimalist way, e.g., carbon emissions from production is always the legal maximum
4 Participative/creative	–	–	–		Business honours the spirit of the law and questions goals and values, e.g., Suncor Energy pulled out of the Stuart Oil Shale Project possibly because the project did not satisfy its sustainability criteria (see box below)
5 Collaborative/excellence	–	–	–		Explicit undertakings that organization plays a positive social role, e.g., Westpac demonstrates this in its Principles for doing business which includes 'care for the environment'
6 Social well-being	–	–	–		Business works for the well-being of society and the environment, e.g., The Bond Building and Lend Lease reflect this orientation
7 Global harmony	–	–	–		Businesses that work to improve the planet and society and operate according to high ideals, e.g., Body Shop

Source: Kramar and Martin 2007.

The following case about the Stuart Oil Project demonstrates how this project reflected different stages of development for different stakeholders. In one sense the joint partner management of the project contributed a low level of social responsibility through its failure to engage community groups and local residents in the development of the project. On the other hand, it reflected a slightly higher level of responsibility for employees through the creation of a number of jobs directly and indirectly.

EXAMPLE

Complexity of environmental ethics

The Stuart Oil Shale Project was a planned Australian–Canadian oil shale development near the Great Barrier Reef in Queensland. It was established in 1995, but in 2004 it was declared bankrupt. It was estimated that the project would contribute significantly to Australia's economic sustainability through the supply of possibly 17 billion barrels of oil and also to the country's social sustainability through the creation of 100 permanent and 6,500 indirect jobs. Grants were therefore provided by the federal and state governments.

The Australian partner, Southern Pacific Petroleum (SPP) proposed a number of ways to offset the carbon dioxide emissions. These included a massive tree planting exercise and design and engineering developments that would provide opportunities to reduce carbon emissions. The Canadian partner Suncor Energy pulled out of the project in 2001, possibly because it considered the proposed development would be unable to meet the company's sustainability criteria. These included establishing performance standards acceptable to stakeholders, greenhouse gas management plans that address the risk of climate change and a mandate from governments and the public to develop oil shale.

The action taken by local stakeholders and Greenpeace demonstrated the project was not acceptable to them. Local residents, environmental, tourism and fishing groups and the Environment Protection Agency opposed the project. Greenpeace took direct action against the project, rallied local support and targeted the partners of SPP so it was unable to obtain buyers for the Stuart Oil Shale product. (Orsato and McCormick, 2006)

Deep change

The implementation of HRM practices used to enhance environmental sustainability and the changes in behaviour they seek to promote are part of deep change management. This sort of change is time consuming, challenging, non-linear and complex (Dunphy and Griffiths, 1998; Dunphy et al., 2003). It is a process which goes through phases in which ideas are initially rejected but then once individuals and then organizations revise their understanding of sustainability and CSR then they are able to develop broader and more sophisticated processes. This is an extremely unpredictable process. The change process involves modifications in roles and contracts, conflict and negotiation, uncertainty, flexible, creative and values based behaviour and it requires individuals to work together. Therefore a critical and essential aspect of understanding how human resources can facilitate the development towards environmental sustainability is to understand some of the capabilities individuals will use while moving through the change.

6.3   The individual

Progress towards sustainable outcomes requires that individuals, including leaders, use a variety of skills and have a number of personal attributes. The approach to leadership will be substantially unlike traditional forms of leadership. The successful implementation of the human resource processes discussed above requires certain ways of thinking, communicating and operating in the workplace. Individuals need to have high levels of self-knowledge, respect for individual differences, an ability to innovate and learn, to share with others and an ability to work in teams. It is also important to recognize the importance of the relationships between these individuals and the way these relationships develop. Relationships between individuals are a 'central point of departure for developing and understanding [of] the dynamics and issues' (Taylor, 2007, p. 21). Before individuals develop and use these capabilities, they need to value the impact their behaviour has on the environment and other people. This can be developed through the provision of information and knowledge about the consequences of their actions and the actions of the wider society on the environment. It involves a process of learning.

Individuals need to recognize the political nature of society and management where systems of power and privilege are embedded in social and economic institutions and in management practice. Decisions about the treatment of humans and the environment typically reflect these systems (Steingard, 2005, p. 231). Therefore progress towards sustainability is a normative, values based and overtly political process which appears to clash with a supposedly neutral, value-free story of management (Alvesson and Willmott, 1996). Individuals and leaders need to develop techniques to understand the nature of the values and assumptions embedded in existing frameworks and understandings. They need to explore social, political, economic, cultural, technological and environmental forces that foster or impede sustainability. These techniques include critical thinking and reflection, affective competence, collaborative learning, participation in partnerships and decision-making, visioning and imagining, systemic thinking.

Critical thinking and reflection

Critical thinking and reflection are essential skills that facilitate uncovering taken for granted assumptions. They require abilities to uncover the real meaning of the information and messages, to formulate a response to the information or message and to not take information at face value. Individuals need to think about the

- assumptions they are making when they interpret the information and message;
- way their values influence their interpretation; and
- structural factors, such as power, culture and gender that influence their interpretation and other interpretations (Schon, 1984; Tilbury and Wortman, 2004, pp. 31–32).

Critical thinking and reflection enable confronting and challenging what is taken as 'truth' and what is regarded as 'logical'. Individuals need to be attuned to their feelings (*affective competence*) and be aware about how these influence their interpretation and response to an issue. To do this, individuals need to take responsibility for and accept a range of emotions. This is more than emotional intelligence, rather individuals 'have intelligent ways of managing their feeling life' (Taylor, 2007, p. 86).

Participation

Another essential capability is the ability to work and learn in a collaborative way. As discussed earlier, the change process is iterative, uncertain and chaotic, and consequently individuals experience a range of emotions. Affective competence assists with this change process. Working and learning for environmental sustainability occurs when individuals participate in decision-making, in partnerships and with a range of stakeholders. All of these collaborative activities require interpersonal skills such as the ability for immediacy of response, attentiveness to others, capacity for self-management, openness to new experiences and openness to others (Taylor, 2007, pp. 112–113).

Participation in decision-making can take a variety of forms. It could involve individuals just being informed of a decision or it could involve active participation in the processes which lead to the outcome. Participation requires individuals to be aware of the different power relations between the groups. A number of skills are necessary for effective participation in decision-making. These include building knowledge through dialogue about the issues and problems, confidence to share knowledge and negotiate with others, persuasion skills, conflict management skills, an ability to think through problems and patience. Patience is essential (Tilbury and Wortman, 2004, pp. 54–56).

The process of collaborative learning involves participating in partnerships. Partnerships can be formed in response to formal requirements often encouraged by governments or they can be voluntary self-organizing partnerships (Tilbury and Wortman, 2004, p. 64). Both types of partnerships require sharing and creating new knowledge (tacit and explicit), sharing information, collaboration, shared responsibilities and cooperative decision-making, innovation and shared goals and resources.

EXAMPLE

Learning about Corporate Social Responsibility

Between 1999 and 2004 the French government funded the National Initiative for Sustainable Development (NIDO). This initiative sought to 'structurally anchor sustainable initiatives in society'. One of the programmes, 'From financial to sustainable profit', was designed to initiate and support change programmes in organizations which developed the relationship between financial performance and environmental and social performance. Nineteen companies were involved in this latter initiative. These companies met every month. At this meeting external stakeholders were involved and representatives from the companies shared and learnt from each other. Each company initiated their own change programme designed to enhance corporate social responsibility (CSR). The companies found that learning about CSR was more effective at the individual level, but for it to become institutionalized at the corporate level it required active support of key people in all levels of the organization. It was also difficult to engage external stakeholders in the process unless there were external pressures to do so. (Cramer, 2005)

Imagining the future and systemic thinking

Before a process of change towards an environmentally sustainable world can occur, such a world needs to be imagined. Individuals need to imagine or vision what such a world would look like. They need to explore what the characteristics of their preferred future or futures would be and examine how realistic this is. Change to this future could require a re-evaluation of lifestyle, values and priorities (Tilbury and Wortman, 2004, p. ix). The envisioning or imaginative process can enhance and integrate any learning that the individual has achieved (Taylor, 2007, pp. 82–83). It can also be driven by imagining what sort of world they don't want in the future.

The Tata Iron and Steel Company (Tata Steel), India's oldest, largest yet most environmentally aware steel plant in India. The founder of Tata Steel, J. N. Tata had a clear vision of the environmental and social context in which the steel plant would operate. He envisioned a city with wide streets, many trees, gardens and shade. Tata Steel is located in Jamshedpur, which is now a 'model for the harmonious co-existence of industry and environment' (Sarkar, 2005, p. 194). Tata Steel takes the lead in maintaining the parks and places of interest (see also Case Study Part II).

A key skill required for environmental sustainability is systemic thinking, which involves synthesizing information and building a whole picture to foster an understanding of the interconnections, relationships and dynamic processes. Once this is done it 'helps [individuals] see how the effects of even a simple action can have effects on social, economic or environmental conditions beyond the original intention across time and geographic space' (Tilbury and Wortman, 2004, p. 89). To do this individuals need to be inquisitive, questioning, accept feedback because of the need to 'look for multiple influences and interactions, rather than single, linear cause and effect; be wary of obvious explanation, and look for deeper issues that might be influencing the problem; take a helicopter perspective "above the issue", to look at the larger picture; look for relationships and feedback by asking, "what does this have to do with that?"; put yourself in others shoes – what is their perspective? And question boundaries and assumptions when an issue is labelled or a solution is suggested'.

An extension of this systems view is the notion that there is a strong level of interdependence between all the elements of the system at a number of levels. Living systems develop new patterns of organizing that could not be predicted by past experience. Systems are therefore 'self-organizing' and at the same time are a reflection of not only the elements of the system but also an understanding of ourselves (Senge et al., 2005, p. 201).

Leadership: mindful and ethical (see also Chapter 4)

Sustainability in all its forms can be promoted by two forms of leadership known as *mindful* leadership and *ethical* leadership. The processes engage many of the skills discussed above. *Mindful* leaders behave – mindfully, collaboratively, taking others with them in personally satisfying and sustainable ways (Sinclair, 2006, p. xv). Just as whole person learning requires individuals to understand who they are, mindful leadership requires individuals understand their motives, values and the way their life experiences influenced their approach to leadership. It requires individuals to understand 'who I am' and 'to lead from within' (Mirvis and Gunning, 2004, p. 70; Senge et al., 2005). This process requires reflection and an awareness of the emotions involved in the leadership process.

A second feature of mindful leadership is that, rather than being individualistic and heroic, it is a collective, shared process (Fletcher, 2004, p. 648). It requires building and valuing relationships with other people. Individuals serve as role models to others and it is a process that is collectively created (Sinclair, 2006, pp. xv, 31). A well-developed form of this is when an individual leader develops a sense of being interconnected to not only one's complete self, but also to others and the entire universe (Mitroff and Denton, 1999, p. 83). This sense, often called, 'spirituality', involves an individual developing a different sense of reality that will lead to decisions which can reflect some form of social justice and to the 'holistic well-being of oneself, humanity and the planet' (Steingard, 2005, p. 235). People who are spiritually aware in business are able to serve outside their own self-interest and see their decisions as part of interests beyond themselves and the business outcomes.

Two of the consequences of this are that leadership becomes a moral activity which impacts well beyond the business. It requires questioning the assumptions that underpin business and the focus on narrow corporate goals. As discussed previously this can be done through critical reflection. This process enables a questioning of the purpose of leadership and the way the dominant view of leadership reflects cultural and gender influences (Sinclair, 2006, pp. 30–31).

EXAMPLE

Mindful Leadership

Unilever Foods Asia (UFA) is seeking to build a sustainable, profitable foods-and-beverage business by creating a 'community of leaders' and a business in which the company's mission is infused with personal values. The processes used to create this reflect the principles of mindful leadership and seek to build interconnections and understanding between individuals.

UFA builds this leadership by enabling each person to understand themselves, to understand other people and their differences and to them build a 'collective consciousness' or a collective dialogue that creates the 'us'. UFA uses learning journeys through different parts of Asia to build its 'community of leaders'. They encourage people to learn about their motives, ambitions and themselves not only through traditional instruments such as personality tests, 360-degree-feedback and coaching, but also through storytelling about their life histories and the lessons they have learnt while on these journeys. The sharing of stories builds a sense of commonality and consensus. Using the process of 'dialogue' individuals are able to confront 'difficult issues' that would normally be avoided. There is also time for reflection and time to observe how the collective is operating.

One such journey was a trip through India that involved 17 'study groups' living in different communities, such as the Dalai Lama's monastery in Dharmashala, Mother Teresa's hospital and cloth-spinning communities. The participants worked through a study guide using their five senses and a sixth one, intuition, to identify how these communities functioned. Participants were prepared to confront their preconceived assumptions, to be open to what they might experience and to examine and consider the lessons they had learnt for themselves and the business. The processes used to develop a 'community of leaders' seek to build a new level of consciousness among Unilever's leaders and foster a sense of caring for the communities in which Unilever operates. (Mirvis and Gunning 2005)

Ethical leadership refers to the exercise of social power which respects the rights and dignity of others in decision-making, influencing and action. Six attributes characterize ethical leadership: character and integrity, ethical awareness, community and people orientation, motivating, encouraging and empowering and managing ethical accountability (Resick et al., 2006, p. 346). Analysis of the data of the GLOBE study which involves 17,000 middle managers in 931 organizations in 62 societies explored ethical leadership in terms of the four attributes of character and integrity, altruism, collective motivation and encouragement. The analysis found all four attributes were supported to differing degrees in all cultures.

Character/integrity was supported most strongly in the Nordic European countries, while South East Asian societies endorsed the altruism attribute most strongly. Latin American and Anglo societies supported collective motivation more than other societies, in particular Middle Eastern societies. Ethical leadership in Middle East countries would probably involve behaviour that models and respects Islamic values (Resick et al., 2006). Just as mindful leadership involves leading in a positive and people-centred way, so does ethical leadership. These forms of leadership are based on respect and dignity for others, including future generations. They would therefore seem to be essential for the adoption of environmental and human sustainability.

6.4   Stakeholders

Effective environmental management and leadership strategies require the management of a range of internal and external stakeholders (Buysse and Verbeke, 2002). Buysse and Verbeke identify some of the implications of this requirement. First, important stakeholders need to be identified and the most important ones selected. Second, effective stakeholder management also requires investment and reallocation of resources in a number of areas, including technology, the strategic planning process, routine-based management systems and processes and employee skills and capabilities. Third, effective environmental leadership involves a long-term vision that broadens the relationship between the stakeholders. Fourth, there could be involvement of companies who are leaders in environmental management with regulators developing environmental rules.

Stakeholder management is at the heart of environmental management. Although there are different definitions (Freeman, 1984, p. 46; Savage et al., 1991, p. 61), a common aspect is a relationship between various stakeholders and flow of communication between them. These stakeholder relationships represent a 'complex interplay of shifting, ambiguous and contested relationships' (Gao and Zhang, 2006, p. 725).

Stakeholder management (Freeman, 1984; Carroll and Buchholtz, 2002) therefore involves incorporating the views of stakeholders such as employees, customers, the regulators, the community and shareholders into decision-making. It is argued that the environment or the Earth needs to also be included as a stakeholder because the health of society, the economy and the environment are connected and depend on each other for survival (Cartwright and Craig, 2006, p. 744) (see second box Section 10.9). The Accountability Standard 1000 (AA1000) specifies that stakeholder engagement involves organizations building relationships with stakeholders through processes such as dialogue, involvement in defining the terms of engagement, providing sufficient information and time to make informed decisions and conditions that enable stakeholders to present their views (Gao and Zhang, 2006, p. 726).

Stakeholders therefore require particular capabilities and resources to engage in effective engagement with each other. These capabilities include the ones specified in the previous section, such as empowerment, visioning and long-term thinking, critical thinking and reflection, ability to manage people with different points of view, systemic thinking, collaborative skills, dialogue skills and conflict management skills. It also requires enthusiasm (Gao and Zhang, 2006) and a willingness to share information and trust other stakeholders.

EXAMPLE

Public–Private Partnerships

The World Summit for Sustainable Development in 1992 stimulated businesses to pursue partnerships with governments, NGOs and international organizations in an attempt to contribute to sustainable development. However, these partnerships are not always possible because of conflict of interests and the activities of secondary stakeholders on primary stakeholders.

TOTAL S.A. was involved in building a pipeline in Myanmar in the 1990s and in order to support the Myanmar code of conduct TOTAL S.A established a socio-economic programme (SEP) in communities living around the pipeline. In 2003 TOTAL S.A. approached UNESCO to further build community development. Although UNESCO was enthusiastic about the opportunity to expand its programmes, the partnership did not eventuate because of opposition from stakeholders with political power and groups with no direct influence on the Myanmar economy. These groups include NGOs/activist groups, local communities, international organizations, the opposition party and the media. These groups were able to highlight the contradictions in TOTAL S.A.'s involvement in a country run by an oppressive regime.

TOTAL S.A. believed its involvement in Myanmar was responsible and contributed an improvement of living standards. However, it hired the military for security and although not proven there were allegations of the use of unpaid labour. In addition, environmental organizations were concerned about the impact on the rainforest along the pipeline corridor. UNESCO decided not to pursue the partnership because of the conflict of interest it involved. (LaFrance and Lehmann 2005)

6.5   Conclusion

Human resources are an essential component of managing towards environmental and social sustainability. Within the corporate context, SHRM provides a basic framework for furthering sustainability. These modifications include specifying a variety of measures of performance, not just financial criteria, specifying a range of outcomes including social and environmental outcomes and seeking to satisfy multiple stakeholders. The HRM processes and policies necessary for sustainability should be designed to create deep organizational culture change and reflect values which are consistent with the organization creating an improved social and natural environment. HRM policies in the areas of OHS, equal employment opportunity and employment relations and environmental performance would be more expansive than that required by legislation. In addition, reward, performance management and selection policies and criteria would be directly linked to environmental and social outcomes.

The success of these corporate initiatives requires individuals, including leaders, to have a range of skills and capabilities. These skills include an ability to manage uncertainty, conflict and individual differences. Success requires individuals to work together, collaborate and be involved in decision-making. Self-knowledge and an ability to reflect, think critically and systemically and to vision are also necessary. Leaders are also required to demonstrate these abilities and to demonstrate that their decisions have impacts beyond themselves and the business. Stakeholders are also important human resources when considering environmental management. Stakeholders can be engaged in a variety of ways in the pursuit of environmental, social and human sustainability and as individuals it is beneficial if these stakeholders also have the skills discussed above.

6.6   Questions

- Discuss some of the personnel selection criteria and performance management criteria organizations could use to further environmental and social sustainability.
- Suggest some of the ways individuals and companies could develop the skills and capabilities required to further environmental and social sustainability.
- Using the information from the above exercises, develop a SHRM strategy to help an organization move to a more sustainable (environmentally and socially) position.

6.7   Further reading

Sinclair, 2006; Dunphy et al., 2007.

Environmental Marketing

7

Michael Polonsky

7.1 Introduction

In this chapter we discuss environmental or green marketing and the issues a firm should consider when developing and implementing environmental marketing. The concept of environmental or green marketing has been around for over 30 years, although it has been called by different names- ecological marketing, environmental marketing, sustainable marketing and green marketing (Chamorro et al., 2007). The idea behind environmental marketing is that firms and consumers undertake exchanges that create value for both parties, which also seek to minimize any negative environmental impacts. According to the American Marketing Association (2008) there are three different perspectives that can be considered to define green marketing:

- *retailing* definition – The marketing of products that are presumed to be environmentally safe;
- *social* marketing definition – The development and marketing of products designed to minimize negative effects on the physical environment or to improve its quality; and
- *environments* definition – The efforts by organizations to produce, promote, package, and reclaim products in a manner that is sensitive or responsive to ecological concerns. (AMA, 2008)

The social and environments perspectives are those that are more generally used today. What this means is that firms think about ways to create value for themselves and consumers through all stages of the exchange process, while at the same time minimizing any environmental harm. Thus environmental marketing can result in firms redesigning their products, amending distribution and logistic activities, communicating additional information to consumers or reconceptualizing how goods are priced. That is, environmental marketing builds on the traditional four Ps of marketing (price, place, promotion and product), which are developed with the firm either independently or in collaboration with partners.

How green should firms go?

Environmental marketing is certainly more than superficial hype, although there has been extensive criticism early in its development that marketers were seeking to exploit the interests of segments of consumers who were socially concerned and wanted to purchase goods that had less environmental impact (Ginsberg and Bloom, 2004). However, there were forms of environmental marketing that were founded based on solid environmental principles where environmental concern was a core plank of the businesses' philosophy (Hart and Milstein, 1999). Other firms saw environmental marketing initiatives as enabling them to operate more efficiently, by using fewer resources which had the benefits of lowering costs while at the same time allowing firms to potentially promote themselves as being environmentally responsible (Porter and van der Linde, 1995a).

7.2   Motivations and types of greening

Motivations

It has been suggested that firms were motivated to undertake environmental marketing for one of three reasons (Keogh and Polonsky, 1998) and that the motivation will potentially shape action. The first type of motivation for undertaking environmental marketing is *affective motivation* where firms' believed that minimizing environmental issues in marketing activities is the right thing to do. Organizations that are affectively motivated will ensure that all marketing activities consider environmental issues. Classic examples of such firms are the Body Shop, Ben and Jerry's Ice Cream and the Australian natural healthcare firm Blackmore's. In all these cases the firms' founder was concerned with environmental issues and ensured that this concern was translated into a core corporate value.

The second type of motivation is a *continuance motivation*, whereby there is a belief that the there is an economic benefit from undertaking more responsible actions. This initially translated into a classical cost benefit analysis for firms. That is, firms decided what environmental improvements could be made, such that costs associated with the changes were recouped. The 'easy' changes were frequently made quickly (Porter and van der Linde, 1995a), such as modifying packaging to use recycled content or increase the efficiency of production facilities. However in many cases these easy changes were not where firms' primary environmental impact occurred.

The third motivation is a *normative motivation* whereby organizations adopt environmental marketing because they want to comply with laws or expectations of stakeholders. Normatively motivated firms tend to be more externally driven. For example, when California indicated it was implementing a law requiring a percentage of all automobiles to be fuelled by alternative energy there was a rush on the part of manufactures to develop such automobiles (Brown, 2001). However, when the law was repealed few automobile firms introduced the alternatively fuelled cars they were working on, although the technology formed the basis of cars they latter developed.

Types of greening

While corporate motivations for undertaking environmental marketing differ, there are also differences in the way that these environmental issues are integrated into marketing activities. Menon and Menon (1997) proposed that there are three levels of greening that can take place. The most significant is *strategic greening* where firms change their overall philosophy as well as their activities. For example, the CEO of General Motors recently stated that petrol-powered automobiles will soon be a thing of the past and auto manufactures will need to shift all activities to biofuelled cars or hybrids (Brewester, 2008). Such shifts will require radical organization change, involving massive investments, that once initiated will be irreversible.

On the other extreme are *tactical greening* activities, where firms seek to make minor changes, frequently related to efficiency, material usage or promotional activities. These are the activities that firms adopted early on in the development of environmental marketing, where the firm sought to promote its environmental credentials without necessarily making substantial changes in its activities. Such actions are potentially seen as cynical attempts to 'jump on the green bandwagon' and as such often have resulted in negative consumer backlash claiming that these are superficial greenwash (Crane, 2000).

In between the two extremes is what Menon and Menon (1997) called *quasi-strategic greening* which involves firms making significant investments and changing practices, but not fundamentally changing the business. For example, Fuji Xerox developed new technologies that allowed them to remanufacture photocopies, that is, reprocessing used parts which resulted in substantial financial benefits as well as environmental efficiencies from minimizing raw material usage (Kerr and Ryan, 2001).

7.3   Customer markets

Internal activates such as motivations and the level of greening also depend on the group of consumers the firm is targeting. As will be discussed in the next section of this chapter there are a range of consumer segments that can be targeted and environmental marketing strategy will vary based on who is being targeted (Ginsberg and Bloom, 2004). The assumption that firms should vary their marketing activities (i.e., marketing mix or four Ps – price, place, promotion and product) for different groups of customers is of course a basic marketing principle. However, this perspective may imply that firms are not necessarily as committed to making environmental improvements, as they are not affectively motivated nor are they undertaking strategic or quasi-strategic environmental marketing activities.

When considered marketing to businesses, segmentation (focusing on meeting the needs of a target market) could potentially be less important in regards to environmental marketing. That is, businesses purchase products because they want to produce their own goods and services. There is a range of recent examples, where suppliers' environmental activities have had negative consequences on their customers and suppliers. One high-profile example is the toy manufacture who had to recall millions of toys because suppliers used paints that were dangerously high in lead and other materials (Associated Press, 2007). When targeting business customers (or individuals in different countries) marketers need to ensure that their goods comply with the appropriate environmental requirements of that country (Kohn, 2003). In cases where customer firms are ISO14000 accredited, it requires that potential suppliers are also accredited. As such, environmental marketing needs to consider the legal environment within each country that it operates, both for consumer and business markets.

Environmental marketing is potentially more complicated when dealing with individual consumer markets, as each individual's interest in environmental attributes of goods will vary. In the early 1970s, such consumers were frequently considered specialized segments (Anderson and Cunningham, 1972). The size of green consumer markets has varied over time (Ottman, 1998). Some consumer groups have become very focused on minimizing their environmental impact by simplifying their consumption overall (Craig-Lees and Hill, 2002). On the other hand, environmental attributes are increasingly becoming important for all consumers even those not generally considered to be overly concerned with environmental issues. There is an increased recognition that consumption may partly relate to society's general increase in concern about global warming (Nesbit and Myers, 2007). However, in some cases it has been governmental regulatory changes that have reinforced consumer's environmental awareness.

EXAMPLE

Legislation and Consumer Awareness

The Australian Federal Government was the first national government to put in place a timeline for phasing out traditional incandescent light bulbs (Johnson, 2007). This initiative sent a clear signal to consumers that they need to change their behaviour, while at the same time serving as a market stimulus for the production of 'long-life' light bulbs. These light bulbs have been available for many years, but recent government action has stimulated changes in purchase behaviour (and possibly attitudes) for all consumers. While past research has identified that green issues are of varying degrees of importance to consumers, environmental issues appear to becoming core expectations of consumers and thus essential parts of marketing activity. (Werther and Chandler, 2005)

Green marketing tools

There are a variety of ways that marketer can implement environmental issues into marketing activities. Polonsky and Rosenburger (2001) identified that there were at least eight activities – targeting, design, positioning, pricing, logistics, marketing waste, promotion, alliances – that could be undertaken **and** that these activities could be undertaken at various levels (i.e., strategic, quasi-strategic and tactical). At various points in time the initiatives proposed by one firm may initially have been seen to be in radical departures from existing practice. Over time environmental marketing activities have been adopted across organizations to such an extent that they now are the industry standard. For example, now all leading firms marketing tuna catch tuna in a way that minimizes the potential of catching dolphins. While modifying fishing practices to be 'dolphin friendly' tuna was initially spearheaded by one manufacture, public interest in the issue ultimately resulted in it becoming a voluntary industry standard (Brown, 2005). As will be discussed in more depth later in this chapter there are a range of issues that are gaining usage in marketing activities. For example, at present many firms offer consumers the option of paying an extra fee to purchase carbon offsets equal to the carbon released in the production of goods and services (Revkin, 2007). At some point in the future this practice may be expanded to become the industry norm or may even progress such that the cost is integrated into the initial price of the good and thus not a purchase option.

7.4   Environmental or green customers

The literature on environmental or green customers has considered the issue from two perspectives (1) firms marketing to final consumers, that is, individuals; (2) firms marketing goods to other firms as products or parts of the other firm's products. Customer firms may then use the environmental attributes of the products they purchase to promote their goods and environmental credentials or they may choose not to promote these links.

Final consumers

The work exploring environmental consumers dates back over 35 years to the early work of Anderson and Cunningham (1972) who explored socially responsible consumers. Since that time there has been extensive research into environmental consumption and environmental consumers (Kilbourne and Beckman, 1998), which has taken a range of perspectives.

Marketers have been extensively concerned with differences in consumer behaviour in regards to environmental issues. The research on environmental consumers has included examining whether a given public policy will bring about positive changes in behaviour such as increased recycling (Davies et al., 2002); whether consumers will respond positively to different environmental promotions (Shrum et al., 1995; Chan, 2004); or whether consumers will modify purchase in regards to environmental marketing activities, such as, will they pay a premium for a green product (D'Souza et al., 2007).

Environmental marketing activity has also focused on changing consumers' attitudes or environmental knowledge. If consumers are not positively disposed to behaving in a given way because they do not understand the underlying issues, than marketing needs to focus on modifying attitudes and knowledge, before it seeks to change actual behaviour (Kahn, 2007; Mostafa, 2007). For example, it might be suggested that the increased realization that global warming is an important issue has resulted in consumers being more willing to modify their consumption (Nisbet and Myers, 2007). For this reason, the environmental marketing literature has often not only examined behaviours but also environmental knowledge and attitudes.

When examining environmentally oriented consumers, a variety of different descriptions have been used in the literature for consumers. Connolly et al. (2006) identified thirteen different 'names' used to describe environmentally focused consumers (see Table 7.1). Within this list two broad philosophies have generally been used. The first and possibly largest set of research has examined environmental consumption – that is, those who seek to minimize their environmental impact or those who behave with more responsibility. This work has frequently sought to define whether there are segments of consumers who wish

Table 7.1   Categorizations of Green Consumers in the literature

Name used in the literature	Emphasis of the approach
Responsible consumers	Responsible
The socially conscious consumer	Responsible
Ecologically concerned consumers	Responsible
Environmentally concerned consumers	Responsible
Environmentally conscious consumers	Responsible
Green, ethical & charitable consumer	Responsible
Green consumers	Responsible
Humane consumers	Responsible
Ethical consumers	Responsible
Ethical simplifiers	Minimalists/responsible
Conserving consumer	Minimalists/responsible
Downshifters	Minimalists
The voluntary simplifier	Minimalists

to minimize their negative impact on the environment. One of the earliest works seeking to develop a profile of responsible consumers was by Anderson and Cunningham (1972) who suggested that there were demographic and socio-psychological factors that differentiated consumer segments.

The determination of what makes a socially or ecologically concerned consumer has been an ongoing theme in the literature. Diamantopoulos et al. (2003) undertook an extensive review of the past work examining socio-demographics as a segmentation tool (i.e., identify consumers who behave in a similar way) for environmental consumers, which includes gender, age, family issues, income and education. In regards to gender they identified that in past research males were often more knowledgeable about environmental issues, but that females were more concerned with environmental issues and females were also more likely to undertake environmental responsible activities. However, in their study of 9700 UK consumers they did not find a gender difference in knowledge, but they did find females were more environmentally oriented and undertook environmental activities more frequently.

Their review of the literature suggested that, in general, there was no difference between older and younger consumers in regards to environmental knowledge, but that younger consumers were more concerned about environmental issues. The past research also found that there were differences in behaviour based on age, although the literature was found to be inconsistent in this regard. Within their work they confirmed the past results in regards to knowledge (i.e., no age affect) and concern (younger people were more concerned); they also found that there were limited differences in regards to behaviour.

According to Diamantopoulos et al.'s (2003) review, some previous research also found that the number of children one has affects individuals' environmental knowledge, concern and behaviour. Additionally, the past literature suggested that the more education one has, the greater his/her knowledge, concern and behaviour. Within their study they found that having children did not affect knowledge, concern or behaviour. However, they found that one's level of education did appear to influence knowledge and to some extent behaviour, but not environmental concern.

Thus, the literature and research by Diamantopoulos et al. (2003) found that demographic factors do appear to impact on consumer environmental knowledge, attitudes and behaviour. The issues are not only important for consumers in developed countries, but have also been found to influence consumers in China (Chan, 2004), Egypt (Mostafa, 2007) and Turkey (Furman, 1998) to name just a few. Thus understanding environmental knowledge, attitudes and behaviour from a final customer perspective has global relevance.

In examining the types of environmental/green consumers studies identified in Table 7.1, there is a smaller, but important set of research that has examined consumers who are often called voluntary simplifiers. These consumers seek to modify their lifestyle so that they consume less or do without certain types of goods, thereby minimizing their environmental impact. The idea of simplification is not new and these types of consumers have existed as far back as the depression of the 1920s. While initially these consumers were motivated by economic constraints (Sharma, 1981), some did adopt a simplified lifestyle because of environmental concerns (Leonard-Barton, 1981).

Individuals may undertake different levels of simplification (McDonald et al., 2006). This will translate into a range of environmental behaviours (Bekin et al., 2005). At the extreme end of the spectrum one might consider the idealized communities that seek to be self-sufficient as simplifiers. That is, they seek to only consume what they (i.e., the commune) can produce, although Bekin et al. (2005) identified that simplifiers are developing more traditional communities where consumption is minimized. Most simplifiers do not seek to cut themselves off from the traditional market; rather they seek to undertake changes in lifestyles that minimize consumption. For example, the increased shift to public transportation is a simplification behaviour, where people choose not to use individual automobiles for transportation. In most cases people keep their cars for some uses. If they were to sell their car (or not purchase one in the first place) this could be considered another type of simplification. As such most simplifiers may be considered 'un-consumers' (Huneke, 2005).

There is less research exploring simplification, but the behaviour appears to be growing as does the research into simplification. Huneke (2005) found that there was a range of differences in simplification segments based on demographic factors and that simplifiers were not necessarily lower income consumers, as had been the case when the movement started in the 1920s. This is important, as it means that targeting un-consumers or simplifiers was equally difficult to targeting different segments of environmentally oriented consumers.

Business consumers

When thinking about environmental marketing we possible traditionally focus on firms targeting final consumers (Ginsberg and Bloom, 2004). However, marketers target business and government customers as well. In thinking about environmental marketing for business customers the research has tended to be fragmented, focusing on specific types of activities. For example, research has explored the design of new goods and the fact that most of the environmental impacts are designed into products at the initial planning phase (Bhat, 1993). As such there are unique opportunities for organizations producing less environmentally harmful production processes to target organizations seeking to design new products and services (Chen, 2001). Take, for example, the increased interest by automobile producers in Hybrid automobiles. They have the choice of developing all the components to be used in these products or to purchasing components from suppliers. For marketers to be effective in dealing with business customers they not only need to have the environmental expertise but also a solid understanding of the business and its processes.

Another example of environmental marketing targeting business customers relates to the removal/disposal of waste (Zikmund and Stanton, 1971). There are a number of markets that exist specializing in providing such services to a range of business customers. For example, the disposal of cardboard packaging is a substantial issue for large retailers and shopping centres. While on one side this is a waste product, as will be discussed later, this is also a resource that has market value.

One of the newer services that have sprung up for business marketers are organizations marketing carbon offset programmes (Lohmann, 2005). These programmes are increasingly becoming important as governments initiate requirements for organizations to reduce their carbon emissions (i.e., carbon targets and taxes). Firms can respond to this legislation by improving their environmental performance, purchasing carbon licenses or purchasing 'carbon offsets'. Carbon offsets in fact do not reduce the firms' environmental impact; rather they indirectly cover the environmental effect of activities. At present there is a range of carbon offset programmes being marketed to organizations and individual firms need to assess which is most appropriate for them. It is unfortunately unclear if all programs deliver equally well on their promises (Ramseur, 2007). For example, in some cases carbon offsets programmes are based on selling new tree plantations. The environmental benefit of these new plantations will only occur in the future when the trees mature but if the plantation is destroyed by drought or fire, the benefits never eventuate.

Environmental marketers targeting business customers have to consider many of the same issues associated with firms targeting final consumers. That is, what motivates the business customer to act (Banerjee et al., 2003)? Business customers' motivations may be as complex as the motives of final customers, although other issues such as the specifics of the organization (i.e., processes, goals, etc.) also need to be considered.

Segmenting consumers

Marketers frequently seek to place consumers (individuals and businesses) into groups that will behave in a similar way (i.e., segment consumers). This allows the firm to develop strategies that can be specifically targeted (i.e., aimed) at each segment, where the strategies used are designed to be most effective in motivating changes in outcomes – knowledge, attitudes or behaviours. In many cases firms marketing environmental goods do not seek to only meet the needs of one segment in the market (often called focused or niche marketing), but also they do not seek to meet the needs of all segments of customers either. Firms using environmental marketing frequently have designed products to target those that are more concerned with environmental characteristics of goods, while at the same time targeting those who might be considered more traditional consumers. For example, many car manufacturers are developing hybrid automobiles, but promote environmental benefits as well as cost benefits (i.e., less operating costs). However, these firms also promote traditional cars aimed at segments that are less environmentally oriented (Kahn, 2007).

When segmenting consumers, firms assume that each segment will behave in a similar way. Thus the research discussed above regarding demographic characteristics of environmental consumers is important. Within the marketing research industry, firms have sought to develop typologies for classifying consumers, based on their environmental motivations. The Roper consulting group has long tracked environmental consumer sentiment in the United States (GfK Roper, 2007) and used this to develop profiles of five groups of green consumers, for which there are significant demographic and psychographic differences between the groups (Ottman, 1998).

Table 7.2 reports the size of each of Roper's environmental segments over time (Ottman, 1998, GfK Roper, 2007). The research has shown that there these segments can be broadly grouped into three categories: committed, middle of the road and laggards. The most committed segment has increased significantly over time, with the True-Blue Greens being the largest segment of US consumers in 2007. While the Green Back Greens declined initially, they have returned to their 1990s' level in 2007.

Those in the middle appear to be approximately 25 per cent of the US population. While this group has shrunk since 1996, this is the result of a shift to more committed consumers. The last segment of green consumers, Laggards, was approximately 50 per cent of the US population in 1990 and 1996, but has fallen to under 35 per cent. What is possibly the most important point to note is that the least green, Basic Browns, were 37 per cent alone in 1996 but are now 18 per cent, thus there appears to have been a significant realization on the part of consumers that environmental issues are important.

Roper's five segments are of course not the only groups proposed by industry for classifying environmental consumers. The Natural Marketing Institute (2007) has proposed an alternative segmentation scheme, which is also included in Table 7.2. The names used to describe their segments are slightly different, which possibly reflects their approach to categorizing consumers. Their most green are called LOHAS, which stands for consumers who have a Lifestyle of Health and Sustainability. While the size of segments differ slightly the overall size of committed, middle of the road and laggards is in fact very similar.

Table 7.2   Segments of green consumers

	GfK Roper green gauge segments			Natural marketing segments	
	Segment	1990	1996	2007	Segment	2007
Committed	True-Blue Greens	11	10	30	LOHAS	19
	Green Back Greens	11	5	10	Naturalites	19
Middle of the Road	Sprouts	26	33	26	Drifters	25
Laggards	Grousers	24	15	16	Conventionalists	19
	Apathetics (basic Browns)	28	37	18	Unconvinced	17

Source: Ottman, 1998; GfK Roper, 2007; NMI, 2007.

Understanding consumers is the first step in developing marketing strategy, as without this, organizations cannot design marketing offerings that meet the needs of consumers (final or business).

7.5   Green marketing tools

There are many different ways in which organizations can build environmental issues into their marketing activities and this can be undertaken at different levels as well: strategic, quasi-strategic and tactical (Menon and Menon, 1997). Firms usually choose to act in a way that will give the firm and its brands some competitive advantage in the marketplace. This means that consumers will, hopefully, prefer the 'green' products over competitor's traditional goods. Ginsburg and Bloom (2004) proposed what they defined as the Green Marketing Strategy Matrix (see Table 7.3) which can be used to determine what environmental marketing focus firms should take. Within this matrix they propose that firms need to consider the size of the segment (how many consumers are there who will be motivated to respond to the firm's actions?) as well as the firms' ability to differentiate itself from its competitors (i.e., how easy would it be for competitor's to copy the initiatives?).

If there is a large segment of consumers who want environmental attributes integrated into your products and you can develop something that cannot be copied (say a patented innovation), then the firm would benefit from undertaking strategic changes that allow them to position themselves as green, 'Extreme Green'. This would include the various companies that position themselves as environmentally responsible. On the other hand, if there are large segments of consumers who are interested in environmental issues, but the firm's environmental initiatives can be easily copied, they will possibly focus on 'Defensive Green' activities. For example, including carbon offsets as part of a product is a positive innovation, but all firms within a sector can easily copy it. Thus firms that act first may have some short-term advantage, but no long-term sustained advantage exists (unless there are some other distinctive environmental activities that can be undertaken).

If environmental segments are relatively small and the ability to differentiate innovations is low, then firms may undertake 'Lean Green' activities. In this

Table 7.3   Green marketing mix

Sustainability of green Market segments			
	High	Defensive green	Extreme green
	Low	Lean green	Shaded green
		Low	High
		Differentiability on greenness	

Source: Ginsburg and Bloom, 2004.

case firms often want to be seen to be doing something, without making substantial repositioning of their activities. This might include firms developing an environmentally friendly version of 'traditional' products that they make in addition to their normal activities.

If there are small market segments, but the ability to differentiate is high, firms may become 'Shaded Green'. This would involve companies undertaking significant changes in their activities, similar to Menon and Menon's (1997) Strategic or Quasi-Strategic activities, where firms make changes that will enable them to take advantage of future developments in the industry, but the changes are less significant than Extreme Green organizations. Firms are not redefining all activities today; rather they are laying the groundwork for ongoing innovation.

The types of environmental marketing tools to be used will vary, depending on how the firm sees itself, its operations and its customers. As will be discussed in the following sections there are a number of tools that can be used to incorporate environmental issues in marketing activities. Authors such as Polonsky and Rosenburger (2001) have proposed that these can be implemented at the Strategic, Quasi-Strategic and Tactical levels.

New product opportunities

Environmental problems create opportunities for innovative solutions to these problems. While in many instances solutions involve redesigning existing products (discussed below), in a few instances solutions result in products or services that are new to the world, thus environmental problems can create business opportunities. Take for example, carbon taxes and carbon trading. It has been suggested that by creating markets for carbon, it will in fact be possible to reduce the production of carbon (Ikwue and Skea, 1994). By creating a market where carbon licenses can be bought and sold, the market will facilitate a reduction in the production of carbon through the supply and demand process.

A somewhat related new product is the development of carbon offsets. These are products that firms and individuals can purchase to 'reduce their carbon footprint or to categorize an activity as carbon neutral. A carbon offset is a measurable avoidance, reduction or sequestration of carbon dioxide (CO_2) or other green house gas emissions' (Ramseur, 2007). There are many global organizations providing carbon offsets. In the first instance these are being bought by firms to reduce the environmental footprint of their activities, but some firms are using carbon offsets as marketing tools to suggest to consumers that the firm is more responsible. Buying a carbon offset does not mean that firm's production of carbon has been reduced; rather it means they have 'purchased' an equivalent amount of carbon savings. While the firm is reducing its environmental impact across the global eco-system, the amount of carbon that it produces is not reduced. It is not clear how well such programmes are understood by consumers. For example, the Australian Competition and Consumer Commission is investigating whether firms promoting carbon offsets are misleading consumers (Australian Competition and Consumer Commission, 2008).

The development of carbon offsets has also stimulated a range of other new products, that is, all those that result in carbon reduction. For example, there are massive investments going into planting new forests, buying old growth forests to be protected and firms exploring ways to capture carbon (i.e,. sequestration). The carbon offset industry has stimulated growth in a second layer of products and services, that is, the firms actually undertaking the carbon savings. As will be discussed below, this also occurs in the redesign of existing products.

Design and redesign

In developing new products, firms increasingly integrate environmental principles into the design process (Sroufe et al., 2000). This is important as negative environmental impacts are designed into products, usually unintentionally (Bhat, 1993). In designing products organizations need to consider broader environmental principles and not focus on simple financial cost benefit analysis. Within various industries there are checklists to assess the environmental issues to be considered. For example, within the electrical area it has been suggested that the following major issues be considered (Clark and Charter, 1999):

- raw material extraction and transport;
- primary material processing and transport;
- product manufacturing and distribution;
- product use; and
- 'end of life'.

Product planning must consider system wide (or life cycle) effects of production, use and disposal of products and therefore firms need to understand the life cycle environmental effects of their products (Clark and Charter, 1999). That is not only what is the impact of producing goods, but also what is the environmental effect of using or disposing of goods. For example, developing long-life light bulbs reduces energy use, yet the disposal of these goods potentially increases environmental harm from mercury (Luther, 2008). In other cases there may be a conflict between consumer value and environmental benefit. For example, the inclusion of a stand-by or sleep modes in electrical appliances may provide more convenience, but this also increases energy use (Fung et al., 2003).

Targeting

Focusing on the specific needs of environmental consumers is another strategy (Crane, 2000; Ginsburg and Bloom, 2004). This approach recognizes that firms produce multiple products, which are often each aimed at a different segment of the market and that each segment has a different set of needs and motivations. Environmentally oriented firms therefore identify segments of consumers that behave more responsibly, that is, leveraging consumers' interest. One example is in the energy sector. Many utility firms have identified that targeting consumers with 'green energy' would enable consumers to purchase energy and feel more comfortable with their decision (Wüstenhagen and Bilharz, 2006). However, most retail electricity providers market 'traditionally' produced energy as well. Thus, the firm targets green energy at consumers who are more environmentally motivated and traditional energy at others.

While targeting makes good marketing sense, it does potentially raise concerns on the part of consumers. How can a firm on one hand say it is committed to making environmental improvements, by marketing 'green' goods, while on the other hand it also markets traditional goods?

Positioning

Positioning is where firms create an identity for the firm which consumers then use to compare the firm to competitors (Hartmann et al., 2005). Environmental positioning is a strategic activity where the firm makes a commitment to support environmental values and undertake Radical or Strategic greening within Ginsburg and Blooms strategy matrix. It has been suggested that corporate social responsibility (Werther and Chandler, 2005), which includes environmental responsibility, is a core part of business and consumers expect firms to behave responsibly.

The question of how to position the firm in regards to environmental issues is difficult. Firms must be able to undertake activities that warrant differentiation (i.e., can they do something significant?). In many cases the environmental changes that are made will not necessarily be identified by consumers. For example, airline travel creates significant negative environmental impacts (Lynes and Dredge, 2006). Purchasing new fuel-efficient planes will significantly reduce environmental harm. Airlines can also purchase carbon offsets to further minimize the negative environmental impacts. The question to be asked is whether consumers will see these improvements as being substantial enough to view the airline as being environmentally responsible. The airline may need to also invest in educating consumers on the real environmental impacts of air travel, as well as how their firm performs relative to competition.

Environmental positioning requires an integrated set of activities that create the right brand identity, which can be demonstrated with underlying changes in behaviour. It requires consistent activities across the organization, to ensure there that the firm cannot be criticized for undertaking superficial opportunistic environmental activities (i.e., 'greenwash'). Environmental positioning requires that firms fully understand all the environmental issues that they need to deal with (Polonsky and Jevons, 2006). Unfortunately, for some firms environmental positioning may not be appropriate. If this is the case, firms must resist any temptation to exaggerate their environmental activities; as such exaggerations will often result in consumer backlash.

Pricing

There is frequently an assumption that environmental goods cost more to purchase than 'normal' goods. While there may be differences on the purchase price of the goods, environmental marketers should focus on the running costs or lifetime costs of goods. For example, a long-life light bulb is significantly more expensive than a traditional light bulb. However, if consumers integrate the operating costs into the price (i.e., electric usage) then long-life light bulbs are in fact less expensive. The same would apply to the purchase of many hybrid automobiles; that the purchase price is higher, but if operating costs are included they may in fact be cheaper. This assumes that the two goods are of an equivalent quality. As in the early days of environmental marketing, this was not the case.

EXAMPLE

Pricing Issues

Early recycled photocopy paper was inferior and could damage photocopy machines (Polonsky et al., 1998). Thus while the paper was 'environmentally better', its usage had a higher costs (i.e., the risk of breaking a photocopier). Thus even if early recycled paper was less expensive firms would have not purchased it because of higher overall cost. Of course this has changed significantly and the quality of recycled paper is as high as or higher than virgin paper. When pricing environmental goods firms must understand how consumers assess prices. Firms can then communicate the full price of their goods and 'traditional' goods.

A second difficultly associated with pricing environmental goods is that the pollution 'costs' associated with traditional goods are not paid for by consumers but are externalities (i.e., costs born by everyone). This may be remedied when carbon taxes come into force, as consumers may have to pay for the environmental harm of all their products. At present environmental costs are not paid for by the owner of the car and thus traditional cars are run at a subsidy.

Firms therefore need to think about how to communicate prices in a way that reflects real cost comparisons. That is, product A's purchase and usage cost is Y over its lifetime and product B's purchase and usage cost is X over its usage. This will allow for a better comparison of the full cost of the two goods (Polonsky and Rosenburger, 2001).

There is one potential proviso, while an environmental good may be cheaper in the long term, if its initial price is too much higher than the traditional good consumers still may not purchase it. Referring back to the fluorescent long-life light bulb, when people could buy normal bulbs at $.98 and long-life light bulbs at $10+, many consumers failed to purchase the environmental alternative, even though they could be shown it was cheaper. It took too long to recover the costs of the long-life light bulb.

Minimizing and marketing waste

A systems perspective considers that all products have value, including waste. Firms who reduce waste or find markets for waste minimizing resource use recover value from the production system. For example, a farmer who has open irrigation trenches is losing water through evaporation but by running water through pipes will use less water. Another example would be an industrial laundry that instead of flushing water down the drain uses its post-wash water to water its lawns or even sells this water to the local golf course to water its lawns and thus uses less drinkable water.

In some cases industrial parks are being designed specifically where the waste of one organization is being used as a production input into another (Côtéa and Cohen-Rosenthalb, 1998). In this way the waste from all firms in the park are minimized or even eliminated. Such a process requires extensive pre-development planning. In addition, the failure of one organization will affect all others, as waste streams will be disrupted. In the case of waste minimization the firm focuses on re-engineering products to use fewer resources (Eichner and Pethig, 2001) becoming more efficient and having a lower environmental impact. The focus of minimizing and marketing waste is to reduce material usage limiting wasted materials.

Logistics and reverse logistics

The movement of components from production to consumption can represent a significant environmental impact. While systems such as just-in-time are designed to minimize inventories, these required additional deliveries and thus higher distribution and environmental costs. Moving components from buyers to suppliers can be streamlined in developing integrated industrial parks. As was mentioned above (Côtéa and Cohen-Rosenthalb, 1998), these systems can also ensure that waste moves from one firm to be used as an input to another firm located next to the producer. Reducing the movement of goods can even be undertaken by transportation firms tracking their distribution fleet, which may enable them to identify more efficient distribution routes, requiring less fuel usage (Murphy and Poist, 2000).

There is also an increasing expectation that producers are responsible for the collection of waste associated with their goods. In some cases this collection of waste (reverse logistics) indirectly involves the reprocessing of valuable resources. For example, many producers of toner cartridges for laser printers are developing systems to recollect used cartridges and refill them, as the cartridges are more expensive than the toner used (Bartel, 1995). In other cases there are legal requirements that producers take back products that are no longer of use, that is, disposed of products (Crotty, 2006) or collecting packaging from retailers or wholesalers. According to Gooley (1998), there are five steps for reverse logistics which will impact on their success:

- Analyse your reasons for reverse logistics, which may include recovering valuable resources, better customer services or legal obligations.
- How will you communicate this with consumers? The objectives may affect how you get consumer participation. Without their support any programme will fail.
- Plan the reverse logistics operation; that is, establish how the process will operate. This stage is critical as if it is poorly designed it can increase costs and effectiveness.
- Develop an information system to track activities. Managing reverse logistics means having information on goods that are outgoing, incoming or passing through the system.
- Understand the implications of a system in regards to the obligations and requirements of the location where you are operating. While a system may meet obligations in one country it may not meet those in another.

While reverse logistics are valuable, there do need to be investments to ensure that the systems and infrastructure are put in place to enable them to operate.

Promotion

One of the most written about topics in regards to environmental marketing has been promotion. The misuse of promotion is possibly the reason that environmental marketing early on got a bad name, as it was suggested that firms were using greenwash, that is, meaningless environmentally oriented claims. For example, early environmental promotion had firms claiming 'we care about the environment', our products are 'environmentally friendly' etc. The statements sound nice, but have limited meaning and the problem of greenwash had become so bad in the early 1990s that governments around the world developed regulations on environmental marketing claims (Kangun and Polonsky, 1995).

In the promotional mix, there are a number of tools, for example, personal selling, advertising, publicity, sales promotion, etc. The focus of these is to communicate characteristics about your products. Advertising is one of the most used promotional tools and is a paid communication. An example would be a firm advertising that its products 'won a UN environmental award', or we use '10% recycled content in the packaging'. The claims being made must have meaning. Often times if the firm can have these verified externally they will have a greater impact, for example, according to environmental group X, our products use less energy than competitors.

Publicity is another effective promotional tool. This is where information is communicated, but it is not paid for. For example, there is a news story when you win an environmental award. Publicity tends to have a higher degree of believability because it is not the firm promoting the information, it is unpaid media. While firms don't pay for the publicity, often they do have to make extensive investments to warrant publicity. For example, being a sponsor of 'Clean-Up Australia Day' may cost several million dollars. It is important to realize that firms cannot control publicity, that is, whether it is used or how. For example, one fast food company that did sponsor clean-up Australia day was heavily criticized in the media by some groups, who claimed that it was that firm's garbage that was being cleaned up.

Sales promotion is another tool that is used in green marketing; this is where there is some incentive associated with purchasing the product. In environmental marketing this is often cause-related marketing where firms make a donation to an environmental cause when consumers purchase the good (Hemphill, 1996). While this is relatively easy to do, it is also open to criticism of greenwash, for example, what is the link between a brand of tyres and planting a tree for every four tyres sold? In this case, Consumer Relations Management (CRM) is potentially seen as exploitive.

The question associated with promotion is how does a firm develop a campaign that cuts through all the advertising clutter, both in regards to its products and more generally? There is no magic answer. Some firms will choose to develop and promote goods that integrate environmental values, but environmental issues need to be relevant to the group of consumers being targeted (Carlson et al., 1996). For example, one firm promoted biodegradable plastic golf tees. While the products could demonstrate on the claims being made, it is unclear that consumers made product selections based on this attribute? The key with promotion is to ensure that claims, however made, are justifiable and these need to be meaningful to your customers.

Alliances

Environmental problems require system wide solutions, often relying on knowledge and expertise outside the firm. The question is how does the firm draw on sufficient environmental expertise that allows it to ensure activities are 'state of the art'? There are increasing collaborations across industries and organizations to enable them to come up with innovative solutions. For example, when Fuji Xerox decided to re-engineer components of its photocopiers, they knew what needed to be done, but did not have the technical expertise needed for some of the reprocessing processes. They sought out collaborators who had the technical expertise to work with them to develop a process that would achieve their aims, while at the same time allowing their collaborator to advance their understanding of the processes being used. Thus it was a win-win solution.

The alliance strategy, while rather straight forward does require organizations to reconceptualize their activities. Firms are frequently wary of sharing information with those outside the firm. This is even more complicated when firms consider sharing information with competitors or even special interest groups that may traditionally be seen as an advisory (Stafford et al., 2000). For example, environmental groups who have extensive environmental information can cooperate with businesses to address system wide environmental solutions. There are risks on both sides: environmental groups collaborating with business may be seen by their constituents to be selling out. On the other hand, firms have to share sensitive internal information with environmental groups, who may potentially publicize this information and harm the firm.

Alliances require that there is a change in how groups view one another from being confrontational to being cooperative, where there is a benefit to both groups. Environmental groups become to be seen as part of the solution and valued for their expertise, but maintain their independence to highlight inappropriate behaviour wherever it eventuates. Firms are still profit-seeking but are seen to be more open and innovative. The sharing of experiences requires a situation where there is mutual trust, which may take some time to develop. Thus collaborations are not an instant solution.

7.6   Conclusion

Environmental marketing is part of the broader tool set that can be used by organizations when seeking to differentiate themselves in the market. Firms need to have a well-crafted strategy as to how they would like to integrated environmental issues into their activities. While they can undertake strategy, quasi-strategic and tactical greening using a variety of tools, they need to ensure that they can demonstrate that any action has real and meaningful environmental impacts.

The specific strategy selected will of course also depend on the segment of the market where the firm is targeting its goods. There is limited value of a petrol or coal company seeking to satisfy the environmental needs of true-blue green consumers who expect that organizations will do no harm. While such a firm can demonstrate that its behaviour is better than the competitors, they would possibly do themselves a disservice trying to promote themselves as an environmentally responsible organization.

The objective of environmental marketing is to develop a realistic strategy, for each organization, that can be delivered on. Trying to be something that you are not will lead to consumer or stakeholder criticism, with all good efforts left forgotten. As such, environmental marketing although a potentially valuable strategy does have some risks and needs to be used only when a firm can truly demonstrate its purported commitment, whatever level of greening it chooses.

7.7   Questions

• Discuss how your organization or an organization you are familiar undertake effective green marketing activities.
• Identify how a firm might use different environmental marketing activities when targeting 'true-blue' green consumers as compared 'sprouts' (i.e., middle of the road green consumers)?

- Look for a product in the supermarket or advertisement in a newspaper/magazine that undertakes greenwash (i.e., meaningless environmental claims) and explain what would be needed to make the marketing be meaningful.
- Why might a firm that is undertaking positive environmental activities choose not to use these to position themselves in the market?

7.8 Further reading

Ottman, 1998; Charter and Polonsky, 1999; Fuller, 1999.

Organization: Structures, Frameworks, Reporting

8

Arun Sahay*

8.1 Introduction

In this chapter we address some general aspects of organizational management in relationship to environmental and social sustainability with discussions on organizational structures, organizational management system frameworks and organizational sustainability reporting. These illustrate changes that need to occur (and are occurring) if organizations are to respond to external and internal pressures to become more sustainable both environmentally and socially.

Organization defined

Organization facilitates proper utilization of men, material and money for the accomplishment of the defined purpose. In modern era, organization is a pervasive phenomenon that has become the identity of people across the globe. Organizations have been studied by researchers from many disciplines, for example, sociology, economics, political science, psychology, management and organizational communication. However, the discipline of management is interested in organization mainly from an instrumental angle. For a business firm, the organization is a means to achieve its goals. An eminent management thinker quotes: 'By organization, we mean a planned system of cooperative

---

*With some supporting information developed by Robert Staib.

effort in which each participant has a recognized role to play and the duties and tasks to perform' (March and Simon, 1958).

The term organization connotes different things to different people. It can be used in three different senses: the act of designing the managerial structure; both designing and building the managerial structure and the management structure itself. Henry (2004) describes organizations as being purposeful, complex human activities which are characterized by impersonal and second-ary relationship; have both limited and specialized goals; are integrated within a larger social system; provide services and products to their environment; and are dependent on exchanges with their environment.

There are many different types and classifications for organization structures which are usually represented in graphical organization charts, for example, functional or departmental or discipline, divisional, matrix, team-based or project-based and of late network and virtual. Within the structure a number of characteristics are used to describe them including: chain of command (show-ing numbers of reporting relationships); authority, responsibility, accountabil-ity, line authority, staff responsibility (showing relationships between people and organizational positions); and span of management control, flat or hori-zontal structure, tall or vertical structure (showing structure of the organiza-tional positions or functions) (Khalil, 2000, ch. 13; McShane and Travaglione, 2003, ch. 15; Samson and Daft, 2005, ch. 10).

8.2   Organizational structures

In this section we firstly outline some of the traditional organizational models listed above, identify their form, some of their advantages and disadvantages and in Section 8.3 we discuss particular issues associated with organizational sustainability. More details and examples of the different types of traditional structure can be found in the three references cited above.

Functional or departmental model

With a functional structure, positions are grouped into departments that require similar skills and resources, for example, human resources, engineering, account-ing, production and marketing. Its advantages can include economies of scale in the discipline; better internal communications in the department; development of in-depth skills; and high quality problem-solving. Disadvantages can include barriers to communications across departments; a slow response to external changes; decisions concentrated at the top of an organization; and employees having a limited view of the organization's goals (McShane and Travaglione, 2003; Samson and Daft, 2005).

Divisional model

With a divisional structure positions are grouped into departments or div-isions that produce a single product or product type, for example, an industrial organization may have separate divisions for the design and building of rail track infrastructure, rail locomotives and rail carriages. Its advantages can include faster response and flexibility to the market including being closer to customers; better emphasis on product and divisional goals; and ability to develop general management skills. Disadvantages can include duplication of resources in different divisions; less depth and specialization in skills; poor coordination across divisions and less top-management control; and competition for in-house skills. The divisions can also be geographical divisions located in separate areas or countries (McShane and Travaglione, 2003; Samson and Daft, 2005).

Matrix

A matrix structure incorporates parts of the functional and divisional structures and is designed to improve horizontal coordination and information sharing. It can have dual lines of authority with the vertical line being to a functional department and the horizontal line to a product division or geographical division. Its advantages can include flexibility, adaptability and more efficient use of people, resources and organizational hierarchy; interdisciplinary cooperation and development of general management and specialist skills and broader tasks for managers. Disadvantages can include a dual chain of command which can create frustration and conflict; extra human resources training and management may be necessary; many meeting are necessary for coordination and communication; and power can be unequally balanced to one axis of the matrix (McShane and Travaglione, 2003; Samson and Daft, 2005).

Team-based structure

Many sorts of team structures exist and these can be cross-functional teams, temporary or permanent teams and project teams. The discipline of project management has evolved many processes and systems to facilitate the management of teams. Often teams form only a part of the organizational structure and focus on completing a particular task or project in a set time and to a set scope. Its advantages can include using components of the functional structure but with reduced barriers between departments; quicker decisions (with adequate delegation); more focus on outcomes and better communication across traditional boundaries; better moral and employee involvement; and can result in less administrative overhead. Disadvantages can include dual loyalties to the team and to the rest of the organization; many meetings necessary for coordination and communication; increased stress due to ambiguity in organizational roles; and unplanned decentralization (McShane and Travaglione, 2003; Samson and Daft, 2005).

Network structures and virtual organizations

There are many types of network or networking structure, for example, extensive use of subcontractors, outsourced services, loose arrangements of designers, suppliers, assemblers and marketers supported by a core company that organizes and manages the company. Another form is the virtual organization which can be a set of (legally) independent and geographically dispersed organizations or people who share resources and skills to achieve its mission and goals, but that is not limited to an alliance of for-profit enterprises. The interaction among members of the virtual organization can be mainly done through computer networks. Its advantages can include less administrative overhead; flexibility with the workforce and this can create a greater responsive to the market and aid global competitiveness. Disadvantages can include weakened employee loyalty; and difficulties of control and management and even difficulties in defining what the organization is (Samson and Daft, 2005).

8.3   Organization structure and sustainability

Atkinson et al. (2000) studied UK electricity companies during and after transition from public to private ownership in relation to how the environmental function was incorporated into the management structure. They identified differences between regional, functional, product-based and decentralized structures but with a trend towards having both a centralized head office environmental management person/group and separate departmental/regional/functional people. López-Fernández and Serrano-Bedia (2008) studied the effects of the introduction of environmental management systems (EMS) into organizations (mainly small- and medium-sized organizations) and identified the following effects: changes in responsibilities and competencies required; increases in formal systems of planning and control; increases in information movement; and greater use of experts (internally and externally). Other than the introduction of specialist environmental people or groups, they did not identify any major structural changes in the management of the organizations.

While not explicitly mentioning organization structure, Kallio and Nordberg (2006) studied the state of research into organizations and the natural environment and suggested that the research is still anchored to traditional organizational study. They point out that although the eco-efficiency of companies does increase with better environmental management, the ecological footprint of humanity is still becoming larger, implying that the research into organizations and the natural environment (and also management of the organizations) needs to move beyond traditional management.

These first two studies (by no means conclusive or exhaustive) suggest the environmental function within organizations is currently being adapted to existing organizational structures not the other way around. The third study suggests that what we are doing environmentally in organizations is not sufficient and this insufficiency may well apply to the structures of organizations and the way they work. Griffiths and Petrick (2001) have taken a broader view and believe that organizational structures need to adapt to address the sustainability issues both environmental and social. They point out that current corporate structures (or architectures) *insulate* organizational systems and process from a broad range of environmental information. Established routines and organizational systems of many organizations seek to protect and promote the *status quo* and limit or deny access to a range of stakeholders needed in the pursuit of sustainability goals.

In reviewing the literature Griffiths and Petrick (2001) have identified some of the characteristics of ecologically sustainable organizations. They include small corporate entities that are more responsive to environmental concerns; limited government regulations combined with corporate environmental management practices such as Total Environmental Quality Management that can be used to reduce waste and pollution; increased power to individuals and local communities can help set agendas for local ecological sustainability; and ecologically sustainable organizations that can help create production and use that aligns with community needs. To respond to environmental issues it is suggested that organization structures need to be capable of allowing open access to scientific and engineering information on the environmental aspects and impacts of an organization including resource usage and emissions; providing information on current environmental legislation, corporate environmental policies and processes to all staff; circulating feedback from customers and stakeholders on environmental issues associated with an organization's products and supply chain; allowing flexibility to be able to respond to external environmental issues; and facilitating communications throughout the organization on a broad range of environmental matters.

Many organizations (as evidenced by their annual sustainability reports) still seem to have traditional structures with a vertical overlay of sustainability people spread throughout the hierarchy of the organization and supported by sustainability responsibilities added to position descriptions as shown in Figure 8.1.

Rather than simply overlaying the sustainability function (social and environmental) over the top of existing traditional structures, managers should consider the criteria that Griffiths and Petrick (2001) have discussed and then combine these with some of the advantages listed for traditional structures to assist in moving organizations towards more sustainable structures and operations.

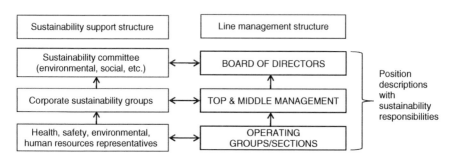

Figure 8.1   Typical sustainability support structure

Source: Based on Rio Tinto, 1998; BHP Billiton, 2008.

8.4 Corporate sustainability issues

Environmental and social sustainability

Pressure for businesses to be more responsible and responsive towards the society and the environments in which they operate has been compounded by the growth of globalization and the Information and Communications Technology revolution which have converted the world into a global village with little of the globe untouched. Problems such as pollution, poverty etc., which earlier had limited geographical existence, now have a global character. For some time, environmental scientists have been claiming that the global economy is slowly being undermined by the trends of environmental destruction and disruption, including shrinking forests, expanding deserts, falling water tables, eroding soils, collapsing fisheries, rising temperatures, melting ice, rising seas and increasingly destructive storms. Moving towards sustainable development on the business level is an important approach. In this regard implementation of business sustainability concepts can increase the interaction among business, society and environment and assist in addressing the environmental and social problems of the world.

Corporate sustainability

Corporate sustainability can be viewed as a new and evolving corporate management paradigm. A review of the literature suggests that the concept of corporate sustainability borrows elements from four more established concepts: sustainable development; corporate social responsibility (CSR); stakeholder theory; and corporate accountability theory. The contribution of *sustainable development* to corporate sustainability is twofold. First, it helps set out the areas that companies should focus on: environmental, social and economic performance. Second, it provides a common societal goal for corporations, governments and civil society to work towards ecological, social and economic sustainability. Like sustainable development, *corporate social responsibility* is also a broad concept. CSR deals with the role of business in society. Its basic premise is that corporate managers have an ethical obligation to consider and address the needs of society, not just to act solely in the interests of the shareholders or their own self-interest (Wilson, 2003).

Stakeholders

Stakeholder theory is a relatively modern concept. It was first popularized by Freeman (1984). The goal of stakeholder theory is to help corporations strengthen relationships with external groups to develop a competitive advantage. Typical stakeholders include shareholders, investors, employees, customers, suppliers, non-governmental organizations, the media, government organizations, community and society in general though it is more difficult to define all (or the most important) stakeholders for particular companies (Grayson and Hodges, 2004, pp. 34–52). Rather than being too worried about multiple stakeholders Grayson and Hodges see it as a *corporate social opportunity* to make a company more socially responsible. Many forms of stakeholder organization have emerged that address particular environmental and social issues and these can have varying impacts on the operation of business organizations. In this section, two environmental stakeholders that the author has experience with in the Indian context are discussed – one governmental and the other private.

The Central Pollution Control Board (CPCB, 2008) is an autonomous government organization of the Ministry of Environment & Forests, India (MEFI). It is a statutory organization, constituted in 1974 under the Water (Prevention and Control of Pollution) Act, 1974 and entrusted with more powers and functions in 1981 and 1986. It serves as a field formation and also provides technical services to the MEFI. Its functions at the National Level are to manage the prevention and control of water and air pollution and improve the quality of the air. Its main functions are to: advise the Central Government; plan and execute a nation-wide programme for prevention, control and abatement; coordinate the activities of State Boards and resolve their disputes; provide technical assistance and guidance to the State Boards, carry out and sponsor investigation and research; plan and organize training; organize awareness programmes through the mass media; collect and publish technical and statistical data; prepare manuals, codes and guidelines; disseminate information; and establish relevant standards.

Greenpeace International (Greenpeace, 2008b) a non-government organization (NGO) is an international movement which has gained momentum around the world. Some may not define Greenpeace as a stakeholder organization but it is an organization (and others like it) that can have an impact on the current operations of business organizations and the future operations of government. In 1971, motivated by their vision of a green and peaceful world, a small team of activists set sail from Vancouver, Canada, in an old, fishing boat. This was the beginning of Greenpeace. This organization works to mitigate adverse impacts of climate change, genetic engineering, nuclear armaments, toxic chemicals, deforestation and it promotes sustainable trade, peace and disarmament. It has worked as a determined pressure group to expose threats to the environment and to set directions for policy formulation and implementation at the level of multilateral organizations, national and local government bodies. Greenpeace does not solicit or accept funding from governments, corporations or political parties or seek or accept donations that could compromise its independence, aims, objectives or integrity. It relies on the voluntary donations of individual supporters and on grant support from foundations. It is committed to the principles of non-violence, political independence and internationalism.

Corporate accountability

The fourth and final concept underlying corporate sustainability is *corporate accountability*. Accountability is the legal or ethical responsibility to provide an account or reckoning of the actions for which one is held responsible. The

Table 8.1   Corporate sustainability framework

Discipline	Concept	Contribution	Other chapters of this book where discussed
Economics	Sustainable	Boundaries & descriptions	5
Ecology	development	of societal goals	1
Social justice			4, 6
Moral philosophy	Corporate social responsibility	Ethical arguments: why corporations should work towards sustainability goals	1, 2
Strategic management	Stakeholder theory	Business arguments: why corporations should work towards sustainability goals	3, 4
Business law	Corporate accountability theory	Ethical arguments: why companies should report on sustainability performance	12, 13

Source: Based on the contents of this book and the structure proposed by Wilson (2003).

contribution of corporate accountability theory to corporate sustainability is that it helps define the nature of the relationship between corporate managers and the rest of society. It also sets out the arguments as to why companies should report on their environmental, social and economic performance, not just financial performance. The contributions of these four concepts are illustrated in Table 8.1. Elkington (1997) of SustainAbility, a UK consultancy firm, called this type of accounting on environmental, social and economic performance *triple bottom line* reporting.

Companies interested in improving their social and environmental performance as part of their business have a wide range of tools available for application. Tools can vary widely in terms of objectives, scope, costs and levels of formality, partnerships, extent of stakeholder involvement and many other characteristics. In some cases the tools may be focused on one element such as environmental protection or CSR and in others may be more comprehensive such as the Global Reporting Initiative (GRI, 2006). These reporting tools can be clustered into the three groups discussed in Section 8.5.

8.5   Management system frameworks

In this section we discuss some of the approaches and frameworks that have been developed to assist business to formulate and implement better environmental and social performance.

Principles, guidelines, codes of conduct

Principles, guidelines and codes of conduct that companies can use to develop their statements of commitment include United Nations Global

Compact (UNGP, 2008); Global Sullivan Principles (GSP, 2008); OECD Guidelines for Multinational Enterprises (OECD, 2008); OECD Principles for Corporate Governance (OECD, 2004); and Caux Round Table (CRT, 2008). The Global Compact is a framework for businesses that are committed to aligning their operations and strategies with ten universally accepted principles in the areas of human rights, labour, the environment and anti-corruption. It is a voluntary initiative with two objectives: mainstreaming the ten principles in business activities around the world; and catalysing actions in support of broader United Nations goals, such as the Millennium Development Goals.

Approaches for developing management systems

Management frameworks and systems are another avenue for improving corporate performance with regard to economic, social and environmental objectives. Businesses recognize the benefits of a management systems approach to managing their operations. Management systems can be employed to demonstrate compliance with legislative obligations, reduce risks and potential liabilities and show due diligence to interested stakeholders. Systems include Quality Management System ISO 9000; EMS ISO 14000; and Health and Safety Management System OHSA 18000 (ISO, 2008). They also include AccountAbility's AA1000 standard based on John Elkington's triple bottom line reporting (Elkington, 1997) and Social Accountability System SA8000 (BSI, 2008).

Indicators, measuring, reporting and benchmarking

Another cluster of tools that are available to businesses involve the means by which companies can become more transparent about their performance on CSR and sustainability through the presentation of information. This includes tools that employ indicators for measuring performance, account and report on corporate performance and assess CSR performance of a business relative to some benchmark such as an acceptable framework, its past activities or to other companies. They include the Global Reporting Initiative (GRI, 2006) and Verité's Monitoring Guidelines (Verité, 2008). The Global Reporting Initiative (GRI, 2006) is a multi-stakeholder collaboration among the Coalition of Environmentally Responsible Economies (CERES) and numerous organizations, united to develop a common framework for global sustainability reporting. Issues reported using these guidelines are not limited to environmental performances but include social and economic indicators. It provides a framework of *how* to report (principles, guidance and protocols) and *what* to report (standard disclosures and sector supplements). Section 8.7 includes examples of companies that use the GRI guidelines fully or in part in preparation of their sustainability reports. Tata Steel (see Part II Case Study) is an example of an Indian company producing its Sustainability Report in GRI format.

8.6   Environmental management systems*

An EMS assists an organization to manage environmental issues by documenting and implementing environmental policies, processes and procedures throughout an organization; formal and on the job training; and using equipment to monitor, measure, collect and store data. Benefits include a structured and systematic approach to compliance with environmental legislation; a legal protection against prosecution; a tool to identify and meet future environmental and legislative change; a clearer definition of the environmental values of the organization; an approach to management and monitoring of environmental performance; better documentation and data management; provision of information necessary for internal and external environmental reporting; support for an improved market image; a basis for taking the organization to a performance beyond compliance and towards sustainability. One fundamental objective of an EMS is to enable an organization to comply with the current and impending legislation. The international standard ISO14001 is a series of codes covering EMSs, auditing, environmental labels and declarations, environmental performance evaluation, life cycle assessment and environmental risk management. Figure 8.2 shows the main EMS processes: environmental policy, planning, implementation and operation, checking and corrective action, management review. The continual improvement feedback loop is to ensure established goals or objectives are achieved by measuring performance and regularly reviewing goals and processes. This framework is similar to other international management system standards.

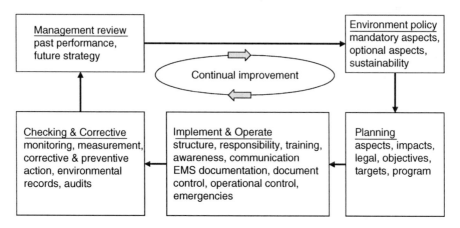

Figure 8.2   Environmental management system elements
Source: Staib, 2005.

---

* Based on Staib, 2005, chapter 12.

Environmental policy

The environmental policy outlines an organization's commitment to environmental management and to environmental achievement. It should be adaptable to changing circumstances and achievements and related to the corporate values. It provides a framework for the setting and achieving environmental objectives and targets and ISO 14001 mandatory requirements are as follows: compliance with environmental legislation and regulations; prevention of pollution; commitment to continual improvement; and making the policy available to the public. Other items include attitude to the environment; establishment of quantified environmental goals; commitment to meeting and exceeding environmental standards; conservation of natural resources; minimization of the effects of its products and services; provision of a healthy workplace; liaison with local communities and society; training of staff and suppliers; addressing all environmental issues, for example, energy, waste, land, water, air; commitment to review of environmental performance; and commitment to moving towards a sustainable company. Also important are obtaining endorsement from top management; making the EMS appropriate to nature and scale of impacts of an organization; and using it as a framework to set quantitative environmental objectives and targets.

Environmental planning

Environmental planning includes the identification of the major environmental issues by listing the main business activities, products and services of an organization; listing for each of these their environmental aspects and environmental impacts; quantifying the impacts to assist in the evaluation of their significance. Tools that can be used include project environmental impact assessment, cleaner production, life cycle assessment and risk assessment. All relevant legal requirements are identified: current, impending and potential ones – particularly disclosure requirements and penalties an organization and its staff could incur for non-compliance. Good planning leads to realistic environmental objectives and targets, implementation programs and projects, for example, one-off projects, ongoing research and development and production improvements. The aim should be to set quantified (and measurable) environmental objectives (indicators and target values for each indicator) so that they can be monitored and reported against and environmental impact of the organization reduced.

The environmental aspects and impacts include emissions to air; releases to water and land; contamination of land; waste reduction and elimination; impact on communities and stakeholders; impact on heritage – natural, cultural and built; use of raw materials and natural resources; use of energy – process and embodied; impact on natural systems and biodiversity; impacts of contractors and suppliers; impacts of users of the organization's products and services; and cumulative impacts and long-term sustainability issues.

Implementation and operation

The implementation and operation of an EMS is similar to other corporate management systems, for example, quality systems. For environmental management to be successful it needs to be integrated into the business operations and into existing management systems. It will mean added personal responsibilities supported by specialists and specialist advice. The following aspects should be addressed: structure and responsibility, training (awareness and competence), communication, documentation, document control, operational control, emergency preparedness and supply chain management. A key issue will be to review and augment the existing organizational structure. Responsibilities will need to be extended to cover environmental responsibilities. There needs to be provision of adequate resources – people, technical, financial and single responsibility for the management of the EMS. The Board and Chief Executive should have overall responsibility.

Training, awareness, competence

The organization needs to identify and provide appropriate training for its people, for example, environmental awareness training; the use of the EMS; relevant legislation and external approvals; roles and responsibilities; specific skills training and the need for recognized external qualifications and environmental experience. External resources may be needed, for example, consultants, and information or services provided by industry peak groups, especially with small- and medium-sized enterprises.

Communication

Communications within the organization for receiving, acting on and distributing environmental information should be established as well as communications with other internal and external stakeholders, for example, suppliers, customers and the general public.

EMS documentation

This could be in the form of an EMS manual with description of each element and maybe a supplementary volume with environmental management procedures, standard forms and reporting formats, integrated into a company's Quality Assurance system as appropriate.

Operational control

Operation control will cover the procedures above and their implementation and management. The procedures should be structured to ensure that the objectives and targets are achieved and the environmental policy is adhered to.

Emergency preparedness and response

Organizations should have in place procedures to mitigate potentially significant impacts of environmental emergencies and incidents. These should be integrated with the organization's traditional emergency procedures so that when an emergency or incident occurs the environmental aspects are included.

Checking, corrective action and audit

A regular process of checking, auditing and corrective action provides information to the organization to help it to achieve targets and make ongoing improvements to take it down the path to continual improvement and sustainability. This includes monitoring and measurement of environmental indicators, identification of non-conformances, instigation of corrective and preventive actions, keeping of records, undertaking EMS audits and process/product audits.

Management review and continual improvement

Regular management review of the EMS will assist the organization to achieve continual environmental improvement and to ensure that the EMS remains appropriate for the organization and the environment. These reviews need to be held regularly, attended by key decision-makers; formally documented with clear actions and responsibilities; related to the business and environmental needs of the organization; address the results of checking and corrective actions, for example, audits, internal reports, external reports, potential changes in legislation, changes in the organization's markets, changes in community and political expectations.

8.7   Sustainability reporting and corporate management

There is an increasing trend for large companies to produce sustainability reports. Using data from a study by KPMG of environmental (and sustainability) reporting of the largest 100 companies in a number of countries, Kolk (2004) describes how reporting has increased from 12 per cent in 1993 to 28 per cent in 2002. In reporting on the Fortune Global 250 companies, Kolk (2008) shows that 64 per cent of them in 2005 were reporting on sustainability compared with 45 per cent in 2001. Over the periods mentioned above, there has been a move from producing purely environmental reports to reports that include a broader sustainability reporting that include economic, social and environmental (Kolk, 2004, 2005, 2008). Some companies are also showing the economic 'value added' of their businesses in their reports (e.g., see the Part II case study on Tata Steel). The Global Reporting Initiative (GRI) has been instrumental in providing a standard approach and framework for sustainability reporting (see Figure 12.4). The above research which relates to companies from Japan, United States and Europe shows how different aspects of reporting vary between the three groups. Reporting in developing countries was not addressed. Sahay (2004) indicates that but for a few notable exceptions sustainability reporting in India is not very well advanced.

There are many factors driving the increased reporting and these can differ between countries, for example, legislation, government guidelines and initiatives that encourage sustainability reporting, external forces operating on companies, actions of non-governmental groups and other strong stakeholder groups as well as individual companies' motivations or reasons for reporting.

Kolk (2008) takes the debate on sustainability reporting a step further by analysing the relationship between accountability in corporate governance and sustainability reporting and suggests that many multinational companies (as evidenced by their reporting) are starting to address the integration of sustainability into corporate governance. She lists some of the issues that illustrate this link as 'the existence of a separate sustainability department or unit; indication of person or body finally responsible for sustainability; separate section on corporate governance in the report; corporate governance specially linked to sustainability issues; the existence of a code of conduct or ethics; existence of complaint mechanisms linked to sustainability; and external verification of a sustainability report'. Many of these relate to how an organization is structured and managed.

Some of the important issues in relation to sustainability (and environmental) reporting relates to

- what is reported in terms of scope and coverage;
- substance (or materiality) of the information, for example, realistic information or 'green wash';
- extent of the use of quantitative indicators;
- use of external agents to verify the extent and accuracy of the data;
- how generation and use of the sustainability information relate to the governance and operations of an organization; and
- how the reporting portrays a company and its operations in terms of its transparency and accountability.

In the examples given below we have used selected aspects of sustainability for two multinational companies to illustrate not only their approaches to sustainability reporting and their use of reporting standards but also their adoption of management systems, external recognition in share-market sustainability indexes and their performance in reducing greenhouse gas emissions. As global warming is a major environmental and social issue facing the world and organizations are likely to be significantly affected by it, we have used green house gas abatement figures to show targets and progress towards reductions (where available), both the tonnes *per unit* of product and tonnes *absolute* to illustrate a company's success firstly at one aspect of eco-efficiency and secondly at the societal aspect of addressing global warming. These could also be considered an aspect of *product stewardship* and *environmental stewardship* respectively. As these reports were produced by the individual companies, we encourage the reader to consider how other independent sources view the companies' performances. Refer also to the Part II case study.

Section 12.5 provides further discussion on sustainability reporting.

Rio Tinto

Rio Tinto is a global mining and resources company. Its business case for sustainable development is stated as:

> We are committed to contributing to sustainable development. Not just because it is right to safeguard the health of the planet for future generations, but because it also makes sound business sense. By earning a good reputation for our care of the environment and contribution to social improvement and the economic conditions of local communities within a strong governance structure, we gain improved access to land, people and capital, the three critical resources on which our business success is built. We believe this yields a range of long term benefits such as: better return for our shareholders; improved management of risks; reduction in our operating costs; greater business opportunities; attracting and retaining high calibre employees; maintaining or improving the value and quality of our products but with less impact on the environment; and better development opportunities for and relations with local communities. (Rio Tinto, 2008b)

Table 8.2 shows selected aspects of Rio Tinto's Sustainability Report for 2007. Rio Tinto acknowledges the difficult task of reducing greenhouse gas emissions and the figure below reflects this difficulty.

Jubilant Organosys

Jubilant Organosys' business composed of three segments: pharmaceuticals and life science products, industrial products and performance polymers. Its sustainability report for 2007 states:

> As responsible corporate citizens we, at Jubilant Organosys Ltd., believe that sustainable growth is possible only when we take all our stakeholders along with us in our journey of growth. The welfare of the communities around our workplaces and the environment forms an integral part of our decision-making processes. We weigh all our commercial activities for its impact on these key stakeholders.
>
> Jubilant Organosys Ltd is the first company in India to have been registered Organizational Stakeholder of Global Reporting Initiative. This is both a recognition and acknowledgement of our adherence to providing a safe working environment to our employees and the communities around our areas of operation. (Jubilant Organosys, 2007)

Table 8.3 shows selected aspects from Jubilant Organosys's 2007 Sustainability Report for 2007. Although the report is based on the GSI guidelines and has

Table 8.2 Selected aspects of Rio Tinto's sustainability reporting

Sustainability item	Comments
Use of GRI approach: economic, environmental, social	Rio Tinto reports in line with the Global Reporting Initiative G3 guidelines; uses a materiality assessment to select what information should be included in its report. Its web-based GRI report is aligned with Application Level A+
Sustainability report externally verified	By Ernst & Young
EMS certified to ISO14001	Majority of the organization
Listed on FTSE4 Good index	Yes
Listed on the Dow Jones Sustainability Index	Yes
Greenhouse gases *per unit* of output: tonnes of CO_2 equivalent per tonne of product (aspect of product stewardship)	0.7 per cent decrease in greenhouse gas emissions per tonne of product compared to 2003 against target of 4 per cent
Greenhouse gas *total output*, million tonnes of CO_2 equivalent. Includes Alcan on an equity share basis. (aspect of environmental stewardship)	On-Site total 2005 14.1 26.7 2006 15.2 28.3 2007 15.6 28.3
'Use of Product' impact	This aspect is not addressed though Rio Tinto provides support to development of alternative energy sources

Source: Rio Tinto (2008a).

Table 8.3 Selected aspects of Jubilant Organosys' sustainability reporting

Sustainability item	Comments
Use of GRI approach: economic, environmental, social	Report for 2007 based on the G3 Guidelines of the Global Reporting Initiative
Sustainability report externally verified	By Ernst & Young
EMS certified to ISO14001	Most manufacturing facilities certified
Listed on FTSE4 Good index	Not mentioned
Listed on the Dow Jones Sustainability Index	Not mentioned
Green house gas (or CO_2) tonnes *per unit* of tonnes of product output	The company has not carried out a detailed study for calculating the greenhouse gas emissions. However, several initiatives were undertaken to reduce the energy consumption
Green house gas (or CO_2) *total output*, million tonnes of CO_2 equiv.	As above
'Use of Product' impact	A majority of the products manufactured by the company are intermediates, not final products. Difficult to assess the direct impact of company's products

Source: Jubilant Organosys (2007).

some quantitative environmental information, it is rudimentary when it comes to reporting on greenhouse emissions.

8.8   Conclusion

In this chapter we have addressed some general aspects of organizational management in relationship to environmental and social sustainability. We discussed traditional organizational structures and how they might need to be reassessed if we are to successfully address global sustainability issues. Broad sustainability issues such as environmental and social sustainability, corporate sustainability, stakeholders and corporate accountability were outlined as a lead into discussing some of the guidelines, codes of conduct and approaches for developing EMSs, indicators, measuring, reporting and benchmarking. We then summarized sustainability reports of two multinational organizations to illustrate not only their approaches to sustainability reporting and use of reporting standards but also their adoption of management systems, external recognition in share-market, sustainability indexes and their performance in reducing greenhouse gas emissions. To address global issues business organizations not only need to reduce the environmental footprint of each of their products but also need to reduce their overall environmental and social footprint.

8.9   Questions

- Select a particular industry and for a sample of companies in that industry establish which externally developed management systems frameworks/standards (referred to in this chapter) are utilized by each company, for example, United Nations Global Compact, Global Sullivan Principles, EMS standard ISO14001 (used as a guide or externally certified), the Global Reporting Initiative, AccountAbility's AA1000 standard, etc. For each company assess why it has chosen to use a particular framework/standard and for the industry determine the most common approach.
- For the companies chosen above review their organization structures to assess how they have been developed to support corporate sustainability environmental and social.
- For a company of your choice review its sustainability report and its website (normally supportive of a company's achievements) and then find more critical information produced by external stakeholders, for example, on their web sites and in journal and newspaper articles which criticize the company's sustainability performance (social and environmental). Analyse the criticisms to determine how real the criticisms are and what the company is and should be doing in response. Supportive information, for example, awards and other forms of recognition could be used if relevant as counter arguments to critical material.

8.10   Further reading

Mintzberg, 1981; Rogers and Roethlisberger, 1991; Griffiths and Petrick, 2001.

Operations

9

Robert Staib and Wang Yong*

9.1 Management of operations

In this chapter we discuss some of the ideas of environmental management and how they are being integrated with operations management and bringing changes to the way organization think about operations management. The management of operations in typical manufacturing organizations involves management of all the processes from the sourcing and receipt of raw materials (the supply chain), transforming these materials through the use of machinery, energy and human intellectual and manual labour (the production process) into finished products and finally delivering to customers.

Typically this involves the following operational management processes: development of operations strategy, making operational decisions, locating facilities, product design, manufacturing process design, production of goods and services (including capacity planning, staffing and establishment of organization structure, supply chain management, inventory control, management of productivity and quality and finally sales and dispatch), planning and control including cost control and reporting, quality management, benchmarking and improvement activities (based on Samson and Daft, 2005).

Establishing and maintaining the management of operations also involves organizing company structures and specialist roles within the production function of a company taking into account the necessary *discipline* areas of management (which are discussed in the chapters of this book). Overlaid on this

---

* Section 9.5 by Wang Yong and the remainder of Chapter by Robert Staib.

are the general management *functions:* planning, organizing, leading and controlling (Samson and Daft, 2005). The description of these types of functions seem to have changed little over the past 30 years, for example Koontz and O'Donnell (1971) described them as planning, organising, staffing, directing and controlling. Probably one aspect that has changed over the years is the emphasis on a feedback loop that includes the processes of monitoring, auditing, management review and continual improvement which has been adopted by the management system codes produced by the International Organization for Standardization: ISO 9001 for quality, ISO 14001 for environment and others for health, safety, risk etc. (For an outline of environmental management systems refer to Section 8.6.)

In this chapter we discuss some of the environmental considerations that need to become a part of the operational aspects of companies, that is, total quality environmental management (TQEM), cleaner production, life cycle assessment. In Section 9.5, we discuss suppliers and the supply chain particularly in relation to China where an increasing amount of the world's manufacturing is taking place, with examples taken from ERM's (2008) experience in working with multinational and Chinese companies in China.

Evolution of management thinking

Samson and Daft describe how management practice has changed over time from the classical perspective during the nineteenth century and early twentieth century to developments in scientific management and then to a human relations perspective of management and a behavioural sciences approach. Since the late 1940s many other approaches have been applied to the management of organizations with a strong emphasis on measurement and 'the application of mathematics, statistics and other quantitative techniques to management decision making and problem solving'. These include operations research, operations management and the use of management information systems supported by the latest information technologies and computer systems. Within or parallel with these broad approaches there are other approaches, for example, a total quality management (TQM) approach which 'focuses on management of the total organization to deliver quality to customers' and 'infuses quality values throughout every activity within an organization, with front-line workers intimately involved in the process' (Samson and Daft, 2005).

Many of the environmental management techniques (some of which are discussed in this book) and the broader sustainable development or sustainability approaches continue this strong tradition of quantitative measurement and analysis applied to the operations of organizations, for example, TQEM, cleaner production, life cycle assessment, greening of the supply chain, eco-efficiency and design for environment. In the following sections, we discuss some of these environmental management approaches and how they are being applied to, and integrated with, operations management to bring about changes in the way organizations think about operations management. Technology management including design management is discussed in Chapter 10.

Environmental management

The objective of applying these environmental approaches to the management of operations of an organization is to considerably reduce the environmental impact of its operations and manufacturing including the environmental impact of its supply chain and its products during their lifetime of use and finally of disposal. All of these approaches require detail knowledge of the production processes and of the organization's manufacturing operations including the flow of supplies, materials, energy, products and wastes supported by a systems approach to its analysis. Equally important is a knowledge and understanding of the organization, its culture, its customers and suppliers and how these stakeholders contribute to the planning and decision-making by the organization's management personnel. These are important as companies move towards greater *stewardship* roles for their products and towards the environment.

9.2   Total quality management

Total quality management aims to take an organization beyond the management of product quality to the management of the quality of management itself across the whole organization (Samson and Daft, 2005, pp. 702, 799). The characteristics of TQM vary between authors but the key management aspects or *inputs* are as follows: top management commitment, participation of people from all levels of the organization (e.g., in the use of quality circles), education and training, customer focus and continuous improvement. This list can be extended to include supplier management, product innovation, benchmarking, inventory control, reward and recognition, customer focus and satisfaction (Chung et al., 2008; Das et al., 2008). The key *output* from the introduction of TQM into an organization is the improvement of product or service quality. TQM shifts the management of quality from specialist departments to the responsibility of all employees, who form cross-functional or cross-departmental groups to solve problems and improve manufacturing processes with the ultimate objective of achieving a high standard in product quality.

Welford (1992) analysed TQM and found many of its characteristics were just those that were needed to address the environmental impacts of organizations. Environmental management should not be an add-on but should be embedded within an organization and among other things it needs commitment, teamwork, communications, monitoring and control and inventory control. With its emphasis on the environmental impacts of organizations, Total Environmental Quality Management (TQEM) builds upon the TQM approach to include and integrate environmental management into an organization. Whereas the aim of TQM is zero defects in production, TQEM seeks to achieve zero negative environmental impacts (Welford, 1992; Jayathirtha, 2001; Curkovic et al., 2008).

Elimination of waste in TQM and elimination of pollution in TQEM are similar concepts and both seek to overcome the under-utilization of resources in an organization and reduce costs. Curkovic et al. (2008) believe that the application of frameworks like LCA (discussed below) and environmental cost accounting in support of TQEM are difficult to apply at the plant level and advocates the need for a cost of quality framework similar to that applied to TQM to be able to identify and quantify environmental costs to support effective decision-making. It would include both environmental operating costs and savings.

One of the key aspects of TQM is the requirement for participation of people from all levels of the organization, facilitated by the formation of cross-functional or cross-departmental groups to solve problems and improve manufacturing processes, for example, process improvement teams or quality circles. Environmental issues can also be addressed, for example, by environmental action teams. It makes sense to coordinate these teams and their functions because they may have similar responsibilities, common people and similar corporate objectives (Welford, 1992).

9.3   Cleaner production*

Many terms are used in the literature for this approach with subtle differences between each of them, for example pollution prevention, clean technology, eco-efficiency and environmentally benign manufacturing (Overcash, 2002). Unless otherwise noted, we use the term cleaner production in a generic sense to mean the application of various process, techniques and tools to the task of reducing the environmental impact of manufacturing. Cleaner production processes and outputs can be used within the framework of TQM or TQEM to assist in identifying continual improvement projects.

Reasons for cleaner production

Cleaner production was initially applied to the prevention of pollution and is an effective response to help an organization comply with the legislation that has sought, increasingly over the past 50 years, to control emissions to land, air and water and to manage the increasing volume of waste produced by urban areas and industry (Overcash, 2002). It is a structured management approach to the analysis of the environmental impact of manufacturing. It requires involvement of the entire organization and seeks to achieve both environmental and cost targets within a business framework. This approach is needed to address the problems of unsustainable resource use (materials and energy), the use of non-renewable resources and increasing pollution (excessive land use for waste disposal, the release of toxic by-products and the emission of greenhouse gases). While compliance with environmental legislation and the desire to improve an organization's environmental performance are important, one of the prime

---

* Based on Staib, 2005, chapter 22.

motivating forces for cleaner production is cost reduction (Cagno, 2005; Gutowski, 2005).

Other forces include pressure from the public, from the market, from stricter emission standards and increasingly legislative pressure for organizations to assume more responsibility for their emissions, wastes and products throughout their life cycles, for example, product take-back or extended product liability (van Berkel et al., 1997). Table 9.1 shows an approximate categorization of cleaner production approaches showing a progression from end-of-pipe pollution control techniques to management orientated and strategic planning approaches. Industrial ecology approaches are in their infancy while pollution control approaches are still common.

In the following sections we discuss some of the management processes associated with cleaner production which include planning and organizing, initial assessment, development of cleaner production options, evaluation of options, development of organizational aspects, identifying cost reductions, presenting

Table 9.1   Evolving categories of cleaner production

Category	Component	Example
Pollution control	Disposal	Construction waste buried in a landfill site
	Treatment	Process waste water treatment plant with disposal to a local creek
Waste management	Energy recovery	Waste wood chips burnt to provide process steam
	Reclamation and reuse	Demolished concrete crushed to produce base for new road
	Off-site recovery	Off-cut steel sheets from manufacture of drums returned to steel producer for re-smelting
Cleaner production	On-site recycling	Process wastewater treated to return to manufacturing process
	Source reduction	Product designed to use less packaging, for example, MacDonald's replaced polystyrene with paper packaging for its hamburgers
	Resource recovery	Car bodies stripped, materials separated, processed for reuse
Cleaner technology	Product take-back	Dutch legislation requiring producers of computers and telephones to take back their products at the end of their lives
	Dematerializing: Supply a human need with a service not a product	Producer owns product and controls use/reuse/recycling by leasing to user e.g., photocopiers
Industrial ecology	Cascading networks of industries and users sharing inputs and wastes	An eco-park where wastes from one industry provide feeds for another, combined waste is processed to supply process heat and electricity to the industries and transport costs reduced because of proximity of industries – see example in Chapter 5.

Sources: From Staib (2005, p. 229) which refers to Gutowski (2005); Environment Protection Authority (2000); Cagno (2005); Overcash (2002); Clift (1997); Hawken et al. (2000, p. 134); Russo (1999, p. 359).

the business case for management approval, implementation, achieving cost and environmental improvements, management review and management feedback. We also briefly discuss some of the tools being used for cleaner production.

Plan and organize

Before embarking upon a cleaner production strategy (or revising an existing) it is important to obtain senior-management support and commitment, as a precursor to seeking approvals for the necessary resources of people and funds. For organizations commencing a new strategy it is advisable to commence with pilot projects and when successful extend to other areas of the organization. Clear and agreed objectives established early will focus the organization's attention on achievable outcomes (Environment Protection Authority, 2000).

Initial assessment

At the start of embarking upon detailed analyses, it is necessary to gather the technical and historical data to establish a good understanding of the organization's products and its manufacturing and production process. This includes collecting existing and new data on manufacturing process inputs (energy and materials), product outputs, unwanted outputs (emissions to air, land and water), wastes and the direct and indirect costs of producing the emissions and wastes. A process flow diagram linked to a mass balance will assist in identifying all wastes and opportunities for eliminating them from the manufacturing process.

Cleaner production options

Much published information is now available to guide companies. Guidelines have been prepared for many industries and these outline options available for cleaner production including specific quantitative data on achievements of environmental and financial gains from cleaner production projects and programmes across many industries. This data is published in hard copy and on the Internet by bodies such as the EPAs, United Nations and industry associations. Table 9.2 is a useful checklist of items to consider, when deciding on options for a cleaner production project. It is important to identify a range of production areas, opportunities and projects for assessment and within a particular project identify several options for implementation. Initial assessment can assist in prioritizing projects to identify which have the greatest potential to achieve initial success with the least expenditure on funds.

Evaluate options

Cleaner production programmes and projects will be subject to the same controls as other programmes and projects and will involve most key departments within an organization and will require justification before senior management

Table 9.2   Cleaner production options

Element	Examples
Raw materials	Reduce hazardous materials Avoid generation of hazardous wastes Buy purer materials Make material substitutions
Technology change	Modify equipment to reduce waste and emissions Use more automation Change process conditions: flow, temperature, pressure, resident times Improve energy efficiency
Better housekeeping	Change management and administrative procedures Change operating practices, provide training Segregate waste Avoid leaks and spills Introduce better production scheduling, handling and inventory practices Change accounting practices e.g., direct charging of wastes to products
Product changes	Improve quality standards Change product composition Improve product durability Make product substitutions Redesign products, use LCA
Reuse and recycling	Reuse waste on-site Make use of recycled raw materials

Source: From Staib (2005, p. 225) which refers to United Nations (1996, 2004).

will agree to their go-ahead. Therefore they will need to be subject to technical and financial assessment as well as environmental assessment. The environmental assessment will need to be rigorous to be able to stand alongside the other two traditional aspects. Because a cleaner production programme could involve, over the medium term, a substantial change to the way an organization does business, the organizational and cultural changes needed should be identified.

Organizational aspects

Three organizational aspects need to be addressed to avoid hampering the implementation of cleaner production (or pollution prevention) projects and programmes. They are the need to change organization culture; have the right people in the right place; and navigate the organization's politics. Failure to adequately address these aspects can affect important decisions-making points associated with identifying the cleaner production opportunities, specifying and agreeing solutions and implementing those solutions (Cebon, 1993). There are many case studies in the literature that provide insight into how to address these issues.

Implementation

Implementation should be progressive, proceeding from pilot projects, multiple projects to a programme involving large parts of the organization. Marketing, education and training are important to the success of the programme.

Management feedback loop

As with other management processes it is important to include the feedback loop of monitoring achievement, evaluating, reviewing and reassessing plans to produce a culture of continuous improvement. Accounting and technical information systems will need to be established to record performance and provide sufficient information to be able to review progress and establish new priorities and programmes.

Cost reduction

As one of the prime motivating forces for cleaner production is cost reduction (Cagno, 2005; Gutowski, 2005), gathering cost information and using it to justify a cleaner production project will be an important part of obtaining organizational approval of a project. Having reliable cost information will enable better environmental decisions to be made. There are many ways to gather and to categorize cost information but the following lists will suffice to illustrate the point (see also Chapter 12).

Internal

- direct cost of materials and energy embodied in emissions and waste;
- indirect cost of producing waste, for example, extra organizational overheads, utilization of extra capacity of staff and manufacturing equipment;
- cost of treatment and disposal of waste and emission fees.

External

- life cycle costs of using and disposing of products; and
- environmental clean-up costs from emissions created in the production and use of products.

Tools and techniques

There are many different tools and techniques that can be used to assist the cleaner production process. Some of these are outlined in Staib (2005) and include life cycle assessment (Section 9.4), environmental design management and auditing. They can be supported by checklists and spread sheets for recording and producing material and energy balances (Environment Protection Authority, 2000).

Summary and implications for business organizations

We have used the term *cleaner production* in a generic sense to mean the application of various management processes, techniques and tools to the task of reducing the environmental impact of manufacturing. Some related approaches have been listed and briefly described, for example, pollution prevention, clean technology and industrial ecology. We have outlined a management approach to the task of undertaking cleaner production assessments and projects within organizations. We refer the reader to the significant literature on specific industries, much of it on the Internet that provides guidance and quantified case studies. Many industries are using an incremental approach to cleaner production though it lends itself to a more revolutionary approach (van Berkel, 2000; see also Chapter 10). There are many reasons why organizations should seek to make their production cleaner including pressure from the public and the market; requirements of stricter emission standards; and increasing legislative pressure for organizations to assume more responsibility for their emissions, wastes and products throughout their lifecycles. While compliance with environmental legislation and the desire to improve an organization's environmental performance are important, one of the prime motivating forces for cleaner production is cost reduction.

EXAMPLE

Cleaner Production Examples

Various Australian State governments and the Australian federal government have for many years been working with industrial organizations to facilitate the introduction of clean production process and to generate demonstration projects. These achieve cost savings and reduce environmental impacts but also alert and educate the companies' personnel to the processes of cleaner production and its possibilities.

BlueScope Steel
BlueScope Steel's Western Port plant converts steel slab into hot rolled coil, which is then processed into a range of downstream coated, painted and uncoated steel products. The plant has the capacity to process some 1.4 million tonnes of steel slab per year. It is in its third five-year Environment Improvement Plan with the Environment Protection Authority of Victoria, Australia. From 1999 to 2006, it has reduced prescribed industrial waste to landfill by 65 per cent – from 4.0 kg per tonne in 1999 to 1.4 kg per tonne in 2006. This represents a saving in disposal costs of A$0.75 per tonne of steel produced (EPA Victoria, Circa 2006).

Datong, Shanxi Province, China
A Cleaner Environment Project in Datong, China was funded by the Australian Government over three years. Datong is a heavily polluted industrial city of three million where coal gasification plants dominate the landscape, with approximately 1000 plants where coal is converted to coke and gas to provide energy for the

region. However, poor environmental management has led to high levels of toxic waste being pumped into the air and leaking into the water system. Coal gasification plants discharge over 15 million tonnes of waste water each year. The discharged waste contains around 3 million tonnes of contaminants, many of which are carcinogenic or otherwise harmful to human or animal health.

The project provided access to Australian and Chinese expertise to implement strategic management systems, in conjunction with Australian environmental and water resource management technologies for improved environmental and social outcomes. The project built capacity within the Chinese counterpart agencies, companies and the broader community, for the sustainable management of natural resources, for example, the Ministry of Commerce (China), Datong Municipal Government (China) and the Datong Coal Gasification Corporation. The goal was to improve the environmental and economic management of China's Datong Coal Gasification Corporation plant in order to reduce greenhouse gas emissions and improve the efficiency of the plant.

The main objectives of the project were to improve the ability of the Environmental Protection Bureau (China) and Water Resources Management Office (China) to manage the economic and environmental impact of coal gasification operations; and to demonstrate the economic and environmental benefits of cleaner production at the Datong Coal Gasification Corporation plant. A concerted effort to reduce water discharge by the Datong Coal Gasification Company allowed the plant to reduce its wastewater discharge by 30 per cent while also extracting pollutants (with the aim of achieving an 80% reduction when all new measures are in place). The project has assisted local workers to develop expertise in the new technology that can be applied to other industries in China. Other achievements include: for the first time the coal gasification company has been able to meet China's most stringent standard for wastewater discharge; the capacity of the Environment Protection Bureau and Water Resources Management Office (Datong Municipal Government) to manage the impact of coal gasification operations has increased; communications and working partnerships have improved between government, industry and communities in Datong; the benefits of cleaner production were demonstrated; the sustainability of the coal gasification process was established; capacity building of many agencies and organizations in Datong and the region on best practice environment and water resource management; and the wider community in Datong has benefited from increased wages, reduced heating costs, improved environmental outcomes and increased environmental awareness through education and training programmes (Australian Government, circa 2007). The author of Section 9.3 was involved in providing training in cleaner production and life cycle assessment to Chinese members of the project team through the University of Western Sydney, Australia.

Hawker de Havilland

Hawker de Havilland is an Australian company and a wholly owned subsidiary of The Boeing Company and it manufactures component parts for aircraft and exports approximately 95 per cent of its output. The company has major contracts with the world's leading aircraft manufacturers such as Airbus, Boeing and Lockheed Martin. The company employs 1330 people at two sites: 550 people work at the Bankstown site, Sydney and 780 at the Fisherman's Bend site, Melbourne. This study is one of a series of case studies featuring companies that participated with the Department of Environment and Conservation of New South Wales Australia in a 'Profiting from Cleaner Production' – Industry Partnership Program. In this programme NSW companies were able to discover that cleaner production not only protects the environment but also reduces operating costs, streamlines processes, boosts profits and improves staff engagement and morale.

What began in 2001 as a simple project to compact and recycle cardboard and plastic has been transformed into a million dollar bonanza for Hawker de Havilland, including aluminium recycling, the recovery of machining cutting fluid and other resource savings. By working with suppliers and treating all waste as a resource, Hawker de Havilland was in 2004 well on its way to reducing waste by 85 per cent. Hawker credits much of its success to working with like-minded metals manufacturers in a group that was facilitated by the Advanced Manufacturing Centre. Hawker de Havilland has diverted the following from landfill each year: 12 tonnes (800 m3) of plastic; 31 tonnes of cardboard; and 300 m3 of silica impregnated plastic. In addition: 500 tonnes of aluminium are recycled per year; 250,000 litres of cutting fluid are available to be reused per year; energy consumption has reduced by about 10.4 million kWh per year from aluminium re-smelting alone (and greenhouse gas emissions are reduced); 60 million litres of water are saved per year; and transportation is reduced. Cleaner production is now an accepted practice and a valuable part of Hawker's overall business strategy. Many other initiatives are planned. As at the date of the report in 2004 Hawker de Havilland had spent $A83,000 on equipment costs and was making savings of over $A 1 million per year in operating costs mainly due to aluminium reclamation and reduced transport costs. (Department of Environment and Conservation NSW, 2004)

9.4   Life cycle assessment*

Background of LCA

Life Cycle Assessment (LCA) is the quantitative assessment of the environmental impact of a product over its life of raw material extraction, manufacture and use, disposal at the end of its life. It is more encompassing that Cleaner Production though it utilizes similar information and some similar techniques. The LCA methodology has now been standardized by the International Organization for Standardization (ISO, 2006a and associated standards). In addition to its

* Based on Atkinson (2005) in Staib, 2005, chapter 24.

primary objective of environmental assessment, it can be used to assist an organization in product development and improvement, strategic planning, public policy making, marketing, decision-making and product comparison.

LCA requires the collection of extensive data and detailed evaluation of this data, not only of a company's own operations but also of the operations of its suppliers, the way in which its products are used and disposed of by its customers and finally how the disposed product is recycled or sent to landfill. Computer software programs have been developed for data entry, evaluation and comparison of findings and worldwide databases have been developed to gather and store data on materials, processes and their environmental impact. LCA was originally developed for use by manufacturers considering options for product development. The example below summarizes a fairly comprehensive LCA analysis undertaken by a consultant for the Environment Agency of the United Kingdom, supported by an Advisory Board which included manufacturers of the products and was finally reviewed by an independent expert.

EXAMPLE

Life Cycle Assessment: Disposable and Reusable Nappies in the United Kingdom

Even though UK recycles (in 2005) nearly 18 per cent of its 25 million tonnes of household waste it still sends the majority of the remaining waste to landfill. It needs therefore to achieve greater recovery and reuse of these materials. Life Cycle Assessment can be used to re-examine the impacts of production and waste generation by providing a framework and a process for examination of the environmental impacts of products and services. 2–3 per cent of UK's household waste is estimated to be from the use of disposable nappies, approximately 400,000 tonnes of waste each year. The alternative is to use reusable nappies to reduce demands on landfill but reusable nappies impact on the environment in other ways such as the water and energy used in washing and drying them. Both approaches therefore create their own environmental impacts. This study reported on the way people used the leading types of both disposable and reusable nappies in 2002–2003. As new nappy products come onto the marketplace there would be a need to update this study. The Environment Agency expects those companies developing these products to use this study to develop more sustainable designs of nappies.

The Environment Agency wanted the main manufacturers of disposable nappies to work with it to find ways to reduce the volumes that go to landfill and wanted reusable nappy manufacturers to help parents review the way they launder and dry reusable products to reduce their water and energy impacts. This LCA study provides the framework against which to judge the success or failure of actions to reduce the impacts of reusable and disposable nappies. There has been considerable debate over the relative environmental performance of reusable (cloth) nappies and disposable nappies. While many people intuitively think that reusable nappies are better for the environment, disposable nappies account for some 95 per cent of the market and around 2.5 billion disposable nappies are sold in the United Kingdom each year. The environmental impacts of different nappy types have been investigated in numerous studies. However, these studies have been limited in their accuracy or in their scope and have often been carried out by, or on behalf of, an organization with a vested interest in the study results. In 2001, the Environment Agency commissioned the environmental consultancy Environmental Resources Management (ERM) Limited to provide an independent and objective environmental LCA of nappy use in the United Kingdom. Life cycle assessment is a technique used to assess environmental performance over the entire life cycle, from raw material extraction through to product manufacture, use and final disposal. The study reported here complied with the latest methods laid down in international standard ISO14040.

Study aims

The aim of the LCA study was to assess the life cycle environmental impacts associated with using disposable nappies and reusable nappies in the United Kingdom for 2001–2002. Three different nappy types were assessed: disposable nappies; home laundered flat cloth nappies; and commercially laundered pre-folded cloth nappies delivered to the homes.

The systems studied

To compare the nappies fairly, the study considered the environmental impacts associated with an average child wearing nappies during the first two and a half years of its life. For each nappy type studied, all the materials, chemicals and energy consumed during nappy manufacture, use and disposal, and all the emissions to the environment were identified. All these 'flows' were quantified and traced back to the extraction of raw materials that were required to supply them. For example, polymer materials used in disposable nappies were linked to the impacts associated with crude oil extraction and the flows associated with the fluff pulp used in disposables were traced back to paper and forest growth. For cloth nappies, the flows were traced back to cotton growth and production. All transport steps have been included. The environmental impact categories assessed were those agreed by the project board: resource depletion; climate change; ozone depletion; human toxicity; acidification; fresh-water aquatic toxicity; terrestrial toxicity; photochemical oxidant formation (low level smog) and nutrification of fresh water (eutrophication). These environmental impacts were calculated for an average nappy system in each case. The study excluded impacts such as noise, biodiversity and the amount of land used by each system.

The total flows of each substance were compiled for each stage of the life cycle and used to assess the environmental impacts of each system. For example, flows of methane, carbon dioxide and other greenhouse gases were aggregated for each system in total. Internationally agreed equivalents that quantify the relative global warming effect of each gas were then used to assess the overall global warming impact of each nappy system. Quantified flow charts were developed for each nappy type over its life cycle. For the three nappy systems, manufacturers provided data for their production processes. Commercial laundries also supplied data. Published excreta data was used for the contents of used nappies. Data on the numbers of different nappies in use and how they were washed etc. were estimated from surveys undertaken for the Environment Agency. Published life cycle inventory data were used to describe commodity material and energy inputs to the stages. Sensitivity analyses were conducted for the following key areas of uncertainty: reusable nappy manufacture; aquatic toxicity impact method; drying methods for reusable nappies; and how excreta were disposed of.

Conclusions

For the three nappy systems studied, there was no significant difference between any of the environmental impacts – that is, overall no system clearly had a better or worse environmental performance, although the life-cycle stages that are the main source for these impacts are different for each system. The study was supported by a stakeholder group representing the interested parties and is the most comprehensive, independent study of its kind. The Environment Agency would like to see it used as the basis for any further studies comparing the impacts of different types of disposable or reusable nappies. The most significant environmental impacts for all three nappy systems were on resource depletion, acidification and global warming. For one child, over two and a half years, these impacts are roughly comparable with driving a car between 1300 and 2200 miles. The study was critically reviewed by an external expert appointed by the Environment Agency. The review and how its findings were addressed are included in the full report available from the Environment Agency UK. (Environment Agency UK, 2005)

It should be noted that although the study showed no significant difference between the three products, the environmental impact of each was significant and as reported above the study and its extensive information can be the basis of identifying and reducing the environmental impacts of each of the products by manufactures, government and consumers. (Edited summary from a report produced by the Environment Agency UK, 2005)

Reasons for LCA

LCA is a quantitative analytical tool that can be used in decision-making to select the product or process that results in the least impact to the environment. To understand the environmental impacts of a product, process or service all the stages and impacts throughout their life cycles need to be considered. LCA can be used with other considerations and factors such as human health, impact, cost and performance data. 'LCA data identifies the transfer of environmental impacts from one media to another (e.g. eliminating air emissions by creating a wastewater effluent instead) and/or from one life cycle stage to another (e.g. from use and reuse of the product to the raw material acquisition phase). If a LCA was not performed, the transfer might not be recognised and properly included in the analysis because it is outside the typical scope and focus of product selection processes' (USA EPA, 2001).

LCA phases and terms

LCA is an established scientific technique that involves four phases: defining the *goal* and scope; compiling an *inventory* of relevant inputs and outputs of a product system; evaluating the potential environmental *impacts* associated with those inputs and outputs; and *interpreting* the results of the inventory analysis and impact assessment phases in relation to the goal of the study. Key terms are: *environmental aspects* – those elements, activities, products or services than can interact with the environment based upon the criteria of significance presented in the study; *significant environmental aspect* – those environmental aspects that have, or can potentially have, a substantial positive or negative impact on the environment; *environmental impacts* – any change to the environment, whether adverse or beneficial, wholly or partially resulting from an organization's activities, products or services; and *environmental significance criteria* – assessment criteria which may be set as aspects regulated by the law. In identifying environmental *aspects* one looks at inputs such as raw materials, electricity, water use and outputs such as finished product, exhaust, waste products.

Goal definition and inventory analysis in LCA

LCAs can be conducted on a variety of elements, products, materials and processes. Defining the *goal* definition and scope is critical and requires the LCA assessors to clearly establish their objectives and the method and process to achieve it. This requires the assessor to document a description of the product, the scope of the study and the required reliability of the findings and the criteria for assessment. *Inventory analysis* requires a systematic description of all the processes in a product's life cycle and then collection of data on each process. The output is an inventory (often tabulated) of all raw material depletion and pollution (emissions or impacts), including those processes controlled by a particular organization and of its supply chain and its customers and the organizations who dispose of or recycle its products.

Steps in Life cycle impact assessment

Life-cycle *impact* assessment (LCIA) starts with sorting of all the raw material depletions, emissions and impacts according to their environmental effect. The calculations require the addition of indicators of different environmental effects, for example, an impact on air quality, an impact on water quality or a depletion of old growth forests, to produce a single overall score. The LCIA is the evaluation of potential human health and environmental impacts of the environmental resources used and emissions released as identified during the inventory analysis. Characterization factors applied in the LCIA stage assist in calculating the impacts each environmental impact has on issues such as global warming. This requires value judgements, for example, air emissions in one location could be a higher concern than the same emission level in another location with better air quality. An LCIA may require seven steps:

- Selection and definition of impact categories – identifying relevant environmental impact categories, for example, global warming, acidification, terrestrial toxicity;
- Classification – assigning life cycle impacts results to the impact categories, for example, classifying carbon dioxide emissions to global warming;
- Characterization – modelling life cycle impacts within impact categories using science-based conversion factors, for example, modelling the potential impact of carbon dioxide and methane emissions on global warming;
- Normalization – expressing potential impacts in ways that they can be compared, for example, comparing the global warming impacts of carbon dioxide and methane;
- Grouping – sorting or ranking the indicators (e.g., sorting the indicators by location: local, regional, and global);
- Weighting – emphasizing the most important potential impacts; and
- Evaluating and reporting LCIA results – including gaining a better understanding of the reliability of the LCIA results.

The results of an LCA are approximate and should therefore be used in context of the precautionary principle which is now enshrined as Principle 15 of the Rio Declaration: 'In order to protect the environment, the precautionary approach shall be widely applied by States according to their capability. Where there are threats of serious or irreversible damage, lack of full scientific certainty shall not be used as a reason for postponing cost-effective measures to prevent environmental degradation.' The precautionary principle should not be confused with the element of caution that scientists apply in their assessment of scientific data.

Strengths and weaknesses

LCA is now a global tool for the assessment of global environmental impacts of products and materials to inform decision-makers by providing information which is often unconsidered.

Performing LCAs can be resource and time intensive. Obtaining data can be difficult and the availability and accuracy of data can greatly impact the accuracy of final results and conclusions. LCA is subjective and often restricted to a limited number of environmental categories such as energy consumption and greenhouse gas emissions. LCA uses approximations, often simplifies the interconnections between natural systems and uses aggregated loadings. One of the biggest criticisms of LCA is that the findings and conclusions are often written without clear disclosure of the uncertainty or application of the precautionary principle. Some industry commissioned LCAs are used as a marketing tool to convince product procurers or stakeholders of the environmental benefits of a particular product or material, for example, in the building industry, architects and interior designers often have no scientific training or experience to evaluate the claims. 'Life Cycle Assessment cannot provide a truly comprehensive and all-encompassing assessment' (Todd and Curran, 1999) because LCA does not directly measure the actual environmental impact, predict environmental effects or take into account technical performance, costs or political and social acceptance. LCA should be used in conjunction with these other parameters (US EPA, 2001) and should not be considered as a definitive answer.

Summary

In this section we have outlined the reasons for and steps in undertaking a LCA. Some of the strengths and weaknesses have been discussed. It is a technique that is being used worldwide and a large amount of data is being generated to help make the LCA outputs more realistic and accurate. It is an important tool for business organizations to help them make decisions on their products and processes and for designers to help them choose materials and systems that have a lower environmental impact.

For further detail guidance in undertaking a LCA the reader is referred to the ISO 14040 code (ISO, 2006a) and associated codes and the guides developed by government authorities and industry associations in many countries. Many are available on the Internet.

9.5   Suppliers and supply chain

This section discusses suppliers and the supply chain particularly in relation to China where an increasing amount of the world's manufacturing is taking place. Unless otherwise noted the information and examples are taken from Engineering Resources Management's (ERM) experience in working with multinational and Chinese companies in China.

We are now living in a small village of the Earth where people are increasingly connected via Internet and mobile; the business world has never been so dynamic due to globalization. As an essential part of the global low-cost strategy, global companies increasingly rely on outsourcing and toll manufacturing in the developing countries such as China and India. Since the mid-1990s, leading electronic companies such as Ericson, IBM, Philips etc. have been restructuring their global resources and the operation through selling manufacturing business and outsourcing more into low-cost areas. In 2006, IBM transferred its global purchasing centre to Shenzhen, China. Many companies establish their global services centres in India.

To some extent, an effective supply chain will lead to a successful business and demonstrate a firm's capability in response to increasingly competitive market, rapid changes in technology and constant shift of costumers' needs. However, globalization imposes increased pressure on companies to be held responsible for supplier behaviour. The business risk associated with supply chain is often underestimated due to lack of understanding of the new regulatory and business environment in emerging markets. It is essential to understand the key issues facing the supply chain managers in the future and identify the initiatives required to close the gaps between today's capability and tomorrow's requirements. Green supplier management will help companies maintain and take the competitive advantage in the dynamic market.

Supplier management – environment, health, safety, social

Since the mid-1990s, the supply chain management has shifted from the upstream to the entire value chain; from the operational supply chain management to strategic supply chain management; from a regional scale to a global network – the Internet facilitates this. Greening supply is increasingly viewed as an essential part of strategic supply chain management.

Figure 9.1 presents the multiple interconnected requirements of a modern supply chain. China and India have become a supply hub for general manufacturing companies and chemical/pharmaceutical companies. This trend also greatly contributes to the rapid economic growth in these emerging markets. In the process, multinational companies are being questioned by their customers and stakeholders in particular non-governmental organizations (NGOs); for example, is the supplier a low-cost supplier, a polluter or a green supplier?

While the companies enjoy the low-cost supply chain, companies are under increasing pressure to comply with a range of issues and stakeholders: *Regulations affecting Chinese companies:* Registration, Evaluation, Authorization and Restriction of Chemical Substances (REACH) (European Union, 2006), China Occupational Health Law (2002), China Safety Production Law (2002), Restriction of Hazardous Substances (RoHS)

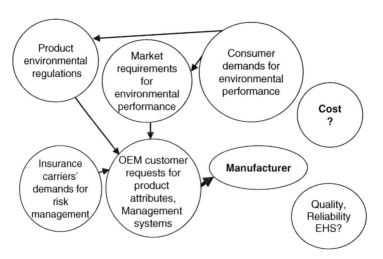

Figure 9.1   Multiple interconnected requirements of supply chain management

Note: OEM is Original Equipment Manufacturers.

(European Union 2002a) (DCA, 2008) and Waste Electrical and Electronic Equipment (WEEE) (European Union 2002b); *Markets:* green barriers and greening of products Greening, Non government organizations (NGO)/customers – influence and preference; *Management:* reputation, liability, business interruption; and *External stakeholders:* sustainability, global corporate responsibility.

According to an ERM survey, one of the major challenges to multinational companies is the increasing pressure to be responsible for its suppliers' behaviour (ERM is one of the world's leading providers of environmental consulting services and health and safety). Foreign companies dealing with China realize that decent Environment Health & Safety (EHS) and labour standards are being demanded by international and Chinese customers, shareholders, media and other stakeholders.

ERM's experience has indicated that the highest area of foreign companies' frustration is the fact that many Chinese suppliers failed EHS audits. Other than the obvious reasons that illegal working practices and missing EHS permits may result in legal action, there are significant reputational risks from ignoring working conditions in a supplier's operations. However, there are also good financial reasons for assuring good operational practices, as there is growing evidence of a labour shortage in China and other emerging market, and increasing enforcement of EHS laws.

In parts of China some factories have shut down through having insufficient labour with factories working below capacity, resulting in variability of supply. Better working practices will be an attraction for those seeking work. In recent times, several facilities have been shut down or fined due to lack of EHS permits, particularly Environmental Impact Assessment (EIA) and related approvals. Local governments and agencies are under increasing pressure to manage the environment in a sustainable manner in line with economical development. Therefore it is imperative to be green with your suppliers – producers and suppliers are linked via supply chain value as illustrated in Figure 9.2.

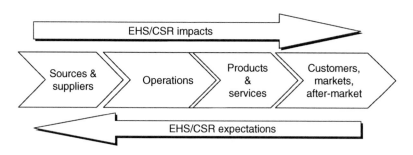

Figure 9.2   Producers and suppliers are linked

Audit approach – Supply Chain Assessments (SCA)

In the supply chain management process, the multinational companies undertake the following qualification process, that is, the audit approach: a market survey to shortlist suppliers; screening based on price, technology, Quality, Health, Safety and Environment (QHSE); self-assessment or pre-audit; and audit (QHSE or environment, health, safety and social (EHSS)).

The SCA is a strategic management tool for cost control, risk management and programme planning. Multinational companies use EHS and labour assessments to identify management system weaknesses; identify short- and long-term liabilities and concerns and their underlying root causes; provide data for sound management decision-making to minimize physical and financial risks; evaluate existing performance or potential suitability of suppliers or contractors; and affirm that the company maintains a proactive stance towards EHS and labour issues, thereby supporting projection of a positive public image and healthier relations with the community and regulators.

ERM experience has shown that companies get the most from assessment approaches that are

Risk-based: A key to success in addressing labour, health, safety and environment within any organization is not only to identify the issues but to understand them in relation to the risk factors which really matter to the organization in question and where action will really make a difference, for example, improvements in legal compliance, liability, business interruption levels and reputation damage which can have different implications for different companies.

Well-informed: Making the right EHS and labour management decisions relies on the most up to date and accurate data. The multinational companies need to fully understand and interpret the impact of local EHS and labour legislation.

Integrated: An EHS system and labour management cannot be considered in isolation. They form an integral part of company culture, production processes and work environment. Only when integration is achieved will risk be managed effectively. It is critical to help suppliers to set targets and measure performance through consistent methodologies thus adding value to their business development.

A variety of EHS and labour issues are found in supplier facilities in China. Some of the common ones are listed below – many of which apply to other countries.

Environment health and safety

- Permitting: failure to obtain all required EHS permits, registration and approvals;
- Pollution: discharge exceeds legal limits or mass loading quota – air emission, wastewater, noise;

- Management of chemicals and wastes: failure to meet relevant standards – Material Safety Data Sheets (MSDS), labelling, licensing of contractors, spillage and leakage control, storage requirements;
- Hazards: failure to properly identify working hazards and associated protection measures – noise, dust, chemical exposure etc.; and
- Safety: problems of machine guarding, electrical safety, insufficient personal protective equipment and emergence response (chemical spillage, fire-fighting).

Labour

- Overtime: exceeding legal limits, no exemption permits and payments associated with this are an issue;
- Contract: illegal compensation terms to employees, neglect of temporary workers and supporting staff (kitchen staff, cleaners) or seasonal workers;
- Social welfare payment: neglect of migrant workers, and borrowed labour, especially pension, occupational injury insurance;
- Minimum wage: in labour-intensive facilities, employee paid lower than regulatory requirements;
- Child labour: especially in labour-intensive facilities with many migrant workers, with false identification cards; and
- Labour union: not in a meaningful function.

Beyond audit approach

High visibility reporting and reputational impacts of supplier performance are derived from increasing scrutiny and reporting by NGOs, the media and the growing relevance to customers and employees. The traditional audit approach often disqualifies suppliers based on the results of audits. To achieve better results many companies are undertaking alternative cooperative approaches, for example, joint audit approaches and partnership programmes and we discuss these below.

The most visible *joint audit program* is the supply chain audit program of the Electronic Industry Code of Conduct (EICC, 2008) and Global eSustainability Group (GeSI, 2008) Project. The EICC/GeSI is a voluntary alliance of companies with approximately 40 brands in the electronics sectors. To streamline the auditing process, and cause less duplication of work and cost to both the brands and the suppliers, the group has developed a joint code of conduct and is in the process of implementing a joint audit process (shared approaches, tools and reports).

More multinational corporations (MNCs) are taking a proactive approach to supply chain management by working in partnership with suppliers. The following approaches have been increasingly adopted by MNCs.

Capacity building: A major chemical and medical company conducted EHS compliance audits for multiple suppliers throughout China. The company then engaged external consultants to provide training of local EHS regulatory requirements and relevant permitting procedures and assist in the implementation of EHS management system.

1 company + 1 supplier + 1 customer + contractor (1+3) Program: This has been initiated by the China Business Council for Sustainable Development (CBCSD, 2008) to help improve the awareness of corporate social responsibility of supply chain. Each company identifies its own prior program with its three partners and three beneficiaries are committed to duplicate the model and share the best practice of supply chain management.

Responsible Care: 52 chemical industry associations and 127 multinational chemical companies have currently signed the 'Responsible Care' global charter. Besides this, more and more emerging economies are joining the programme. Russia for instance, signed the charter this October 2007. In November 2007, Asia-Pacific Economic Cooperation (APEC) hosted the Asia-Pacific Responsible Care Conference in Malaysia, with the purpose of promoting Responsible Care in the region. The Association of International Chemical Manufacturers (AICM) and China Petroleum and the Chemical Industry Association (CPCIA) has been working together to promote and execute 'Responsible Care' in China. The goal of the initiative is to build up a platform for all the players in the industry to share their experience on responsible care and in the end to help Chinese chemical producers, downstream users and government officials to enhance awareness of Responsible Care and to guide green supply chain management (ICCA, 2008).

Conclusion

The supply chain has now become an essential part of environmentally sustainable operations. A *green supply chain program* can help achieve the minimum total environmental impact of the organization, its suppliers and customers. In this section we have discussed different management approaches that can be adopted throughout the supply chain process and they include conducting a proper environmental impact assessment including *risk assessment*; conducting an appropriate Hazardous Operations reviews of the facility and processes at design stage and undertake a *pre-start* safety audit; undertaking ongoing *compliance audits;* building *capacity* through developing awareness training particularly of regulatory requirements, risk assessment tools, emergency response procedures, chemical spill control; creating a *green culture* through partnerships between customers and suppliers, considering Chinese culture in safety management, making senior-management commitment visible; and establishing and implementing a real occupational health and safety management system. While we have used Chinese examples the approaches could apply to companies in any country.

CASE STUDY

Worldtech

Worldtech, a US-based multinational semi-conductor corporation, has moved its operations from California to China. Worldtech built-up a plant in Pudong, Shanghai (East China) three years ago and the plant has operated towards Worldtech worldwide standards. Worldtech is planning to construct a new plant in Xi'an, Sha'anxi Province (West China). In accordance with the current 'go west' policy of the Chinese government, the plant in Xi'an can enjoy preferable tax policy. However, the US-based EHS director is now facing challenges in EHS issues including:

- Chinese EHS legislation is becoming comprehensive but enforcement varies from east to west China;
- Environmental Impact Assessment (EIA) may take six months and a Project Application Report will not be reviewed until the EIA is approved by the State Environmental Protection Administration (SEPA). This will delay the whole project so the development zone people recommend the project approval be undertaken at provincial level;
- The company is required to submit a separate safety pre-assessment according to the newly issued Safety Production Law;
- The proposed greenfield site in Xi'an was a waste dump area and the surrounding areas may be rich in cultural relics;
- The selected construction contractor does not have a Health and Safety Plan and one fatality has been reported at one of its construction sites; and
- The local waste disposal practices are not towards international guidelines but are currently acceptable according to local management.

The Asia-Pacific EHS Director for Worldtech is responsible for working with the business development manager and manager of construction for the transition to the new plants. The recent 'EIA Storm' of SEPA (where many large construction projects were suspended and fined for failure to comply with China's EIA laws) and changes in the Chinese environmental regulations will require that foreign corporations in China take responsibility for compliance with the strict permitting process and historic contamination at the plant site.

It is unclear what Worldtech's exposure will be or what the EHS Director should do about it. The primary difference with the new China plant is that the enforcement of environmental regulations is still in the early stage in China and less stringent in west China, yet the trend is towards more responsibility for the multinational corporations. The EHS Director can't find much guidance though Worldtech has a great reputation for environmental programmes and performance. In the meantime, rumours are circulating about US and European firms finding their facilities fined or even shut down by local environmental regulators.(For study questions on this case study see Section 9.7).

9.6   Conclusion

We have discussed some of the ideas of environmental management and how they can be applied to operations management when considering typical manufacturing processes from the sourcing and receipt of raw materials (the supply chain), transformation of these materials through the use of machinery, energy and human intellectual and manual labour (the production process) into finished products and finally delivery to customers. We discussed some of the environmental management approaches being applied: TQM and TQEM; cleaner production; LCA; and greening of the supply chain.

The links between *Total Quality Management* and *Total Quality Environmental Management* were highlighted with the use of cross-functional or cross-departmental groups to solve problems and improve manufacturing processes – the goal of TQM being zero defects in production and the goal of TQEM being to achieve zero negative environmental impacts. We outlined the management approach to *cleaner production*; with a significant literature on specific industries being available to assist operational managers to make environmental improvements to manufacturing operations. While compliance with environmental legislation and the desire to improve an organization's environmental performance are important, one of the prime motivating forces for cleaner production is cost reduction. We outlined the reasons for and steps in undertaking a *Life Cycle Assessment*. It is a technique that is being used worldwide and a large amount of data is being generated to help make the LCA outputs more realistic and accurate. It is an important tool for business organizations to help them make decisions on their products and processes and for designers to help them choose materials and systems that have a lower environmental impact. Finally we discussed suppliers and the *supply chain* particularly in relation to China where an increasing amount of the world's manufacturing is taking place, with examples taken from ERM's experience in working with multinational and Chinese companies in China.

9.7   Questions

- Choose a manufacturing organization or a manufacturing industry and outline an approach to developing an ongoing programme of environmental impact reduction to meet both current legislation and expected future legislative changes and community expectations, for example, lowering of emission standards, greenhouse gas targets.
- Describe how the programme could fit within an existing manufacturing system based upon the TQM approach, and how it would utilize the techniques of cleaner production, LCA and supply chain management. In particular describe how you would establish cross-functional or cross-departmental groups and how you would define their quality and environmental responsibilities.
- The example of Worldtech raises some significant environmental and social issues for Chinese companies and international companies undertaking

business in China. The student is encouraged to consider and discuss the following questions:

- How do you interpret the local requirements and their potential conflicts with internal corporate requirements?
- How do you plan for expansion, or process changes, during the permitting process?
- How do you qualify local contractors (e.g., waste haulers or land-disposal facilities) and locate pollution control equipment suppliers?
- How do you ensure that your facilities people are aware of specific technical standards prior to the design of facilities and processes?
- How do you organize your internal functional departments to facilitate communication and ensure that you follow all applicable regulatory requirements and meet the planned milestones?

9.8   Further reading

Staib, 2005; ERM, 2008.

Technology Management

10

Robert Staib

10.1 Introduction

This chapter discusses traditional approaches to the Management of Technology and ways in which environmental issues and environmental management can be integrated into it. The management of technology in an organization is a complex process that is becoming more so with the increasing complexity, breadth of scientific and technological knowledge. It has moved typically from traditional engineering management into complex science-based activities and the management of technology is an increasing focus of the business manager. No manager can have more than a general knowledge of all the branches of technology but organizations need the ability to manage them effectively and efficiently. Use of technology enables us to produce and consume the material goods needed or wanted in our lives and to transform the physical assets of the earth, that is minerals, biological matter and energy. Science provides us with the basic knowledge that enables us to develop and use technology. Management provides us with the personal, social and human processes and skills to make this transformation possible through our organizations (Khalil, 2000, ch. 1; Burgleman et al., 2004).

Pure and applied science are generating knowledge at an increasing pace (Khalil, 2000, p. 13; Phillips et al., 2006, p. 193) and offer the prospect of understanding and transforming matter and energy in astonishing and surprising ways, for example, advances in the understanding of the physical and chemical structure of matter, the physical origins of the universe, the workings of the brain and human and plant genomes. Typical technological ages include stone, bronze, iron, steam, electricity, nuclear, electronic, space, information and biotechnology (Khalil, 2000, p. 20). The next technological age needs to be one that is dominated by technologies that reduce our environmental impact to sustainable levels, for example, an age of eco-efficiency, industrial sustainability or sustainable development (see McDonough and Braungart, 1998).

The scientific knowledge is feeding into new technologies, inventions and innovations at an almost uncontrollable rate (Khalil, 2000, p. 28), for example, biotechnology, nanotechnology, computers, Internet, consumer goods, industrial processes, weapons, health products and medicines, entertainment (see 'Examples of Product Developments box in Chapter 3). Use of technology and its support for innovation are widespread in many business organizations and its effective use is 'a key factor in defining competitive advantage in the modern business world' (Harrison and Samson, 2002, p. 2).

Organizations need to seriously consider the environmental impact of the whole technology management process from research and development through product use and finally to product disposal and reuse. Organizations need to adopt a *product stewardship* role over the life cycle of their products and a natural *environmental stewardship* role in relation to their direct and indirect impacts on the environment.

10.2   Technology and change

Management of technology within an organization includes the following: the development and ongoing evolution of technology strategies; the sourcing and development of technological information and knowledge and the application of it to production processes and to products; the establishment, development and servicing of a market; the development of corporate technological capacities within an organization; the continual refinements to the current technology; and continual search for new technologies (Harrison and Samson, 2002, ch. 1).

Many authors have identified a cycle of the application of technology, for example, through periods of research, new invention, technology improvement, mature technology and ageing technology which affects product innovation and process innovation. Other authors have used empirical data to develop and quantify this curve for particular products and industries including sub-curves to identify different technology subsystems for particular products to be able to explain and forecast how technology for an organization or industry might change (Gilmour and Hunt, 1993, p. 284; Khalil, 2000, pp. 80–94; Burgleman et al., 2004, pp. 208–223). Figure 10.1 shows a simple qualitative S-curve, adapted from the above authors, to illustrate how the cycle concept could be used to include the integration of environmental aspects. It illustrates the need to commence thinking about environmental issues and impacts at the earliest part of the cycle when research ideas are being developed and to continue throughout the life of a product.

If companies do not direct their technological developments at satisfying known or potential (or currently hidden) market requirements, they run the risk of their technical developments and investments being commercial failures (Harrison and Samson, 2002, p. 6). Many new products are not commercial

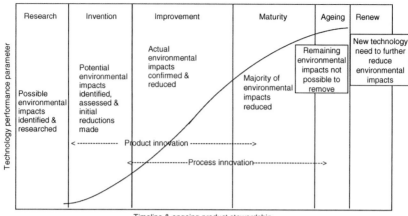

Figure 10.1   Innovation cycle with environmental impact considerations

Source: Adapted from ideas of Khalil, 2000, pp. 81, 88; Burgleman et al., 2004, pp. 35, 229; and Gilmour and Hunt, 1993, p. 284.

successes and many new technologies are not translated into products and services. Approximately 50 per cent of all alliances formed between organizations to develop and implement new technologies fail and approximately 50 per cent of company internal new technology ventures also fail (Tidd et al., 2005, p. 329); only 38 per cent of initial product ideas are successful in the marketplace (Tidd et al., 2005, p. 39). Some of the general conditions for the success of new technology introductions include the requirements for a skilled champion, plans for systems and organizational integration and a balance between technology push and market pull (Harrison and Samson, 2002, pp. 5–15).

Most of the time innovation or technological change is *incremental* but it can also be *discontinuous* (sometimes called disruptive or radical). Etthie (in Tidd et al., 2005, pp. 13, 60) suggests that the level of radical innovation could be of the order of 6–10 per cent. Notwithstanding its sometimes risky and uncertain nature it is important for companies to be able to apply and manage innovation and technological change in disruptive times to increase their chances of long-term survival. Examples of discontinuous or radical innovation include Toyota's introduction of its low fuel consumption car the Prius (see case study) and the phases in the development of photography, for example, the appearance of the digital camera. Large companies have had to radically change their products and business models to ensure their longevity, for example, IBM, Kodak, Vodaphone (Tidd et al., 2005, pp. 13, 22, 39).

Environmental considerations (from new legislation and community expectations) are increasingly putting pressure on companies to continually or radically change their products and technologies, for example, motor vehicle manufacturers with large carbon footprints (Orsato and Wells, 2007). Since January 2006, all automotive Original Equipment Manufacturers and component manufacturers operating within the European Union must comply with the End of Life Vehicles Directive to 'take back' and dismantle all motor vehicles for domestic use at the end of their useful life and reuse or recycle (Smith and Crotty, 2006).

10.3   Technology and the environment

Sustainable development (environmental, social and cultural, economic) is being embraced by many government, community and business groups as a means of solving the environmental issues facing the world. There is a belief that when applied by business organizations it can result in a significant reduction in environmental impacts of businesses while still maintaining the profitability of businesses and economic growth for the community. This view of sustainability is often referred to as ecological modernization (Orsato and Clegg, 2005; Smith and Crotty, 2006; Stubbs and Cocklin, 2006) and some of its aims are as follows: improved eco-efficiency (or less environmental impact) in the life cycle of products (i.e., through production, consumption and disposal); the use of innovative approaches in response to changes in government policy, legislation, technology (research, development and implementation by businesses); and transformation of the social and cultural performance of business. Evidence can be cited confirming significant gains or improvements in environmental and social performance of business (e.g., Hawken et al., 2000; Hargroves and Smith, 2005; Stubbs and Cocklin, 2006) and many of the examples cited in this book. Notwithstanding, while some companies may achieve a level of sustainability and even make radical changes in the way they do business there are many aspects that may be outside their direct control, for example, the operations and behaviours of their suppliers and the consumers of their products (Stubbs and Cocklin, 2006).

There is a counter view that suggests that the application of sustainable development in its many forms has mainly resulted in *incremental* change and this will not be sufficient to resolve our major global environmental problems. The counter view suggests that a more *radical change* is needed in the way we produce and consume material goods. Critics of the incremental approach point out that while there are many good news stories of business sustainable development successes, many of the regional and global environmental indicators show a continuing decline in environmental health and that there is a need for a more radical approach (Orsato and Clegg, 2005; Orsato and Wells, 2007). This point is supported by the recent data showing continuing degradation of the world's environment, for example, the Intergovernmental Panel on Climate Change's report on climate change highlighting the environmental effects of global warming – both current and potential future impacts (IPCC, 2007) and the GEO-4 report from the United Nations (UNEP, 2007) also highlighting 'the dangers of global warming but identifying other issues such as board environmental degradation, the loss of biodiversity and the potential for conflict growing out of competition over dwindling natural resources such as water' (see also Chapter 1).

One approach suggested is a dematerialization of the products we consume by rethinking what service the products provide and subsequently supplying these services in a dematerialized way (Hawken et al. 2000; Hargroves and Smith, 2005). While acknowledging that radical change would seem to be necessary Orsato and Clegg (2005) suggest that a radical change in the institutions of society may not be possible and that real achievement of sustainability may require a combination of 'radical technological innovations and incremental institutional reform'.

EXAMPLE

Product Stewardship

Smith and Crotty (2008) examined the impact of the European Union End of Life Vehicles Directive on United Kingdom (UK) automotive component manufacturers which requires them to 'take back' and dismantle all motor vehicles for domestic use at the end of their useful life and reuse or recycle – a *product stewardship* approach. They considered how a sample of these UK firms (33 firms out of a possible 214) has reacted to it. By a questionnaire, they found limited evidence that the Directive had driven product innovation beyond short-term, incremental technological trajectories and concluded that a more radical approach, in line with the 'dematerialization' thesis by Dobers and Wolff (1999), may be needed to generate more radical, ecological design solutions within the UK automotive industry.

In the following sections, we discuss both the incremental and radical aspects of technology management.

10.4   Technology management

There are many ways of analysing the processes of technology management, for example, it could include the following broad processes:

- Establishing, developing, integrating and evolving a technological strategy, within the organization and its partners;
- Development of corporate technological capabilities;
- Managing the operational systems for design, production, marketing and organizational integration;
- Establishing an internal culture of innovation, research and development, product and process refinement, external market intelligence, research intelligence and identifying societal, governmental and legal trends;
- Implementing and organizing for new technology introduction including organizational development and market feedback. (Based on Khalil, 2000; Harrison and Samson, 2002, p. v; Burgleman et al., 2004)

This list of processes opens up the discussion on how the concepts of environmental management and sustainability (in themselves likely requiring major innovations and changes to an organization) need to (and can) influence and change the management of technology in an organization.

Tidd et al. (2005, pp. 50–52) believe that the so-called current environmental crisis (or sustainability agenda) will open up significant innovation opportunities for organizations: new and sustainable products and processes, new business models and opportunities. There are powerful external drivers like changed social attitudes, changed legislation, for example, requirements for organizations to take into account the long-term use and disposal of their products. These drivers can cause discontinuities in the marketplace but open up new business opportunities, for example, alternative energy sources, green products and services, new transport and construction systems. They emphasize that because these demands arise from societal concerns there is a strong need to address the demand side elements to avoid the likelihood of failure (see the Monsanto 'Negotiating the Future' box in Chapter 3).

This leads into the need to consider the concepts of *product stewardship* and of its ramifications: Product life cycle responsibility and product take back, dematerialization of needs and wants, for example, nanotechnology, miniaturization. These ideas though are confronted with the reality of growing population, new types of products (e.g., iPod which reflect new and increasing human experiences); increasing wealth and materiality. But the question remains what human needs and wants can technology deliver while remaining within growing environmental constraints.

10.5 Technology strategy

Technology management covers both process and product but it is important that a company's technology strategy is matched and integrated with its business and marketing strategies (Tidd et al., 2005). Technology management applies both to the management of the application of existing technology to an organization and to changing technology and the need for innovation in addressing the competitive forces of the market and the changing societal, governmental and legal frameworks of society. Some evidence (Tidd et al., 2005, pp. 5, 401) shows that innovative companies can outperform in measures of market share, profitability, growth and market capitalization. This can also be the case for environmentally aware companies (see Chapter 11 on ethical companies and Figure 1.7 Dow Jones Index for Industrial and Sustainability). Technology management needs to consider the market, the organization and the technology (Tidd et al., 2005) and an organization needs to draw upon many disciplines and increasingly these disciplines include environmental disciplines as illustrated in Figure 10.2.

A technology strategy is a key component of an organization's corporate strategy to remain competitive (Porter quoted in Burgleman et al., 2004). The technology strategy needs to encompass an organization's approach to both

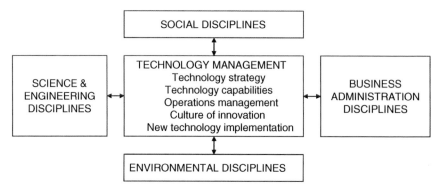

Figure 10.2 Technology management links

Source: Based on Khalil, 2000, pp. 7, 11, 279 and Burgleman et al., 2004, p. 3
with the addition of environmental disciplines.

product and process technology and to encompass the flexibility to be able to respond to changes in technology, changes in the market and changes in legislative forces. Increasingly it needs to be supported by a process of research and development directed towards innovation either in-house, or for smaller organizations to other networks of knowledge.

The environmental strategy of a company as it develops and evolves should be an essential part of the technology strategy. To survive it is important for organizations to have a competitive and enduring technology strategy but with increasing external pressures from stakeholders for organizations to be environmentally responsible it is important for them to integrate the environmental considerations into their technology strategy, that is, product, process and innovation.

EXAMPLE

Integration of Environmental Innovation

Kivimaa (2008) qualitatively studied how well environmental innovation was integrated into product development for four Nordic paper and packaging companies: Stora Enso, SCA, M-real and tetra Pak. He believes that environmental integration is a potential tool to generate environmentally improved innovations. He used six qualitative criteria as indicators of the types and levels of integration: top down implementation, environmental systems implementation, cross-functional integration between departments; cross-functional integration within departments; environmental training and the use of task forces. He found that environmental considerations in research and product development were standard practice in the companies but that practices vary between companies. He found a variable level of integration with some companies using a standardized procedural approach while others used a case-specific approach. In some cases the environmental expertise was located in a centralized corporate function while in other cases the expertise was included within the product development department or product development project group. No quantitative assessment was made of the level of adoption of criteria or the companies' research and development success rate but each company adopted half of the criteria with three adopting close to five of the criteria. Life cycle assessment was used for many of the companies' activities.

The release of the IPCC (IPCC, 2007) report on climate change brings a strong scientific consensus about the causes of human induced climate change and has brought into sharp focus the impact our material life on the earth's climate. The Stern Report (Stern, 2006b) identifies the impact climate change is likely to have on the world's economy and concludes that it is better economically to act now rather than leave it until later when it would most likely be costlier and disruptive to the economy. Business leaders and their organizations (WBCSD, 2006) have realized that failure to respond to the issues of climate change (and other environmental problems) will represent major business risks (see Chapter 3, Strategic Direction and Management).

Therefore, a technology strategy needs to incorporate a strong environmental strategy and a broader Corporate Social Responsibility (CSR) strategy. Indeed it could be called a sustainable technology strategy that both addresses the ongoing commercial viability of the organization and moves the organization away from significant environmental impacts. There is an evolving literature of case studies and methods to assist companies to this new way of thinking (e.g., Hawken et al. (2000); Hargroves and Smith (2005); Cambridge University web site; and various universities who are developing courses in sustainable technology management).

There are emerging techniques to help companies to engage in thinking strategically about sustainable technology, for example, forecasting, scenario-planning, visioning and foresight analysis. Foresighting is 'useful when the past and the present are unlikely to be a guide to the future' (Wehrmeyer et al., 2002). It can be used to develop ideas of what futures are possible, desirable, disastrous or feasible and by backcasting from these futures indicate the paths and processes that could be followed to achieve or avoid particular futures and inform the strategic planning process. It is particularly relevant when the problem is complex with a high probability of significant change, with trends that are not favourable and the time horizon is relatively long (Wehrmeyer et al., 2002, p. 10). These criteria would apply to many major environmental issues (Dewberry and Sherwin, 2002). With an increasingly uncertain environmental future, uncertain human reaction to it and the likely legislative response, it is important that environmental issues are at the forefront of any company's strategic technology planning and not just added as an afterthought or as a compliance issue (Wehrmeyer et al., 2002).

EXAMPLE

Business Responses to Climate Change

Kolk and Pinske (2005) using qualitative data from the Carbon Disclosure Project and data from a questionnaire to the 500 largest companies of the 2002 *Financial Times* Global 500 list (136 valid responses) studied their strategic approaches to climate change and carbon emissions. They identified a framework within the two broad strategies companies could adopt: an *innovation* strategy (sub-strategies: process improvement, product development, new product/market combinations) and a *compensation* strategy (sub-strategies: internal transfer of emission, supply-chain measures, acquisition of emission credits) to reduce emissions. The sub-strategies were set at three levels: internal (within an individual company); vertical (in the companies supply chain; and horizontal (through competitors or companies in different sectors). The authors found that most companies were in the early phases of implementing strategies but use was being made of all six strategies to varying degrees and that companies should consider carefully which are the best strategies for their own company.

10.6   Innovation

Innovation can take many forms within an organization and can depend on the organization's size and market. Authors have categorized innovation into several types in particular: *incremental innovation* which is a gradual or step-wise introduction of new methods, technologies and process innovations and is similar to continual improvement concept of Total Quality Management; and *discontinuous* innovation (or disruptive or radial) which is the introduction of a new technology or the application of existing technology in new combinations or applied in different fields. Some authors see a further split of discontinuous product innovation into architectural (arranging components in new ways) and modular (introducing new technologies to specific components or subsystems). Other authors suggest that innovation is a continuum with various degrees of radicalism from incremental to radical (based on the work of Moors and Vergragt (2002, p. 281); Harrison and Samson (2002, p. 54); Magnusson et al. (2003); Burgleman et al. (2004, p. 3); Tidd et al. (2005, pp. 11, 21)).

Management of discontinuous innovation

The concept of discontinuous innovation is probably nearer to the requirements needed to address major environmental problems than the concept of incremental innovation (Magnusson et al., 2003, p. 1). In the automobile industry, van den Hoed (2007) suggests that if we are to significantly reduce the environmental impact of the industry we need radical innovation and change though he notes that radical change rarely happens in this industry where incremental change is more normal. He believes it is difficult to introduce radical innovation in an industry with such a large corporate momentum.

Some sources of discontinuity that might cause or require an organization to innovate include the following examples with environmental examples shown in italics:

- New market emerges: for example, text messaging, *green power;*
- New technology emerges: for example, mobile phones, digital photography images, *hydrogen fuel cells for cars*;
- New political rules: for example, collapse of communism, *new environmental laws, carbon dioxide emission limits*;
- Running out of road: for example, saturation of a market and diminishing returns, *major weather events*;
- Sea change in the market: for example, MP3 music delivery system;
- Shifts in the regulatory area: for example, deregulation of the electricity generation industry, *extended producer responsibility* in Australia or *end-of-life-vehicles* legislation in Europe; and
- Peripheral issues become mainstream: for example, health concerns about smoking, fast food and obesity, concerns about *genetically modified food*. (Based on Tidd et al., 2005, pp. 33, 50–51; Phillips et al., 2006, pp. 178–179; Department of Environment and Climate Change, 2007)

When these events occur, the routines that a company has developed for managing a more steady state (or incremental) innovation may no longer be adequate. Phillips et al. (2006, p. 175) say that there is relatively little guidance of generic routines that can be used for managing discontinuous innovation other than case studies. Harrison and Samson (2002, p. 54) say it is hard to get a general innovation model because innovation can be highly situational orientated. Phillips et al. (2006) in their study of four companies identified different events that caused companies to innovate: opportunities identified serendipitously by senior management; scanning other commercial opportunities in its area of expertise; an approach from a customer to find a solution to its particular problem; and identifying ways of improving production efficiency by looking at other industries.

Radical or *discontinuous innovation* is characterized by a high failure rate (e.g., solar photovoltaic and wave power in the box given below), can be disruptive and difficult to manage and can be precipitated by a crisis in the company externally or internal driven (Moors and Vergragt, 2002). Management of radical innovation requires the need for specialization on one hand and the integration of knowledge into technology and products on the other hand (Magnusson et al., 2003, p. 3); a strong internal technology framework; a strong external technology network; the creation of new management systems; and dedication of top management towards risky long-term projects (Moors and Vergragt, 2002, p. 296).

Emergent *good practices* include scanning and searching the market, the technology and the research; making strategic choices and structures for innovation development; resourcing and implementing flexible organizations; exploring future scenarios and considering parallel possibilities (see also foresighting in Section 10.8); building a culture that supports innovation; developing long-term strategic alliances; developing learning and capability characteristics; and developing key individuals (based on Tidd et al., 2005, p. 512; Phillips et al., 2006, p. 183).

Environmental innovation

In response to the environmental impact of industrial civilization on the world's natural resources (and on human health) many authors are calling for significant reductions in the use of energy, the use of materials, pollution and impacts upon biodiversity. The Factor Ten Club (Schmidt-Bleek in Hawken et al., 2000, p. 11) believes that we should reduce our environmental impact by a factor of 10, that is, a 90 per cent reduction in energy and material intensity of our products. Moors and Vergragt (2002, p. 279) discuss a factor 20 decrease in environmental burden. The Stern Report (Stern, 2006b) calls for a significant reduction in greenhouse gas emissions by 30 per cent by 2020 and 60 per cent reduction by 2050, that is, a factor of 2.5. Vergragt and Brown (2007) suggest a 75–85 per cent reduction of CO_2 emissions, that is, a factor of 5. It is interesting to note that 'At the turn of the millennium, the internal combustion engines powering (new) cars that entered OECD roads emitted around 95% less pollutants into the air than their counterparts did in 1975' (Orsato and Wells, 2007) that is, a factor of 20 reduction over approximately 25 years.

If we are to make these significant environmental gains, we may need to consider discontinuous or radical innovation. Incremental innovation is important but radical innovation will be necessary though radical changes will only make a significant contribution if it is made along with transformation in social structure, culture and practices that are embedded in current technology (Moors and Vergragt, 2002, p. 282). They say that a 'dedication of top management towards risky, long term research projects is a precondition for the success of radical developments'.

New technologies compete with established and proven technologies and existing organization structures, systems and behaviours and are resisted. When innovation is radical or discontinuous it can raise great difficulties in an organization even threatening its existence, for example, development of digital photography upon companies with traditional photographic technologies. Many of the characteristics of radical or discontinuous innovation management are those faced by organizations seeking to implement *environmentally driven innovation*, for example, the need to establish ambitious environmental targets supported by senior management; seek and develop new scientific knowledge and technologies; coordinate the management of research, product design, manufacturing and marketing; and manage feedback from the market to enable refinement and continuous improvement. Environmental innovation will nearly always have to fight against established technology, organizational and social structure, for example, the replacement of tin-lead based solder for electronic components with lead-free alternatives; the replacement of fossil fuels with energy from renewal sources (Magnusson et al., 2003).

EXAMPLE

Environmental innovation in sustainable power

Christiansen and Buen (2002) describe two cases for innovative power generation technologies whose aim was to produce more sustainable power: solar photovoltaic (PV) and wave power (WP). They describe the difficult process involved in developing the products including the organizational and management strategies, the social issues and the establishment of partnerships and finally the assessment of market opportunities. Both projects were supported by Norwegian Government funding. PV was able to establish more successful partnerships and a niche market and is 'a growing export market despite limited public funding', whereas WP is 'in limbo despite considerable government funding in the period after the energy crisis'. PV is also proceeding down the learning and experience curve in improving costs and production capacity issues through partnership with other specialist suppliers. The PV case 'illustrates that matching effective technology management with market opportunities and well-founded strategies for learning and legitimacy may support and facilitate successful evolution of nascent enterprises'.

10.7   Management of research and development

The management of research and development (R&D) is an important component of an innovation strategy as companies are continually seeking new and improved products to enable them to grow and remain in business. Goffin and Mitchell (2005, pp. 49–51) suggest that large companies in various industrial sectors can spend between 2 and 8 per cent as a percentage of sales on R&D with up to 20 per cent in the Information Technology industry. Most large companies and many smaller companies have R&D processes and it is important that consideration of environmental issues is introduced as early as possible in the process. There are many external drivers of the need for companies to invest in R&D but two of the main ones are the influence of customer demand/requirements and the influence of government regulation (Foster and Green, 2000). This can also apply to environmentally driven innovation (Foster and Green, 2000; Sharfman et al., 2000).

Sources of environmental information

An organization needs to use many sources of environmental information in developing and managing its R&D programme.

Customers (general public, other businesses) are an important source of environmental information brought to the R&D department through a company's sales and marketing departments. Customers are subject to changing regulations and the influence of pressure groups, though some research suggests that expecting customers and other organizational departments to always understand environmental issues may result in organizations missing potential opportunities to green their products or to develop new green products (Foster and Green, 2000; Johansson, 2006).

Communication on environmental issues with *suppliers* need to be undertaken regularly so that the environmental impact of the supplies is understood by both parties, to identify likely changes to regulations and to identify joint opportunities for environmentally friendly products or environmental improvements to existing products (Foster and Green, 2000; Sharfman et al., 2000; Johansson, 2006).

Intelligence needs to be gathered from *regulators* as the lead time between the start of an R&D project and its successful introduction to the market can be long, so an organization needs to be able to anticipate future changes to environmental legislation and regulations. This would apply to both local and overseas if the company is anticipating exporting its products (Foster and Green, 2000; Johansson, 2006).

Non-government organizations and pressure groups often pre-empt public sentiment which influence future markets and legislation. Many of the environmental issues being raised may seem unlikely to affect business but sometimes it is difficult to predict how public sentiment will turn. Hoffman (2001) said 'today's heresy can be tomorrow's dogma'. Non-governmental organizations can also be the harbingers of environmental change (Staib, 1997).

Much basic and applied research in a country that will eventually find its way into products and services is carried out by *external researchers*, for example, universities, government organizations etc. Goffin and Mitchell (2005) suggest that industrialized countries spend on average 1.3 per cent of gross national product on R&D.

Industry partnerships can be an important way to bring environmental information to a company as joint ventures and strategic alliances play an important role in developing and launching new products and services (see Toyota case study at the end of this chapter).

EXAMPLE

Sustainable Technology Management Research

Paramanathan et al. (2004) reviewed issues in the implementation of industrial sustainability to identify how technology management research can help and what are the critical research needs. It is not always clear what industrial sustainability means in practical terms with the business case for implementation often built on individual conviction or motivational case examples, rather than being grounded in solid theory with associated frameworks, guidelines and tools. Challenges facing organizations include the choice of appropriate product and process technologies, life cycle valuation techniques, changing employee and other stakeholder mindsets and possibly the creation of a new business model altogether. With the goal of improving environmental, social and economic performance they discuss cross-functional and cross-organizational issues of implementation (between business units and functions within a company), the supply chain, development of new methods for technology valuation and a wider set of values to underpin the concepts of industrial sustainability.

Critical research needs to include design for sustainability and life cycle concepts; design for assembly and disassembly; design for extended life; design for reuse, re-manufacture, recycling; portfolio based methods for technology assessment, incorporating sustainability measures, in terms of impact on the environment and society; approaches for balancing tensions between competitive, environmental and social sustainability; processes for more effective sharing and transfer of technological knowledge of sustainable industrial ecosystems; improved technology management processes to more effectively extract the benefits of sustainable technologies; better methods for the assessment of technology in terms of social and environmental impact; improved methods and systems for supporting benchmarking of technology and business processes against sustainability indicators; support for learning and transfer of best practice between companies and industrial sectors.

Study of technology management processes and mechanisms are important and include the following: dealing with incremental and radical/discontinuous change; methods that increase the agility of manufacturing and business operations such as modularity, increased product development cycle times and core competence based approaches; the transition to different modes of production to reduce the cost and wastage associated with change; understanding of the life cycles of technologies, products, markets, companies and industries, and their interaction; and understanding likely future technology paths/trajectories which are important in developing an organization's strategy and long-term plan.

Management characteristics

Some of the characteristics needed for managing the R&D function within an organization are listed below. Most are traditional characteristics but ideas from several authors who had written on the need to incorporate environmental issues into the function are included.

An *organizational culture* should support both the need for R&D and the need for environmental considerations. This includes the need for strong senior management commitment and support (Sharfman et al., 1999; Johansson,

2006). *Organizational arrangements* should allow for the use of multidisciplinary teams; considerable organizational flexibility; and strong team leadership which possesses both R&D experience and relevant project-management skills. The R&D team should include environmental expertise or access to that expertise through the corporate environmental manager and/or external consultants. This expertise should cover knowledge of environmental issues and environmental legislation and regulation; the environmental impacts generated by the company's operations and those of its suppliers and the users of its products. Importantly the team should include expertise in environmental impact assessment and eco-design (Sharfman et al., 1999; Foster and Green, 2000; Johansson, 2006).

Effort needs to be put into *communications* both internal and external. Channels need to be established and maintained with all the people involved with providing environmental information and feedback on environmental performance (see Sources of Environmental Information above). Communication channels need to be maintained with all R&D project participants: internal organizational departments of marketing and sales, design and manufacture and supply; corporate management; external organizations – typically suppliers, collaborators in research and manufacture; and organizations providing environmental expertise. Technology is complex and not well understood and ongoing communication and reporting is important. Maintenance of a strong external *technology network* is necessary to identify opportunities and to keep up to date with developments in a company's area of operations (Sharfman et al., 1999; Foster and Green, 2000; Johansson, 2006).

Environmental goals

Some authors believe that setting challenging environmental goals in R&D projects by senior management is important if substantial environmental improvement is to occur (see the Toyota case study at the end of this chapter; Johansson, 2006). This can apply to both products and processes. Some projects may have a high level of environmental complexity and require a substantial amount of management effort to understand the environmental issues and to undertake the eco-design necessary to achieve real environmental gains. Other projects may be less complex environmentally but can achieve environmental gains mainly by setting ambitious environmental performance targets at the start of a project. Examples like the R&D effort involved in finding technological alternatives to overcome environmental problems in a complex iron and steel production process have many conflicting and interconnected issues that could affect overall environmental performance (Moors and Vergragt, 2002). The development of a highly efficient gas turbine whose primary R&D environmental objective was to reduce emission levels of NOx, CO and CO_2 did not have a need for complex environmental impact analysis (Johansson, 2006).

Supporting techniques

There are a range of management and technological techniques and approaches that have been developed and applied to the task of reducing environmental impact on society. Many of these could be applied to the management of R&D, for example, dematerialization of products and services to reduce use of materials and energy, accepting a corporate responsibility for an extended producer responsibility (*product stewardship*) by incorporating product take back and recycling initiatives into a company's operations, applying eco-efficiency concepts as a matter of course into all a company's products, processes and activities. Some form of life cycle assessment should be used as R&D precedes, though Foster and Green (2000) in their study of nine UK companies with various annual turnovers from £15M to £24,000M found a low level of use of the technique.

Many companies now have an Environmental Management System that should, but may not extend to R&D activities. It may cover the environmental aspects of the operations of the R&D function but should also cover the environmental aspects of the products and processes being researched and developed including an approach to life cycle assessment.

Goffin and Mitchell (2005) believe that project-management techniques are particularly appropriate for the management of R&D. This would involve the typical project-management tasks of establishing project objectives and scope, developing budgets, resources and time targets, implementing an appropriate quality management system and regular reporting and management review. The authors advocate the phase/gate approach involving milestones with supporting objectives and at which point the project is reviewed and decision such as go/continue/no go are made (Goffin and Mitchell, 2005). With this approach environmental issues could be a key part of the milestone targets and the project reviews and in line with environmentally responsible *product stewardship*, the precautionary principle should be applied.

10.8   Design management

Design management covers the design of products, processes and infrastructure. In its simple linear form it involves identifying a need, analysing that need, collection data, producing design concepts, undertaking preliminary design and producing a final design for manufacture or construction. In reality it is a much more complex process with many feedback loops and iterations, ongoing modifications and adjustments and input from market analysis, R&D and operations research as well as input from a range of stakeholders and technical standards (Staib, 2005).

Decisions made during the design phases of projects can have a big influence on the function, cost and environmental impact of products, for example, up to 80 per cent according to Graedal and Allenby (Dewberry and Sherwin, 2002). Design management draws upon many of the management techniques of project management as well as many specific to design, for example, value management, brainstorming, prototyping etc. Design is a 'forward-looking, reflective, creative, process-orientated and diverse' (Dewberry and Sherwin, 2002) and the management of the design process is a key component for a company wishing to reduce its environmental impact (Staib, 2005, p. 243). Many new management and technical techniques are being developed to integrate environmental issues into the design process and to even change design from a traditional focus to an environmental focus, for example, design for environment, cleaner production, waste management and industrial ecology (Staib, 2005) and design for sustainability (Dewberry and Sherwin, 2002).

There is a growing literature, for example, Hawken et al. (2000), Hargroves and Smith (2005), that suggest that something more radical than mere integration is necessary. By considering some of the growing environmental trends authors are suggesting that we need to make orders of magnitude reductions in the environmental impacts – see Innovation in Section 10.6. We need to not only consider the product itself but also its whole life cycle from the time the raw materials are harvested until the product has reached the end of its life and its materials are available for reuse. We also need to dematerialize our products, identify what service the product provides and then provide that service in a less material and energy intensive way (Hargroves and Smith, 2005).

The concept of all of life *product stewardship* and product take back legislation are growing trends under various titles, for example, extended producer responsibility in NSW Australia (DECC, 2007) and in the European automobile industry as end-of-life-vehicles (Orsato and Wells, 2007, 2007a). These will put external pressure on designers to design products with the whole of life environmental impact being considered.

Foresighting and backcasting

Earlier we discussed visioning and *foresighting* analysis to develop ideas of what future technologies, products and processes might be possible, desirable and undesirable. Dewberry and Sherwin (2002) believe that much design including design for sustainability is focused in manufacturing organizations towards continuous improvement rather that towards providing alternatives to unsustainable development. They suggest that there is a need for more radical change and that the processes like foresighting and backcasting are needed.

Foresighting involves envisioning futures where products are available to deliver a function (a human want or need) in an environmentally benign way. *Backcasting* involves working back from these envisaged futures to determine ways of achieving these futures. It includes more than technological management and technical design. The process requires a human focused approach that addresses desire and consumption issues, directs attention away from the more traditional product-related thinking to more sustainable life styles. On the part of the participants it needs creativity, risk-taking and innovation developed by group work and the integration of different perspectives (Dewberry and Sherwin, 2002).

Foresighting is different from traditional planning methods in that it is a social process that is iterative and deliberate in helping people make sense of the future; it is creative rather than analytical; and it is participatory rather than dominated by experts. Forecasting asks the question 'What is the most likely future?' Foresighting asks the question 'What futures are possible, desirable, disastrous or feasible?' (Wehrmeyer et al., 2002).

EXAMPLE

Foresighting – Room Heating and Cooling

Dewberry and Sherwin (2002) describe foresighting projects that developed ideas for a sustainable household. One project identified that current heating and cooling systems are extremely inefficient because so much energy goes into heating/cooling the room whereas it should be directed (from an environmental efficiency point of view) to only heating/cooling the occupants. From this foresighting project, they developed a concept of transferring the heating/cooling function to the bodies of the occupants directly from temperature-regulated clothes.

10.9   Production management

The management of technology is a key aspect of the profitable and competitive organization (Harrison and Samson, 2002). There have been a number of important trends in recent years that have affected manufacturing management, including focus on high degrees of quality and low cost 'by systematically eliminating all manufacturing activities not directly or indirectly adding value to a product'; globalization of manufacture and supply with linked and integrated supply chains; international competitiveness with the basic need to address price, quality, customer service and increasingly the need to address product differentiation and customization; and the need for rapid response to changes in market requirements from all parties in the supply chain (Shafaghi and Kerr, 2007).

This has led to the need to minimize the time taken to get a product to market, reduce manufacturing lead times, reduce inventory, maximum utilisation of capital and skills and better management of changing supply chains. Manufacturing needs to be lean and agile by eliminating excess inventory, scrap and rework, that is, it requires more efficient use of resources. Proficiency at these types of manufacturing skills is important if an organization is to significantly reduce the environmental impact of its operations and products. Production management involves both the management of the product and the management of the production process itself. Both are influenced by the design of the product and the design of the production process including the equipment, people and systems, for example, product design needs to consider designs that satisfy customer requirements as well as being easy to manufacture (Shafaghi and Kerr, 2007).

With increasing pressure on the natural environment this design needs to also consider the environmental impact of the product's manufacture, use and disposal. Legislation being introduced to cover extended producer responsibility or *product stewardship* adds a new aspect to production management and to product and process design, for example, the need for design and manufacture for disassembly, recycling and reuse (see box below).

EXAMPLE

Extended Producer Responsibility Promotes *Product Stewardship*

Extended producer responsibility (EPR) is an approach designed to reduce waste from consumer goods and their impact on the environment. It involves producers taking more responsibility for managing the environmental impact of their products throughout their useful life. The Organization for Economic Cooperation and Development defines EPR as 'an environmental policy approach in which a producer's responsibility for a product is extended to the post-consumer stage of the product's life cycle'. The aim is both to keep products and materials out of the waste stream and to reduce their environmental impact. Manufacturers are or will be required to play a role beyond the point of sale, for example, by designing products that produce less waste, use fewer resources and contain more recycled and less toxic components. EPR schemes have been implemented in many other countries and regions including Europe, the United Kingdom, the United States, Canada, Taiwan, Japan and Korea. The scheme in NSW Australia is currently a voluntary scheme and is progressively targeting different waste streams, for example, computers, mobile phones, office paper, paint, plastic bags, televisions, tyres, agricultural and veterinary chemicals and chemical containers, batteries, cigarette butts, end of life automotive vehicle residuals, other electrical products, packaging, polyvinyl chloride, treated timber, used oil and lubricants. (DECC, 2007)

Production management typically involves choice and construction of the manufacturing processes, operation and ongoing development; production planning and delivery including planning and coordination of material supply and delivery (the supply chain); forecasting of demand and scheduling production; capacity planning and management; operational control of the production process including control of quality, scope, timing, cost and maintenance of the production equipment and management of the production workforce; management of the supply chain and suppliers including choosing suppliers and supply arrangements and managing the delivery and quality of their products and information; and a continuous improvement programme supported by various techniques, for example, lean manufacturing (which aims to eliminate all forms of waste) and approaches such as Total Quality Control and Management, Six Sigma and Just-in-time (Shafaghi and Kerr, 2007).

'The quality approach as embodied in Quality Function Deployment (QFD) provides a means to find out from customers what they consider are the important product and service attributes and to keep them firmly in view of all people in the process chain or team' (Gilmour and Hunt, 1993, p. 90; Shafaghi and Kerr, 2007). This is especially so when considering environmental issues, but in this case the voice of the environment must also be heard, for example, through environmental harbingers and scientists, reflected in scientific knowledge (see box below). Finally stakeholders affected or likely to be affected by environmental degradation will raise their voices (Staib, 1997).

Many new techniques and management approaches are being developed and applied to production management to address the environmental issues of production. They include up-front processes such as design for the environment, environmental impact assessment and life cycle assessment. They also include processes that focus on the production processes including: cleaner production, waste management and industrial ecology. Extended producer responsibility for an organization's products after use will start to require integration of many aspects back into the production processes covering the collection and receipt of used products, disassembly, remanufacture, reprocessing of materials and finally reuse. One of the key aspects of extended producer responsibility should be directed to the reuse of the product and its components to the highest level (see box above). This may refocus an organization's strategy to what function, need or service they are supplying or wish to supply away from a sole focus on the product, for example, body air conditioning (see example on foresighting in the box in Section 10.8).

EXAMPLE

Natural Environment as a Stakeholder

Starting from the premise that stakeholders are 'any group or individual who can affect or is affected by the achievement of the organization's objectives' Freeman (1984, p. 46) Haigh and Griffiths (2007) argue that the environment should be treated as a primary stakeholder. Using climate change as an example, taking a strategic rather than an ethical point of view and using the criteria of legitimacy, power, urgency and proximity, they argue that the natural environment has an economic stake in organizations; there is no need for moral obligation to exist between organizations and the natural environment from a strategic standpoint; the absence of will and other human attributes are non-issues; and Freeman's 'affect or is affected by' criterion is solid. They argue that it is important to focus on 'the natural environment's impacts on organizations' as well as the 'impacts of organizations on the natural environment'. Taking this position could lead businesses to learn directly about the natural environment, rather than through proxies; enable organizations to understand services provided by nature and work with them in mutually sustaining ways; and develop a greater understanding of the strategic landscape by forecasting how climatic trends will affect competitors, suppliers and customers.

10.10   Conclusion

In this Chapter we have discussed some of the approaches that are applied to the management of technology including technological innovation and how environmental considerations can be introduced into innovation processes. We have described how technical innovation can be viewed on a scale from incremental to radical and that while incremental innovation (similar to continuous improvement in quality and environmental management ISO standards) is an important part of environmental innovation, a more radical approach is being called for to significantly reduce the environmental impacts of a company's products. To achieve significant reductions in environmental impacts, these considerations need to be part of a company's technology strategy, its approach to design management and production management and importantly its management of R&D – a key point where new products and processes are developed and assessed. A company needs to consider its *environmental stewardship* role both in relationship to the natural environment and to the company's own products.

CASE STUDY

Automobile Industry Toyota Prius

This case study discusses some of the issues of technology management and how they have been applied to a project that has introduced some ambitious environmental targets. The use of the automobile for personal mobility has many advantages: door-to-door transport, access to the necessities of life and employment and a source of pleasure and social status. Its disadvantages in an environmentally constrained world are numerous: local air pollution, greenhouse gas emissions, road congestion, injury and deaths from accidents, loss of open space and vegetation to roads, parking lots and urban sprawl. Despite concerns about the environmental impact of cars, the number of cars in the world and their usage are growing (Vergragt and Brown, 2007).

Cousins et al. (2007) show that despite a 15 per cent reduction in CO_2 emissions in all vehicles in the 15 European Union states, there have been a 22 per cent increase in power and a 10 per cent increase in body mass over the period from 1995 to 2002. This power increase has occurred over all engine sizes. Lane and Potter (2006) found that when it comes to car purchasing in the United Kingdom environmental issues have a very low priority for private and fleet consumers. These facts point to the difficulty the world faces in making radical changes to the greenhouse gases emitted by motor vehicles.

Over the past 50 years or so there has been a significant amount of research and development and government action directed at producing cleaner cars (Cousins et al., 2007). In this case study we consider the development of the Toyota Prius. It is a small car (1.6 litre engine capacity) with a very low fuel consumption of 4.4 l/100km (DTRS, 2008) achieved by using a hybrid power train consisting of a petrol engine, a power battery and an advanced electronic control system (Magnusson et al., 2003). It is seen as a car of the future designed for a world of scarce and increasingly costly fuel supplies and growing greenhouse gas emissions of which the car is a major contributor (Taylor, 2006).

Toyota has never been much of a pioneer but rather a fast follower, a risk-averse company famous for its lean production system. The concept of the Prius began in 1993 when the Chairman Eiji Toyoda expressed concern about the future of the automobile. The vice-president of Toyota R&D set two goals for the Prius: development of new production methods and fuel consumption 50 per cent better than Toyota's Corolla. This was later changed to 100 per cent (Taylor, 2006).

The application of a number of important technology management issues were needed to be applied for the development including the following:

- The existing engineering organization was subject to radical change to bring about close dialogue and coordination between specialists;
- The electronic control system was complicated and extensive use was made of computer simulations and prototypes;
- Toyota had limited experience with battery power systems and established a joint venture with supplier Matsushita/Panasonic and this required close cooperation between vehicle and battery engineers; and
- Ambitious environmental performance targets were set for the vehicle's fuel consumption (Magnusson et al., 2003).

Ambitious time targets were set to get the vehicle to market to gain first mover advantage but acceptance by the marketplace was difficult to achieve because of the comparatively high price and the new and unconventional nature of the vehicle, particularly in the United States. The improved fuel consumption (both less pollution and savings in running cost) was important in its success as were market matters such as pride of ownership of a vehicle in the knowledge that one was contributing to reduced environmental impacts from one's personal transport (Taylor, 2006).

Magnusson et al. (2003) believe that in technology management terms the Prius development was an example of discontinuous innovation mainly in its power train subsystem though much of the change was architectural, that is, using existing technology in different ways and combinations of modules. Taylor (2006) believes that Toyota has a head start in the hybrid technology market as other car makers are starting to develop hybrid vehicles and other fuel efficient models such as electric vehicles and hydrogen fuel cell vehicles (see also Chapter 3, Figure 3.1).

10.11   Questions

- Take one of the case studies from a text book on the management of technological innovation, for example, Harrison and Samson (2002), Tidd et al. (2005) or Khalil (2000) and describe how you would establish an environmental technology strategy and apply this strategy to the chosen case study organization's processes for the management of R&D, design and production.
- Choose an organization which has recently changed its technology strategy and is now delivering or about to deliver a product that has a substantially reduced environmental impact in comparison with its early products. Prepare a case study of the management approaches it has adopted and utilized to bring the product to market with reduced environmental impact.

10.12   Further reading

Hargroves and Smith, 2005; Tidd et al., 2005; Orsato and Wells, 2007.

End of Part Case Study: Tata Steel of India

Arun Sahay and Robert Staib*

Indian steel industry

Steel is one of the most important engineering and construction materials in the modern world. The Indian iron and steel industry is 100 years old. After being public-owned previously for a long time, it was deregulated in 1992. Deregulation was an integral part of the general policy of liberalization, economic reforms and structural adjustment programmes aimed at creating a new regime with its accent on competition and ultimately on the enhancement of economic efficiency. At Independence, India possessed a small but viable iron and steel industry with a capacity of 1.3 million tonnes (MT) per year. In 2005, India ranked in eighth position globally with 38.1 million tonnes (MT)/year production, when total world crude steel production was 1131.8 MT (IISI, 2006). Today it has a diversified output mix globally, covering almost the entire range of products. The first Indian integrated steel plant was set up by the Tata Iron and Steel Company (TISCO).

There are 211 market players (CMIE, 2008) in the Indian steel industry with the top two companies the Steel Authority of India (SAIL) (a public sector company) and Tata Steel (a private sector company) having 27 per cent and 14 per cent respectively of the Indian industry. Globally, Tata Steel with its acquisition of the European company Corus was the sixth largest steelmaker in 2007 with production of about 24 MT/per year – 23 per cent from Tata Steel and 77 per cent from Corus (Tata, 2008).

Tata Steel (previously TISCO)

Tata Steel was registered just over 100 years ago in 1907. It is India's largest private sector steel company. Jamsetji Nusserwanji Tata (1839–1904) realized that political freedom without economic and industrial strength to support and defend it would be a cruel delusion and the foundation of industrial power was to be built of steel (Elwin, 1958). Jamsetji witnessed

---

*Unless otherwise noted, the information for this case study comes from Tata (2008).

the beginning of the transformation of every aspect of Indian life that was to lead this country to ultimate freedom and a high place in the counsels of the world. A few years before his death Jamsetji dreamt of a great iron and steel works which, ultimately staffed and *manned by Indians, would revolutionize the industrial picture of India. 'Be sure to lay wide streets planted with shady trees, every other of a quick-growing variety, be sure that there is plenty of space for lawns and gardens, and reserve large areas for football, hockey and parks. Earmark areas for Hindu temples, Mohammedan mosques and Christian churches'* (Jamsetji Nusservanji Tata, Founder).

At the beginning Tata Steel was mainly concerned to provide the basic materials of the industry, but it soon became obvious that if a number of factories could be established in Jamshedpur to process the steel into more advanced products, it would be of very real advantage to the country. The company passed through various difficulties and disasters of the associated companies (Elwin, 1958) but today, Tata Steel has 21 joint-venture companies and associate companies across the globe and has achieved many Indian and global awards.

In 2007, Tata Steel acquired Corus Europe's second largest steel producer with revenues in 2005 of GBP 9.2 billion, and annual crude steel production of 18.2 MT primarily in the United Kingdom and the Netherlands. It had a global network of sales offices and service centres. Corus businesses have systems in place that focus on managing their operations and minimizing the effects of them. Unless noted the data in this case study does not include data from Corus.

Strategic goals and strategy

Tata Steel's strategic goals are to move from commodities to brands; become an Economic Value Added (EVA) positive core business; continue to be lowest cost producer of steel; to develop value creating partnerships with customers and suppliers; have enthused and happy employees; and achieve sustainable growth. To achieve these strategic goals Tata Steel has adopted the following strategies: manage knowledge; outsource strategically; encourage innovation and allow the freedom to fail; excel at The Tata Business Excellence Model; unleash people's potential and create leaders who will build the future; invest in attractive new businesses; ensure safety and environmental sustainability; and divest, merge, acquire. Strategic divestments from non-core or chronically under-performing businesses, mergers and alliances for synergistic growth and acquisitions for accelerated growth will be important pillars of its strategy to maximize the present value of future EVA. The Tata Business Excellence Model lays stress on results through the processes of customer and market focus, strategic planning, information and analysis, human resource development, partnerships and it is its guiding model for business excellence.

Performance of Tata Steel in past sixteen years (1991–2006)

The performance of the firm notably changed after the introduction of new economic policy in India in July 1991. Figure II.1 summarizes Tata Steel's financial performance over this period. (These figures do not include Corus). Tata has successfully managed the transition from a company working in a protected Indian business environment to a strong, market-focused company on the world stage (Seshadri and Tripathy, 2006). Tata Steel response to environmental issues has included the following: responding to increasingly stricter Indian environmental legislation and regulations, changing processes to reduce pollution, management and reuse of waste, implementation of the environmental standard management system ISO14001, implementing a cultural transformation of its workforce to a more environmentally focused one and efforts to green its supply chain (Sarkar, 2004).

Sustainability policies at Tata Steel

Strategy is supported by a set of corporate policies covering: quality, alcohol and drug, human resources, corporate social responsibility, environmental, occupational health & safety, research and social accountability. Two policies relevant to sustainability are outlined below.

Corporate Social Responsibility Policy: Tata Steel believes that the primary purpose of a business is to improve the quality of life of people. Tata Steel will volunteer its resources, to the extent it can reasonably afford, to sustain and improve healthy and prosperous environment and to improve the quality of life of the people of the areas in which it operates.

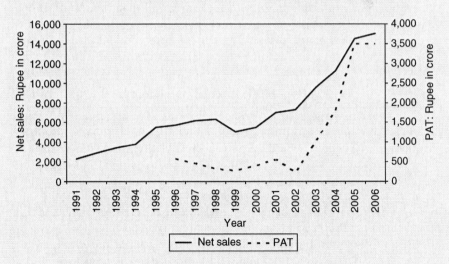

Figure II.1   Net sales and Profit after Tax (PAT), in rupees (crore = 10^7)

Source: Tata, 2008.

Environmental, Occupational Health and Safety Policy: Tata Steel reaffirms its commitment to provide a safe working place and clean environment to its employees and other stakeholders as an integral part of its business philosophy and values. It says that it will continually enhance its Environmental, Occupational Health and Safety (EHS) performance in its activities, products and services through a structured EHS management framework. Most of its operations have been certified to the international environmental management standard, ISO 14001. All of Corus's manufacturing operations have been independently certified as well (Corus, 2008).

To achieve its sustainability goals, Tata Steel has identified key enterprise processes critical to the growth and success of the organization: leadership, order generation, strategic planning and risk management, operation and fulfilment, market development, inbound supply management, investment management, research and development, improvement and change management, information management, human resources and social responsibility and corporate services. Tata Steel produces a Corporate Sustainability Report (externally reviewed) in line with the Global Reporting Initiative (GRI, 2006) Guidelines and Tata Steel's key enterprise processes.

Tata Steel has a complex though fairly traditional, vertical (or hierarchical) organization structure. A separate group covering environmental and occupational health reports directly to a Vice President. It will be interesting to see how environmental and social issues will be integrated with the Corus group (Corus, 2008) and with the larger Tata Group (Tata, 2008).

For Tata Steel 'Sustainable Development' is an important issue in today's world with its three facets: economic, social and environmental. Tata Steel has adopted sustainable policies in tune with international guidelines such as the Global Compact 1998; GRI guidelines for Sustainability Reporting,

Table II.1   Tata Steel sustainability indicators

Sustainability indicators	Unit of measure	World avg.	Tata Steel	Numbers reported*
Greenhouse gas emissions	tonne CO_2 eq/tonne crude steel	1.6	1.48	39
Material efficiency	%	97	85.71	39
Energy intensity	Gigajoules/tonne crude steel	19	19.91	40
Steel recycling	% of crude steel	28	2	39
Environmental Management system	% total employees under EMS/ Total employee under facility.	85	90	39

Note:*Number of member companies who reported.

Source: Tata Steel (2008a).

the 11 sustainability indicators as per the 42 member Brussels-based International Iron and Steel Institute guidelines (IISI, 2006). Summary Sustainable Development indicators are shown in Table II.1.

Greenhouse gas emissions (CO₂ only)

Tata Steel (excluding Corus) has been reporting CO_2 emissions for over a decade. Figure II.2 shows the significant progress in reducing its *process emissions* per tonne of crude steel produced (tcs) by 36 per cent over this period. It also shows the total emissions rate which includes imported electricity, mobile sources and hydrofluocarbons (HFC). Despite the reduction in the process emission rate, *total emissions* of CO_2 have increased roughly in line with growing steel production. Over the period of common data, process improvements have reduced CO_2 process emissions by an average of 2 per cent per annum but total emissions have increased by an average of 4.8 per cent per annum. In addition to process emissions, emissions produced by mainly imported electricity and mobile sources have also increased by 12.5 per cent per annum although these categories only represent approximately 7 per cent of overall emissions. The data reflects a focus (common with many organizations) on efficiency per unit of product. This is very important for a company but in terms

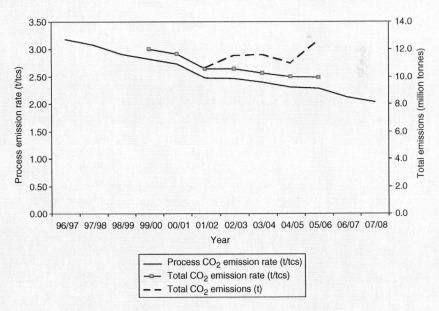

Figure II.2 Tata steel carbon dioxide emissions from steel production

Notes: 1. t/tcs = tonnes CO_2 per tonne of crude steel production. 2. Process emissions exclude imported electricity, mobile sources and HFC. 3. Figures exclude Corus acquired by Tata in April 2007.

Sources: Tata 2007, 2008.

of global environmental impact, total emissions are more important. It illustrates the need for companies to focus and report on total emissions as well. Management of the process emission rate is a part of a company's *product stewardship* role while total emissions are a part of a company's *environmental stewardship* role. The International Iron and Steel Institute is implementing a global sector approach to climate change and is commencing to collect CO_2 emissions data worldwide to help benchmarking good performance and to help in setting national and regional commitment (IISI, 2008).

External commentators

Tata Steel plays a significant role in the economy of India, in the lives of the people in the areas in which it operates and in its impacts on the environment. It has shown itself by its longevity to be a sustainable organization. Although it has shown that it takes sustainability seriously (both social and environmental) not all organizations and people totally agree. Below we present a selection of views of both the Tata group and Tata Steel which illustrate a range of views from external parties on Tata's social and environmental performance. They have been summarized by the book's editor from the sources listed and should only be used for the purposes on the case study.

Social performance*

Comment No 1: Summarized from Ethical Corporation (2008)

The Tata Group (of which Tata Steel is a subsidary) has a long history of supporting individuals, causes and institutions with the objective of improving the quality of life of Indians. It endowers a number of philanthropic trusts (e.g., Tata Institute for Fundamental Research, the Tata Institute for Social Sciences, the Tata Memorial Hospital). It has investment in the Tata Energy Research Institute, an Indian research organization on sustainability. The Tata Centre for Community Initiatives aims to help to 'institutionalise the Tata Group's long-established tradition of community development and welfare'. This now includes environmental management. Tata's major companies produce Global Reporting Initiative and Global Compact reports every year. 'Corporate responsibility experts in India believe the governance structure at Tata group to be extremely good, owing much to the philanthropic nature of the companies' ownership and high-level disclosure about group activities.'

---

*N.B. The views under comments 1 to 7 are *not endorsed or otherwise* by this case study's authors. If readers wish to find out more details or to use the information for publications they *must* consult the original sources.

Comment No 2: Summarized from Kelly (2006)

Tata Steel situated in the north eastern Indian province of Jharkhand, India, has a long tradition of corporate social responsibility and in spite of the fact that it is wholly unionized, it rests on its welfare capitalist origins and traditions. Its headquarters and main plant are in the planned company town of Jamshedpur, where the utilities and infrastructure are run by a wholly owned subsidiary. Throughout its history Tata steel has provided broad education not only for its employees and their families and others within the city of Jamshedpur and the state of Orissa but it has also provided education for literacy and numeracy; assisted farmers and small start-up businesses with training and equipment; supported self-help groups and community groups to identify and achieve community goals; provided HIV/AIDS education and support; provided Adolescent Reproductive Sexual Health programmes a large number of adolescents in slums and villages; and provided general education programmes within the company. In addition it has ensured its undertakings and codes in areas such as ethics and antidiscrimination are realized through comprehensive training, courses and systems of assistance.

Social performance, employees and tribal landowners

Comment No 3: Summarized from Ethical Corporation (2008)

An organization as large as the Tata Group can face many environmental and social issues associated with its operations and the expansion of its operations. In January 2006, tribal people or 'adivasis' in Orissa's Kalinganagar district were protesting against their land being taken by the government for the construction of a Tata Steel plant. The villagers also alleged that 'the government had bought the land from them at a measly price and sold it on to the private sector for a much higher price'. During one demonstration by the adivasis 12 people were killed by police. The company was not involved and denied any wrong doing.

Comment No 4: Summarized from Jayaraman (2006b)

Tata Steel has been in the forefront of India's industrialization and an engine of growth but those struggling for tribal rights in Kalinganagar and elsewhere remain unimpressed by the Tata Steel's size or philanthropic image. The indigenous people's movement for land-rights in the Kalinganagar area points out that the movement became an anti-Tata fight only after October 2004, when it became clear to local villagers that the government and industries were reneging on promises to rehabilitate displaced families. The fight was against any take-over of land, not against any one company, but Tatas sought to overcome people's will with police force. When big industry first came in the early 1990s, it was welcomed. But soon the cultural, environmental and economic costs became apparent. Stone quarries have eaten into hillocks, replaced forests and devastated what little agriculture there was. Families that had lived for generations in a village were asked for deeds establishing their legal claims. The local people joined the ranks of India's indigenous and other marginalized peoples pushed aside in the name of economic growth.

Comment No 5: Summarized from Jayaraman (2006a)

In response to the article described in Comment 4, Mr Jayaraman met with Mr Nerurkar, vice president Tata Steel, to clarify Tata's position. Nerurkar said the people have three main concerns: steel plants pollute; the communities are not happy; and how to trust Tata and government to give compensation and livelihood? The vice president admits that despite 100 years of upliftment programmes for the adivasis by Tatas, the lot of the adivasis could be better. Jayaraman comments that with the proposed onslaught on tribal lands, lifestyle and culture by mining companies and industries, once-self-sufficient adivasi communities in India may become entirely dependent on hand-outs by industry or the State. Rather than question the displace-and-rehabilitate programmes, the vice president of Tata Steel recommends increased 'looking after' of tribal communities. Corporations, governments and even many among adivasi societies seem convinced that adivasis and other marginalized communities have no inherent right to choose their path of development. The right to say 'No' to industrial development is being termed unviable or unreasonable. Instead, corporations and the government are making it seem as if tribal development and the economic betterment of the poor can only piggy-back on some grandiose industrial plan for 'development'. Nerurkar laid out a roadmap according to which Tata will mine ore, build factories in Orissa, and contribute to the upliftment of Orissa in general, and the adivasis in particular including details of a programme to train youth from families evicted to make way for industries to become construction labourers sent to work on industrial and infrastructural projects in various parts of the country.

Environmental issues

Comment No 6: Summarized from Greenpeace (2008a)

Orissa is probably the most significant habitat worldwide for the Olive Ridley Sea Turtle, an endangered species. The nesting beaches at Gahirmatha in Orissa are among the world's largest mass nesting grounds for the species. In October 2004 Tata Steel and Larsen & Toubro signed an agreement for construction of Dhamra port. The proposed Dhamra port is in Orissa's Bhadrakh district and is located less than 5 km from the

Bhitarkanika Sanctuary (a Ramsar Wetland of International Importance) and less than 15 km from the mass nesting beaches of the Gahirmatha Marine Sanctuary. Greenpeace and other environmental groups are opposed to the port on the above environmental grounds and have been calling on Tata to immediately halt construction at Dhamra and assess alternative, less destructive options to the port.

Comment No 7: Summarized from Bisoi (2008)

The Dhamra Port Corporation Ltd (DPCL), a 50:50 joint venture of Larsen & Toubro and Tata Steel, is setting up a deep draft port of international standard at Dhamra on the Orissa coast considered to be strategically important, as it will be closer to South East Asian countries. Despite the protests it appears that the construction of the Dharma port project is on schedule to be made operational by the middle of 2010 with two berths with a total capacity of 25 million tonne per annum. This includes the channel, rail, communications and other ancillary infrastructure. Dhamra is going to be the most environment friendly port in the country. DPCL is committed to proactive measures for conservation to show the world that it too cares for the environment. DPCL has engaged IUCN, the world's premier scientific body on wildlife, to assess the situation and put in place an appropriate environment management plan.

Comment No 8: Summarized Sarkar (2004)

Tata Steel has a strong history of social responsibility towards its employees and the communities in which it works and has developed a reputation as an environmentally responsible company. Sarkar questions how much of Tata Steel's environmental approach has been proactive and how much reactive. She notes that many environmental improvements have come from its strategies of modernization, cost reduction and production process changes and that another important driver has been the ongoing changes in Indian environmental legislation. As of 2004, Tata Steel had only just started to move from a compliance-based approach to a more strategic or proactive environmental management approach.

Exercises

- Review the information provided in the case study from the company's point of view and from the external commentators' points of view and identify the key sustainability issues (social and environmental) that Tata Steel needs to address as it expands its operations to take advantage of its merger with Corus. For some of the relevant corporate and environmental history of Tata Steel read Seshadri and Tripathy (2006) and Sarkar (2004).

- Review the case study outline and the web sites of Tata Steel, Corus and the Tata Group to assess how the groups address sustainability (both environmental and social sustainability). Identify the different approaches, actual and proposed, and how the companies can utilize the best practices from the Indian and European approaches to achieve better sustainable outcomes.
- Make an assessment of how well-prepared organizationally, the three groups are to be able to address a future carbon constrained economy with carbon trading considering what changes might be necessary to Tata Steel's strategy, leadership, human resources, marketing, structure, operations and its use of technology. Consider also how the initiatives being introduced by the International Iron and Steel Institute and the moves by Tata Motors to introduce cheaper Indian cars might influence its approach.

Part III

Support Operations and Business Case

Finance and Investment

11

Rory Sullivan and Craig Mackenzie

11.1 Introduction

This chapter discusses investors' views of corporate responsibility and the role that investors may play in promoting more responsible corporate responsibility behaviour. Companies competing in free markets have a hugely valuable role to play in creating many of the products and services, jobs, tax revenues and investment returns on which modern economies depend. They also have a vital positive role to play directly in providing the investment, research and technology necessary to solve our most pressing social and environmental problems – from renewable energy technologies to medicines to treat AIDS. Despite these important and positive contributions, few would dispute the fact that companies cause or contribute to (whether wholly or partially, directly or indirectly) many significant social and environmental problems, including climate change, loss of biodiversity, social exclusion, bribery and corruption, breaches of human rights and the production of dangerous goods and services.

Over the past ten years, shareholders in the United Kingdom, Europe, the United States, Canada and Australia have used their influence to improve company performance on issues such as climate change, human rights and access to medicines.[1] In some cases this has contributed to important outcomes such as dramatically reduced prices of AIDS medicines, the withdrawal of companies from unhelpful industry lobby groups and improvements in labour conditions in retail supply chains. This has led to increased interest in the potential for institutional investors – a general term for investments managed or controlled by insurance companies, pension funds and investment managers – to contribute to solving corporate responsibility problems (e.g., Hawley and Williams, 2000; McLaren, 2004; Robins, 2006).

11.2   What is responsible investment?

An initial definition for socially responsible investment (SRI) could be something like 'Investment where social, ethical or environmental (SEE) factors are taken into account in the selection, retention and realisation of investment, and the responsible use of the rights (such as voting rights) that are attached to such investments' (Mansley, 2000, p. 3).

It has traditionally been assumed that the only approaches available to investors with strong ethical values (or, more specifically, that wished to reflect their ethical values in their investments) were either to shun certain stocks (e.g., 'vice' stocks such as tobacco, gambling, alcohol and pornography) or to invest in certain positive activities (e.g., environmental technology or healthcare). While such approaches have the advantages of appealing to relatively simple conceptions of right and wrong, they have struggled to become more than a relatively small part of the total institutional investment market. The reason is that most pension funds operate under trust law. This imposes a 'fiduciary' obligation on the pension fund's trustees to serve the interests of those whose money is invested in these funds; these interests are usually interpreted in exclusively financial terms. The consequence is that fiduciary pension funds have tended to reject screened approaches to responsible investment on the grounds that it conflicts with their fiduciary duty to serve the financial interests of their beneficiaries. While the empirical evidence indicates that ethically screened funds may not under-perform (useful overviews are provided in Sparkes (2002, pp. 252–253) and Co-operative Insurance Society and Forum for the Future (2002, pp. 21–23)), and despite the ongoing debate about the exact nature of these conflicts (Freshfields Bruckhaus Deringer, 2005), the consensus (at least in the US and UK) is that ethical screening is not legally advisable for pension funds.

These limitations have created interest in alternative approaches to addressing social, ethical and environmental issues in investment. Two major strategies or responses have emerged, namely (1) enhancing mainstream investment processes to explicitly incorporate consideration of company performance on these issues, and (2) using the formal rights and informal influence available to investors to encourage companies to pay appropriate attention to the management of social, ethical and environmental issues.[2]

11.3   Enhanced analysis

There has been a growing recognition of the financial importance of social, ethical and environmental issues to investment decision-making. Examples of where these issues have impacted directly on company financial performance have included litigation (e.g., tobacco, asbestosis, product liability), regulation, taxation and other market instruments, and company failure as a consequence of probity failings (e.g., Enron). As a consequence, several investment managers have announced initiatives to better integrate these issues into their investment activities. Investment analysts have responded by increasing the amount of research they do in this area and have produced reports on issues such as HIV/AIDS in the southern African mining industry, the effects of the European Union's Emission Trading Scheme on European electricity utility companies, the implications of obesity for food producers and retailers and the effects of climate change on the insurance sector (see, for example, UNEPFI (2004)). Enhanced analysis avoids the legal controversy traditionally associated with SRI because its aims are squarely aligned with the proper goal of fiduciary investors – to maximize financial returns for investors. There is no intention to place ethical considerations ahead of financial ones. Instead the intention is to improve on existing analysis and so deliver financial benefit to pension fund beneficiaries.

From the corporate responsibility perspective, the rationale is that companies will be less likely to behave in ways that are socially or environmentally harmful if their performance on social and environmental issues is properly reflected in their share prices. This argument presupposes that these issues are not presently being taken into account in investment research and decision-making. However, some social and environmental issues are already well understood and accurately analysed by the capital markets. For example, the risks of tobacco litigation – at heart, an issue of corporate ethics, transparency and public health – and the implications of the European Union (EU) Emissions Trading Scheme for the electricity utility sector have already been extensively researched. Notwithstanding these examples, it is probably fair to say that many social and environmental issues have yet to receive the same level of investor attention. The reasons are complex: many environmental and social issues play out over the long term; it can be difficult to assess their impacts on a company's finances or balance sheets; the point at which they become relevant or material to a company's fortunes can be hard to pin point. In some cases, regulation or consumer concern that would trigger companies to respond has been lacking.

However, even if there was greater research into these issues it is not necessarily the case that positive social or environmental outcomes would result. There are two specific issues that need to be recognized: (1) materiality, and (2) market failures. While there is no universally agreed definition, financial analysts frequently use numerical thresholds – 5 per cent of a company's revenue or 5 per cent moves in a company's share price are common rules of thumb – to assess the financial materiality of a particular issue. In this frame of reference, the vast majority of social or environmental issues – notwithstanding examples such as tobacco litigation and climate change – are simply not material. As a result, traditional financial analysts have tended to overlook these issues, focusing instead on other potential drivers of investment value. Furthermore, if analysts conclude that the financial implications of, for example, supply chain labour standards or contaminated land clean-up are relatively insignificant for a particular company in the near term, most mainstream investors will not raise these issues with a company's management. Companies therefore usually conclude that investors are not concerned about how they manage these (financially) non-material issues.

The issue of financial materiality is compounded by the fact that many social and environmental problems are actually the result of market failures, that is,

where the negative social or environmental impacts associated with an economic activity are not borne by the company who causes them, but by wider
society. Where the prospect of government or other social action to internalize
externalities (or otherwise correct market failure) is remote, investment analysts
will have no financial reason to take account of these issues, and companies
will have no incentive to address them. In such situations, the incentives for
companies to take action will need to come from elsewhere – for example, new
regulations, consumer demand, media or NGO attention.

Despite these limitations, enhanced analysis does offer the potential to
encourage improvements in corporate performance on some material social and
environmental issues. To maximize the benefits of this activity, it is essential that
investors actively engage with companies to set out their expectations of how
social and environmental issues should be managed and to explain exactly how
these issues are taken into account in their investment analysis. Unless investors
provide this feedback, companies will not understand the reasons informing
the buy/sell or overweight/underweight decision, or whether or not these decisions were informed by environmental or social issues. Greater transparency of
this nature would also help overcome one of the criticisms made by companies
of investor engagement, namely that there is an apparent disconnect between
the questions being asked by analysts interested specifically in social and environmental issues and the decisions being made by analysts/fund managers.

11.4   Shareholder activism

Shareholder activism occurs when shareholders use their unique power as the
owners of companies to facilitate change. The central focus of this activity has
been on improving aspects of corporate governance (Ryan and Dennis, 2003)
but there is an increasing emphasis on encouraging improvements in the management of specific social or environmental issues. The reasons include the
belief that well-managed companies will tend to outperform over the longer
term and pressure from stakeholders and government for investors to take a
more activist approach to their investments (see, for a general view, Sullivan and
Mackenzie (2006, pp. 150–151)).

As shareholders, large institutional investors have a range of formal and informal rights and powers relating to companies. Formally, shareholders have the
right to vote to approve the appointment of board directors, the board's remuneration policy, the appointment of auditors and, frequently, the annual report
and accounts. Informally, institutional investors can exert influence through
their ability to buy and sell shares and bonds (hence influencing share price or
the cost of capital) through their relationships and frequent contact with management, through encouraging other investors to use their formal powers and
through creating peer pressure (e.g., through benchmarking performance on
specific corporate governance or corporate responsibility issues). These formal
and informal powers mean that shareholders have significant ability, particularly if they act collectively, to influence the behaviour of companies.

To date, most investor activism (in Europe at least) has focused on situations where the goals of activism are broadly aligned with investors' financial interests, allowing investors who wish to encourage improved corporate responsibility to justify their demands by reference to the enhanced shareholder value that is expected to accrue. That is, there is an alignment between the actions of the activist investors and the short- or long-term success of the business. There is a growing body of anecdotal evidence that investor activism backed by a 'business case' in this way can be effective in encouraging companies to improve their corporate responsibility performance.[3] For example, Sullivan and Mackenzie (eds) (2006, pp. 149–213) present a series of case studies that illustrate where UK investors have contributed to improvements in the quality of companies' policies, management systems and disclosures on a range of social, ethical and environmental issues, including climate change, supply chain labour standards, human rights, business ethics and access to medicines, through the following:

- Facilitating dialogue between companies and stakeholders and/or raising stakeholder concerns with companies: For example, institutional investors have helped to raise the profile of human rights issues with companies through supporting specific NGO campaigns and through acting as a conduit for the flow of information between pressure groups and companies.
- Legitimizing specific debates, through encouraging companies to look on issues such as equal pay (see, for example, Henderson Global Investors (2002)) and human rights (see, for example, F&C (2004)), as proper matters for corporate attention because of the risks and opportunities they raise.
- Encouraging companies that fall below standards of good practice set by sector leaders to improve their performance. For example, investors have played an important role in encouraging companies to meet the standards required to allow inclusion in the FTSE4Good indices, whose criteria are based on industry best practice standards.
- Encouraging companies to ensure that corporate governance arrangements are supportive of corporate responsibility, specifically those aspects of corporate responsibility that fall within the proper role of the board – for example, strategic issues such as tax policy or aspects of executive incentives.

In most of these cases, the arguments for improvements to corporate responsibility were supported by business case arguments such as the need to manage potential risks to corporate brand and reputation; the need to pre-empt, or at least be prepared for, potential government regulation; and/or the strategic advantage of being ahead of competitors on a potentially important business issue.

Case study: benchmarking as an engagement strategy[4]

Some observers – in particular non-governmental organizations (NGOs) – have questioned whether engagement actually drives corporate change, and whether objective evidence can be provided to confirm these changes. One way of addressing this question is to benchmark corporate performance and to repeat the benchmark over time to assess whether and how performance has changed. The use of benchmarks in the investment community has been pioneered by Insight Investment which, since 2003, has benchmarked extractive and utility companies' management of biodiversity-related risks, retail sector companies' management of supply chain labour standards and UK house-builders' management of sustainability issues.

Insight's approach to benchmarking starts by establishing an analytical framework that articulates best practice on a given issue, covering companies' governance, strategy, policy, management systems and reporting, as well as the use of specific tools, technologies and processes relevant to the issue at hand. This provides an objective and consistent basis on which to analyse and compare selected companies' performance. It also facilitates dialogue with management by identifying each company's particular strengths and weaknesses. Repeating benchmarks regularly enables each company's progress over time to be tracked.

In January 2004, in partnership with WWF, Insight published a benchmarking study (Insight Investment and WWF, 2004) evaluating how well the UK's leading listed house-builders were managing and reporting on sustainability issues. To prepare the report, Insight – in conjunction with WWF and Upstream, specialist consultants – first sketched out what it considered to be best practice in each of three key areas: governance and risk management, managing environmental impacts and managing societal impacts. This analysis was used to establish a set of 18 criteria against which each company's performance could be evaluated. Companies were first assessed on the basis of their publicly available financial and sustainability reports and material on their websites. Insight then met with each company to review the analysis and discuss the company's practices and performance on each of the issues in question. This process allowed companies to provide further evidence of their work on sustainability issues. The final results of the study revealed that while the house-builders had begun to recognize the growing importance of sustainability issues to their businesses, few had well-developed strategies, policies and practices to address them effectively. The two companies that came closest to meeting best practice were Countryside Properties and The Berkeley Group.

Following the publication of the benchmarking report, Insight and WWF continued to engage with the house-builders through meetings with senior management, explaining the analysis of and suggesting improvements the companies could make. In addition, Insight

- invited all of the companies to take part in the Health and Safety Executive's (HSE's) new health and safety index, CHaSPI (HSE, 2007);
- hosted a meeting for the developers with Keith Hill, the then Housing Minister, to discuss sustainability in the housing sector;
- produced a comprehensive tool-kit to provide companies with detailed guidance on resources available to manage all of the issues evaluated in the benchmark;
- kept companies informed of key research and initiatives.

In order to assess whether companies had made any progress on managing and reporting on sustainability issues, the analysis was repeated during 2005. The results showed substantial improvement in the reporting, management and performance of all of the companies that had been engaged with (see Figure 11.1). Most companies had greatly improved their management and reporting of many of the issues addressed in the benchmark in line with the suggestions that Insight had made to them. Feedback from the companies also reinforced the view that the engagement and benchmarking process had been a major factor in effecting these changes.

Clearly, Insight's engagement was not the only factor at work. Government, market and other trends and pressures had also been driving change within the sector. In fact, one of the critical conclusions from this and other benchmarks is that effective benchmarking relies on the existence of strong incentives (e.g., from government policy) to stimulate the greatest changes in company behaviour. In such situations, benchmarking helps companies understand how best to respond to these incentives. Conversely, in situations where these incentives are not in place, benchmarking is less likely to be effective at encouraging improvements in management practice.

In conclusion, the evidence from this and other benchmarking studies is that properly planned engagement by investors, using rigorous and effective analytical tools, can deliver substantial, demonstrable improvements in companies' governance and management of key social, ethical and environmental issues, thereby also contributing to improvements in risk management. Benchmarking, based on careful research and engagement, helps companies, government and investors to identify leaders and laggards, to identify companies' specific strengths and weaknesses and to highlight the improvements that

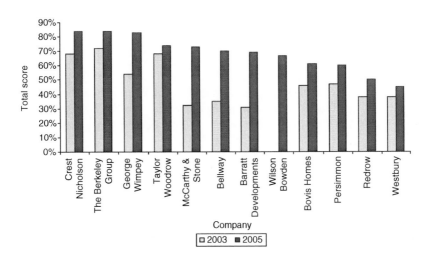

Figure 11.1   The evolution of UK house-builders' sustainability performance

Source: Insight Investment and WWF, 2005.

companies have made over specific time frames. Moreover, it helps to clarify best practice and make clear to companies what investors expect of them on particular issues.

Case study: climate change

The example above relates to the situation where there is a reasonably clear business case for companies to take action on a particular corporate responsibility issue. While such activity may in itself be worthwhile, it does raise the question of whether investors can play a meaningful role when there are conflicts between the interests of companies and society. Unfortunately, economic theory suggests that many of the most serious corporate responsibility problems result from market failures, where the interests of companies are not aligned with those of society (see, for a general view, Mackenzie, 2006). In such situations, there is typically no compelling business case for companies to take action and, by extension, no obvious financial reason for investors to encourage them to do so. If, as a result, investors are unlikely to be prepared to tackle these difficult cases, the hope that investors may be able to play a really significant role in addressing corporate responsibility issues may be disappointed.

Perhaps the one exception to this hypothesis has been in relation to climate change where there is some evidence that investors will seek to take action on an issue that has been described as 'the greatest market failure the world has ever seen' (Stern, 2006a). Even though climate change represents a colossal market failure, it seems to be receiving very substantial levels of investor attention on both sides of the Atlantic. In Europe, 31 institutional investors – primarily UK and French pension funds and asset managers – representing around €2.7 trillion in assets under management have formed the Institutional Investors Group on Climate Change (IIGCC, 2007). In the United States, the Investor Network on Climate Risk now has 50 members with over US$3 trillion of assets under management (INCR, 2007), while the Carbon Disclosure Project (CDP) represents international investors with 225 institutional investors with assets under management of US$31 trillion (CDP, 2007). So far, discussions on the subject of climate change between companies and their investors have primarily focused on reporting and, to a lesser extent, on encouraging companies to ensure that climate change is properly integrated into corporate strategies and risk-management processes. The assumption underpinning this focus on reporting is that the request for disclosure will signal to companies that investors are concerned about climate change, thereby providing an incentive for companies to reduce their greenhouse gas emissions. As yet, however, investors have not asked companies to reduce greenhouse gas emissions beyond those that would be justified in financial terms (Sullivan, 2006). That is, investors' calls for companies to improve disclosure, strategy and risk management can all be justified by reference to relatively conventional business case arguments.

However, investor engagement with companies on climate change is only part of the story. In parallel to engagement with companies, some investors have started to engage much more forcefully with policy-makers, calling for government action to establish a long-term policy framework for internalizing the costs of carbon. Much of this activity has been under the auspices of the IIGCC, a pan-European collaborative initiative between pension funds and other institutional investors to address the investment risks and opportunities associated with climate change (for a detailed description of the IIGCC's work, see Sullivan et al., 2005). IIGCC's public policy work is aimed at encouraging policy-makers to take account of the long-term interests of institutional investors. IIGCC has made submissions (IIGCCa, 2007) to government inquiries and consultations relating to issues such as Phase II of the EU Emissions Trading Scheme, the inclusion of the aviation sector in the EU ETS and EU Action on Climate Change post-2012. In each of these submissions, IIGCC has emphasized the importance of policy certainty, the need for long-term policy targets directed at significant reductions in greenhouse gas emissions, the desirability of extending the use of economic instruments and incentives and the need for better corporate disclosures. IIGCC has also met with key climate change policy-makers to ensure that investors' views on these issues are clearly heard.

Does this provide an example of investors acting against their own interests? If looked at in the context of business cost-benefit assessments, the answer appears to be yes, as the logical implication of IIGCC's work is that, at some point in time, companies will be expected to internalize the costs associated with greenhouse gas emissions, with consequent negative implications for costs, profits and asset values. However, the picture is not as clear-cut as the bald assertion that policy measures directed at internalizing the costs of greenhouse gas emissions will damage investors' financial interests. There are two dimensions to this. The first relates to the macroeconomic implications of climate change. Reports such as the Stern Report on the economics of climate change (Stern, 2006a) and the most recent evaluation by the Intergovernmental Panel on Climate Change (IPCC, 2007) highlight the very significant long-term risks associated with inaction on climate change; the Stern Report suggested that, at its most extreme, climate change could send the world economy into a slump on the scale of the Great Depression following the crash of 1929.[5] An economic catastrophe on this scale is unlikely to be in the interests of long-term investments like pension funds. While carbon taxes or other measures to encourage companies to reduce greenhouse gas emissions may impose short-term costs on companies, there will be significant economic opportunities; overall, therefore, on a macroeconomic basis, the short-term costs should be outweighed by the longer-term economic benefits (see, for example, International Energy Agency (2006) which argues that countries could implement a range of measures directed at reducing energy demand growth and greenhouse gas emissions and increasing energy security, where the benefits of using and producing energy more efficiently significantly outweigh the costs incurred). This conclusion is supported by the so-called 'universal investor' argument (Hawley and Williams, 2000), which suggests that the investment strategies of many large investors, mean that they are essentially permanent shareholders in many of the largest companies in the economy, and their performance reflects that of the economy as a whole more than the performance of individual companies. Hence, the actions that may be in the interest of an individual company – in this case, allowing greenhouse gas emissions to increase – may not be in the long-term interests of the economy as a whole as such emissions may expose other companies to the physical impacts of climate change.

The second reason why public policy activism on climate change may not conflict with investors' interests is that well-designed public policy should present significant opportunities for companies to innovate and create long-term shareholder value through, for example, the identification of new technologies, capturing new markets or through avoiding or reducing the need for defensive expenditures (e.g., to respond to increased risks of floods or extreme weather events). Achieving these kinds of benefits requires that public policy on climate change is focused on long-term goals, with the specific policy instruments being chosen on the basis of their ability to deliver on these goals (i.e., dependability) while also being economically efficient, minimizing transaction costs and stimulating innovation (see for a general view, Helm (ed.), 2005; Sullivan and Blyth, 2006). Far from running counter to companies' interests, it is interesting to note that a number of large electricity utilities have started to make these arguments to government. For example, Centrica has argued that the government should set 'bold' targets for cutting greenhouse gas emissions from 2008 onwards, and RWE has emphasized that companies need greater regulatory certainty and transparency regarding EU Emission Trading Scheme (Bream and Harvey, 2006).

11.5   Conclusion

There are a number of important conclusions that can be drawn from this chapter. The first is that enhanced analysis of social and environmental issues and investor engagement on these issues can – and has – led to significant improvements in corporate responsibility performance, in particular through amplifying the messages being given by regulators and other stakeholders. However, most of the benefits of this action have been limited to situations where there are reasonably clear drivers for action, for example, impending legislation, consumer pressure, media attention.

There is less evidence for the effectiveness of investor activity in situations when the drivers for action are weaker. In such situations, investors appear much less likely to encourage companies to take action. While the case of climate change seems to challenge this pessimistic assessment, it is probably fair to note that the central economic assumption that investors will act in their interests is not overturned; the justification for investor activism to encourage policy-makers to correct the climate change market failure remains rooted firmly in self-interest. However, the scope of this self-interest is substantially broader and longer term than would be expected. The premise that appears to underpin investor activism is that while new regulations to address climate change may be damaging to the interests of individual companies, any such costs will be com-pensated for by the greater benefits investors secure over the longer term. It also appears unlikely that the example of climate change will be replicated in rela-tion to other issues. The reason is that there is probably not another corporate responsibility issue that gives rise to anything like the long-term risk presented by climate change to investors' assets. The lack of similar activity on, to take just one example, access to medicines in developing countries is perhaps a case in point. No doubt interventions by rich world governments could do much to resolve the market failures that deny millions in developing countries access to medicines, but rich-country investors lack a compelling long-term financial interest in encouraging government interventions on these issues.

11.6   Questions

- On a corporate responsibility issue of your choice (for example, bribery and corruption, access to water, human rights), what arguments could you use to encourage investment managers to (1) take account of the issue in their investment analysis (2) use their influence as an investor to encourage indi-vidual companies to improve their performance on the issue?
- What are the key barriers to investor action on this corporate responsibility issue? How could these barriers be overcome?

11.7   Further reading

Sparkes, 2002; Sullivan and Mackenzie, 2006.

Notes

1. For a general overview of shareholder activism in Canada, Australia and the United States, see Sparkes (2002, pp. 311–365). For examples of activism in the United Kingdom, see Sullivan and Mackenzie (eds) (2006).
2. See, for example, the UN Principles for Responsible Investment which have been signed by over 350 asset owners and asset managers around the world, representing some US$14 trillion in assets under management. See http://www.unpri.org/
3. See, for example, the evidence presented by two of the leading activist asset managers in the United Kingdom, Insight Investment (2007) and F&C Asset Management (2007).
4. This section is based on Insight Investment and WWF (2005).
5. Stern's view is not uncontroversial, and the methodology and assumptions used to develop this conclusion have been challenged (see, for example, Nordhaus, 2006 and Dasgupta, 2006).

Sustainability Accounting and Reporting

12

Lorne Cummings

12.1 Introduction

This chapter provides readers with an understanding of the role that accounting systems can play in helping management determine an organization's impact on the natural environment. Accounting involves the definition, recognition, classification, measurement and disclosure of financial information for the benefit of stakeholders. Whilst accountants have specific processes for dealing with how business transactions flow through to the financial statements, environmental information poses unique challenges to the firm due mainly to the holistic nature of the environment, and the difficulty in attributing value to it. Much of what it represents is subjective and its consequences have broader social impacts beyond the firm.

The chapter, in Section 12.2, examines how sustainability is seen from a traditional principal agent perspective of contractual accountability and more formally through corporate fiduciary duty. Section 12.3 examines the systems and processes that help managers coordinate environmental information within the firm namely ISO 14000, life cycle assessment and eco-efficiency initiatives. Section 12.4 deals with measurement and analysis of environmental information on the financial statements including assets, liabilities and the various cost and expense categories. Section 12.5 deals with the various aspects of reporting on environmental/sustainability initiatives including the greenhouse gas reporting system, triple bottom line reporting and the global reporting initiative.

12.2 Sustainability: corporate, director duties, responsibilities

A corporation is governed through a series of contracts. Some of these contracts are formal (written) and are thereby *explicit*, such as those between the organization and its (1) *financiers*, which include repayment conditions and ratio covenants; (2) *employees* in the form of employment contracts; (3) *suppliers* in the form of delivery and costing schedules; and (4) *government*, in the form of taxation payments. Other contracts are unwritten and *implicit* such as those between the organization and society. All contracts contain both principals and agents, as illustrated in Figure 12.1.

Whilst informal or implicit contracts are not written, breaches may still result in penalties that can be imposed through consumer boycotts, class action lawsuits, protests or further government legislation or oversight, all of which can threaten the existence of the organization.

This model is representative of larger private-sector organizations, where there is a separation between the owners (principals) and the managers (agents) of the firm, or between managers (agents) of public-sector enterprises and taxpayers (principals). Under conventional expectations, the primary function of the firm was to produce profits and report to 'shareholders' as principals of the organization. In return, managers as agents would provide audited financial statements, budgets and regular disclosures to principals in the market, to demonstrate organizational accountability and stewardship.

Corporate social responsibility (CSR) was considered, like many ideas at the time, a radical concept during its inception in the 1970s. However, CSR has become more prominent in recent years as issues surrounding employee rights, corporate fraud and environmental degradation pose challenges for society, both developed and developing countries. Consequently, there has been a broadening of what society expects from business. Sustainability accounting and reporting, which are a contemporary manifestation of CSR have been more widely embraced since their inception in the early 1990s. 'Triple Bottom Line'

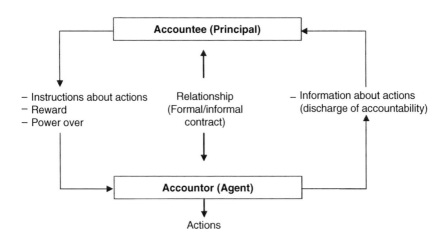

Figure 12.1   A generalised accountability model

Source: Adapted from Gray et al, 1996, p. 39.

(TBL) or sustainability reports, which are the reporting arm of CSR, are widely provided by organizations in addition to their formal reporting requirements.

Early literature on the theory of the firm held that the purpose of the organization was to maximize shareholder wealth. One of the most widely quoted references on the role of the organization has come from leading American economist Milton Friedman (1970) who stated that

> the cloak of social responsibility, and the nonsense spoken in its name by influential and prestigious businessmen, does clearly harm the foundations of a free society', and that 'there is one and only one social responsibility of business – to use its resources and engage in activities designed to increase its profits so long as it stays within the rules of the game.

At issue is what are 'the rules of the game', and do they change over time? Organizations do not operate within a social vacuum, and neither do the laws by which they are governed. What was an acceptable practice 50 years ago in business may not necessarily be acceptable today as changes in social mores and expectations alter what society expects of the organizations that serve it (see Chapter 2).

Neo-conservative scholars continue to oppose most CSR on the premise that the role of a firm is not to provide information to 'stakeholders' who have no direct financial interest in the organization. This would be deemed an unnecessary cost and would breach the long-standing principle enshrined in common law that a 'fiduciary duty' is owed to shareholders as opposed to a broader range of 'stakeholders'. What therefore is the corporate fiduciary duty?

Corporate fiduciary duty

'Stakeholder statutes'[1] in the United States require directors and/or officers to take into consideration the specific interests of 'stakeholders', and by default this fiduciary duty has traditionally been seen as maximizing wealth for shareholders. In Australia, the Corporations Act 2001 (Cth) does not prevent directors from taking into consideration the interests of constituents other than shareholders as the fiduciary duty of directors is owed to the corporation as a whole, as distinct from shareholders. Legislation does exist in Australia with respect to consumer protection, labour and environmental protection, which if contravened, could result in a breach of director duties to the corporation. This can lead to fines imposed on both individual directors and the corporation as a whole.

Of ultimate concern is whether the consideration of environmental and sustainability issues is contrary to the interests of the corporation and its shareholders. Traditionally adopting CSR was seen, at least by some in management, as burdensome and costly to the corporation. However, increasingly there are commercial benefits associated with being 'sustainable'. Being sustainable improves organizational marketability, increases production efficiencies and lowers litigation risks by reducing environmental hazards. Whilst sustainability initiatives involve an outlay of financial resources on new capital equipment and operational items (new systems and personnel), these are, in most cases, outweighed by the longer-term benefits of being sustainable (see Chapter 3).

Academics from a 'critical' perspective in accounting argue that CSR and sustainability accounting/reporting, solely serve the interests of the organization and operate primarily as a marketing and public-relations tool. They identify the lack of provisions within corporate legislation, accounting standards and independent verification (through external audits) as evidence of the failure by government and the accounting profession to treat this issue seriously. Furthermore, the ability by individual organizations and interest groups to influence policy agendas by lobbying politicians and standard setters undermines the importance of the fundamental concepts of sustainability. Standards and legislation are therefore driven by 'economic consequences' as opposed to 'core principles'.

Whilst being motivated by marketing/public relations purposes, CSR and sustainability accounting/reporting can be seen as a genuine means by which to lower overall firm costs by identifying more efficient, safer and cost-effective means of production, that in turn reduces firm risk. Of primary importance is how do organizations, in seeking to adopt a more sustainable approach to their operations, capture this in their accounting systems?

12.3   Accounting management and systems

An environmental management system (EMS) allows an organization to manage, and to a degree control, the effect of its activities on the environment. For sustainability accounting/reporting to be effective, it must be supported by an EMS. An EMS can help facilitate the (1) input of environmental information into the accounting system; (2) tracking of these inputs through the accounting system; and (3) output of this environmental information via the financial statements and annual report. An EMS contains important elements including an environmental policy, objectives and targets of the system, operational procedures, training and education, audit and compliance and system review. An effective EMS can have significant benefits for a service- or production-based organization. Benefits include minimizing wastage associated with paper for IT systems and e-waste raw materials, and promoting a more efficient allocation of resources (Staib, 2005, ch. 12).

ISO 14000

The most widely known EMS is the International Organization for Standardization (ISO) 14000 series, introduced in 1993. ISO 14000 is a broad-based voluntary series of standards which range from ISO 14001 – Core Standard; ISO 14004 – Detailed Guidance explaining 14001; ISO 14020 – Environmental Labelling and Declaration; ISO 14030 – Post Production

Environmental Assessment; ISO 14031 – Evaluation of Environmental Performance; ISO 14040 – Life Cycle Assessment; ISO 14050 – Terms and Conditions; and ISO 14064 – Greenhouse Gases (ISO, 2008).

The intention of the scheme is to reduce pollution, by providing an environmental management system framework by which organizations can assess their policies and strategies and integrate changes into the company's operations to improve profitability. This is critical for an overall environmental accounting framework as organizational policies and strategies, once operationalized, flow through to the financial statements. Peglau (2008) notes that, in January 2007, many have signed up to ISO 14000. Japan at 21,779 has by far the largest amount of registrations of all nations to date, followed by China at 18,979. India, with a comparable population size to that of China, and also being an emerging economy, has only 1,500 registrants. In addition, 1,964 Australian companies have signed up. The number of registrants in Japan and China, countries that have large manufacturing bases, indicate the extent to which these organizations (most likely manufacturing) place emphasis on incorporating sustainability initiatives into their systems.

Whilst a voluntary standard, companies are ISO 14000 certified through a quality certification assessment, which is an audit process to ensure that organizations actually comply with the standard. One of the more important components of an EMS that has a direct effect on the accounting system is that of Life Cycle Assessment.

Life cycle assessment and overhead allocation

To effectively identify, measure and categorize environmental costs within the accounting system, require a specific understanding of the various production or service phases of the organizations operational life cycle. Life Cycle Assessment or 'cradle to grave' analysis requires managers to assess and value the environmental impact of the organizations products and services, from the manufacturing phase (cradle) to the disposal phase (grave) (Staib, 2005, ch. 24). There are various environmental impacts that can be caused by the operations of an organization, including those shown in Table 12.1.

Table 12.1   Life cycle

Phase	Costs of impacts
Raw material acquisition	Costs incurred in extracting raw materials such as harvesting trees for wood, crude oil, i.e., pesticides
Manufacturing process	Costs associated with the manufacture of a product, i.e., oil, lubricants, water, cyanide
Waste management & recycling	Costs associated with the output of the manufacturing process, i.e., sludge, water, plastics, cyanide, airborne emissions

With respect to the *raw material acquisition* phase, organizations need to focus on identifying, and where necessary, reducing and eliminating environmental costs incurred as a result of extracting materials and other inputs into the production process. Reducing water flow rates in the raw material extraction process, using cheaper or alternate fuels to power machinery, using less toxic chemicals, all contribute towards lowering the environmental impact of the raw materials extraction process. Whilst the extraction of timber might involve the use of pesticides, which can be identified, and minimized, clearing of forests (especially old growth and rainforests) also reduces biodiversity. Smoke from burning undergrowth increases pollution, greenhouse gases and health costs, all of which are borne by society instead of the organization.

The organization also incurs environmental costs during the *manufacturing process*, which need to be minimized or if possible eliminated and replaced by other environmentally friendly processes. The use of cyanide as a basis for extracting gold from ore, a process called 'leaching', is one example of how certain high-risk manufacturing processes, can cause environmental costs that are devastating to local communities, reducing the welfare of future generations without the full cost being borne by the organization concerned.

The above-given example highlights that although organizations do bear a certain degree of financial cost associated with environmental negligence, it is impossible to fully capture the overall community and social costs of poor environmental management. Furthermore, alternate approaches do not necessarily eliminate environmental risk; they only reduce it for the organization. The development of cleaner technologies, including more environmentally friendly equipment and alternate chemicals can reduce the environmental impact of the manufacturing process. However, the extent to which these costs/possible delays exceed/do not exceed the costs for 'conventional' equipment and traditional gold extraction methods such as cyanide, and if they do/do not, the short- or long-terms effects on profitability are also important.

EXAMPLE

Cyanide Usage in Manufacturing

Apart from its use as a means for state executions, suicides and extermination during WW II, Cyanide also has a commercial application. It is used as a method of steel hardening and plastics production. It is also present in low concentrations in many plants, in the food we eat, and the cigarettes we smoke. Cyanide is an inorganic compound composed of carbon and nitrogen. It can exist in a solid, liquid or gas state. Levels of two parts per million are considered lethal to humans while concentrations as low as five parts per billion in river waters can inhibit fish reproduction.

Cyanide has been used for more than 100 years as a cost-effective means by which to extract gold from ore, a process termed 'leaching'. The leaching process requires solid cyanide briquettes to be added to a tanked mixture of finely crushed gold ore and water, which is then stirred for a number of hours. The solid cyanide dissolves in the water portion of the mixture, attacks the metal in the ore and forms the water-soluble complex, effectively 'dissolving' the gold from the ore. Thus, the metal has been extracted from a solid state (in the ore) to a liquid state (in the solution). The bursting of a cyanide tailings dam related to a mine owned by an Australian company, Esmeralda, in Romania in January 2000, allegedly caused 130,000 cubic metres of cyanide tainted water to flow into the Lupes, Somes, Tisza and Danube rivers, contributing a reduction in fishing stocks and associated health problems to residents. The tailings dam overflow in Romania is similar to an incident in South Africa in 1994 where 10 people were killed when a cyanide-laced dam bursts its banks, burying a housing complex. In 1995 some 3.2 billion litres of cyanide-laced waste flooded the Essequibo river in Guyana when a dam broke at the Omai gold mine. In June 1998, one woman died from cyanide poisoning after nearly 2,000 kg of the chemical spilled into the Barskoon River in Kyrgyzstan. A spillage by Australian company Dome Resources in Papua New Guinea in 2000, highlight the storage and transportation dangers of cyanide. A crate of cyanide pellets broke away from a helicopter near the company's Tolukuma mine site. Whilst the company reported that it recovered close to 95% of the cyanide in solid form, topsoil had to be removed from the 1250sq m crash site and detoxified. Furthermore, it was reported that a certain amount of cyanide had reached local streams.

There have been civil lawsuits in the United States by Native American Indian Reservations in Montana and Nevada to force companies to clean-up cyanide waste (Chatterjee, 1998). However in one instance, although the community won the lawsuit, the company declared bankruptcy the following year, hampering efforts to clean up the toxic site. Cyanide has been banned in some US states, and restrictions have been placed on its use in many other countries. Increasingly, other less harmful, but still potent chemicals have been used as an alternative to extracting gold from ore, including bromine, chlorine and iodine. Perhaps no single method can be used to totally eliminate environmental risk in gold mining, however alternate methods can reduce the environmental risk associated with the gold extraction process, and consequently lower the litigation costs to the firm. (Commonwealth of Australia (1998); Mineral Policy Institute (2000a, b))

Costs can also be incurred in the *waste management and recycling process.* Land-, water- and air-based emissions need to be identified, reduced and eliminated where possible. Increases in recycling initiatives are one example where product packaging can be made from biodegradable materials.

Much academic research has focused on the form and content of external reporting as a basis for analysing organizational impact on the natural environment but how these impacts are measured and recorded within the accounting system is of critical importance.

Understanding, identifying and subsequently controlling the costs throughout the life cycle process is important as a fundamental accounting concept is that of 'matching'. The matching concept states that expenses should be recognized in the same accounting period as and when the revenues generated from those expenses are recognized. Failure to appropriately account for the expenses that are associated with the gaining of revenue overstates accounting profit.

Management Environmental Accounting is the process of identifying, collating and analysing physical and financial information on environmental-related activities primarily for internal decision-making purposes (see Figure 12.2). Previously, 'Hidden Overhead', if not separately identified, would either be included in both Products A and B, or not captured at all, causing not only product and service mis-pricing (most often underpricing), but also more importantly a failure to address wastage problems in the manufacturing process.

Effective overhead allocation requires not only the ability to identify specific environmental-related activities, but also the ability to be able to accurately capture and allocate this through the accounting system. More specific transaction analysis requires the creation of sub-accounts within the accounting system. As Figure 12.3 indicates, instead of having purely a 'Conventional Overhead' account, an effective EMS would also allow for the creation of specific overhead accounts that would capture environmental-related costs that had been 'hidden' in conventional accounts.

Identifying overhead such as clean energy power costs (wind, solar) that would be in overhead accounts along with general fossil-based fuel costs (coal) allows for better tracking of environmental costs for decision-making purposes and to gauge the extent to which organizations are engaged in sustainability initiatives. Similarly, identifying cleaning costs associated with toxic spillages contained within a 'cleaning' overhead account as opposed to general cleaning and maintenance costs, allows the organization to focus on linking the toxic

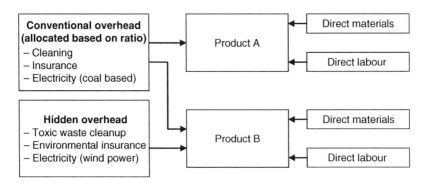

Figure 12.2   Overhead allocation

Source: Adapted from USEPA, 1995, p. 23.

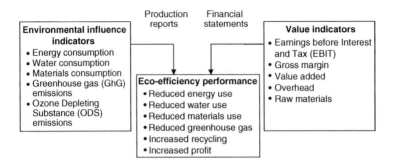

Figure 12.3   Eco-efficiency

costs with specific products or services. This not only allows an organization to target specific areas of concern in relation to environmental management, but also enables proper product and service margins to be determined, and initiatives implemented to address any fall in margins.

Eco-efficiency initiatives

Focusing on ways to reduce environmental impacts contributes to the maximization of eco-efficiency. Coined at the 2002 World Business Council for Sustainable Development (WBCSD) in Rio De Janeiro, eco-efficiency is the concept of creating more goods and services by utilizing less resources and reducing waste in the process, which in turn increases organizational profit. Eco-efficiency requires organizations to utilize both physical and financial indicators to increase eco-performance. Whilst life cycle assessment allows the organization to capture and reduce costs at the three stages (input, process and output) eco-efficiency seeks to link these costs with physical indicators of performance.

There are various ways in which eco-efficiency can be undertaken. Data on water, energy and materials usage and its associated costs can be used as a basis for deciding on the purchase of environmentally friendly equipment to replace inefficient conventional equipment. An organization's land holdings can be partially converted to wetlands which can be used as an effective way of reducing wastewater. Physical indicators along with associated financial data can be used as a basis for identifying cleaner production methods, reducing ongoing operational costs through the purchase of environmentally friendly supplies (light bulbs, recycled paper), installing water-saving devices and encouraging personnel to change their daily behaviour on resource usage (turning-off lights, printing on both sides of paper for computers, proper disposal of waste etc.). As Figure 12.3 illustrates, the range of different indicators on energy, water and materials consumption, in conjunction with the current costs associated with their use, can form the basis for deciding how to implement eco-efficiency initiatives.

E-waste (electronic waste) is a fast-growing category of waste in the world and includes waste associated with electronic or electrical products such as computers, monitors, printers, photocopiers, televisions etc. Many of these items appear as assets on the financial statements and are either replaced in perpetuity on leasing schemes or are purchased outright. If purchased outright, systems must be in place to dispose of such equipment. A large proportion of e-waste is disposed of by way of landfill, however much e-waste contains harmful elements such as mercury, lead and cadmium. A more economical approach for organizations is to upgrade, recycle or donate these materials.

Upgrading can often be as minimal as the replacement of one or more parts, which is less costly that a full capital acquisition of a new piece of equipment. Much e-waste can be recycled through suppliers or local computer stores or through local government initiatives. Certain e-waste can be donated for charitable purposes. Old computers that may not be compatible with new software or operational platforms may still be operational and useful in developing countries, or in not-for-profit or charitable organizations who do not require sophisticated and complex systems. This can be less costly and more practical for an organization than making direct financial donations.

Many organizations are today seeking to monitor their environmental operations through an 'ecological footprint'. The ecological footprint seeks to measure the extent of human impact on nature (WWF, 2006). Whilst it has been used to assess the extent to which local communities can reduce their 'footprint' on society by adopting sustainability initiatives, organizations can undertake their own ecological footprint by assessing to what degree their people and products effect the environment. An organization's ecological footprint can be reduced several ways, including, among others the following:

- organizing car pooling for employees;
- encouraging the use of public as opposed to private transport;
- installing energy saving devices in the office;
- planting shrubbery/trees around the organizational premises that utilize less water; and
- organizing teleconferences between organizations as opposed to flying commercially (where necessary) to reduce carbon emissions.

The footprint is measured using a quantitative approach and its importance from an organizational perspective is that by identifying the extent to which it impacts the environment in quantitative terms, the organization can be motivated to adopt less carbon intensive activities, by identifying and reducing operational inefficiencies associated with high carbon emitting activities (such as costly vehicular and air travel). Furthermore, there are benefits from a holistic perspective by being a good corporate citizen which enhances the corporate image whilst motivating staff, which in turn improves productivity.

Many organizations seek to promote their products as environmentally friendly. One way businesses can capture a greater market share and improve profitability is through 'eco-labelling' their products and services. Eco-label programmes have been instituted in many countries and labels include among others,

- Blue Angel – world's first worldwide environmental label (Germany);
- European Union Eco-Label – Voluntary Scheme to promote green products and services (European Union);
- Forest Stewardship Council – A non-profit organization that helps to promote the sustainable use of forests (Bonn, Germany);
- Good Environmental Choice – (Australia);
- ISO 14000 – International Environmental Management Standard;
- Marine Stewardship Council – A non-profit organization that helps to promote sustainable fishing (London, United Kingdom); and
- Dolphin Friendly Tuna – various labels across different countries. (Greener Choices, 2008.)

Most eco-labels are externally certified and are therefore authenticated. There are also labels which crossover into general social responsibility including 'Fair Trade Certified' which seeks to ensure that farmers from third world and developing nations receive a fair price for their product. All are part of the Global Eco-Labelling Network (2008). Organizational benefits can be achieved, first, through enhanced branding of products and services, which can increase organizational profit in the short term; second, by adopting a holistic perspective and being a good 'corporate citizen', this lower firm risk in the longer term.

12.4   Measurement and analysis

A considerable challenge for the accounting profession has been to determine to what degree the environment itself can be incorporated into the financial statements. Adopting a purely entity-based approach to accounting would limit the degree to which the natural environment can be directly incorporated into the balance sheet and income statement. However, there has been an increasing school of thought which adopts a 'holistic' (the philosophical perspective that the whole is more than a mere sum of the parts) approach to accounting (Ramboll, 2004). Holistic accounting moves beyond the traditional financial statements to include the human intellectual and natural environmental elements which involve aesthetic values and measures.

How then do the definitions of assets and liabilities fit the natural environment, and how do we identify the range of costs associated with environmental activities?

Assets

Is the environment an asset? Under the International Accounting Standards Board's (IASC, 2001) 'Framework for the Preparation and Presentation of

Financial Statements', 'assets' for financial statement purposes are defined as

> ...a resource controlled by the enterprise as a result of past events and from which future economic benefits are expected to flow to the enterprise. (para. 49)

Whilst items such as land, motor vehicles, plant and machinery satisfy this definition, the environment itself does not. The environment by its very nature cannot be 'controlled' by an entity. The environment is often seen as a free good that is for the benefit to all. There has often been debate as to the issue of heritage assets. Controversy often surrounds attempts to place a value on heritage assets such as national parks, as the reliability and relevance of the valuation is called into question. Most public-sector assets are not held for the purpose of sale (they have a value in use), so placing a fair value or market value on national parks is of no use if this information will not be used for decision-making. Even if a value is placed on it, what basis of measurement do we use? How do we account for the aesthetic value of such assets? Should trees and shrubbery that surround corporate premises be valued at the cost incurred to plant them or at their mature stage? Whilst the organization may incur the costs of tree planting and maintenance around corporate premises, these trees once mature are assets which enhance the positive well-being of employees of the organization, thereby increasing organizational value. Yet the environmental value of this is not separately identified in the financial statements but instead is included in overall goodwill upon the sale of the business or in the value of land and buildings as a whole.

Burritt and Cummings (2002) cover an excellent example of environmental accounting in action. Earth Sanctuaries Ltd (ESL) was the only public conservation company in Australia to operate sanctuaries for local wildlife. For the 1995–1998 financial years, ESL produced two sets of financial statements. The 'financial' accounts were produced according to conventional accounting standards, whilst the supplementary 'economic' accounts were voluntarily produced by the directors so as to include a value for 'wildlife' and 'habitat', that were not legally allowed to be recorded on the 'financial' accounts as they could not be sold, but which the directors felt embodied value for the company due to their attraction for eco-tourism, and so were included on a 'supplemental' set of accounts. The problem however was the value that had been placed on this 'wildlife' and 'habitat' which, using money spent by tourists visiting Australia, had no bearing on any fair or market value. In seeking to increase 'relevance' (an essential characteristic of accounting information) in its financial statements, the company compromised another essential characteristic, namely 'reliability' of the valuation method.

Liabilities

Is the environment a liability? Under the International Accounting Standards Committee's (IASC, 2001) 'Framework for the Preparation and Presentation of

Financial Statements', 'liabilities' for financial statement purposes are defined as

> ...a present obligation of the enterprise arising from past events, the settlement of
> which is expected to result in an outflow from the enterprise of resources embodying
> economic benefits. (para. 49)

The environment itself is not an 'entity' and therefore cannot stand before the
courts. As such it cannot be a liability unto itself. However, liabilities can be
recorded by organizations through a court order, statutory fines or voluntary
accepting of responsibility to another party. This can be for past environmental
practices that may have resulted in damage, neglect or breaches of regulations.
Cases often involve 'proof' that the organization committed an environmental
crime or event, and that the damage sustained was a result of this event, which
can be difficult. An accrual or payable is recorded when there is an obligation
for a fixed amount payable to another party.

If a company has voluntarily committed itself to rehabilitation and clean-up
costs, then these can be recognized as 'provisions' in the financial statements.
Under the International Accounting Standards, provisions are defined as a
'liability of an uncertain timing or amount'. With provisions, there is a present
obligation, albeit an uncertainly in timing or amount. This obligation can be a
legal (court or statutory order regarding environmental costs) or constructive
(organizations accept responsibility to another party for past action on environmental matters).

If an organization is defending itself against an ongoing legal action for environmental damage, and no outcome has been determined, then the organization would record a 'contingent liability' in the notes supporting the financial
statements. It would not be recorded as a liability in the organization's financial
statements as the outflow of resources is not 'probable' and the cost cannot be
'measured reliably'. However, as the organization may be liable in a court of law,
the information is 'relevant' information to external stakeholders and therefore
details of the contingent liability would be made via a note disclosure.

Costings and expenses

Some environment costs are *direct* costs to the organization. That is, the cost
can be specifically traced to a particular segment such as effluent output from a
manufacturing facility. Other environmental costs such as fines may be *indirect*
in that they are allocated from a general overhead account. Table 12.2 outlines
that range of different environmental costs and the ease by which they can be
identified.

Whilst conventional and hidden costs can be relatively easy to measure as they
involve costs that have already been incurred by the organization, some of these
may not be specifically categorized correctly. Contingent costs are likely costs,
but the amount is dependent on the outcome of a future judgement, whilst
relationship/image costs are clearly identifiable but the benefits associated with

Table 12.2   Types of environmental costs

Cost type	Measurement difficulty	Description
Conventional	Easy	*Cost accounting and capital budgeting oriented*: capital equipment, materials, labour, supplies, utilities, salvage value
Hidden	Easy	*Hidden from managers*: environmental insurance, storm water management, closure/decommissioning of equipment, feasibility studies
Contingent	Medium	*May or may not be incurred*: penalties and fines for spillages or regulatory breaches
Relationship/image	Medium	*Affect stakeholder perceptions*: sustainability reports, corporate philanthropy, clean-up campaigns
Societal	Difficult	*Cost of business impacts on society to which business is not legally responsible*: loss of natural habitat due to solid- or water-based emissions, health costs associated with air pollution

Source: USAEPA, 1995, p. 14.

these are more difficult to measure. Societal costs are imposed by the organization on its external environment. These include the affect of pollution such as increased health costs, lost productivity etc.

Social costs are extremely difficult to calculate from an organizational or societal standpoint although attempts have been made to estimate the cost of pollution and specific environmental events with respect to the overall GDP of an economy.

EXAMPLE

Societal Cost

Examples of the societal costs of commercial activities were the Indonesian forest fires of 1997–1998. Private agriculture and timber companies regularly engage in 'slash and burn' logging in East Kalimantan, Indonesia. The aim of the 'slash and burn' exercise was to clear the forest for agricultural use, mainly palm oil plantations. Local villagers argue that slash and burn allows the land to be more productive, leading to greater economic income locally. However, much of the logging was illegal and the extent of the burn off caused the fires to blanket Singapore and much of Malaysia with dense clouds of smoke and ash. The net welfare losses were estimated at US$20.1 billion; however, the true social costs are immeasurable. Haze from the fires caused flight cancellations and school closures. Health problems including asthma, nose, and eye irritations arose, leading many to wear surgical masks. As many people could not attend employment, there was a consequential loss of income/productivity to both the individual and the nation as a whole. Whilst the actions are caused by private companies, the effects are borne by

> the citizens. Despite the slash and burning being illegal, prosecutions rarely occur. The costs are therefore borne by individuals despite the fact that these costs are caused by organizations. Only a small proportion of these costs are ultimately incurred by the organization. (Varma, 2003)

There are also opportunity costs associated with failing to adopt environmental initiatives within the organization. Opportunity costs are defined as *the potential benefit that is lost or sacrificed when the selection of one course of action makes it necessary to give up a competing course of action* (Garrison and Noreen, 1994, p. 48).

EXAMPLE

Opportunity Cost

An organization may face a decision on whether to replace outdated machinery with cheaper conventional equipment, as opposed to environmental friendly equipment that may cost an extra $1,000,000. The decision to replace outdated equipment with the cheaper version may result in the organization forgoing $2,000,000 in efficiency savings over time that would have resulted from lower power and water usage with environmentally friendly equipment. The $2,000,000 represents the opportunity cost of not installing environmental friendly equipment.

Whilst there are the tangible benefits of efficiency gains and cost reductions, there are also intangible benefits of being associated with environmentally friendly equipment including a reduction in political costs associated with environmental protests, regulatory action and consumer boycotts etc. Whilst opportunity cost cannot be entered onto the financial statements of the organization, they must be factored into any strategic decision the organizational manager undertakes. Table 12.3 indicates the range of possible accounts that due to their association with the environment may appear on the financial statements.

Whilst certain costs can be easily classified into one of the above-mentioned financial statement classifications, often costs associated with business activity are not easily captured in the business statements. Such an example, as has been mentioned, is that of pollution. Whilst it is commonly understood that organizations often cause pollution, they do not always bear its full direct costs. These costs are absorbed by society though lost production, health complaints and a general decline in the quality of life. Some important criteria that could

Table 12.3   The impact of the environment on the conventional financial statements

Profit and loss account

Revenue	Expense
– Market growth	– Fines
– Market decline	– Health & safety claims
– Product taxes	– Plant depreciation
– Clean-up	– Compliance
– Effluent/emission control or reduction	– Waste minimization
– Waste treatment/disposal	– Licences/authorizations
– Insurance	– Research & development

Balance sheet

Asset	Liabilities	Equity
– Land revaluations	– Capital commitments	– Remediation (pollution damage)
– Plant write-offs	– Greenhouse gas	– Contingent Liabilities
– New plant	Emission provisions	– Natural asset Trust reserve
– Inventory (NRV)	– Breach of consents (fines)	(possible)
– Greenhouse gas Emission allowances		

Source: Adapted from KPMG – The National Environmental Unit in Gray et al., 1993, p. 23.

be incorporated into the text of the annual report, outside of the financial statements include

- the extent of adoption of quality control mechanisms of production;
- past compliance with statutory environmental regulations;
- degree of health and safety requirements;
- prior legal action taken against the organization;
- third-party audits of production facilities; and
- disclosure of physical data on environmental activities.

One of the more fundamental problems associated with accounting for the environment has been whether to measure and report on environmental activities using monetary or physical data or both. Whilst conventional accounting measurements include historical cost (the amount paid for an item), current/replacement cost (the cost to buy a similar item again), and market/fair value (the selling price in the market), there are other approaches that use a degree of estimation. Economic approaches utilize different monetary methods, whilst a physical approach is based on the use of imperial or metric measurements. Economic approaches include the following:

- *Market-price* – for example, loss on value of contaminated land or crops due to toxic emissions;

- *Hedonic-pricing* – estimates economic values for ecosystems or environmental services that affect market prices; for example, impact of air and water pollution, aircraft noise, aesthetics (trees) on housing prices;
- *Travel-Cost* – uses economic value of 'time' as the central indicator of willingness to pay for improvements in environmental quality. The more we visit the more valuable something becomes. for example, the elimination or addition of a recreational site, or changes to its environmental quality; and
- *Contingent-Valuation* – is a survey technique used to estimate an individual's maximum willingness to pay for a benefit/ improvement, or willingness to accept a loss, for an issue; for example, how much extra in taxes to improve the local environment including river streams, parklands and reserves (see Staib, 2005, ch. 8).

A physical approach would record accounts for natural and environmental resources based on physical units, without seeking to place a monetary valuation on the unit (refer Table 12.4). Such approaches are often used when seeking to determine the extent to which a nation's resources of rainforest, minerals etc. have been used or replenished over a given time period. The advantage of a physical approach to environmental measurement is that it is often easier for an organization to implement given the ease to physically account for depletion/replenishment etc. It also avoids organizations having to place dubious financial measurements on items which are often unreliable. However, the main disadvantage is that, unlike monetary measurements, physical indicators lack a common unit of measurement, which raises issues for consistency and comparability, which are essential characteristics of accounting information.

12.5   Reporting

Whilst much of the reporting on social and environmental activities has to date been voluntary, there has been progress towards mandatory reporting. Denmark, Norway, Sweden and The Netherlands have already implemented mandatory reporting requirements in the late 1990s (Scott, 2001, p. 24).

Table 12.4   Physical categories

Issue	Land	Air	Water
Biological resources used (minerals mined, trees cut down)	✓	✗	✓
Habitats protected	✓	✗	✓
Volume and percentage of water usage and recycling	✗	✗	✓
Number and volume of spillages	✓	✗	✓
Amount of acid rain	✓	✓	✓
Land used/eroded	✓	✗	✗
Emissions of ozone-depleting substances including carbon dioxide	✗	✓	✗

The increasing pressure by public interest groups and investors for verifiable, balanced and independent social and environmental information in light of corporate misbehaviour may very well lead to mandatory environmental reporting across most reporting entities in many countries in the not-so-distant future. By having such accounting and reporting systems in place now, organizations can reduce the costs of compliance if and when further mandatory requirements arise.

Arguments for mandatory reporting are that it would

- establish a minimum standard for business, which would require disclosure of both positive and negative information thereby reducing the possibility that the information is purely for public-relations purposes;
- enshrine a stakeholder perspective towards business; and
- prevent a free rider problem whereby only some companies disclose information to the market whilst others would be able to obtain related market-wide benefits.

Arguments against mandatory reporting are that

- the fiduciary duty of the manager is owed to the 'shareholders' not 'stakeholders', and as such social and environmental reporting confuses managerial obligations;
- organizations are of different size and industry make-up, therefore requiring all entities to produce the same information is too costly; and
- voluntary reporting ensures that only information demanded by the market is supplied to the market, thereby reducing information asymmetry.

In absence of significant mandatory reporting mechanisms, environmental reporting can fall into several categories ranging from being purely public relations to being a fully costed system that integrates financial and physical indicators, as indicated in Table 12.5.

Table 12.5   Elkington's five stages of development in environmental reporting

Stage 1	Green glossies, newspapers, videos, short statements in annual report.
Stage 2	One-off environmental report often linked to first formal policy statement.
Stage 3	Annual reporting linked to environmental management systems, but more text than figures.
Stage 4	Provision of full Toxic Release Inventory (TRI) style performance data on annual basis. Available on diskette or online. Environmental report referred to in annual report.
Stage 5	Sustainable development reporting linking environmental, economic and social aspects of corporate performance, supplied by indicators of sustainability.

Source: Elkington (1993).

To date much environmental reporting, whilst comprehensive, lacks structure and verifiability. Attempts have been made in recent years to build structure into the reporting framework. One structure that has emerged has been that of 'triple bottom line' reporting.

Triple bottom line

Triple Bottom Line (TBL) reporting (see Table 12.6) specifically focuses on reporting for the financial, social and environmental aspects of an organization: (1) Financial Reporting involves traditional value-added measures affecting financial statements; (2) Social Reporting involves value-added measures that impact upon human and social capital; and (3) Environmental Reporting involves value-added measures that impact upon both renewable and non-renewable resources.

The elements within TBL have been measured and disclosed by private, governmental and non-profit organizations for decades now, albeit in a rudimentary and ad-hoc form as a means by which to demonstrate accountability. Information in the reports is sometimes extracted from the financial statements themselves, but often involves the display of physical or non-monetary information. This information can be in quantitative (numbers) or qualitative (words) format, and it can include both positive and negative information, although in absence of formal reporting requirements this has been found to be most often positive (Deegan and Gordon, 1996).

Table 12.7 provides an example of a TBL report in financial format. Whilst an extensive TBL report is beyond the scope of this chapter, there are various other forms and structures for these reports. Alternative formats to the following example could include estimated pollution costs, physical data and actual vs budget comparisons (see also Chapter 8 and the case study in Part III).

Table 12.6   TBL reporting disclosures

Category	Positive examples	Negative examples
Financial (profit)	Profit, debt repayment, dividends paid, government taxes, conventional expenses	Loss, interest expenses on debt, political donations
Social (people)	Corporate philanthropy, health and safety programmes, training programmes for disadvantaged employees, gender and ethnic diversity	Workplace accidents and fatalities, sick leave taken, industrial action, cost of regional plant closures, child labour in foreign or domestic facilities
Environmental (planet)	Tree planting programmes, voluntary environmental clean-up campaigns, recycling initiatives, environmentally efficient capital equipment and energy consumption strategies	Carbon dioxide (CO_2) emissions levels, greenhouse gas emissions, ozone-depleting substance emissions, details on levels and locations of water effluent

Table 12.7   Example – TBL report

ABC corporation
TBL operating statement for the year ending June 30, 2XXX

	$
I. Social performance	
A. Improvements	**$**
1. Training programme for handicapped workers	60,000
2. Contribution to educational institutions	100,000
3. Building upgrades to accommodate handicapped workers	65,000
4. Day-care-centre expenses for employee's children	50,000
Total improvements	275,000
B. Less detriments	
1. Postponing installing new safety devices on cutting machines (cost of the devices)	120,000
2. Medical expenses for workplace accidents	36,000
Total detriments	156,000
C. Net improvements in social actions for the year	119,000
II. Environmental performance	
A. Improvements	**$**
1. Reclaiming and landscaping on company property	150,000
2. Installation of pollution control devices on manufacturing plant	30,000
3. Detoxifying waste from product finishing process	20,000
TOTAL IMPROVEMENTS	200,000
B. Less Detriments	
1. Cost that would have been incurred to re-landscape strip-mining site used this year.	80,000
2. Estimated costs to have installed purification process to completely neutralize liquid gases	100,000
3. Fines for Breaches of environmental legislation	60,000
TOTAL DETRIMENTS	240,000
C. NET DEFICIT IN ENVIRONMENTAL ACTIONS FOR THE YEAR	(40,000)
III. FINANCIAL PERFORMANCE	
A. Improvements	**$**
1. Net Profit	200,000
2. Dividends Paid	100,000
3. Government Taxes	90,000
TOTAL IMPROVEMENTS	390,000
B. Less Detriments	
1. Interest Expense no debt	30,000
2. Political donations	20,000
TOTAL DETRIMENTS	50,000
C. NET IMPROVEMENTS IN FINANCIAL ACTIONS FOR THE YEAR	340,000
TOTAL SOCIO-ECONOMIC DEFICIT FOR THE YEAR	419,000
Add OPENING BALANCE OF TBL IMPROVEMENTS AS OF JULY 1, 2003	179,000
CLOSING BALANCE OF TBL IMPROVEMENTS AS OF JUNE 30, 2004	598,000

Source: Adapted from Linowes (1972).

Given the voluntary nature of TBL reports, organizations can place emphasis on different aspects of TBL performance. Some organizations include more financial information than others. Emphasis can be placed on colour codes to demonstrate whether organizations have met environmental targets, or information can be displayed via Pie, Line or Bar charts. Comparative information can be presented to show variances in performance from year to year. Some organizations even have ten-year forward targets for desired emissions levels. Maroochy Shire Council in Queensland Australia is one example of a government organization that prepares TBL reports on an annual basis.

CASE STUDY

Maroochy Shire Council

Maroochy Shire Council in Queensland, Australia, has produced since the 1990s, performance data on economic, community (social) and environmental criteria within its annual report. This is presented over a six-year period, similar to financial statement and ratio data commonly seen in corporate annual reports.

The 2005/2006 annual report includes statistical trends on economic, community and environmental performance. *Economic* indicators include number of rateable properties, number and value of building approvals and number of airport flights and passengers per year. A further nine pages are specifically dedicated to various economic development issues. *Community (Social)* indicators include visits to the libraries per annum and number of library items borrowed, and customer contacts received at the call centre and over the counter. A further ten pages are specifically dedicated to various community issues. *Environmental* indicators include water supplied and sewerage treated in mega litres, kilograms of recycled waste per person and number of properties registered in Land for Wildlife (a voluntary programme administered by the non-profit organization 'Greening Australia' encouraging landholders to provide habitat for plants and animals on their properties). A further 19 pages are specifically dedicated to environmental issues.

Each of the additional sections across the economic, social and environmental categories include (1) services delivered that contribute to the priority of economic, community and environment; (2) other key performance indicators; (3) whether these indicators are increasing or decreasing; (4) highlights of what was achieved in 2005/2006 and what is intended to be undertaken in 2006/2007 and into the future. The text is interspersed with expenditure figures and pictorial content.

Whilst this is very comprehensive, and beyond that which is produced by many other organizations, and therefore is to be commended, the form and content of the report has changed over the years. In prior years there was an extensive list of indicators within a 'Triple Bottom Line' report including operating cash flow, external debt, current ratio, the number of council childcare users, amount of road reseal works (in km), trees planted by the local council and community, water reticulation services (km), sewerage services (km) and the number of complaints regarding drinking water quality. Furthermore, there is no indication that this data has been independently assured by an external auditor in previous years, although there is no reason to doubt its authenticity. For details of the 2006/2007 refer to Maroochy Shire (2008).

Increasing stakeholder pressure both from the community and industry peers has placed TBL firmly on the corporate agenda. High profile corporate collapses both in Australia and overseas have resulted in 'corporate governance' being an increasingly important topic for boards to deal with. Awards ceremonies such as the annual Australasian Reporting Awards (ARA, 2008) acknowledge both the quality of mandatory and voluntary reporting. Organizations are given gold, silver and bronze awards for the extent of their financial, social and environmental disclosure in their annual reports, which are voted on by industry peers and other professionals.

Global Reporting Initiative

Another programme which seeks to increase the level of transparency by organizations has been the introduction of the Global Reporting Initiative (GRI, 2008). Begun in 1997 as a Centre of the United Nations Environment Programme, its purpose is to develop and disseminate globally applicable 'Sustainability Reporting Guidelines'. These guidelines include social and environmental indicators which are applied using technical protocols to ensure consistency with respect to definitions, procedures, formulae and references. These are supported by issue guidance documents and specific sector supplement to ensure flexibility (see Figure 12.4).

The guidelines are voluntary, and like TBL reporting, and report on the organizations economic, environmental and social dimensions of their activities, products and services. The GRI is increasingly being seen as the international benchmark for sustainability reporting. As accounting standards are now subject to an international benchmark, being International Financial Reporting Standards (IFRS), increasingly sustainability reporting is facing similar pressures, given the global nature of social and environmental issues such as climate change, the costs of which do not distinguish between jurisdictions.

Greenhouse gas reporting system

Another area of emerging importance for management with respect to environmental management and reporting is the specific issue of accounting for greenhouse gases, which will become more prominent for accountants and organizations in the years ahead. The Kyoto Protocol to the United Nations International Framework Convention on Climate Change (UNFCC, 2008) requires ratifying

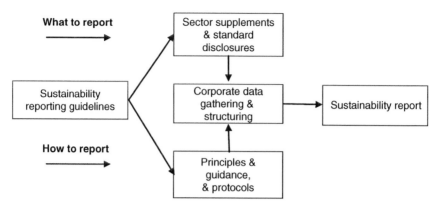

Figure 12.4   GRI reporting framework
Source: Based on GRI, 2006.

countries to commit to reducing greenhouse gases to set amounts below 1990 emission levels by 2012. These gases identified by the Framework Convention on Climate Change (UNFCCC, 2008) are carbon dioxide, methane, nitrous oxide, sulphur hexafluoride, hydrofluorocarbons and perfluorocarbons. There has, and continues to be, political debate surrounding treaty ratification, based on the economic consequences of committing to targets, that to a large extent impose costs on government and industry (Lyster, 2007). Market-based emissions trading schemes are being set up to create incentives and penalties for manufacturing based organizations to adhere to these set targets.

In Europe and the US state of California (and currently under consideration in Australia from 2010), greenhouse abatement schemes involve a 'cap and trade' mechanism, where organizations are allocated permits (capping) allowing them to emit a certain level of emissions. If an organization emits above or below this amount then they can buy or sell permits in an open market (trade). This would be supported by mandatory assurance and verification requirements and reporting requirements.

The greenhouse gas reporting system will raise issues for accountants with respect to how it impacts the accounting system in terms of measurement and formal reporting. From an accounting perspective, and in response to the EU's Kyoto Protocol Commitment on Climate Change, businesses that emit carbon-based emissions can purchase (or be allocated) emissions allowances, which are designated as 'intangible assets' and which diminish in value over time and, as mentioned, are tradable in an open market. Businesses exceeding their allowance, can purchase additional 'emission credits' or incur a liability. That is, as greenhouse emissions are made by organizations, a provision/liability is to be recognized for the obligation to deliver allowances to cover those emissions (or to pay a penalty), which is opposite to the allowance which is to be treated as assets.

The International Financial Reporting Interpretations Committee (IFRIC) 3 *Emission Rights* developed specific requirements to account for emission rights or similar schemes, but the International Accounting Standards Board (IASB) unexpectedly withdrew IFRIC 3 in June 2005 on the basis of an assessment that there was no urgency for such an Interpretation in Europe, despite the introduction of the ETS six months earlier. The IASB claimed that the withdrawal would allow it to address the underlying accounting treatment on the issue in a more comprehensive way than IFRIC 3 (IASB, 2005). However, it was argued that the primary reason for the withdrawal of the Interpretation was the European Financial Reporting Advisory Group's vote against it (Brackney and Witmer, 2005).

In summary, how does an organization seek to develop a sustainability report? What are the steps that organizations need to follow to ensure that a comprehensive reporting mechanism is in place? Seven key steps are outlined in Table 12.8. Overall organizations that seek at least some form of sustainability

Table 12.8   Steps for developing a sustainability report

1 – Investigate rationale
- Identify potential benefits and pitfalls in producing a report
- Identify the scope and coverage
- Assess costs and benefits and attain top management commitment

2 – Identify key stakeholders
- Identify key stakeholders and their needs in a report, both at this initial stage by consultation and at the review stage through feedback mechanisms

3 – Identify key aspects and impacts
- Identify key environmental and/or social and/or economic issues and resulting significant aspects for reporting purposes

4 – Develop performance indicators
- Identify and prioritize relevant (operational and management) performance indicators and condition indicators for reporting purposes

5 – Set objectives and targets
- Set appropriate performance objectives and targets including time lines aimed at meeting established commitments for sustainability performance

6 – Measure and evaluate
- Develop a framework for measurement including data collection, collation and evaluation

7 – Strengthen effectiveness of communication
- In reporting, ensure honesty, clarity, neutrality, credibility, continuity, validity, understandability, relevance, completeness and comparability. Independent verification may also provide additional external assurance to readers

8 – Publish, distribute, use and review
- Choose reporting format(s) and period that suits your organizational and stakeholder requirements
- Distribute and use the report appropriately
- Include a feedback mechanism and contact details for feedback, queries and further information
- Review feedback; environmental, social and economic aspects; environmental, social and economic indicators; stakeholder needs and objectives and targets

Source: DEWaterHArts (2008).

accounting or reporting benefit in that its relationships with stakeholders are improved. Employees are more motivated, customer confidence in the organization's products and services increases, which provides the organization with a competitive advantage over its competitors. This in turn lowers the risk that regulatory bodies will impose penalties on the organization, which increases firm value and improves the organization's investment appraisal and attractiveness for investment (ibid).

12.6   Conclusion

This chapter has sought to highlight some of the issues surrounding accounting for environmental management within the organization. Whilst the principal agent relationship within the firm traditionally encompassed the shareholder (principal), creditor (principal) and manager (agent), a broadening of the social contract has resulted in the need to demonstrate accountability to a wider range of stakeholders. Whilst traditionalists have argued that this undermines the fiduciary duty of the firm, corporate and director duties as they stand in Australia apply to the corporation as a whole as opposed to shareholders specifically.

For sustainability to be effective it is essential that there be an environmental management system to help facilitate the input of environmental data into the accounting system, track the progress of this data through the system and display this information in an effective structured format through outputs in the form of the formal reporting mechanism. ISO 1400 is one example of an environmental management system that is globally accepted. One important element of the ISO 14000 series is the need for organizations to consider life cycle assessment. That is, effective identification, measurement and categorization of environmental costs within the accounting system, requires a specific understanding of the various production or service phases of the organization's operational life cycle, from raw materials acquisition to the manufacturing process to waste management and recycling. Failure to consider and manage the environmental risks inherent within each of these three phases can result in environmental disasters during the production process.

Of equal importance is the need to be able to appropriately identify environmental costs within overhead accounts. Traditionally environmental costs have been included in overall overhead and allocated disproportionately to products and services. However, environmental management systems allow organizations to better trace environmental costs to specific products and services thereby resulting in more accurate pricing. The ability to separately identify environmental costs increases eco-efficiency within the organization. That is, more goods and services are created by using less resources and reducing waste across the areas of energy, water and resource consumption. Organizations can undertake an ecological footprint of their organizations activities to determine their impact on the environment and further reduce costs. Having their products and services certified with a specific 'eco-label' scheme is another way to positively contribute towards environmental management. This promotes the organization's brand which in turn may increase sales and profits.

There are also conceptual issues relating to treating the environment as an asset. From the organization's perspective the environment cannot be controlled, and therefore cannot appear on the financial statements. Consequently it is often treated as a 'free good' to the organization and consequently can be 'misused'. Likewise the organization cannot owe a liability to the environment as the environment is not a legal entity unto itself. Liabilities can only be imposed through statutory or court-imposed costs, or where liabilities for environmental costs have been incurred to another individual or organization. Court-imposed costs for environmental damage may not mirror actual costs imposed on society as a whole as there is difficulty in identifying and estimating the full social costs incurred by present and future generations from organizational activities that harm the environment (e.g., pollution). Whilst some environmental costs are easily identifiable, others like pollution are more difficult.

Organizations can engage in sustainability reporting (environmental, social and financial) as a means by which to demonstrate accountability to the broader constituency. Issues arise over whether this reporting needs to be mandatory or voluntary. Whilst mandatory reporting may impose additional costs on organizations, voluntary reporting suffers from the perception that sustainability reporting will become a public-relations exercise if it is not independently verified and the reporting structure between organizations is not consistent and comparable (as financial statements are). Triple Bottom Line reporting (Economic, Social and Environmental) has emerged as one structure and the Global Reporting Initiative, which is fast becoming the international benchmark for sustainability reporting, builds upon this by providing a range of performance indicators across these economic, environmental and social dimensions of the organizations activities, products and services.

Whilst much sustainability accounting and reporting has so far remained ad hoc, the emergence of Emission Trading Systems (ETS) in Europe and the United States, and a forthcoming ETS in Australia in 2010, has placed increasing pressure on accountants to seriously consider and address not just the reporting aspects of climate change, but also fundamental measurement and recognition issues, that to date have not been the subject of significant attention at the standard setting level.

Given the increasing complexities of global business in the twenty-first century, and the increasing pressure placed on the natural environment to fuel development, an understanding of mechanisms which lead to more accurate and informed organizational decision-making not only provide transparency but also reduce long-term costs associated with business operations, which can only lead to benefits for both business and society.

12.7   Questions

- Access an annual report from the website of an organization, be it private or government. Does it contain any information on sustainability, and if so in what form? Consider the following criteria with respect to sustainability information:
- Is the sustainability information predominantly positive and self-promotional as opposed to being negative and self-critical?
- Does it contain more text-based as opposed to statistical-based material?
- Does it have a structured format?
- Is it independently verified and if so by whom?
- Pollution is given in this chapter as one example of how the negative effects of the organization flow onto the society at large. List down some economic costs to society that result from pollution that do not necessarily appear on the financial statements of the organization. Correspondingly, list some initiatives that an organization can implement that can add value to society by improving the environment that are not necessarily recorded on the financial statements.

12.8   Further reading

Schaltegger and Burritt, 2000; Schaltegger et al., 2003.

Note

1. Thirty (30) states in the United States now have some form of stakeholder constituency statutes that permit directors to consider constituencies other than shareholders in performing their fiduciary duties (Springer, 1999). Polonsky and Ryan (1996, p. 8) state that under the Pennsylvania Statute, corporations
   - 'may in considering the best interests of the corporation, consider the extent they deem appropriate [t]he effects on any action upon any or all groups affected by such action, including shareholders, members, employees, suppliers, customers and creditors of the organisation, and upon communities in which offices or other establishments of the corporation are located' (Pennsylvania, #515(a)(1)),
   - are not to consider any corporate or group interest as 'dominating or controlling' (Pennsylvania, #515(b)),
   - are not to act in any way solely because of the benefit of that action on an acquisition or the price paid to shareholders on an acquisition (Pennsylvania, #515(c)).

Legal Aspects and Compliance

13

Patricia Ryan

13.1 Introduction

Laws support provision and distribution of food, shelter, transport, finance, communications and other services and goods. They are used to protect, and exploit, people, natural resources, relationships, status and products of labour and intellect. Little in human and business life has not been touched by law in either a restrictive or facilitative way. Yet laws rarely eliminate tensions between different values and influences in society; balances struck separately within environmental and business law fields reflect contemporary politics. For governments, regulatory law may also simply offer cheaper options than direct spending on incentives, compensation or infrastructure. Sustainability policy, however, in environmental law has enormous potential to impact upon, and interface with, business law in pursuit of a seamless sustainability culture encompassing governments, businesses, communities and individuals. Significantly, interest in sustainability firmed dramatically after the Intergovernmental Panel on Climate Change advocated massive reduction in greenhouse-gas-related energy consumption (IPCC, 2007). This topic examines sustainability implications for legal controls and compliance.

13.2 Business law overview

Business directly benefits from legal facilitation and recognition of commercial bargains and exchanges, backing of property and other claims and regulation of anti-competitive practices. It also ultimately gains, with society, from government intervention in broader interests of public security, safety, amenity and health. Some business law principles reflect ages-old, culturally universal, commercial customs, enshrining human values of honesty, trust, mutual care, prudence and careful planning. These *stewardship* notions underpin agency, trusteeship, partnership and corporations laws in common law jurisdictions, where fiduciary duties oblige persons exercising discretionary powers in relationships of trust and confidence to act prudently and loyally in the best interests of the duty recipient. Case-law origins of the duties means there is some overlap in different common law jurisdictions because law in one jurisdiction may be informed by case-law in other jurisdictions. Civil law jurisdictions often formulate similar duties to act diligently and prudently in like circumstances.

Contemporary business law struggles to respond to changing business environments comprising giant corporations – with revenues exceeding those of nation-states, rapidly evolving technology and novel markets. Finance, corporations, insolvency, investment and competition laws, for example, often seem to deliver neither good businesses nor good law. In general, too, business law, excepting trade law, has not developed at an international level anywhere near the extent of environmental law.

Sustainability context

Environmental law may inhibit, or expand, business options. Only relatively recently, has it taken both an international and holistic sustainability direction, as distinct from ad hoc domestic responses to environmental issues (Ryan, 2005, pp. 63–64). Some business leaders have also voluntarily embraced a sustainability critique, recognizing that businesses benefit from environmental services, including water management, biodiversity protection and climate change regulation.

Sustainability is not uniformly defined internationally or nationally. The global goal of 'development that meets the needs and aspirations of the present without compromising the ability to meet those of the future' (WCED, 1987, p. 40) is generally referenced to complementary principles necessary for careful decision-making:

- *sustainable use:* prudent or wise use of natural resources so that development improves total quality of life now and in the future by maintaining life processes;
- *integrated decision-making:* effective integration and mutual reinforcement of economic development, social and environmental protection considerations;
- *precautionary principle:* measures to prevent environmental degradation should not be postponed because of lack of full scientific certainty concerning scope and nature of threats of serious or irreversible environmental damage;
- *inter-generational and intra-generational equity:* the present generation should ensure environmental health, diversity and productivity are maintained or enhanced for the benefit of future generations, and equity considerations (environmental justice) must govern enjoyment of clean and healthy environments among sectors and nations of the present generation;

- *conservation of biological diversity and ecological integrity:* diversity of life in terms of genetic, species and ecosystem variety is a fundamental consideration at any stage of development decision-making;
- *internalization of external environmental costs:* environmental factors should figure in the valuation of assets and services, so polluters and waste generators bear full costs of containment, avoidance or abatement; users of goods and services should pay prices based on full life-cycle costs, including use of natural resources and waste disposal; and those best placed to maximize benefits or minimize costs should develop their own solutions and responses to environmental problems.

Sustainability principles do not preclude using Earth's resources or competing for them; nor mandate particular adaptive strategies, internationally or nationally. Typically, business, government and community organizations seek 'balanced' certainty and flexibility, with national laws that define and promote sustainability for specific purposes also offsetting any new obligations with specific public powers and private rights accrued under previous legal regimes. Even decisions made within highly coercive frameworks, however, cannot ultimately remove contextual (including professional, industry-related, educational and personal) decision-making influences. Flexible sustainability decision-making boundaries are further boosted by lack of international mechanisms capable of delivering consistent, principled, enforceable, legal guidance.

13.3   Environmental law overview

Domestic environmental law provides a remarkable raft of techniques (including criminal penalties, licensing, citizen suits, performance bonds, labelling, registration, reporting, audit, special insurance, remediation, community right-to-know, emissions trading, discharge taxes and due care requirements) for addressing concerns including environmental impact assessment and planning; natural ecosystem and resource conservation and management; environmental protection from harmful activities; waste avoidance and management. Unilateral national law, however, cannot redress transboundary and global problems. Internationally, multilateral action has mainly flowed from the 1972 Stockholm Conference on the Human Environment that gave rise to the United Nations Environment Program (UNEP) and 1992 Earth Summit in Rio de Janeiro; with less follow-up from the 2002 Johannesburg World Summit on Sustainable Development.

International environmental law mainly comprises treaties (legally binding agreements among nations, ratified – not just signed – by their governments and voluntarily implemented under national domestic legislation) and non-binding guidelines adopted in international processes, but lacking formal means of enforcement. International agreements may be specific, or general with action-oriented protocols, or codifications of a broad area. They need not be coercive and may exhort action by agreeing on needed policies, development assistance, quantitative targets or timetables. They may involve very small to very large groupings of nations. Treaty obligations potentially bind nations only, and are not even indirectly enforceable against individuals or corporations unless treaties underpin domestic law obligations. Figures 13.1 and 13.2 show trends in making of international agreements. Some of these agreements will be manifest in legislation by ratifying countries and impact the obligations of business organizations.

Environmental matters covered by international instruments (UN, *Treaty Collection*) include the following:

- *international environmental governance:* Global Environmental Facility; Rio Declaration of 27 principles for environmental decision-making; Agenda 21 sustainability policy framework; UN Commission on Sustainable Development; Johannesburg Declaration and Plan of Implementation;
- *marine environment:* Law of the Sea; marine pollution, including oil and dumping of waste and other matter at sea; carriage of hazardous and noxious substances by sea; marine mammal action plan;
- *climate and atmosphere:* long-range transboundary air pollution; ozone layer protection and Montreal Protocol; climate change framework and Kyoto Protocol;
- *biodiversity, heritage and nature conservation:* Antarctic environment and living resources; world cultural and natural heritage; desertification; endangered species of world flora and fauna; migratory species of wild animals; biological diversity and Cartagena Protocol on Biosafety; forest principles; tropical timber;
- *hazardous material:* transboundary movements and disposal of hazardous wastes; hazardous chemicals and pesticides; persistent organic pollutants; nuclear tests and material.

Excepting ozone depletion, environmental treaties have not halted these major problems: acid rain and regional air pollution; climate change from greenhouse gases; deforestation; land degradation, including desertification, erosion, compaction and salinization; freshwater degradation and scarcities; marine threats, including over-fishing, habitat destruction, acidification and pollution; health threats from persistent organic pollutants and heavy metals; declining biodiversity and ecosystem services through loss of species and ecosystems; excessive nitrogen production and over-fertilization (Speth and Haas, 2006). The 2007 Paris Call for Action (seeking a new UN environmental organization to coordinate government action and promote funding, research and technological advancements) foundered because of non-confidence in international governance mechanisms.

Non-treaty norms come from established international customs, general principles of law of civil nations, judicial decisions and writings of eminent publicists. The relatively few non-treaty principles have focused on requiring nation states to ensure activities within their jurisdictions do not harm environments of other states or areas beyond national jurisdiction and requiring states to advise neighbours of activities capable of transboundary harm (Boer, Ramsay and Rothwell, 1998, pp. 4–5).

EXAMPLE

Trends in Numbers of International Environmental Agreements

Figure 13.1 shows that the number of treaties deposited with the United Nations is growing and includes an increasing number of environmentally based treaties since 1980.

Figure 13.2 shows how the increasing trend in the number of Multilateral Environmental Agreements being agreed. 'Multilateral Environmental Agreements (MEA) are a subset of the universe of International agreements. What distinguishes them from other agreements is their focus on environmental issues, their creation of binding international law, and their inclusion of multiple countries. Over the years, many MEAs have been negotiated and agreed at the international and regional levels. Some have a few Parties; some have almost global participation' (UNEP, *circa* 2006).

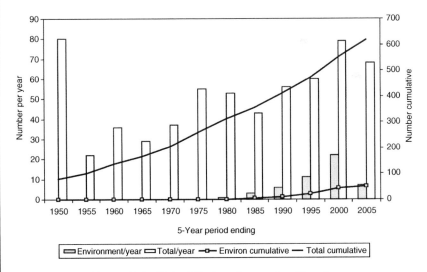

Figure 13.1   United Nations: International Treaties

Note: The numbers include 'major multilateral instruments deposited' as of 1 January 2006 and 'multilateral treaties recently deposited with the Secretary-General not yet published in the United Nations Treaty Series'.

Source: United Nations Treaty Collection, 2008.

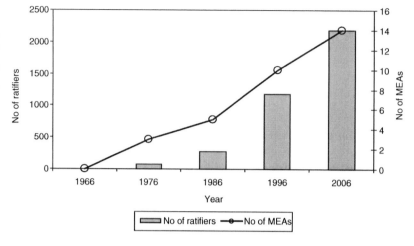

Figure 13.2   Multilateral environmental agreements

Source: United Nations Environmental Program (2007), summary of Figure I.I. Agreements reported are: Basel, CBD, CITES, CMS, World Heritage, Kyoto, Ozone, Ramsar, Rotterdam, Stodkholm, UNCCD, UNCLOS, UNFCCC and Cartagena.

Shaping environmental law

Why is so much environmental law eventuated since the 1970s, despite organized opposition, not fully understood (Percival, 1998, pp. 11–15; Ryan 2001; Speth and Haas, 2006). Part explanations include massive post-World War II social and economic transformations in public values favouring environmental legislation; charismatic public movement leaders; new political activism committed to ongoing influence of, rather than sporadic involvement in, regulatory processes; widening appreciation of environmental impacts, frequently associated with trigger events (such as the 1984 Bhopal chemical leak in India and the 1990 Exxon Valdez oil spill); action-research by academics; environmental advocacy backed by sound science and economics; new technologies for multi-dialogue communications and complex data-handling; multimedia reporting; specialist journalism; reformist champions; emergence of new nations from former Western colonies; and development of an agenda for international action against a mixed background of environmental and development concerns.

Nowadays, diverse environmental organizations exist in various institutional settings, with a major, if not primary, role of influencing environmental legislation. Widely different agendas of these organizations, together with diverse agendas of the regulated community, help shape an intricate policy process; with consensus-building emerging as an important legislative design component. This is evident in the United Kingdom (UK) *Climate Change Bill* (which offers a strategic suite of emissions trading, reduction targets, carbon taxes, regulations, carbon accounting, judicial review of government action and independent expert assessment of government performance), more than in the United States (US) *Climate Stewardship and Innovation Bill*, also introduced in 2007. In common law jurisdictions, like the UK and US, case law may also play a major role in shaping and interpreting parliamentary legislation. (In other jurisdictions, rules tend to be set in codes or other formal instruments, and litigation is not decided on case-law precedents). Despite, increasing climate change litigation (Lyster, 2007, pp. 300–309), however, the common law court role of settling definable legal issues between identifiable litigants provides scant scope for the political exercise of balancing wide-ranging, competing, sustainability interests.

Green political parties are raising sustainability policy stakes by pressuring governments for trade arrangements, which both uphold human rights and protect the environment; reject trade regimes that concentrate control over intellectual property and require privatization or diminished government roles in education, health and welfare; prohibit trade in goods and services produced through exploitation of children, human trafficking and in disregard of core labour standards; and provide incentives to developing countries to encourage local development and participating citizenry. Sharply declining environmental quality also has reinvigorated attempts by IUCN – the World Conservation Union to recast sustainability with greater environmental focus, including ecosystems conservation, payments for ecosystems services and internalization of environmental costs.

Transnational non-governmental and local government policy and action networks underscore the fact that national governments need not be the central players. Yet effective macro-level environmental policy responses are severely hampered by cross-scale and cross-level interactions (Cash et al., 2006). Speth and Haas (2006, pp. 102–103) concluded international efforts were mostly *not* 'notably successful', because of systemic and procedural obstacles, lack of necessary conditions, special characteristics of international environmental issues, the relative importance given to economic considerations and 'morphing' of environmental problems into new ones as corporations skilfully find ways around treaty restrictions. Lyster (2007, p. 321) was more optimistic, believing a heightened cumulative impact of worldwide regulatory efforts, litigation and corporate initiatives would force public and private sectors to reduce their climate change footprints, and correct 'the greatest and widest-ranging market failure ever seen' (Stern, 2007).

13.4   Environmental and business law relationships

If environmental law did reduce consumption and limit growth, business activity would continue, with some businesses developing new environmental products and services. Sustainability adaptation spawns new markets to capture economic value from previously unvalued or undervalued ecosystem resources, through ventures such as water quality trading, carbon and biodiversity off-sets, wetland and endangered species banking (Stigson, 2007). Fundamental concerns over maintaining competitiveness, however, have been identified with respect to Kyoto Protocol and successor climate change measures. For instance, non-Protocol states, not subject to carbon constraints, may enjoy unfair advantages; and treaty implementation by party-states may create unfair advantages for their domestic industries.

International trade law

Major interface issues between the Kyoto Protocol and World Trade Organization (WTO) rules arise with respect to tariff and other trade restrictions to induce Protocol compliance; trade negotiations on environmental goods and services; subsidies such as for biofuels; border tax adjustments to offset competitiveness losses from carbon taxes; design and adoption of energy standards; energy-related eco-labelling about product characteristics and manufacture; government procurement programmes; allocation of emission trading permits; investment conditions for projects granted Clean Development Mechanism status; and tariff preferences for developing countries (Cosbey and Tarasofsky, 2007, pp. v–vii). Although there is little inherent legal conflict, a stable relationship between the two regimes requires clarification of WTO law and selection of compatible Kyoto trade measures (Cosbey and Tarasofsky, 2007, p. 25). This highlights how progress on international law covering environmental and trade issues has been pursued separately within the two areas, without real regard for integration. Consequently, trade and trade regulations remain the general rule, with social and environmental protection the exception (Kennedy, 1996; Albala, 2003).

Corporations and management law

Corporations law preoccupation with internal management might mean environmental issues could be better regulated using this lens (Bubna-Litic, 2007, p. 254). As there is no overarching international law of corporations, myriad national laws govern their creation, dissolution, structure, capital-raising, management, operation and reporting and the democratic machinery of corporate governance. There is a sustained debate about which stakeholder interests, if any, corporations law should recognize as 'corporate best interests'. While directors cannot excuse non-compliance with environmental laws by arguing non-compliance harms corporate or shareholder interests, corporations laws have elevated shareholder-members over other interests, despite stewardship notions being less appropriate for modern dispersed and institutional shareholdings (Hay, 1990).

Under narrow views of corporate best interests, senior managers still need to reconsider any assumptions that preclude their considering major environmental issues. The care and diligence legally required of 'reasonable management' possibly already accommodates such considerations. Building upon recent legal obligations in various countries for corporations to report environmental and social performance and broaden their reporting constituencies (Bubna-Litic, 2007, pp. 269–276), management of sustainability risks as 'material business risks' is becoming seriously associated with good corporate governance principles and practice (Lyster, 2007, pp. 309–313). A strong synergy between environmental and corporate law, however, has been difficult to establish, even in environmentally conscious countries such as Norway and the Netherlands (Bubna-Litic, 2007, p. 257).

The UK *Companies Act* 2006 boldly initiated statutory directors' duties to consider member interests *plus* long-term likely consequences of decisions; employee interests; relationships with suppliers, customers and others; environmental and social impacts of corporate business; fairness between members; and importance of maintaining a reputation for high standards of business conduct, highlighting relationships between responsible business behaviour and business success. Traditionally, corporations laws reduce litigation risks for corporations by leaving broader community concerns like the environment, employment, anti-competitive practices or consumer protection to specific-purposes laws.

Internationally, the UN *Global Compact* promotes voluntary minimum standards of worker protection, human-rights, anti-corruption and environmental protection. OECD *Guidelines for Multinational Enterprises* additionally cover consumer protection, technology transfer, anti-competitive behaviour and disclosure of corporate information (including corporate risk factors potentially including social, ethical and environmental policies). Although *UN Norms on Responsibilities of Transnational Corporations and Other Business Enterprises with Regard to Human Rights* place primary duties upon nation-states to ensure corporations respect human rights, an emerging international law principle would oblige non-state entities to respect human-rights values, including environmental values (Freshfields Bruckhaus Deringer, 2005, p. 34).

Finance and investment law

Nationally, investment decision-making rules comprise specific laws (about permitted asset types, for example) and general duties (such as diversified investment obligations). The rules do not prescribe how to integrate sustainability considerations into investment decisions; mostly, decision-makers are free to determine the approaches most suitable for meeting legal obligations in their particular circumstances. Attempts to negotiate a multilateral investment agreement having failed, there is no agreed international regulation of investment (Freshfields Bruckhaus Deringer, 2005). Financiers and investors do, however, have a real interest in how corporations manage sustainability risks and their effects on financial viability, especially since the market for socially responsible investment has grown substantially and activist campaigns have influenced environmental management policy (Bubna-Litic, 2007, pp. 262–263).

To assist investment practice, the *Global Framework for Risk Disclosure* (CERES, 2006) sets out corporate information needed by global institutional investors for analysing business risks and opportunities associated with climate change, and voluntary UN *Principles for Responsible Investment* (PRI) (UNEP FI, 2006a) recognize direct links from environmental, social and governance practices to investment performance and risk. PRI practice is supported by peer-learning among the largest global investors, and the inaugural 20 institutional signatories in 2006 expanded to over 200 international investment community members (asset owners, investment managers and professional service partners) by the time of the first PRI anniversary, showing strong take-up of the principles especially in relation to carbon disclosure.

Transnational environmental litigation

Since different nations and sub-national jurisdictions have different legal concepts, rules and processes, laws may differ for civil wrongs or torts, contracts, agency, intellectual property, taxation, franchising, competition policy and regulated trade practices, insolvency, industrial relations, business crime, product liability, transport, electronic communications and so on. Contractual strategies for resolving jurisdictional differences are not always available and nation-to-nation interventions on behalf of citizens or corporations are extremely unlikely; leaving redress, if any, to an excessively technical 'private international law'. Non-nation-state litigation (such as business-versus-business or business-versus-stakeholder), involving foreign parties, injuries or events, experiences substantial obstacles when choosing the applicable national law; obtaining standing to sue in foreign courts or pursue other foreign dispute-resolution mechanisms; gaining access to viable enforceable remedies at a distance; and marshalling cross-jurisdictional litigation resources. Difficulties reconciling different jurisdictions and factoring in technological developments have quelled international attempts to codify jurisdiction, recognition and enforcement of foreign judgments in civil and commercial matters (Kaye, 2007, p. 57).

13.5   Reconceptualizing and leveraging compliance

Although business leadership and leverage are strongly connected with learning and ethical values, prevailing regulatory conditions also matter. Unregulated sustainability responses, such as corporate social responsibility, have been driven anyway by tightening regulation in conjunction with changing expectations from consumers, investors, employees and other stakeholders; pressure from non-governmental organizations; and increased demands for transparency (Idowu and Papasolomou, 2007). Assisted by certifiable voluntary standards, strategic environmental management can be embedded in core business objects and build creatively on regulatory requirements and fundamental stewardship to make organizations more efficient and effective; reduce costs of stakeholder stewardship and regulatory compliance; and avoid or reduce adverse environmental impact.

Strategic organizational compliance with regulatory regimes may also deliver organizational benefits, like innovation, that exceed compliance costs when regulation is perceived as an opportunity. Proactive management beyond technical compliance, however, will generally be necessary to achieve meaningful environmental protection, because of inherent failings in regulatory regimes, including political incompetence. An ideal scenario is to achieve an attitude shift by business from victim to partner in concurrent compliance, to yield equally healthy ecosystems and economies (Ryan, 2003, pp. 263, 266).

Future-oriented thinking will not necessarily deliver sustainability outcomes, but the precautionary principle in particular entails onus-shifting and risk-weighting environmental and health consequences in decisions so as to allow for incorrect predictions based on current assumptions and data (Peel, 2005, p. 228). Here, decision-makers need to avoid a tendency to think in terms only of scientifically assessed risk, which omits non-scientific indicators of harm (such as regulatory and litigation experience or customary practice) and situations where scientific understandings do not coincide with broader non-expert, community concerns about what is important (which may be evidenced by particular regulatory instruments setting lower or stricter thresholds for precautionary action or prescribing public participatory processes) (Peel, 2005, pp. 66–75). Change-oriented thinking and strategies similarly need 'multidisciplinary agility' (Krznaric, 2007, p. 46).

13.6   Conclusion

Whereas environmental harm mitigation measures ideally will deliver global benefits and lower overall long-term costs, adaptation measures enable more specific benefits for individual actors. Global mitigation efforts are still largely embryonic and there is no adaptation blueprint (IPCC, 2001, pp. 88–89); the best adaptation strategies will function at organizational and value-chain levels. Adaptation, moreover, should be able to fit well with, and certainly need not involve compromising, mainstream business motivations to seek new markets, leverage core competencies, acquire optimal resources and supplies and generally compete better. There are good fits available between corporate and environmental interests (UNEP FI, 2006b).

Ultimately, corporate integrity grows from interacting formal regulations, informal social actions and corporate self-regulation. Legal strategies with a triple loop that forces corporations to evaluate and report on their own self-regulation, help regulatory agencies to determine whether substantive objectives of improved natural environment and sustainable development are being achieved. This meta-regulatory role enables regulatory agencies to revise their own strategies in the light of corporate self-regulation (Parker, 2002, pp. 245–246). At the same time, corporate due diligence systems must ensure regulatory compliance by connecting all management, administrative and investment decisions and fully implementing compliance decisions having regard to the particular business, its particular regulatory environment and the particular risks relevant to that business (Ryan, 2003, p. 265).

The value-emphasis in stakeholder relationships provides a basis for advancing beyond technical compliance with domestic business and environmental laws. In this regard, the classic role of private contracts to determine, limit and honour agreed relations should not be gainsaid. Although there are private international law enforcement obstacles, innovative contractual arrangements (for example, that avoid surprise, enable change, decide value, achieve efficiency, protect position and oblige others to take extra care) can be legal mainstays of the management role of influencing sustainability directions; taking charge/care (of resources, expenditure, performance, information, training and so forth); and being accountable. Cooperative peer-learning initiatives with UNEP backing, showcasing leaders in specialist industries, also have focused mitigation and adaptation potential, but they are purely voluntary and may rank corporate value before sustainability.

Better laws are still needed (Ryan, 2005, p. 64), and will eventuate, to provide minimum business assurances while delivering enhanced sustainability performance platforms. Fundamental business features will include harmonized business and environmental laws; sustainability targets, standards and verification; responsive proprietary and organizational frameworks.

13.7   Questions

- Using the company you work for (or another know company that you know about), prepare a list of the legislation that would apply to that company and against each law list the company's legal obligations, how it is responding (or should respond) and if it is required to report compliance or performance against that law and whether this compliance reporting is available to the public.
- Discuss how community concerns about the environment and the generation of scientific knowledge about environmental degradation influence the environmental policies of your government. Discuss how these policies are formulated by governments and how they become translated directly into environmental laws that affect business operations.
- Describe an approach and strategy that the company (used in the first question) might adopt to scan information sources (e.g., non-government organizations, research outputs, community and government debates, overseas trends, international treaties) for signs that may indicate the likelihood of some future environmental legislation that would significantly affect the future operation of the company (e.g., carbon trading, *product stewardship*, emission standards).

End of Part Case Study: Sustainability Reporting and Corporate Governance

Robert Staib and Arun Sahay

Further to Section 8.7, where we included two examples of sustainability reporting and its relationship to selected sustainability aspects of organizations, we include four further examples and focus on some of the social aspects recommended by the Global Reporting Initiative (GRI, 2006), to illustrate how organizations are responding to the need for more corporate sustainability. The tables below do not address all aspects of sustainability reporting and do not make a critical assessment of the reporting but have been developed to illustrate different aspects for a sample of organizations. Readers can access the company web sites for more comprehensive data. At the end of this section, we include an exercise for students to undertake which requires a similar assessment of an organization's sustainability performance but from a corporate *governance* perspective and from a more critical perspective drawing on sources external to a company.

Procter & Gamble

Procter & Gamble is a health and cleaning products company with a wide range of products selling to the global market. Its sustainability vision stated by the Director, Global Sustainability includes:

> building P&G's business through Sustainability innovations that delight consumers while improving the environmental profile of P&G products; continuing to improve the environmental profile of P&G operations; continuing to improve lives through P&G's social responsibility programs; inspiring and engaging P&G employees to build Sustainability thinking and practices into their daily work; continuing to work with external

stakeholders to identify new needs and to create new opportunities and solutions for the world's Sustainability challenges and being committed to becoming an even more sustainable company in a sustainable world. (Proctor & Gamble, 2007)

Table III.1 shows selected aspects of Procter & Gamble's Sustainability Report for 2007. While Proctor & Gamble does not appear to have an externally verified Sustainability Report or a certified EMS to ISO 140001 it does state that it follows the requirements of the Global Reporting Initiative (GRI) and ISO14001. It also appears to be marginally reducing both its total greenhouse gas (GHG) footprint and its product unit footprint.

Table III.1   Selected aspects of Procter & Gamble's sustainability operations

Sustainability item	Comments		
Use of GRI approach: economic, environmental, social	Follows GRI guidelines		
Sustainability report externally verified	Not mentioned		
EMS certified to ISO14001	Stated that it meets the requirements but not certified		
Listed on FTSE4 Good index	Yes		
Listed on the Dow Jones Sustainability Index	Yes		
Greenhouse gases *per unit* of output: tonnes of CO_2 per tonne of product. Greenhouse gas emissions include CO_2 from fuel combustion sources	2005	0.17	
	2006	0.14	
	2007	0.14	
Green house gas *total output*: million tonnes of CO_2	2005	3.111	
	2006	2.937	
	2007	2.970	
'Use of Product' impact	Have a policy to reduce or prevent the environmental impact of their products and packaging in their design, manufacture, distribution, use and disposal whenever possible		
Diversity & equal opportunity (LA13)*	Makes commitment to diversity and provides diversity data; e.g., percentage of women in workforce and in management globally and minorities in the US workforce. Founding member of Global Sullivan Principles		
Suppliers and human rights (HR2)*	Includes sustainability guidelines for suppliers		
Customer health and safety assessment (PR1)*	Health and safety of employees addressed and statistics provided		

Note: *Numbers are from the GRI.

Source: Proctor & Gamble (2007).

Electrolux

Electrolux is a manufacturer and supplier of appliances both household and commercial. Its approach as stated on its web site is 'We can make a positive contribution to sustainable development both through our operations and our products. We are continually working to reduce energy consumption from products and emissions from factories; working to ensure that our employees and business partners are treated fairly; and striving to be a good neighbour in the communities in which we operate' (Electrolux, 2008a).

Table III.2 shows selected aspects from Electrolux's Sustainability Report for 2007. Although Electrolux do not appear to conform to the GRI it does appear (from the evidence in its report) to address many sustainability aspects. It appears to be concentrating on the energy and water efficiency of its products because it states that the operational phases of its products use more energy and water than the production phase.

Table III.2   Selected aspects of Electrolux's sustainability operations

Sustainability item	Comments
Use of GRI approach: economic, environmental, social	A separate report provides a GRI matrix for 2005 showing levels of compliance with the GRI components. Also member of the UN Global Compact
Sustainability report externally verified	Not stated
EMS certified to ISO14001	About 95% of its facilities are certified
Listed on FTSE4 Good index	Yes
Listed on the Dow Jones Sustainability Index	Yes
Greenhouse gases *per unit* of output: kg CO_2 per kSEK	2005 30 2006 31 2007 32
Green house gas *total output*: million tonnes of CO_2 equivalent	Not included, but aim to reduce energy use in its *operations* by 15% to 2009
'Use of Product' impact	States that majority of energy use over the life cycle of its products is in the operational phase of its household appliance *products*. Achieved 2% improvement in efficiency improvement in its product offering in Europe for 2007
Diversity & equal opportunity (LA13)	Makes a commitment to diversity and quantitative data provided on percentage of women in workforce and in management
Suppliers and human rights (HR2)	Has a supply chain code of conduct and details of audit programme of suppliers
Customer health and safety assessment (PR1)	Health and safety of employees addressed and statistics provided

Source: Electrolux (2007, 2008b).

Monsanto

Monsanto is an agricultural company and includes its sustainability details in a report called a Pledge Report. Its website focuses on its products that increase agricultural yields that help supply the world's need for increased productivity of food, animal feeds and fibre. It argues that this increased yield is being achieved in a sustainable manner through better products including use of biotechnology and genetic modification. The Pledge Report states:

> We want to make the world a better place for future generations. As an agricultural company, Monsanto can do this best by providing value through the products and systems we offer to farmers. With the growth of modern agricultural practices and crops that generate ever-increasing yields, we are helping farmers around the world to create a better future for human beings,

Table III.3   Selected aspects of Monsanto's sustainability operations

Sustainability item	Comments			
Use of GRI approach: economic, environmental, social	Report covers economic, environmental, social topics and includes a report reference index to GRI indicator information in the report			
Sustainability report externally verified	No			
EMS certified to ISO14001	No mention of			
Listed on FTSE4 Good index	No mention of			
Listed on the Dow Jones Sustainability Index	No mention of			
Greenhouse gases *per unit* of output: tonnes of CO_2 equivalent per tonne of product	Year	direct	indirect	total
	1990	4.96	2.53	7.49
	2005	3.39	1.44	4.83
	2006	3.23	1.45	4.68
Greenhouse gas *total output*, million tonnes of CO_2 equivalent	Year	direct	indirect	total
	1990	0.858	0.438	1.296
	2005	1.397	0.595	1.992
	2006	1.305	0.585	1.890
'Use of Product' impact	As described above, report focuses more on sustainability benefits of its products, with some quantitative data			
Diversity & equal opportunity (LA13)	Makes a commitment to equal opportunity but no data provided on diversity; e.g., on women in workforce or on racial minority peoples in leadership			
Suppliers and human rights (HR2)	Has published Human Rights documents that make commitments to employees, business partners and communities in which it works			
Customer health and safety assessment (PR1)	Health and safety of employees addressed and statistics provided			

Source: Monsanto (2007).

the environment and local economies. Increased yields are the core of this agenda. As agricultural productivity increases, farmers are able to produce more food, feed, fuel, and fibre on the same amount of land, helping to ensure that agriculture can meet humanity's needs for the future. Moreover, increased productivity allows farmers to produce more with the same – or fewer – inputs of energy and pesticide. This results in more responsible use of natural resources, better ecosystem health, increased soil fertility, increased farm income, and more opportunities for farmers and their communities. (Monsanto, 2007)

Table III.3 shows that Monsanto, despite its strong focus on product benefit does record greenhouse gas (both direct and indirect) per unit of product and totally for its operations. Per unit emissions were reduced by approximately 37 per cent from 1990 to 2006 but total emissions increased by 46 per cent. Product output increased by 131 per cent during this period. Another focus on Monsanto is included in the case study box at the end of Chapter 3.

Norsk Hydro

Hydro is an integrated aluminium and hydroelectricity company with a global presence. It is 43 per cent owned by the Norwegian state. Its web site includes the following statements: '

The renewable resource of hydroelectric power has been a core activity in Hydro since the company started up in 1905 ... It is accompanying us on our journey into the future, on which we have now been joined by solar energy – the new 21st century growth area ... The risk of severe climate change requires action now to reduce global greenhouse gas emissions. Technology and long-term sustainable systems must be developed to achieve significant and lasting emission reductions. The viable use of natural resources requires that raw materials are reused and waste production is minimized. We are intensifying our efforts to achieve an optimal use of resources, and can see that this will also contribute to increased profitability. (Norsk Hydro, 2008)

Table III.4 shows that Norsk Hydro has a fairly advanced environmental management system and reporting approach including reporting both unit and total greenhouse gas emissions. It does not address quantitatively the impact of the use of its product on the environment.

Corporate governance audit exercise

Consider yourself as an auditor with the role of externally assuring the publically available *governance* information on a business organization,

Table III.4   Selected aspects of Norsk Hydro's sustainability operations

Sustainability item	Comments			
Use of GRI approach: economic, environmental, social	Yes			
Externally verified	By the state-authorised public accountant			
EMS certified to ISO14001	Hydro's policy is that all production sites shall be managed in accordance with the ISO 14001 standard or equivalent though not necessarily certified			
Listed on FTSE4 Good index	Yes			
Listed on the Dow Jones Sustainability Index	Yes			
Greenhouse gases *per unit* of output: tonne of CO_2 equivalent per tonne primary aluminium output	Year	direct only, no indirect i.e., electricity		
	2005	1.60		
	2006	1.23		
	2007	1.25		
Greenhouse gas (or CO_2 equivalent) *total output*, M tonnes of CO_2 equiv. (Hydro-operated facilities – excluding other companies that Hydro have an equity in)	Year	direct only no indirect i.e., electricity		
	2005	5.3		
	2006	4.5		
	2007	4.4		
Greenhouse gas (or CO_2) *total output*, M tonnes of CO_2 equiv. (Hydro-operated facilities and other companies that Hydro have an equity in) (approx. only)	Year	direct	indirect	total
	2005	7.5	8.5	16.0
	2006	7.0	8.5	15.5
	2007	6.5	8.0	14.5
'Use of Product' impact	No data on product use impacts but emphasizes the long life of aluminium products and their ease of recycling			
Diversity & equal opportunity (LA13)	Emphasizes diversity in the workforce and provides data on percentage of women in the workforce and in management. Also data on non-Norwegian peoples in management			
Suppliers and human rights (HR2)	Has commenced a process on including corporate responsibility into its supply chain			
Customer health and safety assessment (PR1)	Health and safety of employees addressed and statistics provided			

Source: Norsk Hydro (2007).

either one of the above or one of your choices.

• Read and understand the requirements of the Global Reporting Initiative (GRI). Summarize the elements of the GRI that address corporate governance (both environmental and social) particularly the roles, responsibilities and obligations of the Board, senior executives and senior managers.

- Using the web site of a company and its sustainability reports, summarize the extent of information provided on the corporate governance aspects of the GRI and comment on the picture it paints of the company.

- Using sources external to the company, e.g., interviews with company executives (and/or personal knowledge), academic papers, journal and newspaper articles, stakeholder and non-governmental groups' publications, develop a picture of how the organization's reporting and performance at the corporate governance level complies with the intent of the GRI including addressing critical issues identified by external stakeholder groups and pressure groups.

- In assessing corporate governance consider to what extent the company displays and achieves a *product stewardship* role and an *environmental stewardship* role and whether its approach to environmental management is underpinned by an incremental or radical approach to green innovation and green product development.

- If the company is working in overseas countries, assess its consistency of approach to social and cultural issues between its home-based operations and its overseas operations.

- Produce a report of the company which assesses the level of compliance with the corporate governance requirements of the GRI and make recommendations for improvement.

Conclusions and the Business Case

14

Robert Staib

14.1 Introduction

This final chapter brings together some of the ideas the authors have discussed in the preceding chapters. They have covered many topics from many points of view of the management of the business organization and the environment. They have discussed why and how companies should change their business management to cover environmental issues and address *environmental steward-ship*. Most touch on the broader topic of sustainable development (both social and environmental). The subjects and topics are components of management courses and the stuff of everyday business. They do not cover every topic and not in the detail they deserve but they indicate the breadth of knowledge that needs to be understood.

The key theme of the book has been that the way to integrate environmental issues into everyday business operations is to include environmental thinking as a prelude to management action and as a response to management action. Bubna-Litic and Benn (2003) in addressing the state of the degree of Master of Business Administration (MBA) discuss both traditional management and management that addresses the needs for creating a sustainable society and say that 'Our concern is the need for fundamental revisions to be incorporated into management education either by incrementally integrating change or revolutionary redesign of all aspects of the current curriculum through the inclusion of activities that foster broader reflection and critical thinking.'

In the chapters of this book we have not attempted a broad-scale integration of the subject matter from all disciplines but leave this to the student of management to take this step and in this chapter we lead the reader along this path – a path that will be different for each management student, each manager and each organization.

14.2   The business case

Sustainable development (both environmental and social) 'is inherently a learning process through which learners can build capacity to live more sustainably' (Springett, 2005, quoting Scott and Gough, 2004, p. xiv). Banerjee (in Scott and Gough, 2004) describe three key themes that 'underlie teaching about and for sustainability: theoretical analysis and critique, inter-disciplinary and local-global perspectives'.

The World Business Council for Sustainable Development (WBCSD) acknowledged that there is a need for integration of sustainable development ideas into the fabric of business organizations (Engen and DiPiazza, 2005). Willard in Galea (2004) develops a quantitative business case for introducing sustainable development approaches into business and suggests that core courses in business schools should be quantifying the benefits. He attempts this by using a hypothetical organization and identifies potential benefits lying in the categories of the following: people management (easier hiring of the best talent, greater retention of top talent, increased employer productivity); reduced environmental impact (reduced expenses of manufacture, reduced expenses at commercial sites); and business performance (increased revenue and market share, reduced risk and easier financing).

The importance of the people aspects is shared by Porritt (2006, pp. 317–320) though to a much stronger degree. He sees the big difference between sustainable development and conventional environmentalism being that sustainable development brings forth the ideas of human happiness and well-being as a counter to traditional political goals of growth, efficiency and competitiveness. Hamilton (2003) quoted in Porritt uses studies of human happiness and well-being to articulate an argument that growth at all costs does not necessarily equate with people who are happy and in a state of well-being. These ideas are important for managers when considering the future where stakeholder's views are becoming increasingly important.

Van Berkel (2002) in reviewing the World Summit on Sustainable Development in 2002 and the case for sustainable development discusses the qualitative case for business involvement in sustainable development and identifies eco-efficiency and innovation as key components for business. In quoting Weaver et al. (2000) he identifies innovation trajectories and their potential time frames from *environmental care* (0–5 years) through *eco products and services* (5–10 years) and to *sustainable production and consumption* (20–50 years). The WBCSD presented its case for Sustainable Development based on the market, the business framework, eco-efficiency, corporate social responsibility, learning to change, from dialogue to partnership, innovation and reflecting the value of the earth.

Despite these notes of optimism, the United Nations Environmental Program (UNEP) has identified a widening gap 'between the efforts made by industry and the worsening global environmental situation' with the two main reasons being that only a small number of companies are active in trying to achieve sustainability and 'the improvements are being overtaken by economic growth and increasing demand for goods and services'. The UNEP identified five priority areas for action: mainstream decision-making, improvement in voluntary initiatives, reporting, integration of social, environmental and economic issues and global responsibilities and opportunities (UNEP, 2002).

Salzman et al. (2005) in reviewing the literature on the business case for sustainability found that the evidence of a link between environmental sustainability, social sustainability and financial sustainability was inconclusive especially at the individual company level.

The ideas outlined above suggest that there is a growing awareness for the need to establish a business case for sustainable development but that we have a way to go in defining it, applying it to business and measuring its achievement. Each organization and industry is likely to have a different position and approach and it is a long journey – maybe over a generation, over the working life of an individual.

While climate change is not the only environmental problem the world faces it is one that is currently focusing the attention of the world's media. As discussed in Chapter 1, two salient reports have appeared recently: the first confirming consensus on the science of climate change (IPCC, 2007); and the second linking the economy to the effects of climate change (Stern, 2006b). From a business perspective they exemplify the significant business risks that are likely to arise if business ignores the environmental and social impacts of their operations. I suspect that the move of business to sustainable operations will be driven by a combination of stakeholder pressure (through the market and the impact of environmental degradation on peoples' lives), changed legislation and business perception of risk. One thing that the current debates on climate change are highlighting is that business needs to seriously address medium- and long-term business risks likely to be brought about by potential changes to the weather, environmental regulation, the market, insurance and investment.

I think the authors in this book have raised many of these issues and have provided ideas for students of business to mull over and apply their innovative thinking to. In general the authors have taken an optimistic view of the ability of and need for companies to act. *Environmental stewardship* may be an elusive concept and as Dodo Thampapillai and Bo Öhlmer suggest (Chapter 5) it may be difficult to get business to adopt without a significant legislation. The WBCSD, other business organizations and many multinational organizations have started to address the role and responsibilities of business over recent years and have started to develop and communicate a business case for sustainable development – mainly qualitative but hopefully increasingly quantitative too (see also case study Part III).

14.3   Environmental and ethical issues and questions for business

In developing the framework for this book and in working though the contributions of the authors, many issues and questions have presented themselves to me. Some have been addressed by the authors, others remain elusive. Rather than confine them to history, I have set them down in this section to stimulate the reader's thoughts towards future reading and actions. They will also be useful for students attempting the Capstone project that I describe in Section 14.4 below.

Role of business in society

What is the role of business in society? Is it to reflect societal needs or the needs of individuals? What is responsible business and who should it be responsible to: shareholders or stakeholders? Is there a business case for medium-term sustainability? Is there a business case for medium-term environmental stewardship? Is there a significant difference between small business and large business?

Can the concept of a sustainable business be achieved temporally and geographically without strong government regulation? Can business management only attain financial success with some integration of environmental quality and social equity? Is a historical review of business sustainability necessary? Are models of sustainable management overly optimistic? For example, The Natural Step (2008), *Natural Capitalism* (Hawken et al., 2000), *The Natural Advantage of Nations* (Hargroves and Smith, 2005), 'Corporate Sustainability' (Dunphy et al., 2007).

Education of business

How are environmental and ethical values considered by MBA and other business management courses? What is the educational value of MBAs and other management courses (Bubna-Litic and Benn, 2003)? Do the courses need to be changed from their traditional approaches (Aspen Institute, 2008)?

Environmental impact of business

The cumulative impact is not addressed well by corporate environmental approaches, for example, a business may significantly reduce the energy and material content of a product but increase sales of that product so the cumulative environmental impact of the business is increased. Many products are used only once, have limited lives and are not designed for recycling or are not designed for dismantling for ease of recycling and the cost of repair of many products quickly exceeds the purchase price of a new or upgraded product.

Performance of business

How do businesses address their contribution to cumulative environmental impacts? How do businesses reconcile their contribution to the continuing growth in sales with its concomitant growth in material and energy use? Do many businesses use green wash to obfuscate a lack of real environmental commitment and achievement (Beder, 1997, 2006; Trainer, 2001).

Timeframes for social change

Many major societal changes take place over timescales of 20 years or more, that is, it may require a generation or more for the significant change to occur (Staib, 1997, 1998; Bindé, 2001, 2004, pp. 341–345; Hoffman, 2001). For example, the time taken for action and achievement of a solution to the ozone hole problem; the world to be convinced that global warming was reality not speculation; the Kyoto protocol to be signed; and business to react to environmental issues.

Behavioural change in response to sudden or significant environmental change

There is some evidence, that on global and regional scales, it often needs a significant cumulative environmental impact or environmental shock to instigate real societal and business change (Staib, 1997; Hofffman, 2001). Future significant environmental impacts and events may move us to a new suite of environmental management ideas.

Changing economic environment

How do people's commitment to and investment in company shares and private superannuation influence their environmental and ethical judgement? Do their concerns for their own financial outcomes override their concerns and actions on the environmental impacts of businesses and on other ethical questions (e.g., excessive profits, exploitation of ordinary workers, exorbitant salaries for executives etc.)?

Human values

Are human values considered by business as important or are they not considered very relevant for an individual business? For example, considerations of the direction of human evolution from physical to cultural to cognitive to the emerging approach of genetic engineering/biotechnical manipulation with the latter raising issues of the sanctity of human life; the drivers of human happiness or contentment (see ideas in Hamilton, 2003); the rise and continuing rise in excessive consumption, acquisitiveness, materialism; the continuing existence (or change or loss) in a postmodern world of human dignity and universal values (Bindé, 2001, 2004); the right of individuals as opposed to the obligations or duties of individuals; the decline of the social and rise of the individual; the disappearance of cultural values and practices under the rise of globalization. Do business managers need to consider these aspects especially when considering environmental and social issues?

Human cognition

Many of the separate ideas and philosophies coming from science, religion and technology address environmental issues and may have the ability to change corporate and consumer attitudes and behaviour.

For example, brain research seems to oscillate between scenarios of determinism and free will. Are the outcomes of this accelerating research of both psychological and biophysical/biochemical matters likely to influence ideas about humans' relationship to, and exploitation of, the environment?

Environmental sustainability and futures thinking for business organizations

Is environmental sustainability (or sustainable development) an impossible dream? Is too much staked on it? Does it come from an ideal world type of thinking that may never be possible to achieve. On a global scale, one might feel pessimistic about it when one looks at the history of competitive evolution, the violent interventions of nature and the violent history of human wars and conflicts. Despite all our efforts in utilizing our science and social institutions, the world and its natural environment may change in many unpredictable and unacceptable ways and never achieve a global sustainability.

However, we may achieve a rough balance with the environment in some areas or parts (and for some peoples) but in other parts (and for other peoples) it will always be changing and seeking a new balance. Could we at least view sustainable development as best available environmental practice at the moment, but continually strive for a better, more-evolved approach? Is sustainable development enough for business organizations to cope with – recognizing that fundamental change in production and consumption is needed to bring it about?

Can business organizations look beyond consumption and life style? Could the question be changed from: 'Is the product greener, more socially benign and more profitable?' to 'Is the product's environmental impact acceptable and is it necessary for humanity and consistent with human values?'

14.4   Capstone Project

By now readers will have been flooded with a plethora of ideas on business, sustainability, environmental stewardship, social responsibility etc. It is time to reflect and apply the ideas and schemes to a real-life business situation. In this final chapter we outline a Capstone project to help business management students bring together many of the ideas of the book. It is to help students think logically through the issues, consider the separate management-related disciplines, look at the broad, general management picture of a company, review the company's industry and the company itself and prepare short-, medium- and long-term corporate positions. To assist in the project I have extracted and summarized some of the key topics from the chapters of the book and listed them in Section 14.5. The two Capstone projects are described below.

(a)   Existing company

- Select an existing company and its product or product range of traditional products, for example, automobiles, a natural food product, a manufactured food product, house construction, construction supplies, consumer white goods, luxury goods or services, etc.

- Outline a sustainable development approach that will *radically* green the company, for example, with objectives such as no net use of non-renewable energy and materials; no discharge of waste; no net use of water; becoming carbon neutral; becoming socially sustainable. The sustainable development outcomes – financial, environmental and social – should be achievable and measurable.
- Develop and document a corporate strategy, an implementation plan, an operational plan and marketing plan for the chosen organization. The strategy and plans should clearly identify that the company is to become a sustainable company (financially, environmentally and socially) and the time frame and resources required. We suggest using the logical structure provided by the book.
- In formulating the strategy address key ideas of this book, for example, the roles that *product stewardship* and *environmental stewardship* should play and the need for both incremental and radical change.
- From the strategy and plans, develop a succinct sustainable business case for submission to a Board of Directors for approval. The business case should include short-, medium- and long-term business outcomes, funding and resourcing requirements, projected cash flow and yearly financial accounts.

(b)   Start-up company

- Select a new product or product range for a new start-up company, for example, products that service an environmental market such as wind turbines, carbon trading consultancy service or a traditional product or product range (as in (a) above).
- Outline a sustainable development approach to produce a *radically* green company, for example, with objectives such as no net use of non-renewable energy and materials; no discharge of waste; no net use of water; becoming carbon neutral; becoming socially sustainable. The sustainable development outcomes – financial, environmental and social – should be achievable and measurable.
- Develop and document a corporate strategy, an implementation plan, an operational plan and marketing plan for the proposed organization. The strategy and plans should clearly identify that the company is to be a sustainable company (financially, environmentally and socially) and the time frame and resources required. We suggest using the logical structure provided by the book.
- In formulating the strategy address key ideas of this book for example, the roles that product stewardship and environmental stewardship should play and the need for both incremental and radical change.
- From the strategy and plans, develop a succinct sustainable business case for submission to a Board of Directors for approval. The business case

should including short, medium and long-term business outcomes, funding and resourcing requirements, projected cash flow and yearly financial accounts.

14.5   Outline of ideas from chapters

Some of the key topics from the chapters of the book are listed below to help students build a framework for their Capstone project.

Chapter 1   The need for change

- *Environmental thinking* as a prelude to management action;
- *Environmental thinking* as a response to management action;
- Drivers of environmental impacts;
- Environmental impacts of the business;
- Business responses to environmental issues;
- Product stewardship and environmental *stewardship.*

Chapter 2   Philosophies of business, society and environment

- The unexamined life is not worth living (Socrates);
- The primary area of relevance is moral philosophy or ethics;
- The relevance of philosophy to the modern manager;
- The spirit of open, critical inquiry to explore ethical debates within business;
- A philosophical link between environmental and business philosophies;
- Community views on intrinsic and extrinsic values of nature, on stakeholders rights, on ideas of sustainable development and changing the rules of the business game.

Chapter 3   Strategic direction and management

- Establishing a strategic environmental direction for a business;
- Environmental benefits to help maximize returns to investors, minimize environmental harm;
- Environmental problems – opportunities for business but constraints and threats to profitability;
- Excellence in protecting the environment creating opportunities for achieving competitive advantage through pollution prevention, product stewardship, sustainable development;
- Establishing a distinctive competence for managing the physical environment can mean less waste, fewer emissions, less accidents, lower costs, new market opportunities and innovation and better integrated systems development;
- Competence to add value to customers through product differentiation, lower costs, competitive advantage.

Chapter 4   Leadership for sustainability

- Leadership of change, roles in constructing the sustainable corporation;
- Transforming business requires inspiration, energy, skills, effective leaders;
- Easier to hold to traditional ways, to accept the leadership of others who don't question the status quo but for the world to survive, we must change;
- How to equip myself to be an effective leader, where shall I start?
- Organizational change for sustainability, the need to embrace self leadership. Change leadership involves owning our own power and using it responsively and responsibly.

Chapter 5   Environmental economics and environmental stewardship

- Environmental stewardship by firms induced through pecuniary incentives including ownership rights or enforced by regulation;
- Voluntary stewardship is virtually non-existent – omission of environmental capital (KN) from firms' production function;
- Conceptual premises that recognize KN would render voluntary stewardship feasible;
- Taxes, subsidies and regulation are instruments of environmental protection and conservation.

Chapter 6   Human Resources

- Human resources (individuals, groups and their relationships) essential for promoting sustainability;
- Social and human sustainability comprise the development and fulfilment of people's needs (and wants?) and the maintenance of social relationships;
- Human resources policies important as a means of driving change but change requires challenging ideas and practices of organizations, particularly the way people are managed;
- Success requires individuals to work together, be involved in decision-making, to have self-knowledge and ability to reflect, think critically and systemically and to envision desired futures;
- Discusses systems and processes, individuals and stakeholders.

Chapter 7   Environmental marketing

- Environmental or green marketing – exchanges that create value for both parties but seeks to minimize negative environmental impacts;
- Types of greening – strategic, quasi-strategic and tactical greening;
- Require a realistic strategy that can be delivered, if not may lead to consumer or stakeholder criticism;

- Environmental marketing – a potentially valuable strategy but has risks and firms need to demonstrate their purported commitment, whatever level of greening it chooses.

Chapter 8   Organization: Structures, Frameworks, Reporting

- Organization design and structure change to become more sustainable (environmentally and socially);
- Organization structures to allow access to scientific/engineering information on environmental aspects, impacts, resource usage and emissions of an organization; information on current environmental legislation, corporate environmental policies and processes, feedback from customers and stakeholders, environmental issues of products and supply chain; flexibility to respond to external environmental issues; facilitating communications on environmental matters;
- Organization to consider concepts of sustainable development, corporate social responsibility, stakeholder theory and corporate accountability theory;
- Management systems to consider environmental and social principles, guidelines, codes of conduct, standards, for example, United Nations Global Compact, Environmental Management System ISO 14000 and Global Reporting Initiative;
- Trends in the extent of environmental reporting and examples of indicators from two companies.

Chapter 9   Operations

- Environmental management and integration with operations management;
- Typical manufacturing processes: the sourcing of raw materials (the supply chain), transformation of these materials through the production process and delivery to customers;
- Environmental management approaches: total quality management (TQM), total quality environmental management (TQEM), cleaner production, life cycle assessment and greening of the supply chain;
- Links between TQM and TQEM – a goal of TQM is zero defects in production and a goal of TQEM is zero negative environmental impacts;
- Cleaner production with a significant literature on specific industries;
- The reasons for and steps in undertaking a life cycle assessment;
- Suppliers and the supply chain in relation to China, increasing amount of the world's manufacturing; and
- Examples taken from Engineering Resources Management's experience with multinational and Chinese companies in China.

Chapter 10   Technology management

- Technology enables us to produce the material goods needed or wanted in our lives by transformation of minerals, biological matter and energy;

- Advances in the understanding of the physical and chemical structure of matter, the physical origins of the universe, the workings of the brain and human and plant genomes;
- New technologies, new inventions and new innovations at an increasing rate;
- Integration of environmental issues into the management of technology by combining science, engineering and management;
- Environmental impact of technology management from research and development, design management, production management, product use, disposal and reuse to product stewardship;
- Technical innovation on a scale from incremental (similar to continuous improvement) to radical – a radical approach needed to significantly reduce the environmental impacts of a company's products.

Chapter 11   Finance and investment

- Investors' views/roles in corporate responsibility – promoting more responsible corporate behaviour;
- Investment, research and technology to solve pressing social and environmental problems;
- Analysis of social and environmental issues and investor engagement can lead to significant improvements in corporate responsibility performance;
- Most of the benefits of this action is limited to situations where there are reasonably clear drivers for action, for example, impending legislation, consumer pressure, media attention;
- Less evidence for the effectiveness of investor activity in situations where the drivers for action are weaker.

Chapter 12   Sustainability accounting and reporting

- Director duties and responsibilities towards sustainability;
- Importance of environmental management systems in facilitating sustainability accounting and reporting;
- Measuring the environment from an asset, liability and expense recognition perspective;
- Understand the various categories of environmental costs, the difficulty in measuring pollution;
- Reporting sustainability initiatives using triple bottom line and the global reporting initiative;
- Measurement and disclosure issues for accountants with the emission trading systems.

Chapter 13   Legal Aspects and Compliance

- Laws support the provision of services and goods, and they are used to protect and exploit, people, natural resources, relationships, status, and products of labour and intellect;

- Laws rarely eliminate tensions between different values but for governments, regulatory law may offer cheaper options than direct spending on incentives, compensation or infrastructure;
- Sustainability policy in environmental law has enormous potential to impact upon business law;
- Domestic environmental law provides many techniques, for example, criminal penalties, licensing, citizen suits, performance bonds, labelling, registration, reporting, audit, special insurance, remediation, community right-to-know, emissions trading, discharge taxes and due care requirements;
- International environmental law mainly comprises treaties signed by governments and voluntarily implemented under national domestic legislation;
- Corporate integrity grows from interaction of formal regulations, informal social actions and corporate self-regulation;
- Better laws are still needed and will need to eventuate. Fundamental business features will include harmonized business and environmental laws; sustainability targets, standards and verification and organizational frameworks.

14.6   Conclusion

I hope you have enjoyed the book and it has helped you to achieve a good understanding of how businesses can manage environmental and social issues and why business should adopt a *stewardship* role. One hopefully comes away from the book not with a gloom and doom feeling – though not to be concerned would be to miss the point of the book. I believe that businesses needs to be optimistic and to know that they can make a difference not only in aspiring to best environmental and social practice but also in seeking to make radical changes to achieve monumental outcomes in the protection of the environment and in making the world sustainable (environmentally, socially and financially) for all people including current and future generations.

Remember our opening chapter where we outlined the theme of the book. It is a book about *thinking: environmental thinking as a prelude to management action* and *environmental thinking as a response to management action*. Humans can think, the environment cannot, but the environment will react to abuse.

References

AccountAbility (2005) *Towards Responsible Lobbying*, http://www.unglobalcompact.
org/docs/news_events/8.1/rl_final.pdf, accessed 11 May 2006.

Albala, N. (2003) 'Can ordinary people regain their power of decision? International
law: Justice as a commodity', *Le Monde diplomatique*, http://www.MondeDiplo.
com/2003/12/14internationallaw, accessed 14 December 2003.

Albinger, H. and S. Freeman (2000) 'Corporate Social Performance and Attractiveness
as an Employer to Different Job Seeking Populations', *Journal of Business Ethics*,
28(3) 243–253.

Aldrich, H. and C. Fiol (1994) 'Fools Rush in: The Institutional Context of Industry
Creation', *Academy of Management Review*, 19, 645–670.

Alvesson, M. and H. Wilmott (1996) *Making Sense of Management: A Critical
Introduction*, Sage, London.

American Marketing Association (AMA) (2008) *Green Marketing*, http://www.
marketingpower.com/mg-dictionary-view1332.php, accessed January 2008.

Anderson, S. and J. Cavanagh (2000) *The Rise of Corporate Global Power*, http://www.
ips-dc.org/downloads/Top_200.pdf, accessed 19 December 2007.

Anderson, T. and W. Cunningham (1972) 'The Socially Conscious Consumer', *Journal
of Marketing* 36, 23–31.

Andrews, K. (1989) 'Ethics in Practice', *Harvard Business Review*, 67(5), 99–104.

Aragôn-Correa, J. (1998) 'Strategic Proactivity and Firm Approach to the Natural
Environment', *Academy of Management Journal*, 41(5) 556–567.

Aragôn-Correa, J. and S. Sharma (2003) 'A Contingent Resource-Based View of
Proactive Corporate Environmental Strategy', *Academy of Management Review*,
28(1) 71–88.

Aristotle (350 BCE) *Politics*. Book 1, Part VIII.

Ashiabor, H., K. Deketelare, L. Kreiser and Milne, J. (eds) (2005) *Critical Issues in
Environmental Taxation*, Richmond Law & Tax, Richmond.

Aspen Institute (2008) The Aspen Institute Center for Business Education home page,
http://www.aspencbe.org/, accessed 22 August 2008.

Associated Press (2007) 'Mattel Issues New Massive China Toy Recall', *MSNBC*
14 August 2007 http://www.msnbc.msn.com/id/20254745/ accessed January
2008.

Atkinson, M. (2005) in Staib, R. (2005) *Environmental Management and Decision
Making for Business,* London, Palgrave Macmillan, ch. 24.

Atkinson, S., A. Schaefer and H. Viney (2000) 'Organizational Structure and Effective
Environmental Management', *Business Strategy and the Environment*, 9, 108–121.

Australasian Reporting Awards (ARA) (2008) Australasian Reporting Awards web site,
http://www.arawards.com.au, accessed 23 April 2008.

Australian Competition and Consumer Commission (2006) *Carbon Offset Claims – Issues
Paper*, 16 January 2006, http://www.accc.gov.au/content/item.phtml?itemId=808

255&nodeId=7fb158e03286f64038540c9146d08742&fn=ACCC%20Issues%20 paper%E2%80%94carbon%20offset%20claims.pdf, accessed January 2008.

Australian Government (*circa* 2007) *Datong Cleaner Environment Project,* http:// www.environment.gov.au/commitments/publications/datong.html, accessed 1 May 2008.

Bachaus, K., B. Stone and K. Heiner (2002) 'Exploring the Relationship between Corporate Social Performance and Employer Effectiveness', *Business and Society,* 41(3) 319–344.

Bakan, J. (2004) *The Corporation,* Constable & Robinson, London.

Ban Ki-moon (2007) *Secretary-General of the United Nations,* quoted in Global Environment Outlook GEO4, United Nations Headquarters, New York, http:// www.ipcc.ch/, accessed 3 March 2008.

Banerjee, S. (2004) *Teaching Sustainability: A Critical Perspective. Teaching Business Sustainability: From Theory to Practice* in C. Galea. Sheffield, UK, Greenleaf Publishing, 34–47.

Banerjee, S., E. Iyer, and R. Kashyap (2003) 'Corporate Environmentalism: Antecedents and Influence of Industry Type', *Journal of Marketing,* 67(2) 106–122.

Bansal, P. (2003) 'From Issues to Actions: The Importance of Individual Concerns and Organizational Values in Responding to Natural Environmental Issues', *Organization Science,* 14(5) 510–527.

Barney, J. (1991) 'Firm Resources and Sustained Competitive Advantage', *Journal of Management,* 17(1) 99–121.

Bartel, T. (1995) 'Recycling Program for Printer Toner Cartridges and Optical Photoconductors', *Electronics and the Environment,* 225–228.

Bass, S. (2007) *A New Era in Sustainable Development, IIED Briefing,* International Institute for Environment and Development, London, http://www.iied.org/ mediaroom/docs/new_era.pdf, accessed 19 July 2008.

Becker, B. and M. Huselid (1999) 'Overview: Strategic Human Resource Management in Five Leading Firms', *Human Resource Management,* 38(4) 287–301.

Becker, B., M., Huselid, P. Pickus and M. Spratt (1997) 'HR As a Source of Shareholder Value: Research and Recommendations', *Human Resource Management,* 36(1) 39–47.

Beder, S. (1997) *Global Spin: The Corporate Assault on Environmentalism,* Scribe Books, Carlton, Victoria.

Beder, S. (2006) *Suiting Themselves: How Corporations Drive the Global Agenda,* Earthscan, London.

Bekin, C., M. Carrigan and I. Szmigin (2005) 'Defying Marketing Sovereignty: Voluntary Simplicity at New Consumption Communities', *Qualitative Market Research: An International Journal,* 8(4) 413–429.

Benn, S. and D. Dunphy (2004a) 'Case Study in Corporate Sustainability Fuji Xerox Eco Manufacturing Centre Sydney, Australia', *The International Journal for Innovation Research, Commercialization, Policy Analysis and Best Practice,* 6(2) 258–268.

Benn, S. and D. Dunphy (2004b) 'Human and Ecological Factors: A Systematic Approach to Corporate Sustainability', *Sustainability and Social Science Round Table Conference,* Institute for Sustainable Futures, UTS, Sydney.

Benn, S. and D. Dunphy (2007) *Corporate Governance and Sustainability,* Routledge, London and New York.

Benn, S. and L. Bone (2005) *Interview with Mike Hawker, CEO IAG,* 20 April, Sydney.

Benn, S. and L. Wilson (2006) 'Insurance Australia Group: A Case Study', *Case Studies in Innovation and Excellence 2*, School of Management, University of Technology, Sydney.

Benn, S., D. Dunphy and A. Ross-Smith (2006) *Building Sustainable Organizations*, Presentation at Academy of Management Conference, Atlanta.

Benyus, J. (2002) *Biomimicry: Innovation Inspired by Nature*, Harper Perennial, New York.

Bhat, V. (1993) 'Green Marketing Begins with Green Design', *Journal of Business & Industrial Marketing*, 8(4) 26–31.

BHP Billiton (2006) *2006 BHP Billiton Sustainability Report*, http://www.bhpbilliton. com/bb/sustainableDevelopment/reports.jsp, accessed 28 February 2007.

BHP Billiton (2008) *Sustainable Development Governance*, http://www.bhpbilliton. com/bb/sustainableDevelopment/sustainableDevelopmentGovernance.jsp, accessed 19 June 2008.

Bindé, J. (ed.) (2001) *Keys to the 21st Century*, Paris, Berghahn Books and UNESCO.

Bindé, J. (ed.) (2004) *The Future of Values*, Paris, Berghahn Books and UNESCO.

Bisoi, D. (2008) 'The Monday Interview: Santosh Kumar Mohapatra, Dhamra Would Be The Most Modern Deep Draft Port', *The Financial Express, 7 July 2008*, http:// www.financialexpress.com/news/Dhamra-would-be-the-most-modern-deep-draft-port/332113/0, accessed 30 July 2008.

Blount, F. (1999) 'Changing Places: Blount and Joss', *Human Resources Monthly*, December, 10–14.

Boatright, J. (1994) 'Fiduciary Duties and the Shareholder Management Relation: Or, What's So Special About Shareholders?' *Business Ethics Quarterly*, 4(4) 393–407.

Boele, R., H. Fabig and D. Wheeler (2001a) 'Shell, Nigeria and the Ogoni. A Study in Unsustainable Development: I The Story of Shell, Nigeria and the Ogoni People – Environment, Economy, Relationships: Conflict and Prospects for Resolution', *Sustainable Development*, 9(2) 74–86.

Boele, R., H. Fabig and D. Wheeler (2001b) 'Shell, Nigeria and the Ogoni. A Study in Unsustainable Development: II Corporate Social Responsibility and "Stakeholder Management" versus a Rights-based Approach to Sustainable Development', *Sustainable Development*, 9(3) 121–135.

Boer, B., R. Ramsay and D. Rothwell (1998) *International Environmental Law in the Asia Pacific*, Kluwer Law International, The Hague.

Boxall, P. (1998) 'Achieving Competitive Advantage through Human Resource Strategy: Towards a Theory of Industry Dynamics', *Human Resource Management Review*, 8(3) 265–288.

Brackney, K. and P. Witmer (2005) 'The European Union's Role in International Standards Setting', *CPA Journal*, 75(11) 18–27.

Branco, M. and L. Rodrigues (2006) 'Corporate Social Responsibility and Resource-Based Perspectives', *Journal of Business Ethics*, 69(2) 111–132.

Bream, R. and F. Harvey (2006) 'Call for More Certainty on Future Energy Policy', *Financial Times*, 13 April 2006, 3.

Brennan, A. (1995) 'Ethics, ecology and economics', *Biodiversity and Conservation*, 4, 798–811.

Brennan, A. and Y-S Lo (2002) 'Environmental Ethics', *Stanford Encyclopaedia of Philosophy*, http://www.plato.stanford.edu/entries/ethics-environmental/, accessed 26 August 2008.

Brewster, K. (2008) 'Climate Change Forces Car Manufacturing Rethink', *ABC News* January 18, http://www.abc.net.au/news/stories/2008/01/18/2141215. htm?site=victoria, accessed January 2008.

Brouwer, M. (1991) *Schumpeterian Puzzles*, University of Michigan Press, Ann Arbor.

Brown, J. (2005) 'An Account of the Dolphin-Safe Tuna Issue in the UK', *Marine Policy*, 29(1) 39–46.

Brown, M. B. (2001) 'The Civic Shaping of Technology: California's Electric Vehicle Program', *Science, Technology & Human Values*, 26(1) 56–81.

Brundtland, G. (ed.) (1987) *Report of the World Commission on Environment and Development: Our Common Future*, Oxford, Oxford University Press.

BSI (2008) *SA8000 Social Accountability*, http://www.bsi-global.com/en/, accessed 22 March 2008.

Bubna-Litic, D. and S. Benn (2003) 'The MBA at the Crossroads: Design Issues for the Future', *Journal of the Australian and New Zealand Academy of Management*, 9(3) 25–36.

Bubna-Litic, K. (2007) 'Climate Change and Corporate Social Responsibility: The Intersection of Corporate and Environmental Law', *Environmental and Planning Law Journal*, 24(4) 253–280.

Burgelman, R. (1984) 'Managing the Internal Corporate Venturing Process', *Sloan Management Review*, 25(2) 33–48.

Burgleman, R., C. Christensen and S. Wheelwright (2004) *Strategic Management of Technology and Innovation, 4th Edition*, Boston, McGraw Hill.

Burritt, R. and L. Cummings, (2002) 'Accounting for Biological Assets – the Experience of an Australian Conservation Company', *Asian Review of Accounting*, 10(20) 17–42.

Business for Social Responsibility (BSR) (2008) BSR home page, http://www.bsr.org, accessed 3 July 2008.

Buysse, K. and A. Verbeke (2002) 'Proactive Environmental Strategies: A Stakeholder Management Perspective', *Strategic Management Journal*, 24(5) 453–470.

Cagno, E., P. Trucco and L. Tardini (2005) 'Cleaner Production and Profitability: Analysis of 134 Industrial Pollution Prevention (P2) Project Reports', *Journal of Cleaner Production* (on-line http://www.sciencedirect.com) 13(6) (May) 1–13.

Camerer, C. and D. Lovallo (1999) 'Overconfidence and Excess Entry', *The American Economic Review*, 89, 306–317.

Capra, F. (1997) *The Web of Life: A New Synthesis of Mind and Matter*, HarperCollins, London.

Carbon Disclosure Project (CDP) (2007) Carbon Disclosure home page, http://www.cdproject.net, accessed 17 September 2007.

Carlson, L., S. Grove, R. Laczniak and N. Kangun (1996) 'Does Environmental Advertising Reflect Integrated Marketing Communications? An Empirical Investigation', *Journal of Business Research*, 37(3) 225–232.

Carroll, A. and A. Buchholtz (2002) *Business and Society with Infotrac, Ethics and Stakeholder Management*, South-Western College, Cincinatti.

Cartwright, W. and J. Craig (2006) 'Sustainability: Aligning Corporate Governance, Strategy and Operations with the Planet', *Business Process Management Journal*, 12(6) 741–750.

Cash, D., W. Adger, F. Berkes, P. Garden, L. Lebel, P. Olsson, L. Pritchard and O. Young (2006) Guest Editorial, 'Scale and Cross-Scale Dynamics: Governance and Information in a Multilevel World', *Ecology and Society*, 11(2) 8.

Caux Round Table (CRT) (2008) Caux Round Table home page, http://www.cauxroundtable.org/, accessed 22 March 2008.

Cebon, P. (1993) 'Corporate Obstacles to Pollution Prevention', *EPA Journal*, 19(3) 20–22.

CERES (2008) Ceres home page, http://www.ceres.org, accessed 3 July 2008.

Chamorro, A., S. Rubio and F. Miranda (2007) 'Characteristics of Research on Green Marketing', *Business Strategy and the Environment*, published on line, http://www3. interscience.wiley.com.simsrad.net.ocs.mq.edu.au/cgi-bin/fulltext/114204445/ PDFSTART, accessed 29 November 2008.

Chan, R. (2004) 'Consumer Responses to Environmental Advertising in China', *Marketing Planning & Intelligence*, 22(4) 427–437.

Charter, M. and M. Polonsky (eds) (1999) *Greener Marketing: A Global Perspective to Greening Marketing Practice Second Edition*, Greenleaf Publishing, Sheffield, UK.

Chatterjee, D. (1999) *Living Consciously: A Pilgrimage Towards Self-mastery*, Viva Books and Butterworth and Heinemann, Oxford.

Chatterjee, P. (1998) 'Montana Voters Nix Use of Cyanide Poison in Mining', *The Progress Report*, November 1998, http://www.progress.org/mining04.htm, accessed 12 April 2008.

Chen, C. (2001) 'Design for the Environment: A Quality-Based Model for Green Product Development', *Management Science*, 47(2) 250–263.

Chesterman, C., A. Ross-Smith and M. Peters (2003) 'Senior Women Executives and the Cultures of Management', Unpublished Report to a major Australian financial institution.

Chesterman, C., A. Ross-Smith and M. Peters (2004) 'Changing the Landscape? Women in Academic Leadership in Australia', *Mcgill Journal of Higher Education* 38(3) 421–436.

China Business Council for Sustainable Development (CBCSD) (2008) CBCSD home page, http://www.english.cbcsd.org.cn/, accessed 1 May 2008.

Christiansen, A. and J. Buen (2002) 'Managing Environmental Innovation in the Energy Sector: The Case of Photovoltaic and Wave Power Development in Norway', *International Journal of Innovation Management* 6(3) 233–256.

Christmann, P. (2000) 'Effects of "Best Practices" on Environmental Management', *Academy of Management Journal*, 43(4) 663–680.

Chung, Y., S. Tien, C. Hsieh and C. Tsai (2008) 'A Study of the Business Value of Total Quality Management', *Total Quality Management & Business Excellence*, 19(4) 367–379.

Clark, T. and M. Charter (1999) *'ECO-DESIGN CHECKLISTS: For Electronic Manufacturers, "Systems Integrators", and Suppliers of Components and Sub-assemblies'*, The Centre for Sustainable Design, UK, http://www.me.umn.edu/ education/courses/me4054/archives/fall_2005/fall_2005/notes/environment_2. pdf, accessed January 2008.

Clift, R. (1997) 'Overview Clean Technology – The Idea and the Practice', *Journal of Chemical Technology & Biotechnology*, 68(4) 347–350.

CMIE (2008) The Centre for Monitoring Indian Economy, Mumbai, India, CMIE home page, http://www.cmie.com, accessed 22 March 2008.

Coalition for Environmentally Responsible Economies (CERES) (2006) *The Global Framework for Climate Risk Disclosure*, http://www.ceres.org, accessed 25 August 2008.

Collins, R. (1994) 'The strategic contributions of the personnel function', in A. R. Nankervis and R. L. Compton (eds) *Readings in Strategic Human Resource Management*, Melbourne,Thomas Nelson.

Collison, D., G. Cobb, D. Power and L. Stevenson (2007) 'The Financial Performance of the FTSE4 Good Indices', *Corporate Social Responsibility and Environmental Management*, 15(1) 14–28.

Commonwealth of Australia (1998) *Cyanide Management, Best Practice Environmental Management in Mining (BPEM) Booklet series No 16*. Reproduced by the Australian Minerals and Energy Environment Foundation.

Connolly, J., P. McDonagh, M. Polonsky and A. Prothero (2006) 'Green Marketing and Green Consumers: Exploring the Myths', in D. Marinova, D. Annandale and J. Phillimore (eds) *International Handbook on Environmental Technology Management*, Edward Elgar, Cheltenham, UK, 251–268.

Co-operative Insurance Society (CIS) and Forum for The Future (2002) *Sustainability Pays*, CIS, Manchester.

Corporate Register (2008) Corporate Register home page, http://www.corporateregister.com/, accessed 2 July 2008).

Corus Group (2008) Corus home page, http://www.corusgroup.com/en/, accessed 3 August 2008.

Cosbey, A. and R. Tarasofsky (2007) *Climate Change, Competitiveness and Trade*, Royal Institute of International Affairs, Chatham House.

Côtéa, R. and E. Cohen-Rosenthalb (1998) 'Designing Eco-Industrial Parks: A Synthesis of Some Experiences', *Journal of Cleaner Production*, 6(3–4) 181–188.

Cousins, S., J. Bueno and O. Coronado (2007) 'Powering or De-Powering Future Vehicles to Reach Low Carbon Outcomes: The Long Term View', *Journal of Cleaner Production*, 15(11–12) 1022–1031.

Craig-Lees, M. and C. Hill (2002) 'Understanding Voluntary Simplifiers', *Psychology & Marketing* 19(2) 187–210.

Cramer, J. (2005) 'Company Learning about Corporate Social Responsibility', *Business Strategy and the Environment*, 14(4) 255–266.

Crane, A. (2000) 'Facing the Backlash: Green Marketing and Strategic Reorientation in the 1990s', *Journal of Strategic Marketing*, 8, 277–296.

Crotty, J. (2006) 'Greening the Supply Chain? The Impact of Take-Back Regulation on the UK Automotive Sector', *Journal of Environmental Policy & Planning*, 8(3) 219–234.

Curkovic, S., R. Sroufe and R. Landeros (2008) 'Measuring TQEM returns from the application of quality frameworks', *Business Strategy and the Environment*, 17(2) 93–106.

Dahlsrud, A. (2008) 'How Corporate Social Responsibility is Defined: An Analysis of 37 Definitions', *Corporate Social Responsibility and Environmental Management*, 15(1) 1–13.

Daily, B. and S. Huang (2001) 'Achieving Sustainability through Attention to Human Resource Factors in Environmental Management', *International Journal of Operations and Production Management*, 21(12) 1539–1552.

Daley, I. (1992) 'Is the Entropy Law Relevant to the Economics of Natural Resource Scarcity? – Yes, of Course It Is! Comment', *Journal-of-Environmental-Economics-and-Management*, 23(1) 91–95.

Das, A., H. Paul and F. Swierczek (2008) 'Developing and Validating Total Quality Management (Tqm) Constructs in the Context of Thailand's Manufacturing Industry', *Benchmarking: An International Journal*, 15(1) 52–72.

Dasgupta, P. (2006) *Comments on the Stern Review's Economics of Climate Change*, http://www.econ.cam.ac.uk/faculty/dasgupta/STERN.pdf, accessed 17 September 2007.

Davies J., G. Foxall and J. Pallister (2002) 'Beyond the Intention – Behaviour Mythology: An Integrated Model of Recycling', *Marketing Theory*, 2(1) 29–113.

Davis, K. (ed.) (1977) *Discretionary Justice: A Preliminary Inquiry*, Urbana, IL, University of Illinois Press.

Debold, E. (2005) 'New Operating Reality', *Executive Excellence,* 22(11) 8.

Deegan, C. and B. Gordon (1996) 'A Study of the Environmental Disclosure Practices of Australian Corporations', *Accounting and Business Research,* 26(3) 187–199.

Dees, J. and J. Starr (1992) 'Entrepreneurship through an ethical lens: Dilemmas and issues for research and practice', in D. Sexton and J. Kasarda (eds), *The State of the Art of Entrepreneurship,* Boston, MA, PWS-Kent, 89–116.

DeGeorge, R. (1993) *Competing with Integrity in International Business,* Oxford University Press, New York.

Delery, J. and H. Doty (1996) 'Modes of Theorizing in Strategic Human Resource Management: Tests of Universalistic, Contingency and Configurational Performance Predictions', *Academy of Management Journal,* 39(4) 802–835.

Department for Business, Enterprise and Regulatory Reform (BERR) (2007) *Companies Act 2006 Regulatory Impact Assessment,* BERR home page, http://www.berr.gov.uk, accessed 25 August 2008.

Department of Environment and Climate Change (DECC) (2007) *Extended Producer Responsibility,* http://www.environment.nsw.gov.au/education/spd_epr_prodsteward.htm, accessed 31 December 2007.

Department of Environment and Conservation NSW (2004) *Cleaner Production Case Study,* http://www.environment.nsw.gov.au/resources/sustainbus/hawker.pdf, accessed 1 May 2008.

Department of the Environment, Water, Heritage and the Arts (DE WaterHArts) (2008) *Sustainability Reporting: Steps for Developing a Report,* Australian Government, Canberra, Australia, http://www.environment.gov.au/settlements/industry/corporate/reporting/producing.html, accessed 20 April 2008.

Department of Transport and Regional Services (DTRS) (2008) *Green Vehicle Guide,* http://www.greenvehicleguide.gov.au, accessed 5 January 2008.

Design Chain Associates (DCA) (2008) *China RoHS Services,* http://www.chinarohs.com/services.html, accessed 5 March 2008.

Dewberry, E. and C. Sherwin (2002) 'Visioning Sustainability through Design', *Greener Management International,* Spring, 125–139.

Diamantopoulos, A., B. Schlegelmilch, R. Sinkovics and G. Bohlen (2003) 'Can Socio-Demographics Still Play a Role in Profiling Green Consumers? A Review of the Evidence and an Empirical Investigation', *Journal of Business Research,* 56(6) 465–480.

Dobers, P. and R. Wolff (1999) 'Eco-Efficiency and Dematerialization: Scenarios for New Industrial Logics in Recycling Industries, Automobile and Household Appliances', *Business Strategy and the Environment,* 8, 31–45.

Doppelt, B. (2003) *Leading Change towards Sustainability,* Greenleaf Publishing, Sheffield, UK.

Dow Jones (2008) *Dow Jones Sustainability Index World (DJSI),* http://www.sustainability-indexes.com/, accessed 10 February 2008.

Dowling, P. and R. Schuler (1990) 'Human Resource Management', in R. Blanpain (ed.) *Comparative Labour Law and Industrial Relations in Industrialised Market Economies,* vol. 2, Boston, Klumer Law and Taxation Publishers.

D'Souza, C., T. Mehdi and R. Khosla (2007) 'Examination of Environmental beliefs and its Impact on the Influence of Price, Quality and Demographic Characteristics with Respect to Green Intention', *Journal of Targeting, Measurement and Analysis for Marketing,* 15(2) 69–78.

Dunphy, D. (2001) Unpublished Notes, *The Skilled Practitioner Workshop.*

Dunphy, D. and A. Griffiths (1998) *The Sustainable Corporation*, Allen and Unwin, St Leonards.

Dunphy, D., A. Griffiths and S. Benn (2007) *Organization Change for Corporate Sustainability*, Second Edition, Routledge, London.

Dunphy, D., J. Benveniste, A. Griffiths and P. Sutton (2000) (eds) *Sustainability: Corporate Challenges of the 21st Century*, St Leonards, Allen and Unwin.

EICC (2008) *Electronic Industry Code of Conduct*, http://www.eicc.info/, accessed 5 March 2008.

Eichner, T. and R. Pethig (2001) 'Product Design and Efficient Management of Recycling and Waste Treatment', *Journal of Environmental Economics and Management*, 41(1) 109–134.

Eisenhardt, K. (1989) 'Agency Theory: An Assessment and Review', *Academy of Management Review*, 14(1) 57–74.

Eisenhardt, K. and J. Martin (2000) 'Dynamic Capabilities: What Are They?' *Strategic Management Journal*, 21, 1105–1121.

Electrolux (2007) Sustainability Report 2007, http://www.electrolux.com/Files/Sustainability/PDFs/2008_PDF/Electroux_Sustainability_07_low.pdf, accessed 22 June 2008.

Electrolux (2008a) Electrolux home page, http://www.electrolux.com/node18.aspx, accessed 24 June 2008.

Electrolux (2008b) *GRI Matrix*, http://www.electrolux.com/node44.aspx, accessed 5 July 2008.

Elkington, J. (1993) 'Coming Clean: The Rise and Rise of the Corporate Environmental Report', *Business Strategy and the Environment*, 2(2) 42–44.

Elkington, J. (1997) *Cannibals with Forks: The Triple Bottom Line of the 21st Century*, Capstone, Oxford.

Elkington, J. (2001) *The Chrysalis Economy: How Citizens, CEOs and Corporations Can Fuse Values and Value Creation*, Capstone, Oxford, 118–120.

Elmore, R. (1979) 'Mapping Backward: Using Implementation Analysis to Structure Policy Decisions', chapter presented at the annual meeting of the American Political Science Association, Washington, DC.

Elwin, V. (1958) *The Story of Tata Steel*, Commercial Printing Press, Bombay.

Engen, T. and S. DiPiazza (2005) *Beyond Reporting, Creating Business Value and Accountability*, World Business Council for Sustainable Development, Geneva, Switzerland.

Environment Agency UK (2005) *Life Cycle Assessment of Disposable and Reusable Nappies in the UK*, Environment Agency UK.

Environment Protection Authority (2000) *Profits from Cleaner Production A Self Help Tool for Small and Medium Businesses*, NSW Environment Protection Authority and Department of State and Regional Development, Sydney.

EPA Victoria (*circa* 2006) *Resource efficiency case studies*, http://www.epa.vic.gov.au/bus/Resource_Efficiency/casestudies/default.asp, accessed 1 May 2008.

ERM (2008) *Environment resources management* home page, http://www.erm.com/ERM/LOC/erm_china.NSF, accessed May 2008.

Ethical Corporation (2008) *Asia-Pacific: Corporate responsibility in India: Flying the flag the Tata way*, http://www.ethicalcorp.com/content.asp?ContentID=4299, accessed 19 July 2008.

Ethical Investments Research Services (EIRIS) (2008) *Key ethical/socially responsible investment (SRI) statistics*, http://www.eiris.org/, accessed 3 March 2008.

European Union (2002a) *Directive 2002/95/EC on the restriction of the use of certain hazardous substances in electrical and electronic equipment (RoHS)*, http://www. ec.europa.eu/environment/waste/weee/index_en.htm, accessed 5 March 2008.

European Union (2002b) *Directive 2002/96/EC on waste electrical and electronic equipment (WEEE)*, http://www.ec.europa.eu/environment/waste/weee/index_en.htm, accessed 5 March 2008.

European Union (2006) *EC 1907/2006 Registration Evaluation Authorisation and Restriction of Chemical Substances (REACH)*, European Union, http://www. ec.europa.eu/environment/chemicals/reach/reach_intro.htm, accessed 5 March 2008.

Evan, W. and R. Freeman (1993) 'A stakeholder theory of the modern corporation: Kantian capitalism', in G. Chryssides and J. Kaler (eds), *An Introduction to Business Ethics*, London, Chapman & Hall.

Ezzedeen, S., C. Hyde and K. Laurin (2006) 'Is Strategic Human Resource Management Socially Responsible? The Case of Wegmans Food Markets, Inc', *Employee Responsibilities and Rights Journal*, 18(4) 295–307.

F&C Asset Management (2004) *Banking on Human Rights: Confronting Human Rights in the Finance Sector*, F&C, London.

Fisher, I. (1904) 'Precedents for Defining Capital', *Quarterly Journal of Economics*, 18(3) 386–408.

Flavin, C. (2007) *Preface to the State of the World 2007 Our Urban Future*, Worldwatch Institute, W.W. Norton and Company, New York, London.

Fletcher, J. (2004) 'The Paradox of Postheroic Leadership: An Essay on Gender, Power and Transformational Change', *Leadership Quarterly*, 15, 647–661.

Foster, C. and K. Green (2000) 'Greening the Innovation Process', *Business Strategy and the Environment*, 9(5) 287–303.

Frank, R. and B. Bernanke (2002) *Microeconomics and Behaviour*, Irwin McGraw Hill, New York.

Frank, R. and B. Bernanke (2006) *Principles of Economics*, Irwin McGraw Hill, New York.

Freeman, H., T. Harten, J. Springer, P. Randall, M. Curran and K. Stone (1992) 'Industrial Pollution Prevention: A Critical Review', *Journal of the Air and Waste Management Association*, May, 618–656.

Freeman, R. (1984) *Strategic Management: A Stakeholder Approach*, Pitman, Boston, MA.

Friedman, M. (1970) 'The Social Responsibility of Business Is to Increase Profits', *New York Times Magazine*, September 13, 32.

Friedman, M. (1982) *Capitalism and Freedom*, University of Chicago Press, Chicago.

Freshfields Bruckhaus Deringer (2005) *A Legal Framework for the Integration of Environmental, Social and Governance Issues into Institutional Investment*, United Nations Environment Programme Finance Initiative, Geneva, UNEP FI home page, http://www.unepfi.org, accessed 25 August 2008.

Fuller, D. (1999) *Sustainable Marketing*, Sage, UK.

Fung, A., A. Aulenback, A. Ferguson and V. Ugursal (2003) 'Standby Power Requirements of Household Appliances in Canada', *Energy and Buildings*, 35(2) 217–228.

Furman, A. (1998) 'A Note on Environmental Concern in a Developing Country Results from an Istanbul Survey', *Environment and Behavior*, 30(4) 520–534.

Futures Foundation (2001) 'Storming the Mindsets', *Future News*, 6(2), March, Futures Foundation, Sydney.

Gagne, M., J. Gavin and G. Tully (2005) 'Assessing the Cost and Benefits of Ethics: Exploring a Framework', *Business and Society Review*, 110(2) 181–190.

Galea, C. (2004) *Teaching Business Sustainability, Volume 1: From Theory to Practice*, Greenleaf Publishing, Sheffield, UK.

Gao, S. and J. Zhang (2006) 'Stakeholder Engagement, Social Auditing and Corporate Sustainability', *Business Process Management Journal*, 12(6) 722–740.

Garrison, R. and E. Noreen (1994) *Managerial Accounting: Concepts for Planning, Control, Decision Making*, Seventh Edition, Irwin Inc., Sydney, Australia.

Geffen, D. and A. Marcus (1994) *Pollution prevention: overcoming barriers to further progress*, Strategic Management Research Center, Working Paper Series.

GeSI (2008) *Global eSustainability Initiative*, http://www.gesi.org/gesi-the-global-e-sustainability-initiative.html, accessed 5 March 2008.

GfK Roper Consulting (2007) 'Green Gauge' http://www.gfkamerica.com/news/gfk_roper_environment_companies.htm, accessed January 2008.

Ghemawat, P. (2001) *Strategy and the Business Landscape*, Prentice Hall, Upper Saddle, NJ.

Gilmour, P. and R. Hunt (1993) *The Management of Technology*, Longman Cheshire, Melbourne.

Ginsberg, J. and P. Bloom (2004) 'Choosing the Right Green Marketing Strategy', *MIT Sloan Management Review*, 46(1) 79–84.

Gladwin, T. (1993) 'The meaning of green', in J. Schot and K. Fischer (eds) *Environmental Strategies for Industry*, Washington, DC, Island Press.

Glinow, M., E. Drost and M. Teagarden (2002) 'Converging on IHRM best practices: Lessons Learned from a Globally Distributed Consortium on Theory and Practice', *Human Resource Management*, 41(1) 123–140.

Global Eco-Labelling Network (2008) Global Eco-Labelling home page, http://www.gen.gr.jp/, accessed 22 April 2008.

Global Reporting Initiative (GRI) (2006) *Sustainability Reporting Guidelines Version 3.0*, GRI, Amsterdam, The Netherlands.

Global Reporting Initiative (GRI) (2008), GRI home page, http://www.globalreporting.org, accessed 22 April 2008.

Godfrey-Smith, W. (1979) 'The Value of Wilderness', *Environmental Ethics*, 1(Winter) 309–319.

Goffin, G. and R. Mitchell (2005) *Innovation Management: Strategy and Implementation using the Pentathlon Framework*, Palgrave Macmillan, Basingstoke.

Gooley, T. (1998) *Reverse Logistics: Five Steps to Success, Logistics Management* 6 January 98, http://www.logisticsmgmt.com/article/CA126609.html, accessed 25 August 2008.

Gratton, L. (2000) *Living Strategy: Putting People at the Heart of Corporate Purpose*, Financial Times/Prentice-Hall, London, 17.

Gray, R., D. Owen and C. Adams (1996) *Accounting and Accountability: Changes and Challenges in Corporate Social and Environmental Accounting*, Prentice-Hall, London.

Gray, R., J. Bebbington and D. Walters (1993) *Accounting for the Environment*, Paul Chapman, London, UK.

Grayson, D. and A. Hodges (2004) *Corporate Social Opportunity! 7 Steps to Make Corporate Social Responsibility Work for Your Business*, Greenleaf Publishing, Sheffield, UK.

Greener Choices (2008) Greener Choices home page, http://www.greenerchoices.org/eco-labels/eco-home.cfm?redirect=1, accessed 27 April 2008.

Greening, D. and D. Turban (2000) 'Corporate Social Performance As Competitive Advantage in Attracting a Quality Workforce', *Business & Society*, 39(3) 254–280.

Greenpeace (2008a) Dhamra Port Project Backgrounder, *http://www.greenpeace.org/india/turtles/background, accessed 25 July 2008.*

Greenpeace (2008b) Greenpeace International home page, http://www.greenpeace.org/international/, accessed 5 April 2008.

GRI (2006) *Sustainability Reporting Guidelines,* http://www.globalreporting.org/ReportingFramework/G3Guidelines/, accessed 22 March 2008.

Griffin, J. (2000) 'Corporate Social Performance: Research Directions for the 21st Century', *Business & Society,* 39(4) 479–491.

Griffiths, A. and J. Petrick (2001) 'Corporate Architectures for Sustainability', *International Journal of Operations and Production Management,* 21(12) 1573–1585.

GSP (2008) *Global Sullivan Principles of Social Responsibility,* http://www.thesullivanfoundation.org, accessed 22 March 2008.

Gutowski, T., C. Murphy, D. Allen, D. Bauer, B. Bras, T. Piwonka, P. Sheng, J. Sutherland, D. Thurston and E. Wolff (2005) 'Environmentally Benign Manufacturing: Observations from Japan, Europe and the United States', *Journal of Cleaner Production Article in Press,* on-line http://www.sciencedirect.com, 13(1) (January) 1–17.

Haigh, M. (2006) 'Camouflage Play: Making Moral Claims in Managed Investments', *Accounting Forum,* 30(3) 267–283.

Haigh, M. and J. Hazelton (2004) 'Financial Markets: A Tool for Social Responsibility?' *Journal of Business Ethics,* 52(1) 59–71.

Haigh, N. and A. Griffiths (2007) The Natural Environment as a Primary Stakeholder: The Case of Climate Change, *Business Strategy and the Environment,* published on-line in Wiley InterScience.

Hamilton, C. (2003) *Growth Fetish,* Crows Nest Australia, Allen & Unwin.

Handy, C. (2001) *The Elephant and the Flea: Looking Backwards to the Future,* Hutchinson, London, pp. 74–75.

Hanley, N., J. Shogren and B. White (1997) *Environmental Economics in Theory and Practice,* Macmillan, Basingstoke.

Hannan, M. and J. Freeman (1989) *Organizational Ecology,* Harvard University Press, Cambridge, MA.

Hardin, G. (1968) 'The Tragedy of the Commons', *Science,* 162, 1243–1248.

Hargroves, K. and M. Smith (2005) *The Natural Advantage of Nations,* Earthscan, London.

Harrison, N. and D. Samson (2002) *Technology Management,* Boston, McGraw Hill.

Hart, S. (1995) 'A Natural Resource Based View of the Firm', *Academy of Management Review,* 20(4) 986–1014.

Hart, S. (1997) 'Beyond Greening: Strategies for a Sustainable World', *Harvard Business Review,* January–February 1997.

Hart, S. and M. Milstein (1999) 'Global Sustainability and the Creative Destruction of Industries', *Sloan Management Review,* 41(1) 23–33.

Hart, S. and R. Quinn (1993) 'Roles Executives Play: CEOs, Behavioral Complexity, and Firm Performance', *Human Relations,* 46, 543–575.

Hartmann, P., V. Ibáñez and F. Sainz (2005) 'Green Branding Effects on Attitude: Functional Versus Emotional Positioning Strategies', *Marketing Intelligence & Planning,* 23(1) 9–29.

Hartwick, J. and N. Olewiler (1986) *The Economics of Natural Resource Use,* Harper & Row, New York.

Hawken, P. (1993) *The Ecology of Commerce*, Harper Business, NY.

Hawken, P., A. Lovins and L. Lovins (2000) *Natural Capitalism, The Next Industrial Revolution*, Earthscan, London.

Hawley, J. and A. Williams (2000) *The Rise of Fiduciary Capitalism*, University of Pennsylvania Press, Philadelphia.

Hay, D. (1990) *The Public Joint-Stock Company: Blessing or Curse?* Tyndale Ethics Meeting, Cambridge, UK.

Hazelton, J. and K. Cussen (2005) 'The Amorality of Public Corporations', *Essays in Philosophy*, 6(2), http://www.humboldt.edu/~essays/hazelton.html, accessed 29 November 2008.

Health and Safety Executive (HSE) (2007) Corporate Health and Safety Performance Index, http://www.chaspi.info-exchange.com/, accessed 17 September 2007.

Helm, D. (ed.) (2005) *Climate-Change Policy*, Cambridge University Press, Cambridge, UK.

Hemphill, T. (1996) 'Cause-Related Marketing, Fundraising, and Environmental Nonprofit Organizations', *Nonprofit Management and Leadership*, 6(4) 403–418.

Henderson Global Investors (2002) *Closing Britain's Gender Pay Gap*, Henderson Global Investors, London.

Henderson, D. (2001) *Misguided Virtue: False Notions of Corporate Social Responsibility*, New Zealand Business Roundtable, Wellington, NZ.

Henry, N. (2004) *Public Administration and Public Affairs*, ninth edition, Prentice-Hall of India Pvt. Ltd.

Hirsh, B. and P. Sheldrake (2001) *Inclusive Leadership: Rethinking the World of Business to Generate the Dynamics of Lasting Success*, Information Australia, Melbourne.

Hoffman, A. (2000) *Competitive Environmental Strategy: A Guide to the Changing Business Landscape*, Island Press, Washington, DC.

Hoffman, A. (2001) *From Heresy to Dogma: An Institutional History of Corporate Environmentalism – Expanded Edition*, Stanford University Press, San Francisco.

Howard-Grenville, J. (2007) *Corporate Culture and Environmental Practice*, Edward Elgar Publishing, Northampton, Mass.

Huneke, M. (2005) 'The Face of the Un-consumer: An Empirical Examination of the Practice of Voluntary Simplicity in the United States', *Psychology and Marketing*, 22(7) 527–550.

Idowu, S. and I. Papasolomou (2007) 'Are the Corporate Social Responsibility Matters Based on Good Intentions or False Pretences? An Empirical Study of the Motivations behind the Issuing of CSR Reports by UK Companies', *Corporate Governance*, 7(2) 136–147.

Ikwue, T. and J. Skea (1994) 'Business and the Genesis of the European Community Carbon Tax Proposal', *Business Strategy and the Environment*, 3(2) 1–10.

Insight Investment (2007) Insight Investment home page, http://www.insightinvestment.com/Responsibility/investor_responsibility_home.asp, accessed 17 September 2007.

Insight Investment and WWF (2004) *Building towards Sustainability*, Insight Investment, London, http://www.insightinvestment.com/responsibility/project/one_million_sustainable_homes.asp, accessed 17 September 2007.

Insight Investment and WWF (2005) *Investing in Sustainability: Progress and Performance among the UK's Listed House-builders – Revisited*, Insight Investment, London, http://www.insightinvestment.com/responsibility/project/one_million_sustainable_homes.asp, accessed 17 September 2007.

Institutional Investors Group on Climate Change (IIGCC) (2007) Institutional Investors Group home page, http://www.iigcc.org, accessed 17 September 2007.

Institutional Investors Group on Climate Change (IIGCC) (2007a) *IIGCC activities page*, http://www.iigcc.org/activities/activity4.aspx, accessed 17 September 2007.

Intergovernmental Panel on Climate Change (IPCC) (2007) *Climate Change 2007: The Physical Science Basis Summary for Policymakers*, http://www.ipcc.ch/pdf/assessment-report/ar4/syr/ar4_syr_spm.pdf, accessed 3 March 2008.

Intergovernmental Panel on Climate Change (IPCC) (2001) *Climate Change 2001: Impacts, Adaptation and Vulnerability*, Cambridge University Press, Cambridge UK.

Intergovernmental Panel on Climate Change (IPPC) (2007) *Summary for Policymakers of the Synthesis Report of the IPCC Fourth Assessment Report*, accessed 17 November, 2007.

International Accounting Standards Board (IASB) (2005) 'IASB withdraws IFRIC Interpretation on Emission Rights', http://www.iasplus.com, accessed 20 April, 2008.

International Accounting Standards Committee (IASC) (2001) *Framework for the Preparation and Presentation of Financial Statements* (the Framework), London, IASB.

International Council of Chemical Associations (ICCA) (2008) Responsible Care home page, http://www.responsiblecare.org/page.asp?p=6427, accessed 1 May 2008.

International Energy Agency (2006) *World Energy Outlook 2006*, IEA, Paris.

International Iron and Steel Institute (IISI) (2006) *World Steel in Figures 2006*, http://www.worldsteel.org/pictures/newsfiles/WSIF06.pdf, accessed 21 March 2008.

International Iron and Steel Institute (IISI) (2008) World Steel Home page, http://www.worldsteel.org, accessed 28 June 2008.

International Organization for Standardization (ISO) (2000) *The ISO Survey of ISO 9000 and ISO 14000 Certificates Tenth cycle: Up to and including 31 December 2000*, http://www.iso.org/iso/survey10thcycle.pdf, accessed 3 March 2003.

International Organisation for Standardization (ISO) (2006a) *Environmental Management – Life Cycle Assessment – Principles and Framework ISO 14040:2006*, International Organisation for Standardization, Geneva.

International Organization for Standardization (ISO) (2006b) *The ISO Survey – 2005*, http://www.iso.org/iso/survey2005.pdf, accessed 3 March 2003.

International Organization for Standardization (ISO) (2007) *The ISO Survey – 2006*, http://www.iso.org/iso/survey2006.pdf, accessed 3 March 2003.

International Organisation for Standardization (ISO) (2008) home page, http://www.iso.org/iso/home.htm, accessed 22 April 2008.

Investor Network on Climate Risk (INCR) (2007) http://www.incr.com home page, accessed 17 September 2007.

IPCC (2007) Climate Change 2007: The Physical Science Basis, Summary for Policymakers. Contribution of Working Group to the Fourth Assessment I. P. O. C. Change.

Jaffe, A. and K. Palmer (1997) 'Environmental Regulation and Innovation: A Panel Data Study', *Review of Economics and Statistics*, 79(4) 610–619.

Jayaraman, N. (2006a) Interview with Mr H. H. Nerurkar, vice president, Tata Steel, *Corporate Watch* 10 June 2006, http://www.corpwatch.org/article.php?id=14111, accessed 25 July 2008.

Jayaraman, N. (2006b) Stolen for Steel: Tata Takes Tribal Lands in India, *Corporate Watch* 24 May 2006, http://www.corpwatch.org/article.php?list=classt&class=1&type=183, accessed 25 July 2008.

Jayathirtha, R. (2001) 'Combating Environmental Repercussions through TQEM and ISO 14000', *Business Strategy and the Environment*, 10(4) 245–250.

Johansson, J. (2006) 'Incorporating Environmental Concern in Product Development, a Study of Project Characteristics', *Management of Environmental Quality: An International Journal*, 17(4) 421–436.

Johnston, T. (2007) 'Australia Plans to Phase Out Incandescent Lights', *New York Times*, February 20, 2007 http://www.nytimes.com/2007/02/20/world/asia/20cnd-light.html?_r=1&oref=slogin, accessed January 2008.

Jubilant Organosys (2007) *Corporate Sustainability Report 2007*, http://www.jubl.net/pdfs/CorporateSustanabilityReport200607.pdf, accessed 23 June 2008.

Kahn, M. (2007) 'Do Greens Drive Hummers or Hybrids? Environmental Ideology as a Determinant of Consumer Choice', *Journal of Environmental Economics and Management*, 54(2) 129–145.

Kallio, T. and Nordberg, P. (2006) The Evolution of Organizations and Natural Environment Discourse: Some Critical Remarks, *Organization & Environment* 19, 439–457.

Kangun, N. and M. Polonsky (1995) 'Regulation of Environmental Marketing Claims: A Comparative Perspective', *International Journal of Advertising*, 11(1) 1–24.

Kant, I. (1996) *The Metaphysics of Morals*, Cambridge University Press, Cambridge.

Kanter, R. (1986) *When a Thousand Flowers Bloom: Structural, Collective, and Social Conditions for Innovation in Organizations*, working chapter, Harvard School of Business, Boston, Mass.

Katz, D. and R. Kahn (1978) *The Sound Psychology of Organizations*, Wiley, New York.

Kaye, R. (2007) 'Transnational Environmental Litigation', *Environmental and Planning Law Journal*, 24(1) 35–58.

Kelly, D. (2006) Human Resource Development: For Enterprise and Human Development, *Research Online*, University of Wollongong, Australia, http://ro.uow.edu.au/cgi/viewcontent.cgi?article=1116&context=artspapers, accessed 25 July 2008.

Kelman, H. (1961) 'Processes of Opinion Change', *Public Opinion Quarterly*, 25, 608–615.

Kennedy, D. (1996) 'Trade and Environment – an NGO Perspective', in B. Boer, R. Fowler and N. Gunningham, *Environmental Outlook No 2: Law and Policy*, The Federation Press, Sydney, 173–185.

Keogh, P. and M. Polonsky (1998) 'Environmental Commitment: A Basis for Environmental Entrepreneurship?' *Journal of Organizational Change Management*, 11(1) 38–49.

Kerr, W. and C. Ryan (2001) Eco-Efficiency Gains from Remanufacturing: A Case Study of Photocopier Remanufacturing at Fuji Xerox Australia, *Journal of Cleaner Production*, 9(1) 75–81.

Khalil, T. (2000) *Management of Technology, the Key to Competitiveness and Wealth Creation*, McGraw Hill, Boston.

Kilbourne, W. and S. Beckmann (1998) Review and Critical Assessment of Research on Marketing and the Environment, *Journal of Marketing Management*, 14(6) 513–532.

Kilman, S. (2006) 'New Leaf: Seed Firms Bolster Crops Using Traits Of Distant Relatives', *Wall Street Journal*, New York, October 31, p. A1.

King, A. and M. Lenox (2002) 'Exploring the Locus of Profitable Pollution Reduction', *Management Science*, 48(2) 289–299.

Kivimaa, P. (2008) 'Integrating Environment for Innovation: Experiences from Product Development in Paper and Packaging', *Organization & Environment*, 21(1) 56–75.

Klassen, R. and D. Whybark (1999) 'The Impact of Environmental Technologies on Manufacturing Performance', *Academy of Management Journal*, 42, 599–615.

Kohn, R. (2003) 'Environmental Standards as Barriers to Trade', *Socio-Economic Planning Sciences*, 37(3) 203–214.

Kolk, A. (2004) 'A Decade of Environmental Reporting: Developments and Significance', *International Journal of Environment and Sustainable Development*, 3(1) 51–64.

Kolk, A. (2005) 'Environmental Reporting by Multinationals from the Triad: Convergence or Divergence?' *Management International Review*, 1, 145–166.

Kolk, A. (2008) 'Sustainability, Accountability and Corporate Governance: Exploring Multinationals' Reporting Practices', *Business Strategy and the Environment*, 18, 1–15.

Kolk, A. and J. Pinkse (2005) 'Business Responses to Climate Change: Identifying Emergent Strategies', *California Management Review*, 47(3) 6–20.

Koontz, H. and C. O'Donnell (*circa* 1971) *Principles of Management: An Analysis of Managerial Functions*, McGraw-Hill, New York.

Korten, D. (1999) *The Post-corporate World: Life after Capitalism*, Kumarian Press and Berrett-Koehler Publishers, Bloomfield, CT.

Kramar, R. and G. Martin (2007) 'Compliance, ethics and corporate social responsibility', in *Australian Master Human Resources Guide*, Fourth Edition, CCH Australia Ltd, Sydney.

Krznaric, R. (2007) *How Change Happens: Interdisciplinary Perspectives for Human Development*, Oxfam GB.

LaFrance, J. and M. Lehmann (2005) 'Corporate Awakenings – Why (Some) Corporations Embrace Public–Private Partnerships', *Business Strategy and the Environment*, 14(4) 216–229.

Lagan, A. (2006) *A View from the Top*, Corporate Citizenship and Business Ethics Unit, KPMG, Sydney.

Lane, B. and S. Potter (2006) 'The Adoption of Cleaner Vehicles in the UK: Exploring the consumer-action gap', *Journal of Cleaner Production*, 15, 1085–1092.

Laszlo, C. (2005) *The Sustainable Company*, Island Press, Washington, DC.

Lawrence, P. and D. Dyer (1983) *Renewing American industry*, Free Press, New York.

Leach, L. and P. Sabatier (2003) 'Facilitators, coordinators, and outcomes', in R. O'Leary and L. Bingham (eds), *The Promise and Performance of Environmental Conflict Resolution*, Washington, DC, Resources for the Future Press, 148–175.

Leape, J. (2006) *Director General of WWF quoted in the WWF International Living Planet Report*, 2006, http://www.wwf.org/, accessed 3 March 2008.

Lenz, R. (1981) 'Determinants of Organizational Performance: An Interdisciplinary Review', *Strategic Management Journal*, 2(2) 131–154.

Leonard-Barton, D. (1981) 'Voluntary Simplify Lifestyles and Energy Conservation', *Journal of Consumer Research*, 8(3) 243–252.

Leopold, A. (1989) *A Sand County Almanac, and Sketches Here and There*, Oxford University Press US, New York.

LeVeness, F. and P. Primeaux (2004) 'Vicarious Ethics: Politics, Business and Sustainable Development', *Journal of Business Ethics*, 51(2) 185–198.

Levy, N. (2002) *Moral Relativism: A Short Introduction*, Oneworld Publications, Oxford.

Linder, S. and B. Peters (1987) 'A Design Perspective on Policy Implementation: The Fallacies of Misplaced Prescription', *Policy Studies Review*, 6(3) 459–475.

Linowes, D. (1972) 'An Approach to Socio-Economic Accounting', *The Conference Board RECORD*, 9(11) 58–61.

Lipsky, M. (1978) 'Standing the study of public policy implementation on its head', in W. Burnham and M. Weinberg (eds), *American Politics and Public Policy*, Cambridge, MA, MIT Press, 391–402.

Lohmann, L. (2005) 'Marketing and Making Carbon Dumps: Commodification, Calculation and Counterfactuals in Climate', *Science as Culture*, 14(3) 203–235.

López-Fernández, M. and A. Serrano-Bedia (2007) 'Organizational Consequences of Implementing an ISO 14001 Environmental Management System: An Empirical Analysis', *Organization & Environment*, 20(4) 440–459.

Lovelock, J. (1991) *Healing Gaia*, Harmony Books, New York.

Lovins, A., L. Lovins and P. Hawken (1999) 'A Road Map to Natural Capitalism', *Harvard Business Review*, 77(3) 162–178.

Luthans, F. (2002) 'Positive Organizational Behaviour: Developing and Managing Psychological Strengths for Performance Improvement', *Academy of Management Executive*, 16(1) 57–72.

Luthans F., K. Luthans, R. Hodgetts and B. Luthans (2002) 'Positive Approach to Leadership (PAL): Implications for Today's Organizations', *Journal of Leadership Studies*, 8(2) 3–20.

Luther, L. (2008) 'Compact Florescent Bulbs: Issues with Use and Disposal', *Congressional Research Service*, http://assets.opencrs.com/rpts/RS22807_20080213.pdf, accessed February 2008.

Lynes, J. and D. Dredge (2006) 'Going Green: Motivations for Environmental Commitment in the Airline Industry. A Case Study of Scandinavian Airlines', *Journal of Sustainable Tourism*, 14(2) 116–138.

Lyster, R. (2007) 'Chasing down the Climate Change Footprint of the Private and Public Sectors: Forces Converge', *Environmental and Planning Law Journal*, 24(4) 281–321.

Mackenzie, C. (2006) 'The scope for investor activism on corporate social and environmental impacts', in R. Sullivan and C. Mackenzie (eds), *Responsible Investment*, Sheffield, UK, Greenleaf Publishing, 20–38.

Macquarie University (1981) *The Macquarie Dictionary*, The Macquarie Library Pty Ltd, Chatswood, NSW.

Magnusson, T., G. Lindström and Berggren, C. (2003) 'Architectural or Modular Innovation? Managing Discontinuous Product Development in Response to Challenging Environmental Performance Targets', *International Journal of Innovation Management*, 7(1) 1–26.

Magretta, J. (1997) 'Growth through Global Sustainability an Interview with Monsanto's CEO Robert B. Shapiro', *Harvard Business Review*, 75(1) 78–88.

Majumdar, S. and A. Marcus (2001) 'Rules Versus Discretion: The Productivity Consequences of Flexible Regulation', *Academy of Management Journal*, 44(1) 170–180.

Malthus, T. (1798) *An Essay on the Principle of Population*, St Paul's Church-Yard, London, J. Johnson.

Mansley, M. (2000) *Socially Responsible Investment: A Guide for Pension Funds and Institutional Investors*, Monitor Press, Sudbury, Suffolk, UK.

March, J. G. and H. A. Simon (1958) *Organizations*, New York, Wiley.

Marcus, A. (1988a) 'Implementing Externally Induced Innovations: A Comparison of Rule-Bound and Autonomous Approaches', *Academy of Management Journal*, 31(2) 235–256.

Marcus, A. (1988b) 'Responses to Externally Induced Innovation: Their Effects on Organizational Performance', *Strategic Management Journal*, 9, 387–402.

Marcus, A. (1996) *Business and Society: Strategy, Ethics, and the Global Economy*, Irwin Press, Chicago, IL.

Marcus, A. (1998) 'Ringer: Overcoming Obstacles in the Path to Success', *Strategic Environmental Management*, Pollution Prevention Educational Resource Compendium, University of Michigan.

Marcus, A. (2006) *Winning Moves: A Casebook*, Marsh Books, Lonmbard, Ill.

Marcus, A. and D. Geffen (1998) 'The Deluxe Corporation's PrintWise System', *Strategic Environmental Management*, Pollution Prevention Educational Resource Compendium, University of Michigan.

Marcus, A. and D. Geffen (2005) 'Hybrids: Hype or Hope?' *Business & Professional Ethics Journal*, 24(1) 141–161.

Marcus, A. and M. Anderson (2006) 'A General Dynamic Capability: Does it Propagate Business and Social Competencies in the Retail Food Industry?' *Journal of Management Studies*, 43(1) 19–46.

Marcus, A., D. Geffen and K. Sexton (2002) *Reinventing Environmental Regulation: Lessons from Project XL*, Resources for the Future, Washington, DC.

Margolis, J. and J. Walsh (2003) 'Misery Loves Companies: Rethinking Social Initiatives by Business', *Administrative Science Quarterly*, 48(2) 268–305.

Maroochy Shire (2008) *Maroochy Council Annual Report 2006/07*, http://www.maroochy.qld.gov.au/siteresources/documents/ar1_intro.pdf, accessed 23 April 2008.

Marshall, A. (1891) *Principles of Economics*, Macmillan, London.

Marx, K. and F. Engels (1967) *The Communist Manifesto*, Penguin, Harmondsworth, Middlesex.

Marx, K. and F. Engels (1968) *The German Ideology*, Progress Publishers, Moscow.

McDonald, S., C. Oates, C. Young and K. Hwang (2006) 'Toward Sustainable Consumption: Researching Voluntary Simplifiers', *Psychology and Marketing*, 23(6) 515–534.

McDonough, W. and M. Braungart (1998) 'The Next Industrial Revolution, Solving the Environmental Problems that Industry Makes', *The Atlantic Monthly*, 283.4, October, 82.

McDonough, W. and M. Braungart (2002) *Cradle to Cradle: Remaking the Way We Make Things*, North Point Press, New York.

McIntosh, A. (2000) *Do Corporations have Human Rights?* http://www.alastairmcintosh.com/articles/2000_quarrylaw.htm, accessed 20 December 2007.

McLaren, D. (2004) 'Global Stakeholders: Corporate Accountability and Investor Engagement, *Corporate Governance – An International Review*, 12(2) 191–201.

McShane, S. and T. Travaglione (2003). *Organizational Behaviour on the Pacific Rim*, McGraw-Hill Irwin, Boston.

Meadows, D. H., D. L. Meadows, J. Randers and W. Behrens III (1972) *The Limits to Growth*, Earth Island, London.

Menon, A. and A. Menon (1997) 'Enviropreneurial Marketing Strategy: The Emergence of Corporate Environmentalism as Market Strategy', *Journal of Marketing*, 61(1) 51–67.

Miller, J. (2006) Stalk-Raving Mad: French Farmers, Activists Battle Over Rise in Genetically Altered Corn, *Wall Street Journal*, New York, NY. October 12, p. B1.

Mineral Policy Institute (2000a) *Massive Cyanide Spill by Australian Mining Company*, http://www.mpi.org.au/campaigns/cyanide/romanian_esmeralda_cynaide_spill/, accessed 18 August 2007.

Mineral Policy Institute (2000b) *Report on Tolukuma Cyanide Spill*, http://www.mpi. org.au/campaigns/cyanide/report_tolukuma/, accessed 5 March 2008.

Mintzberg, H. (1981) 'Organization design: fashion or fit?' *Harvard Business Review* 59(1) 103–116.

Mirvis, P. and L. Gunning (2005) 'Creating a Community of Leaders', *Organizational Dynamics*, 35(1) 69–82.

Mitroff, I. and E. Denton (1999) 'A Study of Spirituality in the Workplace', *Sloan Management Review*, 40, 83–92.

Mohamed-Katerere, J. (2007) *From Environment and Development to Evolution of Ideas*, from Our Common Future to GEO-4: Brundtland + 20 Seminar Background paper, http:// www.unep.org/geo/geo4/media/Brundtland_24_10_07.pdf, accessed 29 July 2008.

Monsanto (2007) *Monsanto Pledge Report 2007, Growth for a better world*, http://www. monsanto.com/pdf/pubs/2007/pledge_report.pdf, accessed 23 June 2007.

Moors, E. and P. Vergragt (2002) 'Technology Choices for Sustainable Industrial Production: Transitions in Metal Making', *International Journal of Innovation Management*, 6(3) 277–299.

Mostafa, M. (2007) 'A Hierarchical Analysis of the Green Consciousness of the Egyptian Consumer', *Psychology and Marketing*, 24(5) 445–473.

Muller, B. (2007) *Food miles or poverty eradication? The moral duty to eat African strawberries at Christmas*, http://www.oxfordenergy.org/pdfs/comment_1007-1.pdf, accessed 25 August 2008.

Murphy, P. and R. Poist (2000) 'Green Logistics Strategies: An Analysis of Usage Patterns', *Transportation Journal*, 40(20) 5–16.

Nattrass, W., M. Nattrass and B. Horniman (2006) 'New Rules, New Plays in the Changing Game of Business', *Batten Briefings*, Darden School of Business and Batten Institute, University of Virginia, Charlottsville, VA, 1–7.

Nike (2004a) *Corporate Responsibility Report*, http://www.nike.com/nikebiz/gc/r/ fy04/docs/FY04_Nike_CR_report_pt1.pdf, accessed 10 May 2006.

Nike (2004b) *Nike Names New VP of Corporate Responsibility Maria Eitel Becomes President of the Nike Foundation*, Press Release 21 October 2004, http://www.csr-wire.com/article.cgi/3154.html, accessed 12 May 2006.

Nisbet, M. and Myers, T. (2007) 'Twenty Years of Public Opinion about Global Warming', *Public Opinion Quarterly*, 71(3) 444–470.

Nordhaus, W. (2006) The *Stern Review* on the Economics of Climate Change, http:// www.nordhaus.econ.yale.edu/stern_050307.pdf, accessed 17 September 2007.

Norsk Hydro (2007) 2007 Annual Report, http://www.annualreporting.hydro.com/ en/Our-performance/Viability-performance/, accessed 23 June 2008.

Norsk Hydro (2008) Norsk Hydro home page, http://www.hydro.com, accessed 23 June 2008.

Novo Group Academy (2001) 'The invisible movement', *Trendspotter Newsletter no. 2*, Denmark: Novo Group Academy, October 2001, p. 4, http://www.novogroup.dk/ academy, accessed 10 may 2008.

O'Reilly, C. and J. Pfeffer (2000) 'Southwest Airlines: If success is so simple, why is it so hard to imitate?' *Hidden Value*, Harvard Business School Press, Boston.

OECD (2004) *OECD Principles for Corporate Governance*, http://www.oecd.org/ dataoecd/32/18/31557724.pdf, accessed 22 March 2008.

OECD (2008) *Guidelines for Multinational Enterprises*, http://www.oecd.org/ department/0,3355,en_2649_34889_1_1_1_1_1,00.html, accessed 22 March 2008.

Organisations and the Natural Environment (ONE) (2008) Organisations and the Natural Environment home page, http://www.one.aomonline.org/, accessed 21 July 2008.

Orlitzky, M., F. Schmidt and S. Rynes (2003) 'Corporate Social Financial Performance: A Meta-Analysis', *Organizational Studies*, 24(3) 403–441.

Orsato, R. (2006) Competitive Environmental Strategies: When Does it Pay to be Green? *California Management Review*, 48(2) 127–143.

Orsato, R. and K. McCormick (2006) *The Need for Oil: The Stuart Oil Shale Project in Australia*, UTS, Sydney.

Orsato, R. and P. Wells (2007) 'The Automobile Industry & Sustainability', *Journal of Cleaner Production*, 15, 989–993.

Orsato, R. and P. Wells (2007a) 'U-turn: The rise and Demise of the Automobile Industry', *Journal of Cleaner Production*, 15, 994–1006.

Orsato, R. and S. Clegg (2005) 'Radical Reform: Towards Critical Ecological Modernism', *Sustainable Development*, 13, 253–267.

Orsato, R., R. Perey and D. Dunphy (2006) *The Green Building Strategy: The Case of Lend Lease Australia*, UTS, Sydney.

Ottman, J. (1998) *Green Marketing: Opportunity for Innovation*, Lincolnwood, NTC Business Books.

Overcash, M. (2002) 'The Evolution of US Pollution Prevention, 1976–2001: A Unique Chemical Engineering Contribution to the Environment – a Review', *Journal of Chemical Technology & Biotechnology*, 77(11) 1197–1205.

Palmer, I., R. Dunford and G. Akin (2006) *Managing Organizational Change*, McGraw-Hill, Irwin, New York.

Paramanathan, S., C. Farrukh, R. Phaal and D. Probert (2004) 'Implementing Industrial Sustainability: The Research Issues in Technology Management', *R&D Management*, 34(5) 527–537.

Parker, C. (2002) *The Open Corporation: Effective Self-regulation and Democracy*, Cambridge University Press, Cambridge UK.

Passmore, J. (1974) *Man's Responsibility for Nature*, Duckworth, London.

Peel, J. (2005) *The Precautionary Principle in Practice: Environmental Decision-Making and Scientific Uncertainty*, The Federation Press, Sydney.

Peglau, R. (2008) *The Number of ISO14000 Registrations Throughout the World*, Peglau-Federal Environment Agency, Germany, http://www.ecology.or.jp/isoworld/english/analy14k.htm, accessed 4 February 2008.

Percival, R. (1998) 'Environmental Legislation and the Problem of Collective Action', *Duke Environmental Law and Policy*, 9(Fall) 9–27.

Peterson, D. (2004) 'The Relationship between Perceptions of Corporate Citizenship and Organizational Commitment', *Business & Society*, 43(3) 296–319.

Pfeffer, J. (1996) 'When It Comes to "Best Practices" – Why Do Smart Companies Occasionally Do Dumb Things?' *Organizational Dynamics*, 25(1) 33–34.

Pfeffer, J. (1998) *The Human Equation*, Harvard Business School, Cambridge, MA.

Phillips, W., H. Noke, J. Bessant and R. Lamming (2006) 'Beyond the Steady State: Managing Discontinuous Product and Process Innovation', *International Journal of Innovation Management*, 10(2) 175–196.

Polonsky, M. and C. Jevons (2006) 'Understanding Issue Complexity When Building A Socially Responsible Brand', *European Business Review*, 18(5) 340–349.

Polonsky, M. and P. Rosenberger III (2001) 'Re-evaluating Green Marketing – An Integrated Approach', *Business Horizons*, 44(5) 21–30.

Polonsky, M. and P. Ryan (1996) 'The Implications of Stakeholder Statutes for Socially Responsible Managers', *Business and Professional Ethics Journal*, 15(3) 1–35.

Polonsky, M., H. Brooks, P. Henry and C. Schweizer (1998) 'An Exploratory Examination of Environmentally Responsible Straight Rebuy Purchases in Large Australian Organisations', *Journal of Business and Industrial Marketing*, 13(1) 54–69.

Porritt, J. (2006) *Capitalism as if the World Matters*, Earthscan, London.

Porter, M. (1991) 'America's Greening Strategy', *Scientific American*, 264, 168.

Porter, M. and C. van der Linde (1995a) 'Green and Competitive', *Harvard Business Review*, 73(5) 120–134.

Porter, M. and C. van der Linde (1995b) 'Toward a New Conception of the Environment-Competitiveness Relationship', *Journal of Economic Perspectives*, 9(4) 97–118.

Procter and Gamble (2007) *2007 Global Sustainability Report*, http://www.pg.com/company/our_commitment/pdfs/gsr07_Web.pdf, accessed 22 June 2008

Quiggin, J. (1988) 'Private and Common Property Rights in the Economics of the Environment', *Journal of Economic Issues*, 22(4) 1071–1087.

Quinn, R. (1996) *Deep Change: Discovering the Leader Within*, Jossey-Bass, San Francisco, 9.

Raiffa, H. (1982) *The Art and Science of Negotiation*, Harvard University Press, Cambridge, MA.

Ramboll (2004) 'Holistic Accounting and Capitalisation', http://www.ramboll.dk/docs/dan/Pressecenter/Publikationer/generelle/capitalization.pdf, accessed 25 June 2007.

Ramseur, J. (2007) Voluntary Carbon Offsets: Overview and Assessment', Congressional *Research Service*, http://www.assets.opencrs.com/rpts/RL34241_20071107.pdf, accessed 25 August 2008.

Resick, C., P. Hanges, M. Dickson and J. Mitchelson (2006) 'A Cross Cultural Examination of the Endorsement of Ethical Leadership', *Journal of Business Ethics*, 63, 345–359.

Revkin, A. (2007) 'Carbon-Neutral Is Hip, but Is It Green', *The New York Times*, 2 April 2007 http://www.nytimes.com/2007/04/29/weekinreview/29revkin.html?_r=2&oref=slogin&pagewanted=print&oref=slogin, accessed January 2008.

Rio Tinto (1998) *1998 Social and Environment Report*', http://www.corporateregister.com/a10723/rio098-e&ss-uk.pdf, accessed 24 March 2008.

Rio Tinto (2008a) *Annual Report 2007: Sustainable Development Review*, http://www.riotinto.com/annualreport2007/PDFs/p83_95SustainbleDevelReview.pdf, accessed 22 June 2008.

Rio Tinto (2008b) *Who we are, Sustainable Development Review*, http://www.riotinto.com/annualreport2007/whoweare/sustainable_development/index.html, accessed 22 June 2008.

Robins, N. (2006) Shaping the Market: Investor Engagement in Public Policy, in R. Sullivan and C. Mackenzie (eds) *Responsible Investment*, Sheffield, UK, Greenleaf Publishing, 312–321.

Rogers, C. and F. Roethlisberger (1991) 'Barriers and Gateways to Communication', *Harvard Business Review*, 69(6) 105–111.

Raths, D. (2006) 'Celebrating Companies That Excel at Serving a Variety of Stakeholders Well, 100 Best Corporate Citizens for 2006', *Business Ethics Magazine*, http://www.business-ethics.com/BE100_2006, accessed 30 November 2008.

Russo, M. (1999) *Environmental Management Readings and Cases*, Houghton Mifflin Company, Boston.

Russo, M. and P. Fouts (1997) 'A Resource-Based Perspective on Corporate Environmental Performance and Profitability', *Academy of Management Journal*, 40(3) 534–560.

Ryan, L. and B. Dennis (2003) The Ethical Undercurrents of Pension Fund Management: Establishing a Research Agenda, *Business Ethics Quarterly*, 13(3) 315–335.

Ryan, P. (2001) 'Did we? Should we? Revisiting the 70s' Environmental Law Challenge in NSW', *Environmental and Planning Law Journal*, 18(6) 561–578.

Ryan, P. (2003) 'Sustainability Partnerships: Eco-Strategy Theory in Practice?' *Management of Environmental Quality: An International Journal*, 14(2) 256–278.

Ryan, P. (2005) 'Legislation and institutions', in R. Staib (ed.), *Environmental Management and Decision-making for Business*, Hampshire UK, Palgrave Macmillan, 58–66.

Sahay, A. (2004) 'Environmental Reporting by Indian Corporations', *Corporate Social Responsibility and Environmental Management*, 11, 12–22.

Salzmann, O., A. Ionescu-somers and U. Steger (2005) 'The Business Case for Corporate Sustainability: Literature Review and Research Options', *European Management Journal*, 23(1) 27–36.

Samson, D. and R. Daft (2005) *Management*, Thompson Nelson Australia Pvt. Ltd, Melbourne, Australia.

Samuelson, P. and W. Nordhaus (1994) *Economics*, McGraw Hill, New York.

Sarkar, R. (2004) *Environmental Initiatives at Tata Steel-Green Washing or Reality? A Case Study of Corporate Environmental Behaviour*, in Proceedings of the Second Conference in International Corporate Responsibility, Amsterdam, June, 2004, Philosophy Documentation Centre, Virginia.

Sarkar, R. (2005) 'Environmental Initiatives at Tata Steel: Greenwashing or Reality?' in J. Hooker, A. Kolk and P. Marsden (eds) *Perspectives on International Corporate Responsibility*, Philosophy Documentation Centre, Virginia, Carnegie Borsch Institute.

Savage, G., T. Nix, C. Whitehead and J. Blair (1991) 'Strategies for Assessing and Managing Organisation Stakeholders', *Academy of Management Executive*, 5(2) 61–75.

Schaltegger, S. and R. Burritt (2000) *Contemporary Environmental Accounting: Issues, Concepts and Practice*, Greenleaf Publishing, Sheffield, UK.

Schaltegger, S., R. Burritt and H. Petersen (2003) *An Introduction to Corporate Environmental Management*, Greenleaf Publishing. Sheffield, UK.

Schein, E. (1999) *Process Consultation Revisited: Building the Helping Relationship*, Addison-Wesley, Reading, MA, 201–218.

Schnietz, K. and M. Epstein (2005) 'Exploring the Financial Value of a Reputation for Corporate Social Responsibility during a Crisis', *Corporate Reputation Review*, 7(4) 327–345.

Schon, D. (1984) *Educating the Reflective Practitioner*, Jossey-Bass, San Francisco.

Schuler, R. (1992) 'Strategic Human Resource Management: Linking the People with the Strategic Needs of the Business', *Organizational Dynamics*, 21(1) 18–32.

Scott, P. (2001) 'The Pitfalls in Mandatory Reporting', *Environmental Finance*, April, 24–25.

Scott, W. and S. Gough (eds) (2004) *Sustainable Development and Learning: Framing the Issues*, Routledge Falmer, London/New York.

Senge, P., C. Scharmer, J. Jaworski and S. Flowers (2005) *Presence: Exploring Profound Change in People, Organizations and Society*, Nicholas Brealey Publishing, London.

Sennett, R. (2000) *The Corrosion of Character: The Personal Consequences of Work in the New Capitalism*, W.W. Norton & Company, New York.

Seshadri, D. and A. Tripathy (2006) Reinventing a Giant Corporation: The Case of Tata Steel, *Vikalpa*, 31(1) 133–146.

Sethi, P. and C. Falbe (eds) (1987) *Business and Society: Dimensions of Conflict and Cooperation*, Lexington Books, Lexington, MA.

Shafaghi, F. and R. Kerr (2007) *Management of Manufacturing Systems GBAT9102: Course Overview*, http://www.mbt.unsw.edu.au, accessed 1 November 2007.

Shapiro, B. (1998) 'Towards a Normative Model of Rational Argumentation for Critical Accounting Discussion', *Accounting, Organisations and Society*, 23(7) 641–664.

Sharfman, M., M. Meo and R. Ellington (2000) 'Regulation, Business, and Sustainable Development: The Antecedents Environmentally Conscious Sustainable Development', *American Behavioral Scientist*, 44(2) 277–302.

Sharfman, M., R. Ellington and M. Meo (1999) 'Final Report: Regulation, Business, and Sustainable Development: The Management of Environmentally Conscious Technological Innovation under Alternative Market Conditions', http://www.cfpub.epa.gov/ncer_abstracts/index.cfm/fuseaction/display.abstractDetail/abstract/632/report/F, accessed 4 February 2008.

Sharma, A. (1981) 'Coping with Staglation: Voluntary Simplicity', *Journal of Marketing*, 45(3) 120–134.

Sharma, S. and H. Vredenburg (1998) 'Proactive Corporate Environmental Strategy and the Development of Competitively Valuable Competencies', *Strategic Management Journal*, 19, 729–754.

Shell International (1998) *Profits and Principles – does there have to be a choice? The Shell Report 1998*, http://www.shell.com/static/envirosoc-en/downloads/sustainability_reports/shell_report_1997.pdf, accessed 20 December 2007.

Shrivastava, P. (1995) 'The Role of Corporations in Achieving Ecological Sustainability', *Academy of Management Review*, 20(4) 936–960.

Shrum, L., J. Mccarty and T. Lowrey (1995) Buyer Characteristics of the Green Consumer and Their Implications for Advertising Strategy, *Journal of Advertising*, 24 (2) 71–82.

Sinclair, A. (2006) *Leadership for the Disillusioned*, Crows Nest, Allen and Unwin.

Singer, P. (2001) *Writings on an Ethical Life*, HarperCollins, London.

Smith, A. (1998) *An Inquiry into the Nature and Causes of the Wealth of Nations*, Oxford University Press, Oxford.

Smith, M. and J. Crotty (2008) 'Environmental Regulation and Innovation Driving Ecological Design in the UK Automotive Industry', *Business Strategy and the Environment*, 17(6) 341–349.

Sneddon, C., R. Howarth and R. Norgaard (2006) 'Sustainable Development in a Post-Brundtland World', *Ecological Economics*, 57(2) 253–268.

Snow, D. (2006) 'Business Warms to Change', *Sydney Morning Herald*, 10 April 2006, http://www.smh.com.au/news/environment/business-warms-to-change/2006/04/09/1144521210225.html, accessed 12 May 2006.

Solow, R. (1956) 'A Contribution to the Theory of Economic Growth', *Quarterly Journal of Economics*, 70(1) 65–94.

Sparkes, R. (2002) *Socially Responsible Investment: A Global Revolution*, John Wiley & Sons, Chicester, West Sussex, UK.

Sparrow, P., R. Schuler and S. Jackson (1994) 'Convergence or Divergence: Human Resource Practices and Policies for Competitive Advantage Worldwide', *International Journal of Human Resource Management*, 5(2) 268–299.

Speth, J. and P. Haas (2006) *Global Environmental Governance*, Island Press, Washington, DC.

Springer, J. (1999) 'Corporate Constituency Statutes: Hollow Hopes and False Fears', *Annual Survey of American Law*, 85–124.

Springett, D. (2005) 'Book Reviews', *Business Strategy and the Environment*, 14, 198–200.

Sroufe, R., S. Curkovic, F. Montabon and S. Melnyk (2000) 'The New Product Design Process and Design for Environment', *International Journal of Operations and Production*, 20(2) 267–291.

Stafford, E., M. Polonsky and C. Hartman (2000) 'Environmental NGO-Business Collaboration and Strategic Bridging: A Case Analysis of the Greenpeace-Fron Alliance', *Business Strategy and the Environment*, 9(2) 122–135.

Staib, R. (1997) *Solving Major Pollution Problems: A New Process Model*, Macquarie University, Sydney Australia.

Staib, R. (1998) 'Processes in Pollution Management: An Australian Model', *Environmental Management*, 22(3) 393–406.

Staib, R. (2005) *Environmental Management and Decision Making for Business*, Palgrave Macmillan, London.

Stead, W. and J. Stead (2004) *Sustainable Strategic Management*, M.E. Sharpe, Armonk, NY.

Steiner, A. (2007) *Remarks by the UN Under-Secretary General and Executive Director UN Environment Programme (UNEP)*, at the Launch of Global Environment Outlook-4, http://www.unep.org/Documents.Multilingual/Default.asp?DocumentID=520&ArticleID=5711&l=en, accessed, 29 July 2008.

Steingard, D. (2005) 'Spiritual-Informed Management Theory: Towards Profound Possibilities for Inquiries and Transformation', *Journal of Management Inquiry*, 14(3) 227–241.

Stern, N. (2006a) *Stern Review: The Economics of Climate Change*, Cambridge University Press, Cambridge.

Stern, N. (2006b) *Stern Review: The Economics of Climate Change, Executive Summary*, http://www.hm-treasury.gov.uk/media/4/3/Executive_Summary.pdf, accessed 20 January 2008.

Stern, N. (2007) *Stern Review: The Economics of Climate Change Executive Summary*, HM Treasury, UK; full report N. Stern (2007) *The Economics of Climate Change: The Stern Review*, Cambridge University Press, Cambridge UK.

Stewart, D. (1972) 'The Limits of Trooghaft', *Encounter*, 38(2) 3–7.

Stigson, B. (2007) *Why Ecosystems Matter to Business*, reproduced by World Business Council for Sustainable Development, WBCSD home page http://www.wbcsd.org, from *Environmental Finance*.

Strebel, P. (1987) 'Organizing for Innovation over an Industry Cycle', *Strategic Management Journal*, 8, 117–124.

Stubbs, W. and C. Cocklin (2006) An Ecological Modernist Interpretation of Sustainability: The Case of Interface Inc., *Business Strategy and the Environment*, published online in Wiley InterScience.

Sullivan, R. (2006) *Managing Investments in a Changing Climate*, IIGCC, London.

Sullivan, R. and C. Mackenzie (2006) Shareholder Activism on Social, Ethical and Environmental Issues: An introduction in R. Sullivan and C. Mackenzie (eds), *Responsible Investment*, Sheffield, UK, Greenleaf Publishing, 150–157.

Sullivan, R., N. Robins, D. Russell and H. Barnes (2005) Investor Collaboration on Climate Change: The Work of the IIGCC in K. Tang (ed.) *The Finance of Climate Change*, London, Risk Books, 197–210.

Sullivan, R. and W. Blyth (2006) *Climate Change Policy Uncertainty and the Electricity Industry: Implications and Unintended Consequences*, Chatham House Briefing Paper EEDP BP 06/02, Chatham House, London.

Swan, T. (1956) 'Economic Growth and Capital Accumulation', *Economic Record*, 334–361.

Swanston, D. (2004) 'The Buck Stops Here: Why Universities Must Reclaim Business Ethics Education', *Journal of Academic Ethics*, 2(1) 43–62.

Symbiosis (2008) *Industrial Symbiosis*, http://www.symbiosis.dk, accessed 8 February 2008.

Tata Steel (2007) *Corporate Sustainability Report 2005–06*, Tata Steel Limited, Mumbai.

Tata Steel (2008) Tata Steel home page site, http://www.tatasteel.com/, accessed 21 March 2008

Tata Steel (2008a) IISI Sustainability Reporting on Environmental Indicators, http://www.tatasteel.com/corporatesustainability/environment_management.asp, accessed 21 March 2008.

Taylor, A. (2006) 'Toyota: The Birth of the Prius', *Fortune Magazine*, 21 February 2006, New York.

Taylor, B. (2007) *Learning for Tomorrow: Whole Person Learning*, Oasis Press, West Yorkshire.

Teece, D., G. Pisano and A. Shuen (1997) 'Dynamic Capabilities and Strategic Management', *Strategic Management Journal*, 18(7) 509–533.

Thampapillai, D. (2002) *Environmental Economics: Concepts, Methods and Policies*, Oxford University Press, Melbourne.

Thampapillai, D. and B. Öhlmer (2000) Environmental Economics – for Business Management, Swedish University of Agricultural Sciences, Uppsala.

The Central Pollution Control Board (CPCB) (2008) The Central Pollution Control Board of India home page, http://www.cpcb.nic.in, accessed 5 April 2008.

The National Marketing Institute (NMI) (2007) *NMI's 2007 Consumer Segmentation Model*, http://www.nmisolutions.com/lohasd_segment.html, accessed January 2007.

The Natural Step (2008) The Natural Step home page, http://www.naturalstep.org/com/nyStart/, accessed 8 April 2008.

Thomas, T., J. Schermerhorn and J. Dienhart (2004) 'Strategic Leadership of Ethical Behaviour in Business', *Academy of Management Executive*, 18(2) 56–65.

Tidd, J., J. Bessant and K. Pavitt (2005) *Managing Innovation: Integrating Technological, Market and Organizational Change*, John Wiley & Sons Ltd, Chichester, United Kingdom.

Tilbury, D. and D. Wortman (2004) *Engaging people in sustainability*, IUCN, Gland Switzerland and Cambridge, UK.

Titenberg, T. (2004) *Environmental Economics and Policy*, Pearson- Addison-Wesley, Boston.

Todd, J. and M. Curran (eds) (1999) *Streamlined Life Cycle Assessment: A Final Report from the SETAC North America Streamlined LCA Workgroup*, Society of Environmental Toxicology and Chemistry, Pensacola, Florida.

Toyota (2008) *Worldwide Prius Sales Top 1 Million Mark*, News Release 15 May 2008, http://www.toyota.co.jp/en/news/08/0515.pdf, accessed 10 August 2008.

Trainer, F. (2001) Natural Capitalism Cannot Overcome Resource Limits, http://www.mnforsustain.org/traner_fe_simon_lovins_critique.htm, accessed 8 April 2008.

UNEP (2008) *The Industrial Symbiosis in Kalundborg Denmark*, http://www.unep.fr/pc/ind- estates/casestudies/kalundborg.htm, accessed 8 February 2008.

UNEP (*circa* 2006) *Guide for Negotiators of Multilateral Environmental Agreements*, http://www.unep.org/DEC/docs/Guide%20for%20Negotiators%20of%20MEAs. pdf, accessed 17 August 2008.

United Nations (1996) *Cleaner Production, a Training Resource Package*, United Nations Environment Program, Paris, http://www.uneptie.org/pc/cp/library/catalogue/cp_training.htm, accessed 29 July 2004.

United Nations (2004) Cleaner Production Activities Internet Site, United Nations, Paris, France, http://www.uneptie.org/pc/cp/home.htm, accessed 27 July 2004.

United Nations Environment Program Finance Initiative (UNEP FI) (2006a) *Principles for Responsible Investment*, http://www.unepfi.org, UNEP Finance Initiative and UN Global Compact.

United Nations Environment Program Finance Initiative (UNEP FI) (2006b) *Show Me the Money: Linking Environmental, Social and Governance Issues to Company Value*, http://www.unepfi.org, UNEP Finance Initiative.

United Nations Environment Programme (2008) *Global Environment Outlook GEO4*, United Nations Environment Programme, Malta, http://www.unep.org/geo/geo4/report/GEO-4_Report_Full_en.pdf, accessed 23 May 2008.

United Nations Environment Programme (UNEP) (2002) *Industry as a Partner for Sustainable Development, 10 Years after Rio*, United Nations Environment Programme, Paris, France, http://www.uneptie.org/Outreach/wssd/docs/global/UNEP_report-english.pdf, accessed 17 April 2008.

United Nations Environment Programme (UNEP) (2007) *Global Environment Outlook (GEO4)*, United Nations Environment Programme, Kenya.

United Nations Environment Programme Finance Initiative (UNEPFI) (2004) *The Materiality of Social, Environmental and Corporate Governance Issues to Equity Pricing*, UNEPFI, Geneva.

United Nations Framework Convention on Climate Change (UNFCC) (2008) UNFCC home page, http://www.unfccc.int/2860.php, accessed 22 April 2008.

United Nations Global Compact (UNGP) (2008) United Nations home page, www.unglobalcompact.org, accessed 22 March 2008.

United Nations Treaty Collection (2008) United Nations Treaty Collection home page, http://www.untreaty.un.org/English/access.asp, accessed 22 May 2008.

U.S. Environmental Protection Agency (US EPA) and Science Applications International Corporation (2001) *Introduction to LCA (LCAccess – LCA 101. 2001)*, accessed 12 December 2004.

United States Department of Agriculture (USDA) (1999) *Arkansas WRP Success Story: Raft Creek Bottoms in Northeast Arkansas*, http://www.nrcs.usda.gov/programs/wrp/states/success_ar.html, accessed 8 February 2008.

United States Department of Agriculture (USDA) (*circa* 2001) *Success Story: Waterfowl flock to new WRP site*, http://www.ar.nrcs.usda.gov/programs/wrp_success.html, accessed 8 February 2008.

United States Environmental Protection Agency (USEPA) (1995) *An Introduction to Environmental Accounting as a Business Management Tool: Key Concepts and Terms*, June, reproduced by The Chartered Association of Certified Accountants, Washington DC.

van Berkel, R. (2000) 'Cleaner Production in Australia: Revolutionary Strategy of Incremental Tool?' *Australian Journal of Environmental Management*, 7(3) 132–146.

van Berkel, R. (2002) 'The Business Case for Sustainable Development', *Waste & Recycle Conference 2002*, Centre of Excellence in Cleaner Production, Curtin University of Technology, Perth, Australia.

van Berkel, R., E. Willems and M. Lafleur (1997) 'Development of an Industrial Ecology Toolbox for the Introduction of Industrial Ecology in Enterprises', *Journal of Cleaner Production*, 5(1–2) 11–25.

van de Ven, A. and R. Garud (1989) 'A Framework for Understanding the Emergence of New Industries', Research on Technological Innovation, *Management and Policy*, 4, 192–225.

van den Hoed, R. (2007) 'Sources of Radical Technological Innovation: The Emergence of Fuel Cell Technology in the Automotive Industry', *Journal of Cleaner Production*, 15, 1014–1021.

Van Marrewijk, M. (2001) *The Concept and Definition of Corporate Responsibility*, Triple P Performance Centre, Amsterdam.

Van Marrewijk, M. (2003) 'Concepts and Definitions of CSR and Corporate Sustainability: Between Agency and Communion', *Journal of Business Ethics*, 44(2–3) 95–105.

Varma, A. (2003) 'The Economics of Slash and Burn: A Case Study of the 1997–1998 Indonesian Forest Fires', *Ecological Economics*, 36, 159–171.

Vergragt, P. and H. Brown (2007) 'Sustainable Mobility: From Technological Innovation to Societal Learning', *Journal of Cleaner Production*, 15, 1104–1115.

Verité (2008) Verité's home page, http://www.verite.org/, accessed 22 March 2008.

Vogel, D. (2005) 'Is There a Market for Virtue? The Business Case for Corporate Social Responsibility', *California Management Review*, 47(4) 19–45.

Wahba, H. (2007) 'Does the Market Value Corporate Environmental Responsibility? An Empirical Examination', *Corporate Social Responsibility and Environmental Management*, 15(2) 89–99.

Walley, N. and B. Whitehead (1994) 'It's Not Easy Being Green', *Harvard Business Review*, 72(3) 46–52.

Walsh, J., K. Weber and J. Margolis (2003) 'Social Issues and Management: Our Lost Cause', *Journal of Management*, 29(6) 859–881.

Way, S. and D. Johnson (2005) 'Theorising about the Impact of Strategic Human Resource Management', *Human Resource Management Review*, 15(1) 1–19.

WBCSD (2006) *From Challenge to Opportunity, The Role of Business in Tomorrow's Society*, http://www.wbcsd.org/DocRoot/4lcRHbx7NPrVWlwpGxaL/tomorrows-leaders.pdf, accessed 15 July 2008.

Wehrmeyer, W., A. Clayton and K. Lum (2002) 'Foresighting for Development', *Greener Management International*, Spring, 24–37.

Weick, K. (1995) *Sensemaking in Organizations*, Sage Publications, Beverley Hills, CA.

Welford, R. (1992) 'Linking Quality and the Environment: A Strategy for the Implementation of Environmental Management Systems', *Business Strategy and the Environment*, 1(1) 25–34.

Werther, W. and D. Chandler (2005) 'Strategic Corporate Social responsibility as a Global Brand Insurance', *Business Horizons*, 48, 317–324.

Westpac (2007a) Our Principles for doing business, http://www.westpac.com.au/internet/publish.nsf/content/WICRSR+Our+Principles,

Westpac (2007b) Stakeholder Impact Report, http://www.westpac.com.au/internet/publish.nsf/content/WICRSR+2007+Stakeholder+Impact+Report, accessed 26 August 2008.

Westpac (2008) Westpac home page, http://www.google.com.au, accessed 25 July 2008.

Wheeler, D., R. Rechtman, H. Fabig and R. Boele (2001) 'Shell, Nigeria and the Ogoni. A Study in Unsustainable Development: III. Analysis and Implications of Royal Dutch/Shell Group Strategy', *Sustainable Development*, 9(4) 177–196.

Wilkinson, A., M. Hill and P. Gollan (2001) 'The Sustainability Debate', *International Journal of Operations & Production Management*, 21(12) 1492–1502.

Willard, B. (2004) 'Teaching sustainability in business schools, Why, what and how', in C. Galea (ed.) *Teaching sustainability in business schools, Volume 1*, Toronto, Greenleaf Publishing.

Wilson, M. (2003) 'Corporate Sustainability: What is it and where does it come from?' *Ivey Business Journal*, http://www.iveybusinessjournal.com/view_article.asp?intArticle_ID=405, accessed 21 March 2008.

Windsor, D. (2006) 'Corporate Social Responsibility; Three Key Approaches', *Journal of Management Studies*, 43(1) 93–114.

World Business Council for Sustainable Development (WBCSD) (2006) *From Challenge to Opportunity – The role of business in tomorrow's society*, http://www.wbcsd.org/DocRoot/4lcRHbx7NPrVWlwpGxaL/tomorrows-leaders.pdf, accessed 20 December 2007.

World Business Council for Sustainable Development (WBCSD) (2008) WBCSD home page, http://www.wbcsd.org, accessed 2 July 2008.

World Commission on Environment and Development (WCED) (1987) *Our Common Future*, Oxford University Press, Oxford.

World Commission on Environment and Development (WCED) (1992) *Our Common Future*, Oxford University Press, Oxford.

World Economic Forum (2008) *Global 100's Most Sustainable Corporations in the World*, http://www.global100.org/2008/index.asp, accessed 12 February 2008.

World Trade Organization (2003) *Understanding the WTO*, http://www.wto.org, accessed 15 September 2004.

Worldwatch Institute (2007) *Vital Signs 2007–2008: The Trends That Are Shaping Our Future*, W.W. Norton & Company New York, London, http://www.worldwatch.org/, accessed 3 March 2008.

Wüstenhagen, R. and M. Bilharz (2006) 'Green Energy Market Development in Germany: Effective Public Policy and Emerging Customer Demand', *Energy Policy*, 34(13) 1681–1696.

WWF (2006) 2006 Living Planet Report, http://www.assets.panda.org/downloads/living_planet_report.pdf, accessed 23 April 2008.

Zikmund, W. and W. Stanton (1971) 'Recycling Solid Wastes: A Channels-of-Distribution Problem', *Journal of Marketing*, 35(3) 34–39.

Index